The Disordered Mind

The Disordered Mind: An Introduction to Philosophy of Mind and Mental Illness examines and explains, from a philosophical standpoint, what mental disorder is: its reality, causes, consequences, and more. It is also an outstanding introduction to philosophy of mind from the perspective of mental disorder.

Revised and updated throughout, this second edition includes new discussions of grief and psychopathy, the problems of the psychophysical basis of disorder, the nature of selfhood, and clarification of the relation between rationality and mental disorder. Each chapter explores a central question or problem about mental disorder, including:

- What is mental disorder and can it be distinguished from neurological disorder?
- What roles should reference to psychological, cultural, and social factors play in the medical/ scientific understanding of mental disorder?
- What makes mental disorders undesirable? Are they diseases?
- Mental disorder and the mind–body problem.
- Is mental disorder a breakdown of rationality? What is a rational mind?
- Addiction, responsibility and compulsion.
- Ethical dilemmas posed by mental disorder, including questions of dignity and self-respect.

Each topic is clearly explained and placed in a clinical and philosophical context. Mental disorders discussed include clinical depression, dissociative identity disorder, anxiety, religious delusions, and paranoia. Several non-mental neurological disorders that possess psychological symptoms are also examined, including Alzheimer's disease, Down's syndrome, and Tourette's syndrome.

Containing chapter summaries and suggestions for further reading at the end of each chapter, *The Disordered Mind* is a superb introduction to the philosophy of mental disorder for students of philosophy, psychology, psychiatry, and related mental health professions.

George Graham is Professor of Philosophy and Neuroscience at Georgia State University, USA. He is the author, co-author, or co-editor of more than a dozen books, including *When Self-Consciousness Breaks* (2000), *Reconceiving Schizophrenia* (2007) and the *Oxford Handbook of Philosophy and Psychiatry* (2013).

The Disordered Mind

An Introduction to Philosophy
of Mind and Mental Illness

Second Edition

George Graham

Routledge
Taylor & Francis Group

LONDON AND NEW YORK

First published 2010
by Routledge
This edition published 2013
by Routledge
2 Park Square, Milton Park, Abingdon, Oxon, OX14 4RN

Simultaneously published in the USA and Canada
by Routledge
711 Third Ave., New York, NY 10017

Routledge is an imprint of the Taylor & Francis Group, an informa business

© 2010, 2013 George Graham

British Library Cataloguing in Publication Data
A catalogue record for this book is available from the British Library

Library of Congress Cataloging in Publication Data
Graham, George, 1945-
The disordered mind : an introduction to philosophy of mind and
mental illness / by George Graham. – 2nd ed.
p. cm.
Includes bibliographical references and index.
1. Mental illness. 2. Philosophy of mind. 3. Psychiatry – Philosophy.
4. Psychophysiology. I. Title.
RC437.5.G726 2013
616.89 – dc23
2012035211

ISBN: 978-0-415-51877-2 (hbk)
ISBN: 978-0-415-50124-8 (pbk)
ISBN: 978-0-203-06988-2 (ebk)

Typeset in Franklin Gothic
by Taylor & Francis Books

For Patricia

We are … subject to infirmities, miseries, interrupt, tossed and tumbled up and down … uncertain [and] brittle, and so is all that we trust unto. *And he that knows not this, and is not armed to endure it, is not fit to live in this world.*

Robert Burton, *The Anatomy of Melancholy* (1621)

And I have asked to be
Where no storms come,
Where the green swell is in the havens dumb,
And out of the swing of the sea.

Gerard Manley Hopkins, *Heaven-Haven*, Poems 1918

To try to be happy is to try to build a machine with no other specification than that it shall run noiselessly.

J. Robert Oppenheimer, *Letters and Recollections* (1980)

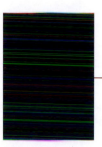

Contents

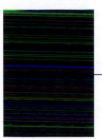

Acknowledgements

Special thanks to Richard Garrett and G. Lynn Stephens. Thanks also to Reinaldo Elugardo, Owen Flanagan, Gary Gala, James Hitt, Max Hocutt, Daniel Moseley, Jeffrey Poland, Jennifer Radden, and Marga Reimer. Two anonymous referees for the press made helpful comments on a draft of the second edition. I am grateful to them.

I am grateful to Tony Bruce, Adam Johnson, and the crew at Routledge for overseeing the second edition through to completion. Special thanks to Tony for inviting me to write both the first and the second edition.

In writing this second edition I continue to remember my parents, George and Catherine Graham, for their support for my interest in philosophy as a young man, and my brother, Paul, for his example of compassionate understanding of people who suffer.

My sister, Kaolin, and sister-in-law Catherine Sedgeman also deserve thanks, as does Cynthia Garrett. Each offered special forms of support and enthusiasm.

Last and most important: love and deepest thanks to Patricia, my wife, and to our daughter Kathleen, her husband Bill, and to their wonderful little son, our grandson, William George, wisdom in progress. This book is re-dedicated to Patricia, without whom it would not contain a single word.

Preface to the second edition

It is with considerable appreciation that I accepted an invitation from the press to produce a second edition of this book. Below I repeat some remarks from the preface of the first edition, but I also add descriptions of where the second edition attempts to improve upon the first and contains material unavailable in the first.

This book tells two tales.

The first is a tale about mental illness or disorder. (I use 'mental illness' and 'mental disorder' interchangeably.) The book offers a theory of mental disorder. It provides an account of mental disorder's reality, sources, causes or propensity conditions, contents and consequences, both symptomatic and therapeutic. The second tale is an introduction to elements of philosophy of mind, to the essentials of the subject. The book tells each of these two tales simultaneously. Each is tied up in the other. The two tales compose one story.

The second tale of elements of philosophy of mind derives its plotline from the first. It assumes that no sound and sensible philosophy of mind can be constructed without attending to the topic of mental illness and to human vulnerability to mental disorder: to such conditions as addiction, clinical or major depression, dysfunctional anxiety, paranoid distrust, and disorders of thought and comprehension.

The first tale of a theory of mental disorder inherits much of its cast of main characters from the second. It assumes that no conceptually regimented and normatively informed theory of mental disorder can be devised or constructed without taking philosophy of mind seriously and knowing something about this subject area of philosophy. This includes knowing of such topics as consciousness, Intentionality (I follow the philosophers' common if not universal convention of capitalizing this technical word), personal identity, the mind/body problem, and rationality.

The book is written for multiple audiences. It is designed for undergraduate and graduate courses in various fields of study, philosophy foremost but not exclusively. So, for example, an instructor in philosophy of mind may use it to introduce the subject in an interdisciplinary and clinically informed manner. For another example, an instructor in clinical or abnormal psychology may use it to complement exposure to clinical literature and case studies. I hope it may also be read with profit by academic philosophers, mental health professionals, and interested general readers. Comments received on the first edition have come from all such readerships. I am grateful to readers for sharing reactions.

Partly for the benefit of students, I include short chapter summaries and suggestions for further reading at the end of each chapter. Partly to avoid visual distractions, no footnotes or endnotes are used. Whatever is in the body of the text literally is in the body of the text. Partly for the benefit of selective users and browsers, some chapters or their parts have been composed so that they may be read independently of each other. Someone interested in, say, the topic of addiction could go directly to the seventh chapter and discover there a more or less self-contained discussion of that disorder. Or someone curious about the goals of a theory of mental disorder could read the second section of the second chapter and find there a unified statement of those goals. When read in order as a single book, however, the chapters offer the continuous development of a theory of mental disorder as well as of the role of philosophy of mind within that theory. The first three chapters introduce the topics of the book and offer suggestions for how to construct a theory of mental disorder that respects both the mind and disorder of a mental disorder; the middle chapters cover questions about the empirical reality of and evaluative standards or assessment norms for a mental disorder; and the final three chapters examine specific disorders in the light of the theory.

The book presents my own views. It argues for my own positions. This is not to banish other positions, but to provide unity and purpose to the book's philosophical theorizing, which is to seek a general philosophical and, in particular, philosophy of mind perspective on mental disorder or illness.

Given that this is a second edition, readers familiar with the first edition may wish to know what revisions and changes have been made. The most obvious change is that the Epilogue has been dropped. Some new section heads appear in the Table of Contents. In content the book has been revised and reworked in a number of conceptually substantive or major ways.

Some changes were motivated by the desire to further describe what I mean by metaphysical realism about mental disorder as well as by the thesis that the explanations proper to a mental disorder or to conditions of mind and behavior that deserve to be classified as mental disorders are rooted in a distinction between rational person respecting explanations and brute causal or mechanical explanations. Theoretical understanding of a mental disorder or illness involves deploying these two types of explanation in joint or interactive concert in order to gauge and grasp different features of a disorder and integrate that understanding with effective and compassionate treatment of a person with a mental disorder.

Other changes were motivated by the desire to reinforce or clarify controversial distinctions or claims made in the book. One of these is that a mental disorder is or may be based *in* the brain without also being *of* the brain or a neurological disorder. Another is the proposition that mental disorders represent impairments or special sorts of truncations or incapacitations in the reason-responsive or rational operation of basic or fundamental psychological capacities. Still another is the related claim that failures of rationality (loosely and contextually understood) play, or should play, key roles in the diagnosis and classification of mental disorders.

There are no serious changes to the original positions put forward by me in the first edition. But I hope that the positions are more clearly stated here in the second edition and better defended as well as more accessible to a wider audience.

Some brand new material on the American Psychiatric Association's (APA) *Diagnostic and Statistical Manual of Mental Disorders* (DSM) has been included. This includes a new discussion of whether grief should count as a disorder in certain extreme cases, which possibility has been a subject of controversy in the construction of DSM-5, and of whether psychopathy (sometimes also known as anti-social personality disorder), a moral failure, also may deserve to be classified as a mental disorder or illness. Some additional information from relevant sciences (especially brain science) has been added, but this is not a book on philosophy of science and mental illness. It is a book on philosophy of mind and mental illness. Philosophy pursued with respect and admiration for relevant sciences, but not as subordinate to them. Mind disordered, not science regnant, is its main focus, and when a mind is disordered or ill that is character enough for a single book.

Introduction

STABILITY AND INSTABILITY

Alice trusted Howard, her husband. She had reason for doing so. He was devoted to her. Or so she thought.

When Howard died unexpectedly, Alice, in preparing for his memorial service, opened his computer file only to discover that Howard recently had been leading a secret and complex second life. He had married another woman, fathered a child with her, and periodically lived with both second wife and child, as he described things, while "out of town doing regular business" in Kansas City.

Alice's grief over Howard's death, which was profound, was mixed with anger and pain, which was deep. A positive interpretation of her husband's character ("Howard was a good man; he loved me and our children; and, I will miss him terribly") may have led to a better emotional and behavioral adjustment to the loss than her bitter negative evaluation ("He lied to me and to the children; I did not really know him"). Alice fell into a protracted despondent mood. Two years later, still despondent, she was diagnosed with clinical depression.

Ian believes that he is the victim of a government plot. He is convinced that he is the object of a conspiracy conducted by the Federal Bureau of Investigation (FBI). "The FBI believes that I am running a terrorist cell." Ian refuses to leave his home for fear that he will be arrested. The business he owns, a men's clothing store, is faltering in his absence. When asked to describe evidence of being persecuted, Ian says that he cannot discuss the matter lest agents overhear the conversation. "The shirts in my closets are bugged with voice detectors." "The cuffs on my trousers contain electronic devices that signal my physical position to the FBI." He is diagnosed with paranoid delusional disorder.

What to do with the Alice's and Ian's of this world? How should they be understood? Treated? Sigmund Freud (1856–1939), the Austrian psychologist and founder of psychoanalysis, famously fretted over them. He tried to fathom the mind's emotional and behavioral fault lines: the creaks, cracks, and crevices of persons divided within themselves. Freud also recognized that mentally disturbed human beings may and often do reclaim mental health and well-being. People recover from a mental illness. For Freud, though, there is a prudent precondition for taking wise and measured aim at reclamation or construction of mental health. This is not to set the bar for emotional and psychological well-being too high.

The philosopher Owen Flanagan eloquently writes of the "wish to flourish, to be blessed with happiness, to achieve eudaimonia – to be a 'happy spirit'" (Flanagan 2007: 1). If Flanagan is right, that's a wish we all share. Truly to be happy, to be blessed. Freud, however, promoted a more modest aspiration. When asked by a despondent patient how he hoped to assist her in regaining mental well-being, he had this to say: "No doubt fate will find it easier than I do to relieve you of your illness." "But you will be able to convince yourself that much will be gained if we succeed in transforming your hysterical misery into common unhappiness" (Breuer and Freud 2000: 305).

Common unhappiness? Was Freud being ironic? In part, yes. Mainly, however, he was trying to be pragmatic or realistic. The conditions or circumstances of human existence, Freud thought, are such that an absolutely healthy, unified, orderly, stable, trouble-free mental life is much too optimistic for a person to expect, whether recovering from a disorder or not. Why so? Why not absolute mental health, behavioral and emotional well-being? Why not total and pure flourishing? Because, he said, "our body is doomed to decay and dissolution", "the external world [rages] against us", and suffering comes from our relations with other people. "The suffering which comes from this ... source is perhaps more painful to us than any other" (Freud 1989/1930: 26). We are psychologically vulnerable and unstable creatures, whom the vicissitudes and tragedies of life may inevitably wear down or pull apart. As persons we must therefore try to live dignified, productive lives, all the while remaining susceptible to periods, perhaps pronounced or protracted periods, of distress, discord and instability.

In order to elicit an intuitive sense of our vulnerability to instability or distress, consider a brief thought experiment. The experiment is counter-factually presumptuous to be sure. Contrary-to-fact presumption, however, is no impediment to imagination.

Suppose you are none other than Mother Nature, although endowed with powers of deliberation, foresight, and decision making of which she herself is not privy. Imagine that humankind has yet to appear on the earthen landscape. You wish to build the sort of mind that will help us as human beings to engage with life on the planet. You are not going to rely on Father Time to do this. (He takes forever.) You are going to do it yourself. If a supernatural or divine agent is behind your efforts, you are not aware of its assistance. You are, as you conceive of the task, utterly on your own.

You wish the human mind to have different and various modes of operation and component psychological competencies, faculties or capacities. You want us to perceive, reason, desire, feel, remember, learn, intend, deliberate, and decide. You want us to enter into productive social relationships. You want us to be properly situated or embedded, not just in the natural landscape, but in multiplex social ecologies and forms of social and cultural life. You want our mental activities to initiate, guide and complete goal-directed behavior and bodily movement. You want us to walk, grip, grasp, run, swim, open, close and climb. You wish us to achieve complex and ennobling purposes: to do philosophy, write memoirs, make art, organize religions, uncover scientific laws, found universities, and discover cures.

Suppose that for reasons of imaginative playful contrast and heuristic comparison, you narrow your conceptions of the possible human mind down just to two. Think of these as a *stable* and an *unstable* mind. You picture each as follows.

The Stable Mind. A human mind that is inherently stable and orderly. It possesses purity of heart and soundness of reason. It does things because it believes them to be desirable and is willing to face down the often and unanticipated aversive consequences of its actions. It assesses itself with equanimity, free of regret and self-doubt. It never loses control of itself. When entering into interpersonal relationships, it aims to insure that these are harmonious, coordinated and cooperative. When it confronts the vicissitudes of life, chronic pain, physical illness and death, it does so with courage and fortitude. It loves with magnanimity, dreams contentedly, and harbors a firm sense of personal dignity and self-respect. Its life, far from being an anarchic master, is the object of single-minded dedication and intelligent direction.

The Unstable Mind. A human mind that is inherently unstable and disorderly. It possesses conflicting motives, impulses, and inhibitions as well as biases of thought and impediments to reason. It does things because it believes them to be desirable, but is unwilling to accept the negative consequences of its actions and frequently is conflicted or befuddled about just what is desirable. It is prone to regret and self-doubt. It often loses its grip on itself. When it enters into social relationships, its agency is prone to be disharmonious, discordant and uncooperative. When it confronts the vicissitudes and heartaches of life, it seeks refuge or escape. It loves with rapturous passion but also with breathtaking infelicity and self-destructive inconstancy. Its self-criticisms are harsh and unforgiving. The demands of life drive it into disarray and dissolution.

Which sort of mind would *you* make if you were Mother Nature? "An absolute no-brainer", you say. "The answer is obvious." "Stability, most certainly." True, stability lacks high drama. Its theatricality is thin. Instability, however, is riddled with dissonance and burdened with discomfort and unhappiness. It is also, of course, grossly incompatible with the desired ends of your creation. An utterly unstable mind could never do philosophy or do so sagaciously. Discover cures? Found universities? What sort of academic institutions would these be like? (If you answer, "Like those that exist today", then you must be a professional academic.)

What has the real Mother Nature actually done? Here's what, to the naked anthropological eye, she has designed for us. She has composed a type of mind that is both stable and unstable. She has mixed each form of mentality in us. She has made us orderly and disorderly, content and discontent, facing life's vicissitudes but also seeking refuge from them. True, some folks are more temperamentally secure than others. True, some people are much less able to undergo various trials and tribulations than others. But beneath our individual differences, however, is a fusion of both. Each of us is endowed with a stable/unstable mind. No person has all of the one but none of the other. Even the most unstable or discordant individual is not without some small slice or sliver of stability. Even the most stable is not without a shadow of instability.

Periodically, of course, instability holds sway. When it does so, we become anxious about small things, develop imprudent patterns of thought, and slip or slide into emotional conflicts. Small influences may unhinge a person. Then, in more sadly serious cases, dissonance, distress, and disturbance may seize truly powerful and persistent if, hopefully still only, temporary dominion. A person's mind may break down or become disordered or ill in a psychiatric or clinical sense. One or more mental capacities or psychological faculties may dissemble into harmful or hurtful incapacity, dysfunction or impairment. Thoughts may become obsessive, preferences addictive, perceptions hallucinatory, beliefs delusional, and post-traumatic amnesia may impose ignorance of significant parts of one's past. Paralyzed by phobic anxiety, a person may avoid any and all public places. Numbed by major depression, an individual may listlessly disengage from people and projects once held near and dear.

Mental disorder, depending on its pulse and purport, may require professional mental health treatment or clinical address. One hopes that assistance is sound and sensible, but treatment and attention are unhelpful and even dangerous when resting on false or improper assumptions about mind and illness. The history of medical treatment for mental disorder is a checkered affair. It is benevolent and sensitive on occasion, given the state of medical knowledge at a time or in a culture. But other chapters in that history are characterized by superstition, ignorance, intolerance and inhumanity. The history of theory and treatment for mental illness is recounted in numerous texts. (It is also briefly available in a short chapter of a long book that helps to carry my name [see Fulford, Thornton and Graham 2006: 143–59].) I do not wish to repeat it here. I do, however, want briefly to sketch more recent phases. This short historical sketch should help to show why it's important to have a sound and sensible understanding of mental disorder. Such an understanding is one, I claim, in which the subject of philosophy of mind, in particular, ought to play a prominent role, to be outlined in a moment and presented in detail throughout the book.

ONE BRIEF HISTORY

In late nineteenth and early twentieth century in Western Europe the category of mental illness or disorder was applied only to the most serious problems and pathologies of mentality, viz. those identified, in effect, with psychoses, severe manias or depressions. Emil Kraepelin (1856–1926), arguably the leading psychiatric taxonomist of the period, attended primarily to three main types of disorder. Kraepelin spoke of dementia praecox (roughly, schizophrenia), depressive illness, and paranoia, a term he used broadly to refer to delusional disorders (one form of which is persecutory). For him mental illnesses fell into a small set of discoverable types, identified by symptom and family history. Hospitals and asylums purported to treat (even if all that they sometimes succeeded in doing was house) persons with such illnesses. Most people who wished help for less severe or disabling disturbances, which went by names such as "nerves", "neurasthenia" or "hysteria", did so with general medical practitioners. These were doctors who did not identify themselves as specialists in mental health. Rest and diet were popularly recommended cures for less severe cases. For the wealthy but worried well, occasional respites at health spas aimed to regenerate one's spirits. For all battered souls, the clergy were available for counseling.

Then, later into the early twentieth century, mental illness diagnosis and treatment underwent a dramatic transformation. Freud was the major force for change. He and his disciples helped to turn clinical insight and therapeutic resource into a distinct medical specialty. This field is known now, of course, as psychiatry.

Freud published his first major work, *The Interpretation of Dreams*, in 1900 (1958 [1900]). He died in 1939. By the time of his death, in the words of Rutgers University's Allan Horwitz, "the most basic ways of thinking about mental disorder had changed" (2002: 40). Psychiatry had become a distinct specialty within medicine. Its range of application had expanded to consider less severe disturbances than psychosis or incapacitating depression. The mental malaises or psychological infirmities that formed the focus of Freud's psychological theory, such as anxiety, obsession, and sexual frigidity, were described as manifestations of unconscious conflicts festering within the lives of all human beings: the severely ill, the worried well (or non-severely ill), and even the well. The primary function of therapy or treatment was to uncover those hidden conflicts and the manners in which people effectively adjust, or fail to adjust, to social and cultural demands. Some attention was given to diagnosis and to identifying categories of disorder, but one and the same set of symptoms or patient complaints was thought, in theory, to stem from just about any form of disorder. So, taxonomic labels failed to carry uniform and reliable conditions of application. Chronic fatigue, headaches, and weight loss may signify obsession in one individual, phobia in a second person, or sexual frigidity in a third. Horwitz aptly sums up Freudian diagnostic practice: "only deep, extensive, and intensive exploration of the individual personality could indicate the true meaning of any symptomatic presentation" (2002: 45).

Freudian thought was widely endorsed and medically institutionalized. It dominated thinking about mental disorder until the 1960s, when it fell into quite rapid decline. The organizational, economic, and social situation of psychiatric medicine, once again, underwent a transformation. Weaknesses in the Freudian framework became apparent. To be sure, Freudian psychology was not well suited for understanding the nature of or best treatment for truly severe psychoses (Hobson and Leonard 2001; Beam 2001). A desire for detailed and reliable clinical diagnosis became widespread (Bentall 2004; Horwitz 2002). Psychiatry grew biomedical. Not without dissenters. (In Britain, R. D. Laing was one of the more prominent opponents of the biomedicalization of psychiatry.) But overall the field became convinced that patient distress and complaint were symptoms of specific and tractable illness types or disease categories, much like somatic or bodily illnesses, though housed in the brain. A proliferating range of ailments of consciousness and behavior were thought to merit classification as distinct and distinguishable disorders.

Drugs emerged as critical for the understanding and treatment of mental disorder. In many cases they were regarded as the first-line of treatment. The aim was to restore biochemical func-tionality or normality to a neural base of mental disorder and to reduce symptoms. Chlorpromazine was introduced in the 1950s for the treatment of severe psychoses like schizophrenia. Monoamine oxidase inhibitors and tricyclics were widely deployed for the treatment of major depression. Presuppositions of drug therapy, foremost, the assumption that specific illnesses require specific drugs, imply that it makes a difference for care and treatment whether a set of symptoms is diagnosed as, say, clinical depression or schizophrenia. Depression should be targeted with one drug. Schizophrenia addressed with another. No longer was one Freudian style of therapy sufficient for all disorders. References to Freudian phenomena such as "repression", "sub-limation, "oedipal dilemma" as well as to the Freudian unconscious were charged with being unscientific and clinically unsound (Grunbaum 1984; Horwitz 2002). Freudians, as they do today, continued to function in the profession, although Freudian style psychiatry and its conceptual brethren moved to the perimeter of psychiatric medicine. Freud was often cast as a scapegoat for problems or false-starts in the profession. Psychiatry as a profession did not blame Freud for contributing to its social and cultural prominence. Few professions lament prominence. Freud, however, was criticized for burdening the specialty with opaque concepts and elusive forms of clinical treatment. No doubt, certain effective counter-criticisms of the anti-Freudian momentum in psychiatry were willfully ignored (Lear 1998: 23). But non-Freudian biomedical trends became secure. Fine-grained diagnostics and illness-specific medication became the prescribed aspiration of the medical specialty.

The twentieth century has ended, of course, and the twenty-first has more than just begun. Understanding and treatment of mental illness is in post-Freudian biomedical full bore. Psychiatry has moved from the language of mind and mentality to that of brain science or to mixes of the languages of mind and brain science, in such fields as cognitive neuroscience and cognitive neuropsychiatry, but in which brain science more or less is the aspired canonical tongue. Preference for reference to the neural holds the day. The methods and manner of neuroscience, it is widely presumed, offer the best understanding of and treatment for mental disorder. It is only a matter of time, some say, before psychiatry will become a sub-discipline of neurology (Ramachandran 2003). Indeed, just such neurological sub-disciplinary status exactly is what one prominent observer says already has taken place in psychiatry. "Psychiatry and neurology [is] one specialty" (M. A. Taylor 1999: viii).

True, interest in the brain is not new to psychiatry. When Wilhelm Griesinger (1817–68), a professor of psychiatry at the University of Berlin, authored the first editorial of the *Archives for Psychiatry and Nervous Disease*, a journal he founded in 1867, he wrote: "Patients with so-called 'mental illnesses' are really individuals with illnesses of the nerves and brain" (see Bentall 2004: 150). (Freud himself attempted to take brain science seriously. After, however, an early effort to reconcile his developing psychological insights with the limited knowledge base of neuroscience available during his lifetime, he abandoned the attempt [Kitcher 1992].) But the immense popularity of neuroscience within psychiatry is a distinctively post-Freudian phenomenon and represents the "culmination of [the biomedical] trend within the profession" (Bentall 2004: 151).

Brain science, of course, is deeply and urgently relevant to the explanatory understanding and clinical treatment of mental disorder. No one should deny that. But does a danger of post-Freudian neuro-mechanical hubris lurk within preference for brain science and associated reliance on drugs and somatic disease modeled modes of treatment? Consider drug treatment. So-called 'atypical' antipsychotic medications (viz. drugs that produce fewer side effects than 'typical' antipsychotic medications) that were so vigorously endorsed, as recently as several years ago, for being more efficacious than psychotherapy and even more so than their immediate pharmaceutical predecessors (like the tricyclics), are now, in the words of psychiatrist Paul Appelbaum, "recognized as having substantial therapeutic limitations and often problematic effects of their own" (Applebaum 2004: vii). (One of the therapeutic limitations is that success with a drug does not necessarily correlate one-to-one with removal of the causes or sources of a disorder. Pathology may persist, although various evident symptoms may disappear or be reduced.)

Some critics complain that while Freud 'pathologized' or medicalized normal variations in human psychological diversity by portraying behavior as the expression of unconscious and unresolved conflicts, the pharmaceutical industry today exerts its own independent 'pathologizing' effect on our understanding of a mental disorder. Drug companies encourage the creation of what often in fact, if perhaps not necessarily in intent, are suspect categories of mental disorder (Horwitz 2002). Neuroscience may have exorcised the elusive Freudian Unconscious from the mind/brain. But commercial forces, critics say, are selling a bill of mixed neurochemical goods to a specialty of psychiatry that is over-enthused about an image of mental disorder as a subtype of brain disorder or neurological disease or neuro-biomedical condition (Luhrmann 2000; Elliott 2003 and 2004).

Is it wise to assume that mental disorders are forms of brain disorder or disease? Might not this assumption be an unreasonable or premature piece of conceptual legislation imposed on the domain of mental disorder? Might it not dangerously obscure the research validity and diagnostic and therapeutic utility of a category of disturbance or distress, like that of a mental disorder, which, although certainly involving the operation of neurobiological and neurochemical processes, does not mean that something is damaged or wrong with brain activities at levels describable by neuroscience? No doubt, mental disorders are problems or disturbances involving pathologies of various sorts, but might this be consistent with a healthy brain bearing a role in a mental disorder? Normative considerations relevant to the diagnosis of mental disturbance and distress, as well as to the explanation of such conditions, may not be identical to those for describing the physical biological base of distress. As a consequence, to the extent that mental disorders or illnesses constitute a coherent type or domain of disorder, it is most plausible (I believe and as the book argues) to maintain that they constitute primarily a psychological kind of some sort, not a neural or neurobiological kind or a condition specifiable at the level of biological neuroscience, although a kind that cross-cuts with descriptions of parts of its causal foundations in brain science terms.

Two analogies may help to explain the conceptual possibility that I have in mind here. Just because there are misspelled words on a book's page does not mean that there is something wrong with its publisher's printing press. Or again: just because when I gaze at a perfectly straight stick, which is submerged in a pool of water, it appears bent (at the point where it meets the surface of the water), and my visual system fails to compensate for the optical effect of refraction, does not mean that my visual system is damaged or disordered. The norms or standards for spelling words are not those for proper printing presses. The standards for perceptual veridicality are not those for computing and correcting for Snell's law (about the path of light rays through refractive media). The printing press produces ink marks. The visual system implements the gazing. But at the levels of description of the activity of the press as a press or of the visual system as a visual or perceptual system everything may be in proper or healthy order, even if neither the page nor the visual information is as we desire or wish, that is to say, even if the spelling is a mistake, and the visual information is in error.

To assume that just because or if the brain is the physically existential base of a mental illness that therein neural processes are ill, disordered or diseased (or of the wrong or improper kind) is an unlicensed inference or non sequitur. Appreciating that the inference is a non sequitur is important because the effect of insisting that mental disorders are brain disorders (i.e. disorders *of* and no just *in* the brain, as I wish to put matters) is to suppose that mental disorders are not even potentially compatible or consistent with normal (or normatively normal) brain function or neural activity.

There are heated debates in the neuroscience literature about just how to determine whether neural processes or activities are functioning as they normatively should in order to qualify as healthy or proper. The consensus of opinion, sometimes not explicit, but at least implicit in the clinical and experimental procedures that neurologists use to test whether a brain is functioning as it should, is that although it certainly is useful, on occasion, to distinguish between desired and undesired forms of brain activity, it is important not to confuse whether a brain itself is healthy or diseased with whether this, that, or another form of neural activity is desired, preferable, or prudent for a person.

When a person is mentally ill, there is necessarily something wrong or undesirable with their condition. But the relevant norms for mental illness wrongness are not necessarily neurological norms. So, just because Alice cannot cope with her husband's death and adultery does not mean that her brain is not functioning as it should relative to biological norms. She is not functioning well or as she should or wishes, to be sure, but her neural processes may be, depending upon the criteria, in proper working order nonetheless.

WHAT IS THIS BOOK ABOUT?

This book articulates and defends a theory of mental disorder. It offers a conception of what a mental disorder both is and is like to its subject, how best to explain and understand it as well as to appreciate what human vulnerability to mental disorder reveals about the nature of mind and mentality.

The theory that the book proposes is distinguished by its attention to issues in empirically and clinically informed philosophy of mind and to questions about norms or standards for how best to assess, explain and understand a mental disorder. A rival brain science centered theory of mental disorder, which may be called the *neurological disorder* or *broken brain* conception of a mental disorder, is outlined and rejected. Not rejected because brain science does not or should not contribute to our understanding of a mental disorder. Clearly, brain science does and must contribute. I say 'rejected' because, I believe, if a disorder is mental, then human psychology (and not just neurobiology or neurochemistry) is part of its causal explanatory foundations.

The theory of mental disorder that the book defends is characterized, in part, by promotion of a concept of mental disorder that is closely tied to a description of the nature or character of the human mind as a *rational* mind or as reason-responsive, broadly understood. We persons are rational agents. We think, act or do things for reasons. We respond to reasons that we have for thinking and doing things. The theory of mental disorder offered in this book defends the proposition that elements of reason and rationality help to constitute or define distinctively mental activities such as believing, hoping, desiring, deciding, thinking and the like. The theory also holds that (i) the reason-responsiveness of a psychological faculty or capacity is impaired, truncated or significantly incapacitated in a mental disorder, but (ii) not obliterated, destroyed or totally incapacitated (as it occurs in severe brain disorders). Reason or rationality is partly but not fully disabled in a mental disorder. It is also partly although not fully responsible for the occurrence or onset and progression of a disorder. So, no behaviors should be considered as symptoms of a *mental* disorder, as opposed to those of a purely neurological or brain disorder (such as cortical blindness or Parkinsonism), unless they satisfy (no matter how deficient, incapacitated or gummed up' in manner) at least some minimal standards of rationality, coherence, or 'logic'.

I describe various ways in which the reason or rationale associated with different mental disorders is truncated or impaired. In analyzing these impairments, I also claim that we need to refer not just to the role of reason-responsiveness in a disorder, but also to neural mechanisms functioning as instances of (what I like to call) unreason or as brute, a-rational forces.

Here is a short imagined illustration of what I have in mind. Suppose that Alice's grief and depression over the death of her husband and her disappointment with his adulterous behavior is so enduring and intense that she becomes a victim of insomnia, weight loss, and an inability to properly care for her children. Now imagine that certain cortical regions of the brain have been shown to be implicated in the production and regulation of affective or emotional states. A background mechanical story about brain regions (that applies to her case) may go something like this.

Suppose two reciprocally connected neural systems help to underlie emotions and emotional activity. One is the so-called 'ventral' system (including, in part, the amygdala and insula), and the other is the so-called 'dorsal' system (including, in part, the hippocampus and dorsolateral prefrontal cortex). Suppose that the ventral system is partly responsible for the recognition of emotionally significant stimuli, whereas the dorsal is partly responsible for effortful responses to emotional states (see Whittle et al. 2009: 43). Suppose also that these regions or systems have been designed by Mother Nature with a kind of emotional threshold or shear pin device that under the strain of protracted grief and dramatic disappointment puts a person into a state of lethargy or virtual tonic immobility (see McKay and Dennett 2009: 501). The associated action of the shear pin device is not 'abnormal', 'improper' or unhealthy in these situations, at least by strictly or narrowly biological or adaptational/genetic fitness standards. Alice's brain is (I am assuming for purposes of illustration) functioning just as Mother Nature has designed brains to function under conditions like those of Alice. However, in upshot, in consequence of such a device, Alice fails to get out of bed. Although unwelcome as behavior and surely unhealthy psychiatrically as well as symptomatic of her diagnosis as a subject of clinical depression, Alice's lethargy or immobility expresses the proper operation or designed function of relevant neural regions. Nothing in the brain is damaged or literally 'broken' or not functioning biologically as it should when she does not get out of bed. The threshold device temporarily shears a people off from the world and renders them more or less motionless, at least with respect to normal daily activities, so as to prevent (whether an individual like Alice's appreciates Nature's purpose or not) more harm to themselves – perhaps more losses, more disappointments, more shocks to the emotional system.

So pictured, Alice's depression is best understood by deploying two general sorts of vocabularies or causal-explanatory languages. One is in terms of the annihilating loss of and disappointment in her husband. These are terms of (what I am calling) the reason-responsiveness or 'rationale' of the depressive or grieving process. If Alice did not believe that her husband was dead or if she was not disappointed in his adulterous behavior, she would not be psychologically disturbed or upset.

The other parts of the story are couched in terms of emotional managerial processes operative at a neurobiological/neurochemical level of analysis i.e. in terms (like those mentioned above) that refer to brain processes as mere mechanisms. The mechanisms may be sub-personally purposive or teleological (to use a technical term of philosophers' art) in certain operations (such as those of the imagined shear pin device) if selected for their ability to produce such effects by Mother Nature. However, they are not themselves therein *rationally* operative in such operations. They do not therein help to produce prudent behavior on Alice's individual part. They operate in interaction with or 'beneath' Alice's personal reasons for being disappointed and grieving. The mechanisms 'weigh' Alice's body in bed. Her disappointment 'stitches' her mind beneath its sheets. Together both mechanism and mind significantly incapacitate Alice.

Reason's deficiencies should be no surprise in a disorder, of course. Approach Ian and it is hard not to notice that he is devoid of good evidence for his fear that the FBI is conspiring against him. Spend time with Alice and it is difficult not to miss that her depression takes a heavy toll on her ability to care for herself and her children, whom she loves. Within the gloomy throes of a form of grief turned into depression, her volitional capacities are stymied. She lacks the will or sufficient energy to face the day.

It may help readers if I had a name for the theory of mental disorder that I offer in this book. Since I claim that our explanatory understanding of a mental disorder requires the twin frameworks of psychology and brain science, I am tempted to call it the *twin theory*. Since I give prideful or primary place in the theory to the truncated or impaired presence of rationality or reason-responsiveness in a disorder, I am also tempted to call it the *truncated* or *impaired reason-responsiveness theory*. In the end, though, I have no name for it. A thorn by any other name would still hurt as much.

The sort of theory I offer is not without kin or precedent. Various other discussions of mental disorder assume that mental disorders result from the interplay of rational and a-rational or brute causal sources. Freud made such an assumption. He proposed that psychiatric patients should be treated as rational agents, but whose reasons for behavior are distorted by the irruption of various forms of 'a-rational noise' (instincts, cultural and other forces) into their psychological space of reasons (a phrase of Wilfred Sellars 1997). Freud tried to finesse his ignorance of the neurobiological/neurochemical details. He relied imaginatively on the fact that remarkably good first approximations of explanations of disturbed behavior may be achieved by proposing that self destructive instincts and other forces operate beneath the horizons of a patient's conscious and deliberate self-control. But whatever the theory's name or label, this book offers a theory of mental disorder, a theory that is connected in robust measure with concerns in philosophy of mind.

Philosophy of mind. What is that?

Philosophy of mind is the subject or sub-discipline within the discipline or field of philosophy that systematically addresses several deep and puzzling problems of mind and mentality. The problems are deep and puzzling, in part, because they resist straightforward or direct scientific dissolution or empirical or clinical resolution. Psychiatry is not philosophy, of course, but it does presuppose philosophic commitments and in philosophy of mind uppermost. If certain deep and puzzling philosophical problems are resolved in one manner rather than another, then much of psychiatric theory and clinical practice may thrive or flounder on such results (depending upon the resolution).

Once we excise the presumption that mental disorders are or must be brain disorders from our understanding of a mental disorder, a primary task for philosophy of mind in the theory of mental disorder, I believe, is to show how notions of consciousness, rationality, Intentionality, and psychological explanation (among others) can and should be deployed within a theory of mental disorder. They can be deployed without facing threat from neuroscience of being rendered explanatorily irrelevant or conceptually enervated or dismissed.

To take a quick example of the germaneness of philosophy of mind to the topic of mental disorder, clinicians and researchers schooled in a biomedical categorical approach to psychiatric diagnosis sometimes presuppose that disorders and ordinary mental disturbances are utterly different and belong to two exclusive and discontinuous categories or domains of distress. Think, for instance, of the phenomenon of delusions. 'Either delusional or not delusional' is a presupposition of this school of thought. But an 'either/or' pattern of botanizing a delusional/non-delusional distinction is indulged at the expense of truth. No matter how false or bizarre the attitudes of a mental health patient, it usually is possible to find people who hold equally false or bizarre attitudes, but who are quite normal and healthy. Avidly searching for a definitive or precise criterion of a delusion is hunting for a hard and fast border where none exists. A suitably philosophy of mind informed theory of delusion, based on exploration of notions such as rationality and self comprehension, should serve to caution clinicians about just when and how to proceed with a delusional diagnosis.

References to neither the unwelcome causes nor bizarre contents of a delusional attitude fully suffice to explain what makes a delusion a delusion. Or so I argue. Rather, in my view, the consequences of an attitude, by which I mean, in a case of delusion, the harmful or imprudent and reason-unresponsive manner in which a person manages the attitude and acts in terms of it helps to make it delusional. As between cause, content or consequence, it is on the cusp of consequence that the nature of delusion ultimately courses.

Ian is in the grips of paranoia. Understanding his delusional attitude requires a proper description of its consequences. Locked doors. A bankrupt business. Fear of others as unwelcome intruders. Inability to knowledgeably manage his own frame of mind.

That, in a nutshell, is what the book is about. It offers a theory of mental disorder that does not relinquish the theory to, but deploys, brain science. The theory also exhibits how elements from philosophy of mind should or at least may operate in an account of mental disorder. In pursuit of such ends and related others, the book argues that it is absolutely essential for understanding a mental disorder to appreciate the truncated or impaired presence of reason-responsiveness or rationality in a disorder. By talk of 'reasons' I do not mean to over-intellectualize the complexities of human psychology. In daily life, for instance, the recognition of reasons for thought or action often is achieved by feeling or emotion, and we are much more likely to be better off as rational agents if we are skilled in fearing, braving, loving or trusting the right things and people, then if we seek to purify our rational powers of emotive content.

The book promotes at least one other big thesis as well. This is metaphysical *realism* about mental disorder. A metaphysical *realist* about mental disorder is someone who claims that mental disorders truly or objectively exist. They are real. By contrast: Those who assert that no condition of a person should ever be thought of as a mental disorder are mental disorder anti-realists. Mental disorders are not real. They don't exist.

I am a mental disorder realist. How so? What does mental disorder realism mean to me and in this book?

The planet Mars illustrates one way in which something may be real. Mars depends upon no mind whatsoever for its existence. It is mind-independent. Objective. Real. If no mind existed Mars still would.

Not so a mental disorder. A mental disorder is a condition of mind. It is mind-dependent. If no mind existed, no mental disorder could exist. But the existence of mental disorder is not mind-dependent in the same way in which Mahler's Fifth Symphony or the baby sitter's favorite TV shows are mind-dependent. The existence of such things depends upon people's thoughts about and classifications of them. The Symphony, for example, depends upon Mahler's composing the score. The existence of the sitter's favorite TV shows depends upon her selection of which specific shows to watch rather than others and her entertainment preferences and tastes. But no one composes a mental illness. No one selects which disorder to suffer.

Another way of thinking of something as real is to think of its existence as perceptually obvious or readily recognizable by the naked eye. For example, the fact that this or that table or mountain exists is perceptually obvious or readily recognizable by the naked eye.

Again, this is not true of a mental illness or disorder. A wide and complex range of behavioral activities are relevant to recognizing a mental disorder. When a disorder as such is observed, it is observed only in the context of a broad range of human practices and with a proper storehouse of empirical and normative concepts and categories at the observer's disposal. No naked eye can spot the fact that a person has a mental disorder. Only one properly conceptually clothed and informed can recognize that fact.

Still another way of thinking of something as real is to think of it as something whose actual existence is so widely believed to be the case that no reasonable person doubts it. Again, though, that is not the case with mental illness or disorder. A goodly number of intelligent people deny the existence of mental disorders. Some theorists say that to speak of certain mental disturbances or distresses as mental disorders is an arbitrary or unwarranted medical convention. Other ways of talking about human mental distress can and should be deployed. Just as, say, we no longer classify phlogiston as a real or existing substance (although the phenomenon of combustion that we human beings used the concept of phlogiston to help to explain remains real), we should no longer classify conditions of depression or obsession as mental disorders or illnesses (although as disturbances those conditions remain real).

When I speak of mental disorders as real, I don't mean that they are mind-independent. I don't mean that they are obvious observationally. I don't mean that their existence is immune to the skeptical doubts of reasonable people. I mean at least four things, each of which is defended in one place or another over the course of the book.

First: Mental disorders exist independent of whether we have a theory about them, think about them as such, or classify people as subjects of mental illness. Just as a person may have a somatic illness or bodily injury independent of whether we realize it, so a person may suffer from a mental disorder without anyone's recognition of this fact. Mental disorders are not mind-independent. But they are, as it were, act-of-classification-independent (or act-of-recognition-independent). Mars would exist whether we classify or recognize the orb or not. But this is because Mars could exist if no mind existed. Mental disorders could not exist in a mindless world. However, they could exist in a situation or world in which no one classified or recognized mental disorders. If our world was devoid of terms or concepts for a mental disorder, there still could be mental disorders.

Second: Mental disorders are empirically discoverable. By this I do not mean that mental disorders are precisely distinguishable from non-disorders or that they possess sharp edges or precise borders. Instead, I mean that they are suitable foci of investigation and analysis, that empirical or scientific generalizations can be made about them, and that whether someone is the subject of a disorder cannot be settled just by appreciating that they are disturbed or upset. To qualify as a disorder, a condition or disturbance must meet certain standards or norms. A disturbance's success or failure in meeting relevant standards or norms also is discoverable.

Third: The evaluative standards or norms for being a mental disorder are such that, when a person is the subject of a mental disorder, there is something wrong with them, wrong, in particular, with their mental and behavioral activity. They are in a condition that they ought not to be in. Their behavior is not just harmful to them (and perhaps also to others), whether they realize it or not, but it represents a truncation or impairment in the reason-responsive operation of one or more of their basic psychological faculties or capacities. The behavior is no mere performance error, judgmental lapse, regrettable personality trait, or character flaw like laziness or nosiness.

Finally fourth: In speaking of realism about mental disorder, I also mean that fears about the displacement or dispensability of reference to mentality or psychology in our description and explanatory understanding of a disorder on grounds of its neurological basis are unfounded. In order to explain some human afflictions, such as blinding brain lesions, hemiplegic cerebral palsy, quadriplegia, conduction deafness, and so on, brain science and the associated language of neural disease or illness is canonical and exclusionary. Psychology as a science or discipline may help to describe some of the consequences or symptoms of those afflictions, but the discipline itself is not truly fit for grasping such afflictions' immediate origins or causal explanatory foundations. However, psychology is needed to account for a condition that deserves to be called a mental disorder. A-rational (mechanical) and mind-infused rational (non-mechanical) factors each interact to produce a mental disorder. Though not the only signatory, the mind *qua* mind puts its inscription on the sources and progression of a disorder. We cannot recognize a condition as a mental disorder without uncovering that psychological mark or autograph, or so I argue.

Here are more advance details.

Numerous mental disorders are discussed in the book, some more than once. These include among others: clinical or major depression, dissociative identity or multiple personality disorder, acute anxiety (in some forms), addiction (in some forms), grandiose/religious delusions, and paranoia. Several non-mental neurological disorders that possess psychological symptoms also are examined. These include among others: Alzheimer's disease, autism, Down's syndrome, and Gilles de la Tourette syndrome.

In this book I outline a way in which to understand the distinction between mental disorders and (non-mental) neurological or brain disorders with psychological symptoms. I do this, in part, in terms of exemplars, prototypes or more or less uncontested examples of each. (I use 'exemplar' and 'prototype' interchangeably.) I claim that the partition or boundary between mental and non-mental physical or neurological disorders is not a sharp chasm, although it is no less real or objective in spite of that fact. The boundary is, if not a hard fact, a soft fact.

Exemplars of a mental disorder may be displaced or dethroned, of course, if theory advances and clinical and scientific evidence progresses in new and different directions. The seizures understood as symptoms of an exemplary mental disorder decades ago may be reinterpreted today as brought about by damage to the temporal lobe and reclassified as signs of a neurological disorder.

Many mental disorders have features in common with non-mental physical or somatic illnesses including their forms of apposite or appropriate treatment. Drugs may help with an anxiety disorder as well as with Tourette's. Psychotherapy may assist with some symptoms or aspects of Parkinsonism as well as of major depression.

While no single chapter is devoted to ethics, over the course of the book I briefly consider a few moral problems surrounding mental health research, clinical practice, and social policy. These considerations are influenced by stands I take on the place of philosophy of mind in the theory of mental disorder. One is the problem of whether benevolent or compassionate treatment of a victim of delusional paranoia morally requires empathetic understanding of their paranoid worldview. We persons, of course, differ in our capacities for empathy or emotional projection, just as we differ in our moral motivations. Some of us possess rather limited capacities to imaginatively simulate the inner lives or attitudes of others. But, morally, should possessing *some* empathy for deluded persons count as part and parcel of clinical care? That is one of the moral questions I examine in the book.

Generally speaking, one criterion for me in the proper treatment of mental disorders is to help people to maintain or recover their dignity and self-respect. The problem of dignity and self-respect preservation is viewed by me as a special instance of a challenge that we all face as human beings. The challenge is to achieve a responsible and productive response to life's heartaches and misfortunes by giving them a "meaningful place in one's progress through life" (Velleman 1991: 55).

To mend or heal from a disorder in a self-respecting and dignified manner requires discovering a positive or purposeful place for past or present episodes of disorder in the future course of a person's life. The fact that a person has or has had a disorder is no personal discredit or sign of poor judgment or faulty character. It is an expression of vulnerability to instability that all of us harbor in our psychological makeup.

Achieving a purposeful place for episodes of disorder often consists of dealing with conflicting alternative interpretations of one's past. Caution in interpretation is required however. Exaggerated emphasis or endless rumination on past episodes of disorder runs the risk of missing lessons that are present in other phases or chapters in one's history.

Influential among efforts to emphasize thinking about the past in a process of recovery is the Freudian presumption that acquiring truths about one's childhood is critical for mental health. Revive the distant past, remember forgotten experiences, and return to recollected trauma. As two observers put it, "to Freud … falling like a shadow over every … life is the significance of early injuries to the self." "A kind of … scar that then must burden … later development." (Gross and Rubin: 2002: 94).

I confess that I am personally leery about the therapeutic efficacy of persistent rumination upon past scars. Especially scars inflicted in the distant past. Two reasons constitute warrant for caution. One is sociological and comes from research on different ways in which people respond to bad experiences. Ruminative responding seems, for many people, to be immensely unhelpful. It leads to the recall of more negative memories, more negative interpretations of past events, and more pessimism about finding effective solutions to present and future personal problems (see Bentall 2004: 264).

The other basis for caution is epistemological or evidential and stems from appreciating that a person's past often just is too vast, inaccessible, and riddled with heterogeneous and ambiguous events to serve as the primary focus of reconstruction or recovery. The past, especially the personally distant past, may be a highly indeterminate place when viewed from the vantage point of one's current evidential or epistemic perspective. Not just in the ambiguities it presents to our feelings and recollections, but, perhaps more profoundly, in the indeterminacies it poses to our efforts at discovering interpretative significance. More helpful and optimistic, for me, is the forward-looking attitude of the philosopher and psychologist William James (1842–1910). James urges us to aim at constructing interpretations of the past that help to secure good results for future behavior. Past accuracy is less important than future utility, assuming that, normally, there often are numerous ambiguous past events about which factual surety cannot be achieved. "Few of us," writes James, "are not in some way infirm [but] our very infirmities can help us unexpectedly" (James 2002: 29). To be helped, however, he notes, a person must realize that "there are dead feelings, dead ideas, and cold beliefs, and there are ... live ones and ... everything has to re-crystallize around [them]" (2002: 218).

James's admonition to focus or crystallize on live ideas or attitudes that assist in future reclamation is not aimed at denying the past suffering and misfortune that is part of a disorder, but at trying to reverse its polarity. Negative past experiences of depression, acute anxiety, or delusion may become positive in delayed and deliberate consequence when they contribute to reconstruction, reconstitution or reformation – to determining how to behave or to think purposively in the future – and are viewed in a progressive light. Getting the past in accurate pictorial detail is less important than sculpting the future properly.

"My residents and I," writes one senior psychiatrist, "end up teaching [patients] how to situate their symptoms, problems, and miseries within a larger life trajectory" (Sadler 2004a: 359). Constructing a future trajectory rather than achieving a past accuracy – if one has to choose where to devote one's energies between them, the first, the future, is to be preferred.

Ask Alice. To overcome her anger and despondency, Alice should not deny that her husband lived a lie. He did. That fact painfully is obvious. But there may well be other aspects of her relationship with Howard that fail to admit of so obvious and negative an interpretation. One such aspect may be whether he loved his second wife more than he did Alice. Perhaps he did not. Perhaps Howard's trips to Kansas City stemmed from a desire to hide a shameful and embarrassing relationship with the second woman rather than from a deep and preferential love for his second spouse or a child who may have been accidentally conceived. The attempt to hide is not a welcome trait on his part, to be sure, but it does not necessarily reflect a preference for the second woman.

Alice needs emotionally to breathe again. She needs to feel that she mattered much to Howard. If it is not obvious whom he preferred, then, other things being equal, she may have good reason to believe or hope that she herself was his deepest and most important love. Persistent brooding over the fact that he deceived her and fathered another child offers no such relief.

A few brief and final words are in order in this introductory chapter before beginning the project of theory construction that I have described above.

If mental disorders are real, and qualify as conditions aspects of whose occurrence are controlled or explained, in part, by reference to forces described in mind-language terms, a theory of mental disorder should illuminate just what it means for mentality to exert partial control over a disorder. The problem of finding a role for mind in a disorder is especially challenging for a theory of mental disorder like the one offered in this book. This is because the theory offered here also locates or describes some of the controls behind a mental disorder in the language of brain science, although it says that subjects of mental disorders do not suffer from damaged brains or neurological disorders. Meanwhile, if it is empirically possible for neurological disorders and mental disorders to pull apart in a causal-explanatory way, although the boundaries between them may not be sharp or precise, considerable theoretical or conceptual elbow room is then left open for mental disorders to be real and theoretically distinct disorders.

One aim of this book is to delineate that theoretical or domain space for mental disorder. It is to identify categorical elbow room for a type of disorder that deserves to be classified as a mental disorder. It is to show how if a disorder harbors certain psychological features in its pathogenesis or causal explanatory foundations, it should qualify as a mental disorder. Philosophy of mind, then, can help us to identify and understand those features.

In psychiatry most problems are not those of philosophy of mind, to be sure, but helping, along with other disciplines, to conceive of conceptual or categorical elbow room for a category mental disorder partly is a job for philosophy.

SUMMARY

This first chapter introduced the main topics of the book and outlined the general manner in which I plan to address them.

The chapter offered a general orientating and heuristic description for why we persons are vulnerable to mental disorder. The human mind is a mix of the orderly and disorderly, the stable and unstable. When this mix goes awry, mental disorder may ensue. It noted the importance of Freud to the history of psychiatry. It urged that a theory of mental disorder should acknowledge its need for assistance from philosophy of mind. It noted that, in order to recognize that disciplinary dependence, this book describes elements in philosophy of mind of special relevance to the theory of mental disorder.

All of us are prone, at least at times, to spiral out of rational or reason-responsive control. Such spirals or episodes, when they constitute a mental disorder, cannot fully be understood just in terms of the language of mind. Brain science, too, must enter into the explanatory picture. But the chapter claimed that mental disorders need not be brain disorders even if or though mental disorders somehow are based in the brain. This claim awaits detailed defense in the book. It is one of its main themes and central to what I mean by realism about a mental disorder.

SUGGESTED READING

Fulford, K. W. M., Thornton, T., and Graham, G. (2006). *Oxford Textbook of Philosophy and Psychiatry* (Oxford: Oxford University Press).

Graham, G. (1998). *Philosophy of Mind: An Introduction,* 2nd ed (Malden, MA: Blackwell).

Graham, G. and Stephens, G. L. (eds) (1994). *Philosophical Psychopathology* (Cambridge: MIT Press).

Murphy, D. (2006). *Psychiatry in the Scientific Image* (Cambridge: MIT Press).

Radden, J. (ed.) (2004). *Philosophy of Psychiatry: A Companion* (Oxford: Oxford University Press).

2 Conceiving mental disorder

I state an obvious fact. The task of describing the conceptual makeup of the category or domain of mental disorder is truly daunting.

Mental disorder is such a big and varied category of states and conditions. How can it be meaningfully decided what mood disorders, anxiety disorders, personality disorders, delusional disorders, impulse control disorders, etc., have in common? But this chapter aims to give the task a try. Or more exactly: it aims to begin the task. The chapter is about how to construct a sound and sensible concept of mental disorder. Not just of disorder and not just of the reference of the term 'mental' in the expression 'mental disorder', but of the category of *mental disorder*. This chapter helps to set the stage for the theory of mental disorder to be constructed and applied in the rest of the book.

MENTAL DISORDER HAS CONSEQUENCES

The very idea of a *mental disorder* has numerous consequences of diverse types. Classification deploying the concept affects millions of people in a variety of different ways and settings.

Scientists and mental health professionals specialize in the study and treatment of mental disorder. Patrons, benefactors, and governments support mental disorder research. Psychiatric drugs and therapies are dedicated to the amelioration of mental disorder. Lawyers and legal advocates argue that if their clients suffer from certain disorders this reduces liability for crimes. Consumers select insurance companies on the basis of whether they reimburse for treatment of mental disorder. Scientific journals, professional associations, patient support groups, book publishers, and websites devote themselves to the topic of mental disorder. Reference to mental disorder is prominent in the autobiographies, biographies, and memoirs of scientists, statespersons, soldiers, scoundrels and saints. People's self conceptions, family aspirations, and social goals often are affected by whether they or those whom they love are classified by mental health professionals as subjects of a mental disorder. Talk of disorder, albeit in this particular type of case, more often than not, loose and informal, appears in descriptions of ordinary moods, problems and emotional disturbances. We speak of ourselves as 'seriously depressed', being prone to 'panic attacks', or 'addicted to work', and so on.

It is difficult to escape from the idea of mental disorder. Indeed, difficult, it seems, to escape from disorder oneself.

A recent survey by R. C. Kessler and associates, published in the prestigious *Archives of General Psychiatry*, claims that nearly half of the citizens of the United States suffer from a mental disorder at some point in their lives (Kessler et al. 1994). Is that true? Does a label or concept with *that* many personal and social consequences apply to so many individuals in just one country alone? The accuracy of statistics like those offered in the survey depends, of course, on the validity or legitimacy of the concept of a disorder that it deploys or presupposes. Skeptics charge that such surveys typically fail to deploy sound and sensible concepts of a mental disorder (see Elliott 2003; Horwitz 2002; Horwitz and Wakefield 2007; Wakefield 1999). Unsound and insensible instruments, they charge, misclassify numerous cases of non-disorder as disorders and therein overestimate the prevalence and epidemiological range of instances of mental disorder. Some skeptics assert, too, that legitimate boundaries have yet to be drawn around a concept of mental disorder (see Bentall 2004; Poland, von Eckardt, and Spaulding 1994). One well-situated observer even claims that "psychiatrists do not know what they mean explicitly by mental illness/mental disorder" (Columbo 2008: 70).

Robert Schumann (1809–56), no doubt, had a mental disorder. To all informed ears Schumann is one of the greatest composers of classical music who has ever lived. But, tragically, Schumann suffered from a profound and periodically recurring depression. So profound, in fact, that he starved himself to death in an asylum, where he had insisted that he be placed after a failed suicide attempt. He had jumped into the Rhine River (Ostwald 1987).

Just as we don't wish people who lack mental disorders to be classified as if they harbor them, we don't wish people, like Schumann, who are subjects of a disorder being treated so poorly or incorrectly that they become suicide statistics. So: We need a *good* concept of mental disorder. We need a concept that identifies real cases of disorder and helps us to properly treat people with disorders. We need to enact what may be called conceptual rectitude in the very idea of a mental disorder. Or we need to do this as best we humanly can.

A tangle of different and competing concepts of mental disorder is available in the literature. I do not intend to survey them all, though some will be examined in the course of the book. This is because I assume that no concept of a mental disorder other than that which is proposed by a good theory of mental disorder suffices as a good concept. A concept with rectitude. We need a good theory before we can have a good concept and assess the strengths and weakness of competing concepts.

WHAT SHOULD A THEORY OF MENTAL DISORDER DO?

So, what should a *theory* – a good theory, a sound and sensible theory – of mental disorder do?

A theory of mental disorder should consist of several components. Five in all.

First and foremost, it should describe what a mental disorder *is*. It should offer a *concept* of mental disorder. This means it should offer a concept that captures the basic nature or constitution of a mental disorder and helps, in concert with other concepts, to distinguish mental disorders from disorders that are not mental, such as purely somatic illnesses like breast cancer or diabetes, as well as from non-disorders or 'mere' problems or disturbances in living, such as normal grief over the death of a loved one, anxiety over exams or fear about the possible loss of a job.

The need to offer or describe a concept of mental disorder does not mean that the concept must be constituted by a clinically tractable list of necessary and sufficient conditions for membership in the category *mental disorder*. That is, it does not require a hard and rigid categorical definition of mental disorder. If a hard and rigid definition for a mental disorder was to exist, disturbances or distresses would count as in the extension or compliance class of 'mental disorder' just in case they satisfy each and every condition on the list. No non-mental disorders would be corralled into the category of a mental disorder. No mental disorders would be outside the conditions in the list.

Consider an imaginary template for a list of the necessary and sufficient condition type.

C_1 –.
C_2 –.
C_3 –.
C_4 –.

Now imagine filling in the blanks with descriptions of purported conditions or characteristics of a mental disorder, whatever they may be. Once filled in, if the list is correct or accurate and captures necessary and sufficient conditions, and we wish to know whether a particular distress or disturbance counts as a mental disorder, then we should consult the list and compare the con-stitution of the list with the character of the disturbing condition. When a disturbance possesses each and every element in the list, *then and only then* does it count as a mental disorder.

Lists of necessary and sufficient conditions or hard and fast definitions for being a mental disorder are notoriously hard to devise. No such list has attracted the consensus of informed professionals. Indeed, whenever such a definition or list is proposed by someone, which occurs rarely, other theorists tend to be skeptical. Rightly so, I believe.

I assume that the concept of a mental disorder lacks necessary and sufficient conditions for its application. In so doing, I am agreeing with psychiatrist Nancy Andreasen, when she says that it possesses "debatable boundaries" (Andreasen 1984: 35). I am, however, disagreeing with various other theorists who charge that its debatable boundaries mean that the concept of a mental disorder just is a catchall concept, utterly resistant to regimentation or conceptual rectitude (Gorenstein 1992: 14). Plenty of good and useful empirical concepts have debatable boundaries, even if they don't have necessary and sufficient conditions for their application. Take the notion of a 'book', for example.

You, I assume, are holding an instance of the proper application of this concept in your hands right now. You know how to talk about books and to recognize them. But, I suspect, you appreciate that there is plenty of conceptual elbow room for debate over what exactly counts as a book. There are fuzzy borderline (non-exemplary, non-prototypical) cases. Must a book have pages? Must it be printed? Can it be stored in a computer file? Can an author carry a book around in their head? Is a comic book truly a book? To debate how best to answer questions like those is neither to deny that, objectively speaking, books really do exist nor to doubt whether you are reading a book. It is not to assert that 'book' is a catchall term or that we don't have the foggiest idea whether books are housed in libraries or may be purchased in stores.

Eleanor Rosch understands how sound and sensible empirical notions like that of a book or of a mental disorder are best defined (Rosch 1978; see also Margolis and Laurence 2003). Rosch, a psychologist at the University of California at Berkeley, says it goes something like this. People begin by using a word to describe cases to which the word initially is intended to apply. Over time the word's application may then be extended to novel cases by a successive series of similarities, resemblances, and analogies with the initial cases. So, for instance, someone first calls an object a 'book' if it is a set of written printed and bound pages, and so on. Then someone calls a second object a book because it resembles the original object in certain ways, if not in every way; then, the process continues. Up to a point. What point? That depends. Sometimes the resemblances in the mind of the speech community are too thin, metaphorical, or confusing to merit the term 'book'. Or other terms may do a better job. The book on my desk is a book. The 'neural code' in my head, unwritten and unbound, is not. It's just a neural code. But extensions sometimes stick. Comic books cost much more today than they did when I was a child. They're also books despite not possessing truly protective covers.

Failure to possess necessary and sufficient conditions is no liability for an empirical notion that like of a book. Nor, I assume, is it a liability for the empirical notion of a mental disorder. Besides which, for a concept like that of a mental disorder to possess such conditions (or more exactly conditions believed to be necessary and sufficient) arguably is not a blessed event. A list of purported necessary and sufficient conditions (especially depending upon the alleged necessary conditions) may overly or unwisely constrain whatever empirical investigation may discover about a disorder.

Suppose the American Psychiatric Association decrees that something is a mental disorder *only if* it is a brain disorder or a neurological malfunction, impairment, disease, deficit or disability viz. the expression of a broken brain or 'mechanism'. Mental disorders are types of neurological disorders, so dictates the higher councils of the Association. Call this purported necessary condition 'C_3'.

Faced with this piece of judgment or legislation, psychiatrists, neuroscientists, neuropsychologists and others would be encouraged or urged to try to discover, identify, and describe impaired or disabled mechanisms within the brain that C_3 says are properly referred to as mental disorders. If C_3 is true, it must be possible, in theory at least, to tell a brain damage or neural malfunction story for any and all properly classified mental disorders. Indeed, a lot of mental health professionals are already attracted to a broken brain/neural disorder conception of a mental disorder. A psychiatrist, for example, may tell her depressed patients that depression is "a brain disorder, just like epilepsy". "Just as you would take drugs for epilepsy, you should take them for your mental disorder."

Some of the reasoning behind the broken brain conception of a mental disorder is represented by the following line of argument.

1. The mental is physically based or realized in the brain or the neural.
2. *X* is a mental disorder.
3. So, *X* is a neural physical disorder, a disorder of the brain.

Consider, though, a somewhat analogous inference about your computer. A software state of your computer is physically based in a hardware state. So, a software malfunction is a hardware malfunction. Or:

1*. A computer software state is based or realized in a hardware state.
2*. *Y* is a malfunction in the software.
3*. So, *Y* is a hardware malfunction, a disorder of the hardware.

But, of course, it does not follow that if a computer's software fails to function properly, then its hardware base is broken. If my computer finds the wrong price for a desired airline ticket, this could be a hardware problem, a software problem or a simple, albeit frustrating, instance of misinformation at the airline's website. Peculiarities in software or in an environmental source of information may be responsible for errors in processing even if there is no corresponding malfunction in the computer's physical machinery (see Arpaly 2005: 283).

I believe that a distinction between a brain disorder and mental disorder, if it can be established, and a mere analogy with a computer does not establish it, for that's a big and complex 'if', would be immensely important theoretically. I am in favor of drawing it (a topic discussed throughout the book). I am in favor of saying that a mental disorder may be based in an unbroken or healthy brain. I am not alone in holding the view that mental disorders may be based in unbroken or healthy brains (see Arpaly 2005; Poland 2013; Nesse and Jackson 2011; see also Graham and Stephens 2007 and Stephens and Graham 2009a), although I may be willing to understand, extend, develop or hold fast to this possibility in ways in which other theorists are not, such as by making it central to the very idea of a mental disorder in which conceptual rectitude is enacted as well as to metaphysical *realism* about mental disorder.

If we understand a mental disorder as a type of brain disorder and recount its story just in terms of a damaged or malfunctioning brain, while this does not imply that we are mistaken in thinking of the condition as a disorder (after all, it is a neurological disorder), it does rule out thinking of the disorder as a *mental* disorder (or so I hold and plan to argue). Realism, for me, about mental disorder says that mental disorders are honest-to-goodness *mental* conditions or states of persons. While this needs not entail that they are non-physical in nature, it does preclude, as I plan argue, understanding a mental disorder in exclusively and exhaustively neuroscientific or neuro-mechanical malfunction terms – as is the case with conditions that are brain disorders or cases of broken or malfunctioning brains.

Of course, it may be objected that any pattern of neural activity that serves as the physical or existential basis of a mental disorder qualifies, by this very fact alone, as a brain or neural disorder. Such a piece of conceptual legislation, however, is not what neurologically enamored investigators typically mean when they propose that a mental disorder is nothing other than a type of neural or brain disorder. An enormous scientific investment is being made in many quarters in finding the neural mechanisms that underlie mental disorders. Often this investment is based on the premise that mental disorders are nothing other than disorders or impairments of brain mechanisms – or brain diseases, as the premise sometimes is put. Nancy Andreasen writes in a chapter of *Brave New Brain* entitled (and note the title) "Broken Brains and Troubled Minds" that "Psychiatrists ... have steadily recognized that mental illnesses are ... cells in our brain [gone] bad [and] this is expressed at the level of systems such as attention and memory [in disorders] such as schizophrenia and depression" (Andreasen 2001: 7; see also Andreasen 1984: 8). (Here and hereafter in this book words in brackets that appear in quotations are inserted by me.)

What normally is meant by referring to mental disorders as disorders of the brain or cells gone bad is that various neurologically specifiable breakdowns or malfunctions occur in the brain (due to a developmental trauma, anatomical injury or chemical pathogen, just to name three sorts of causes) and that such breakdowns help to constitute or compose the conditions that are referred to as mental disorders. So, a mental disorder is a type of brain disorder. It is not merely realized or existentially embodied in the brain (in its cells, as it were), but is itself a form of bad cells or neural damage or impairment.

Given the purpose or intent behind the broken brain view, it is contrary to its scientific aspiration to propose that 'brain disorder' should be defined first in terms of the conceptually prior notion of a mental disorder, and then and then only recommend that the notion of a mental disorder should be re-described as that of a brain malfunction or disorder, all the while continuing to use the criterion of a mental disorder as the criterion for a brain disorder. The whole effort of identifying a mental with a neural impairment would be viciously circular. It would make the notion of a brain disorder depend on the notion of a mental disorder rather than the other way around. The identity of a mental with a neural disorder (urged by Andreasen and others) is supposed to mean that the very ideas of a neural disorder and of how the brain is supposed to operate if healthy, properly regimented or explicated, should be used to describe what makes something a mental disorder. It is not supposed to mean that the *mere* fact that the brain is the physical basis of a mental disorder means that the brain itself is disordered or damaged in cases of mental disorder, viz. possesses 'cells gone bad', to restate Andreasen's catchy phrase.

As it happens, the general distinction that I am suggesting here between that of a disorder being *in Z* (in Z, the brain, as its existential base) versus *of Z* (a *brain* disorder) is quite orthodox in medicine. Consider the domain of somatic or bodily illness or disease. The presence of pain, fever, cough, nausea, vomiting, diarrhea or fatigue does not necessarily mean that something is wrong or malfunctioning with a person's body or soma even though, of course, such events are unpleasant and often need to be addressed medically. Fevers and diarrhea, for instance, may, on occasion, be a body's defenses against disease, danger or bodily damage (see Nesse and Williams 1996). Fever or diarrhea may mean that the body is functioning well by personal preference-indifferent biological standards. Perhaps it is ridding itself of dangerous toxins. So: Some somatic distresses, including discomforts whose aversive or harmful qualities warrant medical treatment and amelioration, may not therein actually be physical illnesses or diseases (depending upon the criteria for such). In such cases we need not speak of a disorder (an impairment, dysfunction, breakage or incapacity) *of* the body in order to identify the physical sources of discomfort. A fever or case of diarrhea may be a disturbance in the body without being an illness or malfunction of the body.

I am suggesting that insisting upon brain disorder status for qualifying as a mental disorder goes conceptually overboard. Of course, even assuming the conceptual possibility of being able to distinguish between explanatory standards for brain and mental disorders, it may be difficult *empirically* (even given the theoretical wisdom of the distinction) to tell apart the identity of a healthy or 'ordered' brain that underwrites a mental disorder from that of a broken brain that underwrites a neurological illness with psychiatric symptoms. Consider Tourette's Syndrome, which, I assume, is a neurological disorder. It is marked by facial tics, forced vocalizations and involuntary profanities. There are number of hypotheses for the possible forms of brain disorder responsible for the Syndrome, early brain damage or childhood infection among them. But it is not obvious just from what the Tourettic person says whether they are suffering from a neural impairment (brain damage or infection) with psychiatric symptoms or, instead, angrily, as part of a mental disorder (paranoia perhaps), intending to indulge in hateful speech acts under conditions, say, of stress or emotional arousal. We may be inclined to say things about them like "As part of her illness she really hates me and wants to insult me". But suppose the proper scientific picture is: "No, no, no, she does not hate you or intend to insult you". "Her speech reflects no deliberate intention and is not infused with real conceptual content" "She is undergoing a burst of impaired electrical activity in her brain." "The sounds appear as speech, real profanities, but they aren't." "Her cells have gone bad."

There is a difference between saying that the subject of Tourette's irrationally hates or distrusts the people at whom they curse and that this explains why they curse, and saying that their profanities are not speech acts (or real or intended curses) at all, but the expressions of impaired electrical activity. The first would be apposite in describing or understanding Tourette's symptoms as expressions of a mental disorder (wherein explanatory reference to the neural is incomplete and psychological explanation partly is called for). The second is the sort of remark appropriate to thinking of Tourette's as a neurological disorder.

As for conceptual rectitude and the concept of mental disorder: If conceptual rectitude cannot be achieved by reference to necessary and sufficient conditions or to disorders using bio-neurological criteria or standards of brain damage or malfunction, then how is it best achieved? Fortunately, there is another way in which to begin to characterize *mental disorder* – at least as a revisable working hypothesis or starting position for a theory of mental disorder. It has been hinted at above in the example of a book. This is to recognize that the concept of a mental disorder has uncontroversial or prototypical instances of application or exemplars, as they may be called. An uncontroversial instance or exemplar is a case that competent and clinically informed observers or qualified judges agree (or at least currently widely agree) is a mental disorder. Then, reference to prototypical or exemplary features of such cases provides some initial working information about how best to characterize the idea of a mental disorder. Reference to a disorder's prototypical features also *fallibly* characterizes a disorder. If a disorder now is consensually classified as mental but somehow later is discovered to be a neurological disorder, then the condition should fall out of the category of a mental disorder. It should be reclassified as a deficit or disorder of a broken or diseased brain. A condition may fall out (or in) the evolving compliance class of mental disorders.

Ian's paranoia may be thought of as a mental disorder until perhaps it is discovered that a specific site in his limbic system is damaged and is responsible for his reason-unresponsive or general distrust of other people. If so, it would be time then for brain science to take over the explanatory understanding of his condition.

So, what about a good theory of mental disorder? A good concept of disorder is needed from that theory. A theory of mental disorder should have elements other than a concept for the domain of mental disorder. It's not all about the idea of a mental disorder. And it's not all about disentangling relationships, if they deserve to be disentangled, between the idea of a mental disorder and that of a brain disorder.

Second, there should be a list that specifies types or kinds of mental disorders. Such a list is known as a taxonomy or nosology of mental disorder. The taxonomy should identify categories of mental disorder, such as 'major depression' and 'paranoid delusional disorder'. It should contain descriptions of the compositional or constitutive details of particular disorders. What makes depression a case of depression? Delusion a delusion?

Third, the theory should explain why disorders are undesirable conditions of persons and normally require medical/psychiatric address or clinical amelioration. Or as I like to put it: The theory should answer the following question: What impairments of *basic* or *fundamental* psychological capacities or mental competencies or faculties make them disturbances of clinical importance or psychiatric significance? These may be conditions that need to be 'fixed' or repaired.

Fourth, the theory should offer or provide explanations of the occurrence or onset of disorders as well as of the emergence and progression of their symptoms. This fourth element is worth a short pause or commentary.

Explanations clarify or illuminate. They identify how something comes to be, or why things happen as they do. So, for instance, an explanation of the occurrence of a mental disorder, say, a case of major depression, MD, may claim that the immediate origins or proximate causes of the disorder lie in certain sorts of conditions or events (X) rather than others (Y). In so doing, the explanation may deploy counterfactual claims or statements of the following sort. If, contrary to fact, X had not happened, or Y had happened rather than X, then the mental disorder, MD, would or probably would not have occurred. An explanation may therein contain predictive power among its warrant or grounds. If reference to X (rather than to Y) explains the present occurrence of a disorder, MD, then the reappearance of those very same conditions predicts the future or likely future occurrence of the very same sort of disorder. If this prediction holds true, then this is one good reason for preferring the explanation of MD in terms of X rather than the explanation in terms of Y.

Finally, fifth, a theory of mental disorder should tell us how to treat or care for people with a mental disorder and how persons may recover or reconstitute their mental health. One of the main goals of medicine is the care and cure (if possible) of those with a malady. It is immensely consistent with the rest of medicine, of course, for a theory of mental disorder to be aimed, in important part, at the care and ideally cure of individuals with a mental illness. Indeed, I think this is one of the background considerations relevant to how we should try to explain the occurrence and progression of a mental disorder. With multiple and sometimes conflicting theories and descriptions competing as explanations of a mental disorder, our notion of a best theory of disorder calls for some connection with clinical demands and the morality of care and treatment of disorder. When we widen our purview to take in not just our scientific research but our clinical practice, and not just clinical practice but its moral or ethical dimensions, we should be cautious in embracing explanatory hypotheses about a disorder that are not focused on or applicable to therapeutic recovery and reconstruction of mental health and well-being.

Philosophers sometimes talk of so-called 'superempirical' virtues of a scientific theory, by which they mean things like its simplicity, power of explanatory unification, and coherence with background knowledge and understanding. To this I would add, in the case of a theory of mental disorder, a theory's clinical utility or promise of positive therapeutic applications. This 'superempirical' medical virtue should not force dismissal of a theory with independently strong evidential and explanatory grounds. Sometimes the truth does not help but hurts. But a theory's clinical utility should encourage (other things being equal) the theory's at least pragmatic adoption or temporary embrace over less useful competitors.

A concept of mental disorder. A nosology of disorders. An identification of undesirability. Explanations of disorders. A path to clinical utility. These are the foci of a theory of mental disorder. I will have things to say about each of these five topics or elements over the course of the book, although not much about the fifth. First things first, however.

The question being asked is: What is *mental disorder*? How should the category or concept of a mental disorder be characterized? At this point, since we do not yet have a theory of mental disorder, we cannot trot out and fully describe the concept that is or should be part of our theory. But a foretaste or pre-statement of it may prove useful, prior to development or analysis.

Consider a real case of a mental disorder or least one that I assume is a real mental disorder (if clouded in history and contestable in interpretation). Consider the case of Virginia Woolf (1882–1941), English novelist and essayist. Woolf committed suicide by drowning herself. Why did she do such a dreadful thing? Here's a plausible hypothesis: Woolf feared a complete depressive breakdown (having had major depressive episodes in 1895 and 1915) from which she believed that she could not recover. In a suicide note to her husband, Leonard Woolf, she wrote that "I shan't recover this time." "I begin to hear voices." "I can't fight it any longer" (quoted in Slavney and McHugh 1987: 31). Quentin Bell wrote of Woolf's episodes as follows: "Her sleepless nights were spent in wondering about whether her art, the whole meaning and purpose of her life, was fatuous, whether it might be torn to shreds by a discharge of cruel laughter" (quoted in Slavney and McHugh 1987: 31). Woolf's disorder, in the words of Philip Slavney and Paul McHugh, two psychiatrists at Johns Hopkins who have studied her case in retrospect, "shaped her development as a person and as a writer, affected her closest relationships, and eventually claimed her life" (Slavney and McHugh 1987: 116).

The symptoms of Woolf's particular disorder consisted, in part, of a complex set of conscious experiences of self and world: anxious sleepless nights, doubts about her art, fear of public humiliation, grief over the loss of her London homes during the Blitz, and so on.

A large body of research examines the general sort of subjective situation and social circumstance in which someone like Woolf appears to have been embedded (see Klinger 1977; Emmons 1999; see also Abramson, Metalsky, and Alloy 1989). When a person is committed to a life defining goal (in Wolfe's case, that of being an accomplished and admired writer), persists in intense and challenging efforts to achieve it, but simultaneously fears or believes that the likelihood of success is negligible or slim-to-none, they may feel trapped or intractably stymied, helpless or impotent. They may believe that they can neither approximate that goal nor effectively disengage from its pursuit, since so much of their labor has already been mixed with its land, so to speak. Perhaps such a person's conception of their own merits as a person may depend on the goal's pursuit but is, as the person fears, most likely to be frustrated. When this happens, when a person is driven to succeed but feels bound to fail, their commitment to themselves and to their own personal well-being may collapse or tumble. They may become incapable of prudently taking care of themselves or of protecting their own welfare or well-being. Whether this describes Woolf's situation and some of the psychological forces behind her depression (viz. a sense of entrapment or helplessness) may be debated, of course. (I am assuming, for purposes of illustration, that it does describe such things.) But certainly Woolf lacked a prudent capacity for responsible self management. Despite her successes and the attentions of those who loved her and admired her work, she ended up committing suicide.

So, what, then, is a sound and sensible concept of mental disorder? Rather than travel through this and a number of chapters to reveal my final answer, I shall state it now. Then, after working through the next several chapters, I plan revisit the statement in the sixth chapter, having in the meantime detailed both its meaning and rationale and adding additional features to it.

There are four main and different, although interconnected, parts to the concept of a mental disorder that I propose. It goes like this (remember, subject to later refinement and addition).

The notion of a mental disorder, prototypically understood and conceptually regimented, is the notion of (i) a disability, incapacity or impairment in one or more basic or fundamental mental faculties or psychological capacities of a person – not a complete and utter or total incapacity, but an incapacity or impairment, that (ii) has harmful (or likely harmful) consequences for its subject. The disability, incapacity, or impairment possesses a special sort of proximate or immediate origin or source. It is (iii) brought about by an interactive mix of mental forces, on the one hand, and (what may be called) brute a-rational neural mechanisms (although not of the pathological sort operative in a case of brain damage), on the other, and (iv) in which the interaction or intersection of these two forces endows the disorder with a truncated 'logic' or an impaired or compromised rationale that is distinctively a disorder's own.

A depressed Alice may not get out of bed. A paranoid Ian may remain locked inside his home. Woolf may commit suicide. Just why such people do such things rather than others is explained, in part, by the rationales behind or within their depressions and paranoia. The depressed Alice does not wish to face the day, so she stays in bed. The paranoid Ian does not wish to engage with other people and possible agents of the FBI, so he locks his door. Woolf fears another breakdown. For her death is the answer.

If I am right and this notion of a mental disorder is sound and sensible, then Woolf's depression, Alice's depression, and Ian's paranoia qualify as instances of mental disorders if each reflects a harmful disability of one or more of their basic psychological capacities, and springs from two sorts of factors, one characterized in mental terms, the other in neural terms (see just below), and that put each of them at serious risk for harm (e.g. for committing suicide). For instance (to oversimplify for illustrative purposes): One possible neural mechanism behind certain aspects or features of depression may be high levels of emotional activation or arousal produced by the limbic system. Eventually, this activity may cascade into the hypothalamus and from there into the autonomic nervous system, preparing a person for, for example, a suicide attempt. Meanwhile, one set of mental forces (among others) behind a depression (or certain cases of depression) may be a belief in one's personal helplessness, impotence or inability to reach desired goals. This belief may lead a person to a severe decline in self care. "I can't help myself, so why bother to try?" The mood effects of levels of emotional arousal combined with belief in personal helplessness and a decline in prudent self care may help not only to bring about a depression but to 'rationalize' some of a depressive's behavior. Committing suicide may possess a sad, sorry and truncated rationale.

Andreasen appears to recognize the power and relevance of the two sorts of forces that I mention as responsible for a disorder (in [iii] above). She writes: "As we think about mental illnesses, we will be mindless if we address only the brain and brainless if we address only the mind" (Andreasen 2001: 29). Properly interpreted, that's part of my position or of the concept of a mental disorder that I believe we should adopt. However, I hasten to add that in identifying mental disorders with disorders of the brain (or with cells that are gone bad), as she does, Andreasen accepts a form of explanatory reduction of mental disorder to that of a neural disorder. And that most certainly is not my view: neither the identification nor the reduction.

How do I come up with the above characterization of a mental disorder? Is it warranted? What does it mean? Which concepts in philosophy of mind are presupposed by it? What do those concepts mean? The four sub-theses (of [i] through [iv]) of the concept that I propose require substantial analysis and motivation. This they hopefully do receive over the course of the next several chapters. One key concept must also be added to the mix of notions in the concept of mental disorder. This is appeal to the notion not just of mind or mentality, but of the rationality or reason-responsiveness of a person.

I plan to proceed as follows. I will divide up the question of 'What is mental disorder?' into two sub-questions. One is: What is *mental* about a mental disorder? The other is: What constitutes the *disorder* of a mental disorder?

In one way or another, these two questions occupy me all the way up to nearly the end of Chapter 6, when I return to the above concept of a mental disorder. Hopefully, by then, I will have successfully explained what a proper concept of a mental disorder is like or is best understood to mean and why it is worth endorsing. I am acutely aware that my concept and its background theory may not strike each and every reader as plausible. But I shall stand by it. At best, it is a sound and sensible theory and worthy of further development. But even at worst, if the theory is grossly mistaken, its mistakes may be illuminating. The theory may serve as one example, an extended case study, of possible connections between philosophy of mind and mental disorder.

THE MIND OF MENTAL DISORDER

A huge book sits on my shelf. It's a reference book that I sometimes consult when conducting research on mental disorder. It's nearly 1,000 pages long and entitled *Neurobiology of Mental Illness* (Charney, Nessler and Bunny 1999).

It's a book with a big hole in it. Not a physical hole. A semantic hole. For despite its title, the word 'mental' is not mentioned in the index, let alone described or defined in the book. So, then, how on earth was it decided by the editors which illnesses to examine in the book?

Anxiety and mood disorders are examined. But so, too, are tic disorders. Schizophrenia is examined, but so, too, are Alzheimer's and autism. Depression surely is a mental disorder. But tics? Alzheimer's? Such classifications are dubious and need argument. It needs to be shown why, say, Alzheimer's possesses not just mental symptoms (which, of course, it does) but the sort of causal origin or immediate source that makes it a mental disorder. The big book offers no such argument. In the title the word 'illness' wears the conceptual pants. 'Mental' is left conceptually naked or without explication.

In the literature on mental disorder, applications of the term 'mental' are often deployed without conceptual attire or semantic explication. Bengt Brulde and Filip Radovic note with a tone of lament that in "almost everything that has been written about the concept of mental disorder ... focus has not been on what makes a disorder *mental*, but on what makes a mental disorder a *disorder*" (Brulde and Radovic 2006: 99). The philosopher Dominic Murphy bemoans this same neglect. "Psychiatry," he says, "contains no principled understanding of the mental" (Murphy 2006: 61).

Brulde, Radovic, and Murphy are right. The very idea of the mental deployed in psychiatry as well as in the theory of mental disorder typically is unexamined or at least under-examined by psychiatrists and others writing on mental disorder. That is unfortunate. Witness the book on my shelf.

Murphy does try to offer a start, however. He writes: "'the mental' covers states and processes that play a very direct role in intelligent action, including processes such as perceiving, remembering, inferring, and a wide variety of motivational states" (Murphy 2006: 63).

Not bad – for a start. But the question arises as to just what constitutes the mentality of the states and processes that he mentions. What is the principal or foremost difference between mentality and non-mentality? Why, for instance, is my perceiving or remembering the hair on my head mental, but growing the very same hair not? Murphy seems skeptical about being able to answer such general questions about mentality without, as he says, waiting to learn what the "sciences recommend" (Murphy 2006: 64). But we don't need to hold our semantic breaths. There is no need for that. We may offer *some* analysis of mentality and then empirical science, broadly understood, so as to include cognitive science and the neurological and social sciences, may, of course, try to refine or revise our effort. In the meantime we are not in the pre-scientific dark.

We may pick out the domain of mental by identifying various prototypical examples of mentality (e.g. thinking, sensing, perceiving, and so on), as Murphy in effect does, and then extrapolating a general description. As the philosopher Eric Olson remarks:

> We agree on a wide range of typical and characteristic ... mental phenomena. ... No one doubts that beliefs, memories, intentions, sensations, emotions and dreams ... are mental phenomena, and that earthquakes and temperatures are not.
>
> (Olson 2007a: 264)

If we do so, if we extrapolate a general description, and this is the actual technique used in philosophy of mind, then what do we find? What we find, I believe, is that states of mind or mentality are constituted by either or both of two elements, aspects or features. These two features are consciousness or conscious phenomenology, on the one hand, and Intentionality (a technically named feature to be explained just below), on the other.

"The mental begins and ends with consciousness and intentionality." "Consciousness and intentionality help to define the mental *qua* mental." So write Terence Horgan, John Tienson and me in summarizing what the philosophy of mind tells us about the very idea of mind (Graham, Horgan and Tienson 2007: 468). That's what philosophy of mind says is the mental: states or conditions of persons (and of other creatures) that are conscious as well as states or conditions possessed of Intentionality. I need to explain.

Presumably, among all the things that there are, some are mindless, some minded. A brick is mindless; so, too, is an earthquake. But we persons possess minds of our own. What is the basis for this distinction? Between being minded and mindless, between person and brick? In what does it consist? It consists, in the broadest sense, in the fact that neither bricks nor earthquakes harbor perspectives or possess the power or ability to consciously represent their selves or the world. A brick is unaware of itself. A quake, although it may bring devastating horrors to the world, bears no thought of the world that it effaces. By contrast, all sorts of things (including us ourselves) appear to us persons in all sorts of different and distinct ways. A box of chocolates may appear to us as a thank-you for a job well done. An architect's papers may appear as a blueprint, prescribing the construction, measuring the spaces and places of our intended home.

To say that we have perspectives or powers of representation is to say two things. One is that representations of self or world are subjective, in the sense that they exist only as had by us as subjects. They mean something for us as well as to us. They mean something for us insofar as they give us reasons for acting in one way rather than another. It is because I see a snowball heading at my face that I duck rather than confront another person head on. It is because I can distinguish between wine that was bottled in France and wine that was bottled in North Dakota that explains why I purchase the French wine rather than the Dakotan variety. Perspectival representations mean something to us, insofar as, if we notice differences in how we experience or represent our selves or the world, we can do something about those representations or how we experience the world. We may learn that we are addicted and decide to try to refrain. We may inherit religious attitudes and aim to replace them with secular attitudes. We may try to modify our own perspectives.

The other feature of our perspectives or power of representation is that our experiences and conscious representational states are about things, or directed at things, other than themselves. This second or directedness aspect of possessing a perspective means that our mental states are about something – the world or ourselves. Franz Brentano (1838–1917) called this aspect of mindedness 'Intentionality'. (The adjectival form of the word is 'Intentional', but use of this term should not be confused with calling something intentional in the sense of its being purposeful or deliberate. See just below.) The word 'Intentionality' refers to the aspect of a mental state or representational attitude in virtue of which it is directed at, is of or about, or represents something other than itself (Brentano 1995 [1874]; see also Searle 1983). Intentionality is exemplified when a desire is for dark chocolate, a fear is of flying, or a mathematics professor wonders how best to describe a Cauchy sequence for her students.

Intentionality, it should be noted, has no special connection with intending or being intentional in the common English sense, in which, for example, I intend to eat dinner tonight or intend to begin a new aerobic exercise regime. Intending is but one form of Intentionality, among numerous others. (So as not syntactically to confuse 'intending' or 'intentionally' with 'Intentionality', I deploy a convention, rather common among philosophers, of capitalizing the first letter in 'Intentionality' when used to refer to Intentional phenomena i.e. mental phenomena possessed of aboutness or directedness.) Thus, for examples, beliefs, perceptions, desires, intentions, and memories are Intentional (note the "I" in a capital) states (i.e. states with Intentionality or directedness), as are emotions such as fear and joy, pride and shame, love and hate. Any mental state that is directed at or about something other than itself is an Intentional state. Your visual perceptual experience of this page, for instance, is possessed of Intentionality. Note, too, that although this page certainly exists, some purported things or events that a mental state or attitude is about or that fall within someone's subjective perspective may fail actually to exist. A song says, "I saw Mommy kissing Santa Claus underneath the mistletoe last night". Mother was there. Mistletoe was in place. But Santa, of course, was nowhere to be found. Mother cannot kiss Santa for he does not exist, although children may sing of him or misperceive of Daddy as Santa (see Harman 1998).

While the basic idea behind that of Intentionality or Intentional states or attitudes is that of directedness to a thing or object, 'thing' or 'object' is interpreted in a very broad way: material entities (cars), abstract (numbers) objects, properties (standing under the mistletoe), states of affairs (kissing mommy), or facts (that Dad is dressed up like Santa). Indeed, anything what-soever that a person may think about, or direct their attitude towards, may count as an object of thought. Even, as just noted, non-existent objects may count as the Intentional objects of Intentional states.

A perspective may be conscious, too, of course. Some things that we do we do for reasons that are not conscious. I place a food receipt in my pocket without thinking about it. But some elements or episodes in our perspectival life are conscious – we experience what is it is like to undergo them.

Conscious (also called 'phenomenal') experiences come in many varieties. Talk about consciousness permeates all discourse, prose and poetry, ordinary and special. Consciousness is the most vivid or explicit feature of our mental lives – of our being minded or possessing a perspective. As William James (1997/1910: 71) put it: "The first and foremost concrete fact which every one will affirm to belong to inner experience is the fact that consciousness of some sort goes on."

One of the most striking features of conscious experience is that the content or directed character of experience or of a conscious representation is directly apparent or immediately evident to its subject. You know directly of what you are thinking. You know, for instance, whether you are thinking of, say, chocolate ice cream or mother kissing Santa. You needn't observe the expression on your face in a mirror to decipher such facts. Mirror observation does not tell you. You know immediately or non-inferentially of the content of your thought. If, however, another individual is sitting next to you, they must rely on your behavior and verbal report to identify what you are thinking of or even if you are thinking about anything at all. As the head of a coma research group recently put it, "conscious awareness is a subjective experience that is inherently difficult to measure in another human being" (Laureys 2007: 87). Indeed it is.

Jones shot Phaedeux (pronounced 'Fido'), his dog. Jones gave a lot of conscious thought to shooting Phaedeux. Jones did so on purpose or deliberately. But we may wonder, what was

Jones thinking about in shooting the poor little creature? That the dog barks too much? That Phaedeux is getting too old and arthritic and needs to be put out of his misery? That the dog had bitten his little son, Jones Junior? (Jones would not tolerate that.) What was on his mind?

Jones had a conscious perspective, a conscious perspective of his own, in shooting his dog. But what was it? We need to ask him. He, by contrast, knows first-hand. "Phaedeux bit Junior", he thought to himself and then shot the poor creature.

A second prominent feature of consciousness is that even if some conscious states are not possessed of Intentionality, an important and pervasive number of conscious states are Intentional or possess directedness or aboutness. Your present visual experience, for example, would not be the visual experience that it is if it did not seem to you to be directed at a book on the subject of mental disorder. My present thought would not be the thought that it is unless it appears to me that I am thinking of Jones and Phaedeux.

Intentionality, if perhaps not as dramatically vivid as consciousness, is just as central to mindedness or to our being minded or having a perspective. One of the most significant aspects of Intentionality, evident on reflection, is that Intentional states have a structure analogous to acts of speech. Just as I may ask whether such-and-such is the case or promise that so-and-so will be the case, so I may hope that something is the case, fear that it is the case, or desire that it be the case. In each instance, the Intentional or representational content of an Intentional state (what it's about) is describable by a sentential clause or propositional phrase or *that*-clause. I fear *that* Woolf suffered from a severe form of depression. I know *that* Santa was not under the mistletoe last night.

Many items in the world other than minds seem to possess Intentionality or aboutness. They serve as apparent vehicles of Intentional content. They include things like the blueprints of a house, maps, representational paintings, words of a language, speech acts, novels, and road signs. The Intentionality of mentality, however, is unique. Mentality has Intentional content built right into it, as it were, as opposed to the map of a city, which derives its Intentionality from the manner in which it is designed or interpreted. A map expresses a perspective (that of the cartographer). But it does not have a perspective. The perspective is not in the map. It must be read into the map. The mind's Intentionality or aboutness is underived. It inheres in or is intrinsic to it. Something literally was on Jones's mind when he shot his dog.

Underived or intrinsic Intentionality is sometimes referred to as original Intentionality. The words or verbal inscriptions in this book mean and refer, and thus have a form of Intentionality, but it is extrinsic to them and originated or derived from me, when I wrote them down. For instance, suppose I write the string of letters or word 'bello'. If I were a speaker of Latin, I might mean *war* by this word; if Italian, I might mean *beautiful*. The point is not that such a string is devoid of Intentionality. The point is simply that the string's Intentionality (that is, what the string symbolizes, represents or is about) is a function of what I and other speakers use the word to mean or refer to.

The notions of consciousness and Intentionality are critical (as we will learn in detail later) for understanding the role of the mental in mental disorder. The philosopher Jennifer Church, in discussing the conscious Intentional states distinctive of depressed people, quotes a remark of a forlorn character in a movie by the distinguished late Swedish film director, Ingmar Bergman (1918–2007). Everything in the world, the character says, is getting "meaner and grayer"

(Church 2003: 175) An explanation of what it is like to be depressed, Church observes, "must take account of [a] correspondence between *what* is ... felt and *what* is ... perceived" (175). "The felt qualities of [a] depressed state ... are the perceived qualities of the objects around" the depressed person (Church 2003: 176). Depression is the state; grayness and meanness appear in the world outside the depressed person. To feel depressed is (in part) to perceive the world as mean and gray.

Church's observation generalizes to other sorts of mental disorders. In disorders the mental or psychological states typically cited as conscious and Intentional or possessed of Intentionality (such as being depressed or anxious about something) possess Intentional contents that are inseparable from their subjective, what-it's-like or phenomenal character. 'The ... qualities of a depressed state are the perceived qualities of the objects around.' Woolf's conscious Intentional states of depression, for example, were part of her experience of self and world – a self and world that had particular depressing qualities to her and that, to use Church's term, corresponded to her depressed mood or feelings. The same may also be said of, say, an anxious state. The qualities of an anxious state are the perceived qualities of various objects around the anxious person. My present state of agoraphobia, for instance, would not be the state that it is if it did not seem to me as if the crowd in the mall where I shop is dangerous, not to be trusted and threatening.

While philosophers of mind agree that the marks of mentality are consciousness and Intentionality, they disagree over how best to understand these features as well as about the relationships between them. Brentano, for his part, claimed that Intentionality is irreducible to and not constituted by anything physical. It's something non-physical. The challenge presented by Brentano is to characterize the relation between vehicles (like brains) of Intentionality and contents of Intentional states or attitudes. But some philosophers try to show that Intentionality can and should be understood in physical and impersonal terms. Fred Dretske (1988 and 1997) has been one of the leading theorists in trying to formulate a response to Brentano that is compatible with thinking of Intentionality and Intentional content in physical and not inherently subjective terms.

Some philosophers claim that Intentionality and consciousness are inseparably connected and that neither Intentionality nor consciousness, in an ultimate sense, can occur or is possible without the other (see Graham, Horgan and Tienson 2007 and 2009). But other philosophers argue that Intentionality can and commonly does occur without consciousness and/or that consciousness can and commonly does occur without Intentionality. Some Intentional states or attitudes (say, unconscious beliefs or desires) are not conscious. Some conscious states (say, generalized moods of anxiety or nervousness) are not about anything. The relevance of such claims and debates to our effort in this book to enact rectitude in the concept of a mental disorder and construct a theory of disorder is difficult and complex to appraise. This is because such claims are rarely raised in the context of discussions of mental disorder (remember the big book on my desk), and because debate about the nature of consciousness and Intentionality is one area in which something like Murphy's hesitancy to speculate about the mental before science has contributed may be methodologically prudent. As we talk more about mental disorder and about the roles of the mental in a disorder, we may be in a better position to assess claims about just what Intentionality and consciousness may involve.

So, how does mentality (Intentionality and consciousness) figure in mental disorder? What role or roles do conscious and Intentional states or attitudes play in a mental illness? I offer a few brief remarks about this topic here, but plan to return to it in more detail periodically throughout the rest of the book.

M. S. Moore claims that whether a disorder is mental is "related in some way to the symptoms exhibited by the person, not to the species of causation involved" (Moore 1980: 57). I agree with the first half of Moore's claim.

Appearing as symptoms and in the content or character of symptoms constitutes a truly important role for the mental (for consciousness and Intentionality) in a mental disorder, as witness the list of exemplars that I plan to offer in the next section of the chapter. Each and every disorder on that list is constituted, in part, by vivid and often harmful symptoms of consciousness and Intentionality. As Richard Bentall puts it: "[C]ommonly recognized forms of psychopathology involve some kind of abnormality of conscious awareness" (Bentall 2007: 130). Bentall offers two brief examples of the relevance of conscious symptoms with Intentionality to the concept of a mental disorder:

> [D]epressed patients are usually excessively aware of negative aspects of themselves, and are often tormented by memories of enterprises that have ended in failure. Anxious patients ... are typically extremely vigilant for potential threats in their environment.
>
> (Bentall 2007: 130)

Vigilance directed to the outside world and its threats are distinctive of anxiety. Tormented negativity about self haunts the severe depressive. Each of these sorts of states is both conscious and Intentional (possessed of directedness). There is something it is like to be tormented about oneself as well as to be anxious about perceived threats.

Moore denies, in the second half of his statement, that mentality plays a definitive role in the causation of a mental disorder. He says it helps to constitute symptoms, but fails to help to constitute the proximate origins of a mental disorder. We should disagree. Visual blindness is a mental symptom, certainly, but if it is caused by a cortical lesion, or damage to the retina, it is not a mental disorder. Contrary to Moore, mental causation (or causal-explanatory reference to a disorder's proximate psychological origins or propensity conditions) is also an important role for mentality in a mental disorder. None of the exemplars as exemplars (again, to be discussed momentarily) are best understood in their conditions of immediate onset or emergence without some or partial reference to conscious and Intentional states in which the contents of these states are causally efficacious in helping to bring about the disorder. Mere mental or psychiatric symptoms are insufficient for calling a condition a 'mental disorder'.

Consider depression. Strokes affecting the frontal area of the brain, especially the orbito-frontal cortex, can trigger something called "vascular" depression (see Kramer 2005: 174). But should we call the stroke a mental illness, just because depression is a symptom? It is necessary to look more closely at the causes of a stroke and the role that the mental may play (or not play) in the condition before a symptom can be categorized as a symptom of a mental disorder. A sound understanding of the causal foundations of a disorder is necessary before we know what kind of disorder a disorder it is.

Did Woolf kill herself and do so intentionally because she felt hopelessly trapped or did she do so accidentally because of a defective alteration of neurotransmitter function due to, say, Parkinson's disease? It's critical to know what causes or helps to cause a set of symptoms if we are to grasp what sort of disorder a disorder is and often just what sorts of behavior its symptoms themselves are. Depression-related deliberate suicide is one thing; accidentally annihilating oneself because of a prefrontal lobe dysfunction in episodic of loss of motor control is another. Did Woolf come to be depressed partly because of her assessments of her situation and habits of punitive self-evaluation – despite the fact (if it was a fact) that nothing was wrong with her brain?

Moore's view confuses the type of disorder a disorder is (whether mental or non-mental) with the type of symptom. Moore also unwisely assumes that symptoms themselves may be properly individuated and understood, at least for purposes of classifying a disorder type, independent of uncovering a disorder's origins. Often symptoms cannot be so identified. Remember Tourette's and the strange symptoms (involuntary cursing) and tics that Tourette's patients may suffer from. We may not know the explanation of Tourette's yet, but if its curses stem directly from damaged bits of electrical discharge, they are not *really* curses or intentionally nasty speech acts. The same sounds are perhaps curses from the mouth of someone else, an angry client or irate neighbor, but not from the tongue of someone in the verbal fits of the disorder.

Here is an analogy for mental disorder (and *pace* Moore) from somatic medicine about the importance of causation for nosology or classification. Suppose that each of us has a sore throat, which *type* of sore throat do we have? If mine is caused by streptococci and yours is not, mine is a strep throat and yours is not. Or: If mine is caused by tonsillitis and yours by mono-nucleosis, we each have a different sort of sore throat, and each sort requires a different sort of treatment. Causes make a difference. Symptoms reveal a disorder. Causes help to determine a disorder's type as well as the foundations and underlying identity of many of its symptoms.

So, we have to be careful in using disorder words or terms for disorders. Given that each of us is 'depressed', does this mean that we each are subjects of a mental disorder? No. It does not. Words can be used with different senses. If my depression is part of the fact that I have had a stroke or have Huntington's disease, which is a chronically progressive neurogenerative disorder characterized by a movement disorder, dementia, and psychiatric disturbances (including paranoia and depression), my depression, so-called, is an aspect of a neurological disorder (or so I assume). But if your depression is caused, in part, by the stressful experience of job loss, perception of marital decay or career entrapment, and if, more generally, it somehow requires partial reference to causes in psychological or Intentionalistic terms (terms that presuppose Intentionality) for its explanation, then, in my view, it is a mental disorder. It is (what I would call) a clinical or major depression of the sort that belongs in a manual of psychiatric taxonomy.

Note, I say, 'in part' or 'partial'. I am not claiming that for the explanation of a mental disorder nothing needs to be said about neurobiology, neurochemistry or neural circuitry or (in a fuller or more synoptic account) about more or less distal causes (background culture or sub-culture, autobiographical histories, problematic inter-personal relationships etc.). I am speaking of the proximate causes or sources of a disorder and of psychological descriptions contributing essentially, but not exclusively or exhaustively, to their specification and analysis.

I have much more to say about the causes or sources of disorder as well as of symptoms in the course of the book. Right now, though, I want quickly to turn to the problematic question of how to identify exemplary disorders.

EXEMPLARS OF MENTAL DISORDER

Here in a nutshell is a problem. How can we at least begin to conceive of forms or examples of mental disorder or of types of mental illness? There are no sacred texts to consult. Naked eyes fail to perceive disorders as disorders. Word worship will not help. Just because the word 'depression' or 'obsessive-compulsive' (or 'addiction', etc.) is used does not mean that a mental disorder is being spoken of. Sometimes these words are deployed as colloquial terms, picking out conditions that involve suffering or disturbance, but without implying or meaning to imply that an illness is present. Or sometimes they may be used to identify symptoms or instances of brain damage. Not mental disorders but brain disorders.

Perhaps the demands of clinical diagnosis and theoretical (psychiatric as well as anthropological and sociological) research may help to keep the very ideas of mental disorders under some sort of semantic control. So I assume the following: A good general way in which to introduce or devise a list of mental disorders is to pick out the most conspicuous and frequently identified disorders as exemplary, using distinct but overlapping standards of clinical and theoretical conspicuousness and frequency. This in itself is a complicated procedure, but a brief effort along these lines will, I believe, serve to identify a set of disorders that attract sufficiently wide consensus and consent.

Anthropology first. Arthur Kleinman, a professor of psychiatry and anthropology at Harvard, remarks that "many medical anthropologists are suspicious about the idea of culture-bound disorders" (Kleinman 2000: 302). The suspicion is not unfounded. A mental disorder if prototypical is not a disorder just of the Chinese or French Mind but of the Human Mind. Symptoms may be culturally or environmentally variable, of course, but a disorder, prototypically speaking, lays more firm or exemplary claim to qualifying as a disorder of mind if it afflicts people across distinct cultural or contextual niches. (Compare: Diabetes is not Canadian diabetes. It is, as it were, diabetes-diabetes. True, an outbreak of diabetes may appear in one place. But being place-bound is not essential to the condition.) So, one way in which to identify an exemplary disorder is to assume that a disorder is exemplary or prototypical when it is cross-cultural and then seek to identify cross-cultural disorders. Non-exemplary disorders may be culturally unique, and certainly certain symptoms may be niche specific, but not a disorder of a broadly consensual sort.

A possible example of a culture bound (hence not exemplary) disorder that Kleinman mentions is known as Chinese railroad psychosis, which also is known as *shenjing shuairuo*, although this perhaps is more likely to be a culturally specific manifestation of neuroasthenia (chronic fatigue) or a symptom of (the more general disorder of) depression. But what are some cross-cultural disorders?

Kleinman claims that five general types of disorder are cross-cultural. These are: Major or clinical depression, bipolar depression, schizophrenia, brief reactive psychoses, and a range of anxiety disorders "from panic states through phobias through to obsessive compulsive disorder" (Kleinman 2000: 302).

Insisting that exemplars must be cross-cultural is not free of empirical difficulty. It may be tough to distinguish between, on the one hand, cultures functioning as varying and shifting contextual scaffolds for a cross-cultural disorder's expressed symptoms and, on the other, cultures as harbors of specific disorders. Might not the defining features of a disorder include *niche specific* features, wherein a disorder is "comprehensible only in relation to some [cultural] norm or other cultural factor" (Murphy 2006: 253)? Take eating disorders, for instance, such as bulimia. Young white American females feel pressure to be thin more so than do their Navajo Indian counterparts. Quite generally, the epidemiology of bulimia tends to follow Euro-American ideas of beauty as they spread through other cultures. The conscious perception by young women of Euro-American ideas of thinness and beauty and the attendant social pressures on them to be physically attractive reinforce thinness as something desirable. This may help to explain the incidence rates and epidemiology of bulimia in certain cultural settings.

Is bulimia more like Chinese railroad psychosis (culture specific) or more like major depression (cross-cultural)? If Kleinman's list is sound and exhaustive, bulimia (not mentioned on his list) is not an exemplary disorder. It's more like Chinese railroad psychosis (assuming this is a culture specific disorder). Or perhaps it is a culturally tethered or socially structured set of symptoms of one of the general disorders which Kleinman lists. Perhaps it is a form of depression, anxiety or obsessive compulsive disorder with a distinctive grip on young women. One female victim of anorexia nervosa, a condition similar to bulimia, reports: "I knew that I had a certain strength … that would really show up somewhere." "I skipped breakfast." "I just couldn't fit the calories into my regimen." "I always 'watched it'." (Costin 1998: 243–44). She obsessively compulsively watched it.

Allan Horwitz remarks that "in the broadest sense symptom profiles … fit the illness norms of particular cultures" (Horwitz 2000: 116). Symptom profiles may be culturally tethered, but exemplary disorders themselves? With Kleinman I shall assume not. To be an exemplar or prototype (I am using these two notions interchangeably) is to be cross-cultural. In this way suitably informed observers, whether in Dakota or Singapore, should be able to reach agreement on certain cases of a disorder viz. an exemplary disorder.

Another sort of challenge arises when a list, like Kleinman's, contains one or more disorders that some observers are inclined to believe reflect brain damage or impairment – like bipolar disorder, which appears on his list. For me, if this were true, if conditions that are brain disorders may be on the list, it would force a relevant disorder off of the list and into the category of a brain disorder. Or perhaps it would serve notice that there are two variants of the disorder. One is in the domain a mental disorder; the other in the domain of a brain disorder. This possibility might show that the category of, say, bipolar disorder is poorly unified or disjoint, and that diverse perspectives need to be applied to the disorder's disjuncts, psychiatry in one type of instance, neurology in another. However, for the nonce, I want to postpone hard questions about the *ultimate* categorization of and presuppositions behind the exemplars until more is understood about just where there is conceptual elbow room for the category of mental disorder.

In any case: It would reinforce the wisdom of adopting a list of exemplars like or similar to that of Kleinman if its same or similar members were also identified on grounds other merely than cross-cultural presence. Are there other grounds? Yes, at least two of them.

So, here is a second and connected way in which to devise a list of exemplary disorders. Epidemiology. It consists of examining surveys or reports of the prevalence or incidence rates of mental disorders worldwide and then picking as exemplars only those that are most prevalent or possess the highest rates of global incidence. Skeptics do question, as earlier noted, and perhaps sometimes should question, the methods employed for gathering prevalence rates in statistical surveys. Methods used in such surveys? Sometimes just self-reports of symptoms when elicited in standardized interviews conducted over the telephone. "Diagnoses based on [personal] recollection," Randolf Nesse complains, "are biased by strong tendencies to forget" (Nesse 2001: 180). For that and other reasons, self-reports may be unreliable. But the following two facts are striking and useful for us to note about the main surveys that, to my knowledge, have been conducted to date.

One is that reports come from several different sources and survey instruments including the World Health Organization, the United States Epidemiological Catchment Area (ECA) survey, and the National Comorbidity Survey (NCS) (Kessler 2005; Kessler, Bergland et al. 2005; Kessler, Chiu et al. 2005; WHO World Mental Health Survey Consortium 2004). The other is that whether occurring in the United States or elsewhere depressive disorders and anxiety disorders are thought to be the most prevalent, often followed, in some countries, such as the United States, by substance or alcohol abuse or impulse control disorders (also known as addictions) (see also ESEMeD/MHEDEA 2000 Investigators). This fact about prevalence rates for depression and anxiety disorders dovetails more or less with part of Kleinman's list. Depression and anxiety disorders are prominent on his list. Substance abuse or addiction also is present on his list, if understood as instances of (what Kleinman calls) compulsive disorder. (Later in the book, in Chapter 7, I explore whether addiction is a form of compulsion.)

Taxonomic apostasy. A third method for identifying exemplars is owed to a mental health theoretician and clinician who is one of the most prominent critics of standard manners and modes of disorder categorization. "Psychiatry", he says, "has suffered from a poverty of ideas" (Bentall 2011: 167). It treats superficial and artificial categories as identifying homogeneous groups of illnesses, when the domain of mental illness itself is filled with heterogeneity at all levels of analysis and treatment.

I have already mentioned the critic in this chapter. It is Richard Bentall (2004). Bentall's rather iconoclastic (albeit not totally idiosyncratic) alternative idea about categorizing types of mental disorder goes something like this.

Popular taxonomies of mental disorder are either, at best, grossly unhelpful and misleading or, at worst, rest on a serious category mistake. The category mistake is that they encourage or presuppose a biomedical disease model of mental disorder. Disease models should be rejected, says Bentall. (I myself plan to examine disease models of mental disorder in the next chapter.) Mental disorders, says Bentall, are not diseases. Diseases typically have discrete edges, which distinguish themselves from each other and are discontinuous from normal variations in health. The sorts of mental health problems faced by the patients of psychiatrists just are not like that, says Bentall. Psychiatric troubles or maladies do not have discrete edges. They are hard to distinguish from normal, albeit otherwise immensely distressful, conditions. There is, for example, no obvious cut off point in the diagnosis of depression that suggests a uniform basis for distinguishing between being grief stricken or profoundly sad, on the one hand, and being clinically depressed, on the other. So, it is best not to think of people's psychiatric troubles or complaints as disorders if this means thinking of them as diseases – as hard edged, homogeneous phenomena. It's best to think of them, says Bentall, as just that viz. troubles or complaints with which people need help. As Bentall puts it, once troubles or complaints have been identified and explanatorily understood, there is no "ghostly" illness, disorder or disease "remaining that also requires explanation." "Complaints are all there is." (Bentall 2004: 141). Complaints are classes of disturbances that are "troublesome" and "worthy of [professional] attention" (Bentall 2004: 142). They are symptoms, to use the parlance of psychiatry. And it is pointless to try to bring tighter disease-like unity to them.

Bentall is not making Moore's claim that causation or causal explanatory understanding is irrelevant to the classification of a mental disorder. He is saying that a 'disorder' consists in symptoms or complaints plus causal origins of a non-disease type. Origins may operate at several different levels of analysis involving individual life-problems, failures to perform social functions, distress, and so on, but sums of such causes issue in "specific types of abnormal and cognitive functioning (Bentall 2011: 168).

Complaint- or trouble-orientated lists of 'disorders' like the one I am about to mention of Bentall are not without critics. Bentall is not without replies (Bentall 2004: 144). I don't wish to endorse his approach or complaint terminology in this context. I simply wish to cite his list.

Bentall mentions the following complaints as the ones most commonly seen by clinicians (Bentall 2004: 488). Complaints about or disturbances of: depression, mania, paranoia, cognitive incoherence, hallucinations, and negative symptoms (including flat affect, affective blunting, anhedonia, apathy, impoverished speech, among others)

What is striking about Bentall's list, at least to me, is that it overlaps with Kleinman's in certain respects as well as with global prevalence rates and incidence data, although it is devised from an utterly different taxonomic perspective. This is the perspective of someone who is deeply skeptical about current diagnostic practices and labels. Depression (major or clinical depression) is mentioned on each list. 'Mania' is part of what it means for a depression to be bipolar. But mania may also count, depending upon how it is described or understood, as a feature of a range of anxiety and impulse control disorders. Blunting, apathy and anhedonia are features of depression as well, of course. Incoherence and hallucinations are constituents of schizophrenia that are mentioned by Kleinman. Paranoia may be part of depression as well as mania and anxiety.

We certainly don't get a perfect match between the three lists. Perhaps such imperfection spells doom for thinking of mental disorder in terms of prototypes or exemplars. I think not. The proposed list of exemplars (which follows below), which is for something as complex as a mental disorder, unlike something as simple or relatively straightforward as a book, just is (in my book here) a sort of heuristic or organizational device. It offers reference points for regimenting or constructing a concept or notion of mental disorder. The proposed list is not, as noted above, intended as an unquestioned creed or without potentially contestable conditions of application. Some members may need to be deleted as we learn more about various conditions. Other conditions may need to be added. In any case, the three lists overlap in various ways. Some items are mentioned or appear on each. So, with such similarities or overlaps in mind, I assume that we are warranted in considering the following as mental disorder exemplars or prototypes.

- Depression (including major depression and depression with mania).
- Anxiety disorders (including phobias and some types of paranoia).

- Disorders of incoherence (including delusional disorders).
- Disorders of reactivity or impulse (including addiction or substance abuse and some forms of both mania and obsession).

So, back to the question: Just what chores or functions does mentality (consciousness and Intentionality) play in disorders or conditions of the above mentioned sorts? For a disorder to be a prototypical or exemplary disorder, it must include roles for the mental. What are they?

ROLES OF THE MENTAL IN MENTAL DISORDER

The mental plays various roles in a mental disorder. I mentioned the two primary roles earlier in this chapter. The first consists in its role as main or central symptoms or symptomatic contents of an illness. The second consists in being part of a disorder's proximate propensity or onset conditions, origins or causes.

Figuring in both symptoms and onset conditions or immediate causal sources are not the only roles of mentality in mental disorder. Psychotherapy for mental disorders, with reliance on reasoning and conversational address, focuses directly on a subject's conscious Intentional states. So, mentality or states of consciousness and Intentionality may also play roles as focal points for a disorder's therapeutic address.

Still another role? Some subjects of certain disorders know that they have a disorder or that something is wrong with them. This first-person knowledge is sometimes referred to as diagnostic 'insight' and is, as a form of self knowledge, constituted by conscious Intentional states. I say "some disorders", since for other types of disorder diagnostic insight on the part of a subject is absent. In delusional disorders, for example, diagnostic insight is missing and often disturbingly so, making it difficult to offer therapy voluntarily to a person (Fulford 1989 and 1994; Currie 2000). Deluded people don't think of themselves as deluded. After all, how could they? If I believe that I am God incarnate, but also believe that I am deluded in believing this, then the conviction that I am God incarnate will impress me as unwarranted or unfounded. So, in my own eyes, I should abandon it. It will hold no grip on me. Insight, however, is present in certain other sorts of disorder. Victims of obsessive thinking, for example, often complain of the obsessive and interruptive character of anxieties and thoughts, and this fact helps to distinguish, clinically, between a deluded subject (who may think that nothing is wrong with them) and a victim of obsessive thinking (Goodwin and Guze 1996: 4).

Aside, however, from certain forms of therapy and cases of illness insight, consciousness and Intentionality have two *main* roles, as already noted, in a mental disorder. In symptoms. In sources or causes. What, then, about sources?

To be brief and to pick up on threads of our earlier discussion: Something is seriously incomplete and over-broad in a concept of mental disorder if it is applied only on the basis of a disturbance's being mental in symptoms alone. Only if our causal explanatory understanding of a condition refers to feelings, beliefs, memories and other mental states or attitudes as causes or sources is a disorder mental. Why so? The answer, as noted in criticizing Moore, is that to understand what type of disorder a disorder is (whether mental or non-mental), it is necessary to go behind or inside symptoms to learn how the symptoms arose, as part of what sort of condition, otherwise even symptoms themselves may not be properly describable or understandable. This is a point I have made earlier but it bears repeating. The causes of a disorder help to contribute to the identity of symptoms.

Parkinson's disease is a degenerative disorder of the brain characterized by progressive tremor, slowness of movement, and rigidity (Litvan 1999: 559–64). Mental symptoms may be part of the symptom profile of this disorder in the form of failing memory, problems with concentration, and difficulties in initiating intentional or goal-directed activity. But do such symptoms make Parkinson's a mental disorder? No, they do not. Consciousness and Intentionality play no role whatsoever in the proximate onset or course of the condition. Degeneration of part of the midbrain (known as the substantia nigra) with subsequent decrease of a chemical messenger known as (striatal) dopamine is a probable cause of Parkinsonism. It is a purely neurological disorder or disease, viz. a disorder *of* the brain, albeit a disorder with harmful symptoms of a mental sort. (Or so I assume.) Neurological problems or deficits irrupt into the space of reasons or reason-responsiveness in Parkinsonism and in severe cases essentially swamp a person's ability to control various forms of bodily activity.

How do the rigid motions of a victim of advanced Parkinsonism compare with Alice's remaining in bed in the morning? How much like the slow movement of the Parkinson's patient are the lethargic and unwelcome motions taken by Alice, when she spots a window that needs to be closed from a bitter winter wind and tries to rise from underneath her bed covers, but can't? Compare the explanation for Parkinson's disease with that for Alice's loss of motivation (which, I am assuming, for purposes of illustration) stems in part from her protracted grief and perception of personal helplessness (Abramson, Metalsky, and Alloy 1989; Abramson, Seligman, and Teasdale 1978). To explain the failure of Alice's effort we must refer to her self conception and to how she thinks of her personal situation. We may ask: Why does she perceive herself to be helpless? No doubt, the experiences that led to her becoming depressed offer part of the answer. Her grief and disappointment (in her husband's behavior) may have strengthened her expectation of negative results for other commitments or behavior. So: If we are to intervene in her depression, we may try both to influence how she understands her husband's attitudes towards her and to provide optimal conditions for her learning to be more optimistic. In a case of Parkinson's, we would aim directly to manipulate its neurobiology/neurochemistry (no small chore as diminishing returns from dopaminergic therapy may sometimes contribute to further motor performance deterioration [Litvan 1999: 563]). No causal connection or association between impaired motor performance and a person's self comprehension is at all evident.

A key feature of Alice's sort of depression is that her conscious representations of self and world, viz. her states of consciousness and Intentionality, play (I am assuming for purposes of example) critical roles not just in the symptom profile or progression of her depression but in its immediate origins or conditions of onset. It is, in particular, in attitudes of a self-referential or self-interpretative nature that people experience themselves as helpless or as personally overwhelmed and therein may become depressed.

That a depression (or a type of depression like Alice's, sometimes labeled as a learned helplessness depression) may spring from such mental sources as perceived helplessness and a sense of hopelessness, does not mean that the psychology at the foundation of a disorder functions to the exclusion of brute a-rational somatic/neural conditions. It is my view (mentioned earlier and to be discussed throughout the book) that mental disorders are produced by a mixture of mental and brute mechanical factors. In mental disorders both mentality and neurobiology/neurochemistry partially incapacitate or 'gum up' the operation of (basic faculties) mind and behavior. Perhaps the brain of a subject of learned helplessness depression suffers a decline (not to be confused with 'cells gone bad') of neurotransmitter function, which is derived in part from interpretations of their own helplessness or frustrated efforts to avoid negative outcomes. The subjective experience of a helplessness depression may exemplify the interplay between such perceptions and an underlying neurobiology/neurochemistry.

One proposal for understanding the interplay in a mental disorder between psychological factors and neural activities is to think of them as operating at different levels of analysis or description and to depict the causal foundations of (or propensity conditions behind) a mental disorder or illness as consisting of the two different levels operating in interactive or dynamic concert and in a two-dimensional final pathway leading to disorder. The result is an inter-level inter-active organization of a mental disorder's causal explanatory foundations, in which any given psychological state or condition is influenced by and in turn influences mechanisms described in neurobiological terms. For example: Perhaps lowered serotonin does not as such cause depression directly or on its own, but permits hopeless attitudes and beliefs in one's own helplessness to get stuck in a person's stream of consciousness and to produce depression.

It's easy to see, by comparison and contrast, that nothing like a key causal explanatory role for psychology (consciousness and Intentionality) occurs in exemplary cases of somatic or bodily illness. Breast cancer neither immediately arises from nor disappears under pressure from a person's Intentional states (states with Intentionality). Cancer growth has somatic sources and may remit only under chemical forces. It would be ridiculous to try to cure breast cancer by, say, doses of Freudian psychotherapy.

Assuming that mentality plays a key causal role in exemplary mental disorders, it is worth wondering how we should answer questions about the *legitimacy* of the diagnosis of a mental disorder. Behavioral symptoms often present a nasty practical problem to the diagnostically conscientious clinician, who must spend time and effort in deciding (i) whether a particular cluster of mental symptoms expresses a mental illness rather than a brute somatic or neuro-logical disorder or perhaps (ii) whether the symptoms represent compensatory psychological adjustments that a patient makes in a case of brain damage. Borrowing a term introduced by the philosopher Nelson Goodman to distinguish, in the visual arts, between original paintings and inauthentic copies, exemplary mental disorders in their proximate origins bear an *autograph* (stamp or mark) of mentality (Goodman 1968: 113). They carry the mark of the mental on some of their sources or immediate propensity conditions. A mental autograph on some sources of a disorder helps to distinguish a disorder that is authentically or legitimately mental from one that is not.

Compare and contrast a case of mental disorder with Alzheimer's disease. Alzheimer's is characterized by progressively worsening memory, language and visual spatial skills, as well as changes in personality. Victims may also become depressed, apathetic, aggressive, and lose insight into their condition. As the disease progresses, delusions and paranoia may occur. But is Alzheimer's a mental disorder? Although its precise proximate physical origins are not known, it is wise, I assume, to classify Alzheimer's as having exclusively brute somatic or neuronal sources viz. likely degeneration of various sorts of processes in cortical and possibly sub-cortical neurons. So, it is not a disorder in which consciousness and Intentionality figure in its onset. No 'autograph of mentality' is present in its immediate sources, although mental decrements are present in symptoms and some of its symptomatic contents do, in fact, help to produce or sustain their own elements of dramatic personality change. (The disorientation or sense of helplessness produced by severe memory loss may be responsible, for example, for the depression and paranoia often observed in victims of Alzheimer's.) Moore may wish to classify it as a mental disorder for this reason. I believe we should not.

There is much more that can, should and will be said as the book continues about exemplary mental disorders being mental in aspects of their production and persistence as well as symptoms. For the nonce, however, I am done with the topic of the mind of mental disorder. I plan to turn in the next chapter to our second question about mental disorder. This is: What makes a mental disorder disorderly – a disorder? I approach this question by asking what makes a mental disorder undesirable.

SUMMARY

Mental disorder? What's that? Properly counting anything as a mental disorder requires having a sound and sensible theory of mental disorder. This chapter offered a brief sketch of the aims of a theory of mental disorder. Coming up with a good concept is one of them. It argued that exemplars or prototypes of mental disorders may serve as a constructive basis for a concept of mental disorder. The character of each exemplar is not written in stone and each example or case of disorder must ultimately be understood in terms of its proximate origins or sources and symptoms.

The chapter also described the concept of mind that applies to a mental disorder. It is that of a condition that possesses both consciousness and Intentionality. The chapter claimed that in mental disorders consciousness and Intentionality play two primary roles. One is in helping to constitute the symptoms of a disorder and the threat that the contents of such symptoms (say, the persistent global sadness and pessimism of depression) pose to a person. The other is in a mental disorder's immediate origins or sources.

SUGGESTED READING

Andreasen, N. (2001). *Brave New Brain: Conquering Mental Illness in the Era of the Genome* (Oxford: Oxford University Press).

Bentall, R. (2004). *Madness Explained: Psychosis and Human Nature* (London: Penguin).

Graham, G. (2013). 'Ordering disorder: mental disorder, brain disorder, and therapeutic intervention' in K. Fulford, M. Davies, R. Gipps, G. Graham, J. Sadler, G. Stanghellini and T. Thornton (eds) *Oxford Handbook of Philosophy and Psychiatry* (Oxford: Oxford University Press).

Hobson, J. and Leonard, J. (2001). *Out of Its Mind: Psychiatry in Crisis: A Call for Reform* (Cambridge, MA: Perseus).

Searle, J. (2004). *Mind: A Brief Introduction* (Oxford: Oxford University Press).

3 The disorder of mental disorder

WHAT MAKES MENTAL DISORDER UNDESIRABLE?

Writers on mental health and illness sometimes complain that the psychiatric use of the term 'disorder' is a conceptual embarrassment. "I am wary of the word 'disorder'," writes Ian Hacking (Hacking 1995: 17). Wary or not, however, the term serves as a potentially useful alternative to a number of other terms. It is common to speak now not just of a mental illness, for example, but of a mental disorder. This is not because the expression 'mental illness' is no longer used. It widely is used. I use it in the subtitle of this book. I use it interchangeably with talk of disorder.

The general intention behind the concept of a disorder when applied to a mental disturbance or distress is to try to capture at least three facts central to a disturbance. These three facts help to explain why a mental disorder is undesirable and something bad or disorderly as such. A condition that people *ought not* to be in. (I say 'help' because other features are also proper to disorders as such, as we will learn in later chapters.)

It is important to recognize, in preparation for describing the three facts, that the classification of a mental condition or state as undesirable or bad for a person is different from saying that it is undesired or believed to be bad by the person themselves. A disorder may be undesired, depending upon the condition, but it may not be. An addictive behavior pattern may be undesired, for instance, but perhaps not when its subject is high on a drug or winning wagers at a casino or horse track. Such a pattern, however, still is *undesirable*, whether or not the person appreciates this fact.

So, what are the three facts that help to explain why disturbances or distressing conditions which are classified as mental disorders are undesirable and 'disorders'? The first fact is that a disorder is harmful or dangerous. A person is much worse off or markedly more poorly off when the subject of a disorder than if mentally well-ordered, sound and healthy. So, for example, a person in the midst of, say, a major depressive episode, or someone in the grips of an obsessive compulsive disorder, is poorly off. Not only may these particular conditions feel bad (again, not all disorders or episodes of a disorder feel bad), but they are associated with harmful or deleterious behavior. The harm of a disorder may take the form of pain and suffering. It may take the form of death or a significant risk of death or of a severe decrement in personal freedom and mobility. Or it may take the form of being unintelligible or incomprehensible to oneself.

To speak briefly of one of these: Being incomprehensible to self is no mere insignificant occurrence, like the transient ignorance associated with occasional absentmindedness or garden varieties of forgetfulness or muddled thinking. Self incomprehensibility is a severe burden, a self-stultifying impairment. Victims of certain disorders just do not understand why they think, feel or act as they do. They vigorously distrust their own husband, although he has done no harm to them. They are deeply despondent, although they have just won a Pulitzer Prize. They are in the dark about themselves.

Being in the dark about one's own person means that an individual is incapable of rational self-scrutiny or taking proper responsibility for self. Consider the disorder of clinical depression. One of the most intriguing hypotheses in Freud's psychopathology is his notion that in a case of depression a person may develop free-floating or content-diffuse anxieties or concerns as well as loosened affective or emotional connections with previous sources of pleasure and satisfaction. Some depressed people care indifferently or are emotionally equally concerned, to employ Jennifer Church's apt terminology, "for everything and nothing" (Church 2003: 181). Which is to say: Everything matters just as much to them, but also alas, just as little, as everything else. So, in effect, nothing matters or stands-out, neither the activities of daily living nor normal bonds of home or heart. A person loses resonant emotional connectivity with previously cherished goods. Engagement with the world may go flat or become sullen. Yet such an individual has perhaps just won, say, a Pulitzer Prize or married a much desired soul mate. So, why can't the person in such a situation get their world to be emotionally resonant again – to be affectively and perhaps passionately cared for again, and with a set of emotional priorities which reflects that some things or persons matter much more to them then others? A depressed person just may not know why. They may be in the dark about themselves. "How could this happen to me?" "Why aren't I happy?" "I should be happy." "Shouldn't I?" "I used to care for my spouse and children or my physical health much more than I do."

Depression is commonly classified as a mood disorder. But, of course, depression is much more than that. A remark made by Annette Karmiloff-Smith about neurodevelopmental disorders applies to depression as well as to other sorts of mental disorder. This is that "a totally specific disorder [is] ... extremely unlikely," (Karmiloff-Smith 1998: 390). Depression, for instance, is not just a mood disorder or specific to a person's feeling or affect. It also is a disorder of care and commitment as well as, oftentimes, of self-comprehension and self-understanding.

The second fact about disorder that helps to make a disorder undesirable concerns its non-voluntary and personally uncontrollable nature. Experiencing a mental disorder is not something a person willfully does. The onset of a disorder is not deliberate. It is not a self "disordering" – not a self-authored or deliberate effort to become disordered. One becomes disordered without intending and despite wanting not to be disordered. So, too, getting oneself out of a disorder is not under direct or voluntary control. A disorder "gums up the works" and upsets the "proper working order" of mind and behavior (Feinberg 1970: 287–88). It psychologically impairs or incapacitates. So, a person can no more 'snap out of it', say, out of an obsessive compulsive or paranoid delusional disorder, than a person can snap out of scurvy or malaria.

I do not mean by this that a mental disorder is all-over involuntary or that each and every one of its parts, elements or phases is involuntary. Disorders are temporally persisting conditions. They stretch out over time. They are patterns of mind and behavior that recur, with different variations, in the texture and trajectory of certain pronounced phases of a person's life.

Take addiction. An addict may find it just too hard to free themselves of a self-destructive behavior pattern. But the ambivalence about such patterns that characterizes many addicts, and the complex series of choices in which they engage while in pursuit of a drug or opportunity to make wagers, means that some aspects of the condition are under voluntary control (see Chapter 7 for detailed discussion).

Or take the example of clinical depression. Depressive conditions include characteristic thoughts, feelings, judgments, and dispositions to behave in different ways in interaction with other people and the environment. Some of these elements may, on occasion, be under voluntary control. For example, in thinking about whether to tell a clinician or family member that one is contemplating suicide, a depressed person may deliberately pick one or more circumstances or forms of expression in or through which to reveal their state of mind.

My point about being involuntary is this: A person does not choose to be addicted. Or choose to be depressed. Also: a clinically depressed person cannot be persuaded to cease having the disorder just by being told of the costs, risks or liabilities associated with being depressed. Being depressed is not a choice to be frowned upon and rejected after a concerted risk assessment or analysis of its costs and benefits. A person can't help it. Often depressed people are acutely aware of its costs, but they cannot do anything about them. The same is true with addiction. Many addicts eventually do stop, apparently of their own accord (just as a depression remit or fade away seemingly of its own accord). But, in the meantime, addicts pass through numerously repeated cycles in which the ability to refrain becomes a depleted resource and 'snapping out of it' cannot be expected of a person. All of which may mean that an individual in the grips of a disorder, like depression or addiction, may require help or assistance from others or mental health professionals to be free of its incapacitation or to reduce its range or prominence. A person with a disorder may be unable to live decently, if live at all, without the aid or assistance of others, especially during crises or periods of reason-unresponsive and imprudent risk.

We are used to people needing aid and assistance with somatic disease or injury. A victim of breast cancer may be unable to survive without assistance (drugs, surgery, and so on) and the generosity and competence of others. So, too, a person who suffers, say, from a mental disorder like agoraphobia or delusional disorder (or depression or addiction) may be unable to function well or appropriately without the aid of others.

The third fact presupposed by the concept of disorder is that a disorder is not excised or extirpated from a person's psychological makeup or economy just by the mere addition of other psychological resources. The mind of a mental disorder is not made orderly or healthy merely by endowing it with other psychological assets. So, someone who suffers from, say, paranoid delusional disorder and is incorrigibly and imprudently distrustful of others, is not released from the grip of paranoia just by being fed with added doses of creative imagination. Added imagination may make their paranoia worse. A vivid imagination may more deeply entrench unwarranted convictions about why other people should be distrusted. A depressed patient who suffers from low self-esteem is not automatically cleansed, psychologically, of their excessively self-critical habits merely by being given special opportunities for social affiliation (a larger family, extra friends, and so on). Social contact may worsen a depressive condition when, in a darkly mood-ridden contrast and comparison with others, a person feels less successful, lovable, or worthy of the betterments of social life than other people.

Compare the situation of a mental disorder with a somatic injury in this respect of not being excised merely by compensatory additions. A person with a broken leg is not freed of this misfortune, the misfortune of the break does not disappear, just if they are endowed with more muscular arms or enhanced ocular acuity. As long as the leg remains broken, they are injured or in ill-bodily health. Likewise, as long as a depressed patient remains pessimistically self-critical, or a paranoid person persists in unwarranted social distrust, they are worse off. They are in mental ill-health. Such is the undesirability of a mental disorder. It gums up, impairs or partially incapacitates not just the mind's works but the ready or simplistic repair of those works.

So, a mental disorder is no mere "alien condition involuntarily suffered" (like a transient headache, for example), to use an apt expression of the philosopher Joel Feinberg (1926–2004), quoted also just above, but it is something for which the simple grafting on of other psychological capacities, so to speak, neither heals nor covers up its wound (Feinberg 1970: 287–88). Unless the disorder itself is addressed, and its 'gum' removed by means that are proper and specific to a condition's content and character, a disorder gets in the way of a person with the condition. It makes life worse.

Just how much worse depends on circumstances, cases and contexts. Being worse off does not mean that disorders are always and utterly devoid of some measure of compensation or secondary gain. It has been claimed, for example, that susceptibility to paranoia may encourage a healthy distrust of others in aberrant and truly threatening social environments or sub-cultures (Jarvik and Chadwick 1972). It also has been said that several prominent scientists and creative artists have flourished in certain particulars of their craft, if not whole person, despite (because of?) the travails of a bipolar disorder or other mental disorders (Simonton 1994). Different contexts or cases may offer different forms of compensation. But who would voluntarily and knowingly pay such steep prices for those 'professional gains'? The alleged gains, no matter how arresting, do not eliminate the disorder. A disorder leaves an individual in harm's way and typically in need of reconstitution or address.

So: It's no wonder that conditions classified as disorders are undesirable or thought of as 'disorders'. They are harmful, non-voluntary impairments and not directly addressed or treated with mere added ingredients, no matter how worthwhile such ingredients may otherwise be or for other purposes. Added doses of imagination, for example, may be wonderful for a writer, but not if he or she suffers from delusions of persecution or paranoia.

MORALLY THERAPEUTIC INTERLUDE AND LURE OF THE DISEASE MODEL

Given that mental disorders or illnesses incapacitate or impair the works of mind, persons with disorders often require special care, intervention or treatment. Questions of care, intervention or treatment may be immensely complicated. Care of a person with a disorder usually is not some one thing, like dispensing a medication, and (as noted above) it should not be depicted as a mere add-on or graft to a disorder. The character or type of care should stem from the character of the disorder as well as from the uniqueness and circumstances of the individual affected or harmed by the condition and their interests and needs.

Care should also morally respect the person with a disorder as a person. It should treat them as still, to some degree, responsible and rational agents, capable with assistance of controlling their own behavior, and participating in their own recovery or reconstruction of mental health. So, whatever care or aid is given to a person with a disorder should be consistent, as best we can tell, with a person's self-respect and sense of personal dignity or self-worth (see Nussbaum 2006). We certainly shouldn't try to 'heal' or restore 'mental order' to a person in a manner that demeans or disrespects them as persons, in spite of the fact that thinking of them as non-responsible is tempted by the often obvious fact that they may have no clear sense of how to alleviate or manage their own disturbance, together with the fact that (temporarily at least) they are impaired and require help and care.

One form of disrespectful or undignified treatment is to encourage unquestioned and imprudent reliance on psychotropic drugs. Prescriptions for antidepressant and antipsychotic medications have skyrocketed in the last decade, due, in part, to the resistance of health insurers to pay for cognitive psychotherapies and the hours and labor often required in psychotherapeutic treatment. Psychotropic medications are among the best selling drugs and best selling new drugs. Among the most popular patented drugs in 2005, for example, was a drug named *Cympalta* (duloxetine), an antidepressant medication, which had secured FDA approval only in 2004 and earned $667 million for its manufacturer Eli Lilly (Klume 2007). Drugs, however, often have deleterious side or long-term negative effects, both known and unknown.

Richard Bentall (2004) offers the following striking example of the unwelcome effect of a drug on none other than himself.

> I was a [volunteer] participant in [an] experiment … in which I received 5 mg of droperidol, and became restless and dysphoric to the point of being distressed. I burst into tears. … I had a hangover for days. … The doses in these experiments were far lower than those typically given to patients.
>
> (2004: 500)

Overenthusiastic use of or reliance upon medication, Bentall adds, has "led to a worldwide epidemic of avoidable iatrogenic [treatment induced] illness, causing unnecessary distress to countless vulnerable people" (Bentall 2004: 501). It is not Bentall's position that "the use of psychiatric drugs is always wrong" (Bentall 2004: 504). But drugs, he cautions, harbor risks that must be factored into their use and application. Even the most popular medications may be harmful.

A timely example may help to illustrate what I mean. One of the most widely prescribed medications for depression is a family of drugs called specific serotonin reuptake inhibitors (SSRIs). Here, roughly, is how they work in the brain. Signals are sent between brain cells (neurons) by chemicals known as transmitters. One of the most common of these chemical messengers in the brain is 5-hydroxytryptamine, known more commonly as serotonin. This chemical is also found in the intestine (as well as in bananas). When a transmitter like serotonin is released and activates a receptor on the adjacent brain cell, its excess is delivered back into the releasing nerve ending in a process known as reuptake. There it is stored for later recirculation. In serotonin's case a specific reuptake process operates through a transporter molecule. SSRIs block that process of reuptake. So, serotonin 'washes over', as it were, the adjacent cell. This increase of serotonin is thought to combat or help to combat depression on the hypothesis that depression is due, in some measure, to a decline of serotonin in the brain. A critic may question that particular empirical hypothesis or its purport for mental health, of course, although that is not the point I wish to make here. I am aiming for another caution.

One difficulty with SSRIs is that they are not designer drugs. That is, they do not target just depression, for although they do block the reuptake of serotonin, they also work wherever the same chemical process occurs elsewhere in the body. This includes the intestine. So, some patients experience intestinal side-effects, such as diarrhea and nausea.

Alas, for all we know, the side or long-term and not designed effects of certain drugs may stymie some perfectly healthy reactions. Some evidence from non-human animal models suggests that social animals undergo fluctuations of serotonin levels in response to natural or normal stresses in their species' life, such as a rise or fall in social status (see Edwards and Kravitz 1997). So, an animal that otherwise enjoys high social status, but experiences a decline of its place in a social hierarchy, may undergo a drop in serotonin levels and exhibit depression-like symptoms such as withdrawal and body self-absorption. To speculate: This behavior may be an evolved or adaptational defense mechanism, like some cases of fever or diarrhea in instances in which a toxin has been ingested by a person. As Neil Levy notes, in a human case perhaps social withdrawal "allows one time to recuperate from the ... decline in status" and to ensure that "the decline ... is reversed or at least halted" (Levy 2007: 82; see also Watson and Andrews 2002). A person who merely shrugs off dramatic loss of social prominence may fail to appreciate that it often takes hard won social labors to deserve, merit or achieve prominence. So, an episode of moderate depression (not something truly harmful or clinically deleterious) may help a person to get their act and energy together or to secure other benefits of a more personal or private nature (see Graham 1990). A serotonin decrement is not necessarily a bad or unhealthy thing from an adaptational or evolutionary point of view.

The power of drugs to restore mental health derives from the ways in which they are used and, often, from how they are understood or interpreted by the people who consume them. One cautionary fear is that drugs may create unnecessary psychological dependencies as well as autonomy or personal responsibility losses that are imprudent and debilitating. If your house is broken into or your job is lost, and you become depressed, this may not indicate, of course, that you should be prescribed anti-depressant medication. Carl Elliott, a philosopher trained also as a physician, complains that people may rely on "beta-blockers or Paxil to take the edge off business presentations, Ritalin to improve our attention and concentration, Prozac to give ...

the confidence to apply for a promotion" (Elliott 2003: 153). Elliott notes: "some situations call for depression or ... anxiety." But "some things call for fear and trembling" (Elliott 2003: 157.)

Drugs and chemical manipulations are not alone in posing dilemmas in the diagnosis and treatment of disorder. Diagnostic taxonomies and psychiatric labeling also raise difficulties – Ethical and moral difficulties. Erving Goffman's studies of the potential stigma of mental illness show that diagnostic categorization sometimes constitutes an affront to a patient's dignity and self-respect (Goffman 1961 and 1963). Dignity and self-respect are undermined by labeling when a person suffering from a disorder is perceived not as the individual or person whom they are, but as one of a general type "without significant individuality and diversity, defined entirely by their [diagnostic] characteristics" (Nussbaum 2006: 191). To classify someone who is not well and in need of help into a de-individuating impersonal pigeonhole is a recipe for prescriptive tyranny.

Prescriptive tyranny may take different forms. I mention two.

One consists of causing a person to lose hope in their condition or circumstances. One mental illness patient describes the effect on him of being labeled as follows.

> By approaching my situation in terms of [my] illness, the system has consistently under-estimated my capacity to change and has ignored the potential it may contain to assist that change. ... The major impression I have received is that I am a victim of something nasty, not quite understandable, that will never really go away and which should not be talked about too openly in the company of strangers.
>
> (P. Campbell as quoted in Radden 2009: 173)

Another form of prescriptive tyranny is described by the philosopher Nomy Arpaly (Arpaly 2005). The fact that a person possesses a mental disorder does not automatically mean that they are not blameworthy, praiseworthy or personally responsible for each and every aspect of their illness-associated behavior. Suppose a woman's husband is clinically depressed and diagnosed as such but, as a result, she treats him like an impotent child – utterly helpless. Suppose also that in "treating his suffering [in this demeaning way] she misunderstands [the condition] and aggravates it" (Arpaly 2005: 297). Treating him like a child humiliates him. She should be forgiving and supportive, true, but she may also harbor legitimate resentment or warranted negative reactive attitudes for certain forms of misbehavior on his part. On occasion, label or no label, he does misbehave and he needs to know this. Anything less fails to respect him as a person. The label 'depression' should not cover all of his sins or enervate her person-respecting reactive attitudes towards them. "We are not limited", the philosopher Ferdinand Schoeman aptly remarks in a paper on alcoholism, "to one response" (Schoeman 1994: 201). Schoeman observes: "Our thinking about what is fair to expect of people must respect the ambiguities implicit in our understanding of what individuals can do" even when they are subjects of a disorder (Schoeman 1994: 195). Anything less is treating them less than they deserve. Anything less treats a disorder as completely and utterly involuntary in each and every element of is temporal persistence, when amongst its multiplicity of states and attitudes may be elements over which an individual has or can learn to have some measure of responsible self-control.

Colin King is a stigma survivor. At 17 years old King was misdiagnosed with schizophrenia. He has since completed a Ph.D. in institutional racism at the University of London and worked as a mental health practitioner. He is a black man.

King remembers, during one period of hospitalization, "looking at the open ward, my acne making me look like I had a second face, mortified, life became morbid, with no purpose, no pride, no joy, and no ambitions, cut off; you begin to think that life is like that all the time" (King 2007: 21). Diagnostic labeling and treatment, he says, may make a person feel as if their personhood had been "objectified … under rigid labels" (26).

When various mental health professionals observed King, they thought they saw an illness in need of treatment. They reacted to him as a person who would function better on medication; an underachieving, social misfit. The mental health profession would have done much better service for King, of course, and treated him with dignity and compassion, if they viewed him not primarily as a patient with a medical problem, but as a person in a behavioral predicament, facing a personal challenge. King's primary challenge was not the medical problem of, say, controlling his angry outbursts, but the personal problem of becoming a more able and stable person, whatever the impediments of his disorder or situation.

Is there any way in which to guard against over-reliance on drugs and the overblown power of labeling? No doubt, we need a conception of mental disorder that helps to reveal when as well as how drugs should be used and diagnostic labels applied. That's a tall and complicated order. It may not be possible to cleanly and clearly deliver on it. But one model for the disorderliness of a mental disorder that has been proposed in response, in part, to that tall order and which attracts numerous clinicians and mental health professionals on other grounds as well is that of a somatic disease or bodily illness. This is sometimes called the Biomedical Disease Model of Mental Disorder. In broadest terms it goes something like this: Somatic diseases and bodily illnesses constitute a class of negative health conditions recognized by medical and lay people alike. We know or often seem to know when a condition should be classified as a somatic disease, treated with drugs, and labeled as, say, malaria not measles, syphilis not scurvy, carbon-monoxide poisoning not cancer. For these and other reasons it is both sound and sensible to conceive of a *mental* disorder on the model of a somatic disease. A person may be classified as someone with leukemia with no miss-reliance on drugs or as victim of ovarian cancer with no harsh social stigma. So, why not aim for the same with a mental disorder-as-disease diagnosis? This is not to say that somatic diseases are never treated with unnecessary drugs or that social or cultural stigmata never affix to somatic maladies. (Just think of the early years of AIDS diagnosis and its contribution to homophobia.) However, still, some say, it's promising and helpful to picture depression as like epilepsy or paranoia as similar to breast cancer or diabetes. The semantic admonition behind such a biomedical program (sometimes said to be part of the discipline of Biological Psychiatry) is to classify each condition, whether somatic or mental, as a disease entity or process.

Is it fit, proper or wise to think of disorders as diseases? It would help in answering this question if there was true uniformity or consensus over just what a disease model of a disorder is or precisely means. Truth be told, there is not (compare Andreasen 2001 with Guze 1992). But still the question is worth exploring. What exactly is to be said for a biomedical disease model of disorder? Are mental disorders disease or disease-like entities or processes? I now wish to explore this question.

ARE MENTAL DISORDERS DISEASES?

The very idea of a disease has its primary residence and first literal home in the diagnosis of somatic or bodily illnesses or disorders. It is in this home or with that family of illnesses that it possesses prototypical or exemplary conditions of application. (Again, I use such terms as 'prototypical' and 'exemplary', adding 'paradigmatic' to the mix, all interchangeably.) Consensus applications of the concept of a somatic disease pick out conditions or states of persons that *tend to have* certain properties or features in truth conditional robustness. States with consensus features are paradigms, prototypes, or exemplars of somatic disease.

Reference to paradigms, prototypes or exemplars doesn't help to classify each and every disease, to exclude non-exemplary diseases from the class or to preclude vagueness and controversy in the concept of disease. Prototype-semantics is like that. Analogy: Each of a Rembrandt self-portrait and the self-portrait of a weekend hack is described as a painting, although only the first is an exemplar, and an art critic may object that a hack job is no real portrait. Each of the Boston Marathon and Monty Python's Marathon for People with Directional Disorder (when the gun goes off folks run in dozens of different directions) is a marathon (though etc.). But acknowledging the existence of prototypes or exemplars and learning from them about what a concept may best mean is incompatible with a laissez-faire spirit of *hands-off conceptual rectitude* that permits people to define 'diseases' pretty much as they please. For example, suppose a notion of disease is introduced that describes diseases as collections of symptoms or unwelcome behaviors that occur together and tend to develop in more or less characteristic patterns, but the notion takes a hands-off attitude towards or is silent about the causal or causal-explanatory foundations of a disease or whether diseases possess an underlying pathology or damaging proximate causes. Such a syndrome- or symptom-tethered approach (as it may be called) would fit nicely with application of the concept of disease to the categorical scheme of *DSM*, which is designed to be agnostic or a-theoretical about the causal foundations of a mental illness. But it does not fit with the practice of somatic medicine, which thinks of diseases as causally destructive processes or pathologies that are manifest in symptoms and not taxonomically classifiable or distinguishable in terms of mere symptoms alone.

So, just which somatic conditions or bodily states are exemplars of a disease? Here is a very partial list:

- Infectious diseases (for examples, malaria and encephalitis)
- Diseases of the bronchopulmonary system (for example, emphysema)
- Diseases of the kidney (for example, medullary cystic disease)
- Diseases of the liver (for example, hepatitis)
- Diseases of the blood (for example, leukemia)

The list may go on, alas, almost indefinitely: diseases of the heart (such as atherosclerosis), diseases of nutrition (like scurvy), metabolism (like lipomas), endocrine system (like Cushing's syndrome), bone and joints ... and so on. We are somatically fragile creatures.

Are mental disorders sufficiently akin to somatic diseases to be classified diseases? Are delusional disorder, agoraphobia and depression (understood as mental disorders) sufficiently similar to malaria, scurvy, atherosclerosis, hepatitis or leukemia to qualify as disease entities?

In asking if mental disorders are diseases I am not asking if mental disorders are *physical* or possess an existential base of some sort in a broken brain or damaged central nervous system. That is an issue I have said a few things about in earlier chapters and plan to re-examine later in the book. I am asking here if mental disorders are disease-like on *other* grounds, grounds that are not directly connected with the issue of basal physicality, but which are sufficient to qualify disorders as diseases or conditions of disease types.

The best answer to this question depends upon at least two factors (three actually, but right now I discuss two). The first concerns symptoms. The second causes.

First symptoms. Prototypical or exemplary symptoms of a mental disorder are complex, variable, and heterogeneous. So, there are no symptomatic hard edges or discrete boundaries between symptoms of a mental disorder and normal variations in human mental health and well-being. Take clinical depression, for instance, of the sort exhibited in what is called a Major Depressive Disorder. Unlike malaria, scurvy and other typical bodily diseases like leukemia, there are no blood tests, X-rays, biopsy results, or skin sores that are available to make a diagnosis of depression. Symptoms of a major depressive disorder include what are called a "syndrome" or "sydromal cluster" of symptoms, such as: feeling sad, blue, tearful; loss of pleasure; change in appetite (either increased or decreased); sleep disturbance (either trouble falling asleep or sleeping too much); being agitated, restless, or slowing down; feeling worthless or extremely guilty; thinking of killing oneself; and other symptoms. The sheer multiplicity and contextual variability and cultural scaffolding or availability of symptoms is a source of major problems in diagnosing the condition as well as in distinguishing depression not just from periods of sadness, unhappiness or demoralization but also from personality traits such as melancholia and negative global attitudes like nihilism or pessimism. "Everywhere we look," writes Richard Bentall, "it seems that [mental disorders] exist on continua with normal behaviors and experiences" (Bentall 2004: 115).

By comparison and contrast, the symptoms of a prototypical somatic disease (like malaria or scurvy) tend to be both few and discontinuous with normal variations in human physical health. Neither malaria nor scurvy is continuous with normal variations in human somatic health. Malaria, for example, is an infectious disease in which people suffer from fever and anemia (its symptoms). It is not a normal variation in body temperature or in the oxygen carrying component of the blood. (I will have more to say about symptoms momentarily.)

Second, consider the factor of immediate or proximate causes.

The more or less remote causes of somatic diseases (sometimes called etiologies or risk factors) often are both many and various and involve life patterns (e.g. dietary and exercise habits) and genetic or biological vulnerablilities interacting with environomental and cultural forces and individuals' learning histories. Much the same is true of mental illnesses or disorders. Just as excessive consumption of fried foods and cigarettes are risk factors for atherosclerosis, a host of background conditions (the death of a parent or loss of a sibling when a child) may be a risk factor for certain sorts of depression. But in a case of somatic disease these distal risk factors find (what may be called) final and specific pathogenic pathways that are causative of the disease, such as tangled arterial plaques or atheromata in atherosclerosis or the rupturing of red blood cells caused by a species of parasitic protazoa (carried by mosquitoes that inject the malarial parasite into the bloodstream) in malaria.

By comparison and contrast, there are no successful causal explanations of (exemplary) mental disorders that cite a single main cause or a final common pathway for their pathogeneses. Any and all victims of clinical depression, for example, do not suffer or appear to suffer from any one single more or less proximate cause of their depressions. More or less immediate losses or disappointments or setbacks of major and heterogeneous sorts are among proposed candidates for vulnerability conditions for depression. Loss of an intimate relationship or of a loved one with whom one has had a deep attachment. A setback in self-respect after a sudden and unexpected decline in social or economic status. Diminishment of health after a person has become the victim of a somatic disease (cancer, chronic nutritional ailment, and so on). Loss of effective personal purposive agency in a situation of learned helplessness. Stress (often associated with the threat or perceived prospect of loss) has also been proposed as an influence or causal-explanatory factor. Financial hardship, marital decay, or a move to a new city among strangers, these are among the stresses associated with some instances of depression. So, too, guilt has been cited as a possible influencing condition. Religious guilt, for example, may make one vulnerable to depression, and may take the form of an intense and unforgiving sense of sin.

Any process whereby distal or vulnerability factors help to feed into a specific final path or pathogenesis for depression of a prototypical disease-like sort currently is not just unknown for any exemplary mental disorder but arguably non-existent. Certainly, the motley assortment of losses, stresses and setbacks associated with cases of depression seem unassociated with specific identifiable underlying pathophysiologies, proximate neuromolecular causal mechanisms or psychobiological triggers that may be proposed as responsible for the condition's symptoms. Some scientists may hope for an as yet unfound underlying molecular neuropathology ('cells gone bad', as it were) for a mental disorder. Indeed, more than one medical scientist has said that such a hoped for discovery of "one biological abnormality" or "biologic marker" is something that would help to warrant depicting a mental disorder as a disease-like entity or condition (Heninger 1999: 89). The assumption behind this sort of claim must be that a disease as such does have a final common pathway as its pathogenesis. Given, however, the variety of depression's diagnostic syndrome and the diverse and contextually various and culturally scaffolded ways in which a depression's symptoms are expressed, such a neurochemical discovery seems quite unimaginable at least given our current state of knowledge.

The variety that characterizes both the causes and symptoms of a typical mental disorder not only makes for an ultimately imperceptible grading from the prototypically or frankly non-disordered to the disordered, but it tempts some observers and researchers to extend the category of mental disorder into shady and conceptually contestable and unregimented areas. Harvard psychiatrist John Ratey, for example, has written of something he calls "shadow sydromes", which are, he claims, milder or loosely graded forms of mental disorders and which, he notes, if accepted as disorders (and he urges that they should be) would mean classifying far more people as disordered or in need of medical treatment than do current and already super-generous schemes of diagnostic classification like *DSM* (Ratey and Johnson, 1998).

However, back to the issue of the proximate causes or more or less immediate forces responsible for mental disorder. Explanatory references to different proximate sources or contributing immediate causes of a disorder like depression help to form what I like to call a causal *propensity explanation* of a disorder. Propensity explanations (as I mean to use this expression) identify factors or processes that contribute to a strong tendency, likelihood or disposition for events to occur. Dynamically, such tendencies evolve over time, at various temporal scales, along various phases and in a variety of different pathways. Propensity explanations are at work in the disciplines of history and political science, for examples.

Consider a political revolution. Why, for example, did a certain violent political revolution occur? Suppose the following is part of its best explanation: In the summer of 2012 there was a growing and seething discontent among a large portion of the population, and when the economy dramatically collapsed late that October, the discontent turned to violence. The combination of discontent and economic collapse brought about the revolution. It did not do so simply double-handedly (discontent plus collapse). Some more or less distal inflammatory remarks of a popular right-wing political entertainer and radio commentator also played a provocative role. So, too, did other factors, such as the absence of strong political leadership in the minority political party. But revolutionary tendencies hit a feverish pitch when the stock market imploded.

Such is a sample propensity explanation. It is eminently compatible with a successful propensity explanation that the explained or partially explained event, contrary to fact, may not have occurred or eventuated. Propensities as such are not necessitating forces. They don't make effects inevitable. Propensities (as I am using this notion) are strongly affecting, robustly influencing, or profoundly encouraging. Insofar as it makes sense to speak of them as causes (as I am willing to say that it does) it must make sense to speak of causation in probabilistic terms. Causes then may, in some way, only make their effects more likely. The onset of revolution originated in discontent and economic collapse insofar as the discontent and collapse made the revolution more likely or insofar, that is, as the objective chance of the revolution's occurring was greater given the occurrence of the discontent and collapse than if those two events had not occurred.

In speaking of a propensity explanation, I do not mean to refer specifically to what is sometimes called a quantified statistical explanation or to an explanation that refers to measurable statistical probabilities. Some propensities may be modeled or quantified as mathematical probabilities, of course, but not, I believe, those streaming towards mental disorders of exemplary sorts. Rather, I mean to refer to a type of what may be called a *how-likely explanation*. Take, for example, the fact that a certain person had a major depressive episode. This episode, if explained by a propensity explanation, is not necessitated or made inevitable by loss of a job or spouse or predisposing features of a sour or dour personal temperament. Reference to a job loss, supplemented by reference to aspects of temperament or to other biographical or situational as well as to neurobiological and neurochemical contingencies, account for why the episode should have been expected or anticipated by a knowledgeable observer. So: A questioner may ask, "How likely was it that the person would become clinically depressed?" Such a question may be answerable by pointing to facts about tendencies that more or less strongly contribute to the onset of the depressive episode. The tendencies themselves may pass through temporal phases in the onset of a disorder that are classified as vulnerability, prodromal and acute (the onset itself). And their ripple effects may resonate through post-acute or post-onset recovery as well as perhaps into continuing or periodic interference after recovery or reconstitution.

Neurobiological and neurochemical factors no doubt play roles in mental disorders (which is one of the main themes of this book, of course). But this does not mean (again) that the mechanical brute a-rational dynamics of the brain inevitably led to depression or that there must be a simple albeit as yet unknown one-to-one relationship between interactions between neurotransmitters (and other brain chemicals) and the empirically tractable onset of a clinical depression. Many different neurotransmitter and neurohormonal systems interact with one another in different ways and phases in the production of depression, and there is some evidence (partly from effects of antidepressant drugs that directly act on the serotonergic system) that decreased production of serotonin (a neurotransmitter) contributes to mood changes in depressed persons.

Why only a partial or non-necessitating causal-explanation of a depression – if I am right? (Or of any other exemplary mental disorder, again, if I am right. Depression is the example considered here.) Arguably, this is because an episode of a disorder like depression has many different and complex aspects. It is immensely difficult to get a causal explanatory grip on the phenomenon. Stephen Haynes briefly describes the sort of complexity confronting explanation of a mental disorder as follows:

> The task facing the [explainer] is overwhelmingly complex. Each client typically presents several concomitantly occurring behavior problems and is imbedded in a complex social setting. [T]here are multiple potential causal factors for these behavior problems.
>
> (Haynes 1992: 3)

In accounting for a mental disorder, our understanding comes up against a multiplicity of partially contributing sources, not just background or distal forces and situational variables but proximate or immediate influences, and into an overall configuration of conditions that help to bring about a disorder. There is no apparent immediate causal trigger (as there is in some cases of somatic illness) in the total configuration of a disorder nor is the set of sources as a whole trigger-like. This is not to deny a priori that there may be necessitating causal triggers for certain aspects or features of a disorder. (A despondent mood, for instance, may possess its own precipitant neurochemistry.) But it is to deny triggering for the complex whole – at least by current empirical lights.

Consider, again, depression. A propensity explanation for a major depressive episode may put into focus the role that, say, death of an intimate or loss of a job may play in the tendency to feel helpless and pessimistic. Then, it may trace a path from the occurrence of such events through to deteriorating aspects of a person's self-confidence or to intense or frequent stressors. Stressors may generate an excess of adrenal stress hormones, which, once initiated, may precipitate or exacerbate a negative mood. In some cases, there may be a point, a threshold perhaps, at which the gradual accumulation of otherwise unremarkable changes in a person's outlook or mood yields a large and overt transformation. An episode of clinical or major depression may then emerge in exemplary form. A great deal of background activity may be needed to build the person up (or down) to such a threshold point, or a person may, perhaps by virtue of temperament or learning history, be pre-possessed with vulnerability for a major depressive episode. A simple loss, a mere disappointment, a routine stress, may somehow swell in some individuals into a profoundly negative and despondent condition. For other people only a dramatic calamity may help to serve as a source for depression, and then (in a case of a calamity) aspects of the causal explanatory landscape, even when informed by the languages of neurobiology and neurochemistry, may elude reference to precise powers of necessitation.

In speaking of the probabilistic or momentum-like nature of a path to a disorder, I do not also mean to preclude *a priori* the operation within a condition of an unknown main single underling neurobiological/neurochemical spring or unified causal mechanism. But the glaring absence of evidence to date for the operation of such springs in certain distressing conditions offers, I believe, good inductive warrant not to expect them of such conditions and helps to classify them as mental disorders.

Propensity or how-likely explanations for a disorder like depression, it should be noted, are compatible with referring to the natural law-likeness or lawfulness of processes that may be part of or contribute to propensity to depression (or more generally, to any mental disorder). Perhaps certain sorts of neural processes, such as a sudden and dramatic decline in serotonin levels, if they could somehow be isolated from other neurochemical forces, do in a lawful manner produce, say, a protracted bleak or despondent mood.

Similarly, nothing in a propensity explanation precludes thinking of various forces behind or processes within a disorder as constituted by types of events, processes or entities classified (in the language of philosophy of science) as *natural kinds*. Natural kinds are special sorts of substances or processes in the world. Natural kinds are types of events, processes or entities studied by the natural sciences (like the quarks of physics or the neurons of neurobiology), referred to in scientific laws or represented in mechanical or mechanistic models, and assumed to be parts of the act-of-human-classification independent causal structure of the world. Chemical substances like lead, gold, and water are standard examples of natural kinds in the literature. Types of neurochemical processes, say among neurotransmitters like serotonin or dopamine, may be natural kinds and, if so, then insofar as reference to such processes is part of the successful propensity explanation of a disorder, natural kinds may help to govern certain specific aspects of a disorder's emergence.

I am reluctant, however, to classify mental disorders themselves as natural kinds. My reluctance to classify mental disorders as natural kinds is not that disorders are unnatural. Disorders are naturally occurring events. Human beings naturally are vulnerable to them. Nor is it based on the assumption that only processes or entities that are discretely bounded and fail to admit of borderline instances qualify as natural kinds. Types of mental disorders lack such boundaries and contain borderline instances, to be sure, but this is not why they fail or should fail to count as natural kinds. Some writers on natural kinds claim that taxonomic classifications of animal species refer to natural kinds. If that is true (and I don't wish to appraise the claim here), and if, for example, terms like 'monkey' or 'dog' refer to organisms that qualify as natural kinds, certainly those categories admit of borderline instances. Spineless-armless-monkeys. One-legged hair-less three-eyed dogs. Nor, finally, is my reluctance premised on the assumption that disorders are not objective states of affairs or that they are conditions that are perniciously culturally relative or otherwise unfit objects of medical scientific discovery and analysis. Mental disorder anti-realism is not the proper line.

My reluctance about bestowing natural kind status upon a mental disorder stems from at least two facts. The first is that mental disorders (or those conditions that I am arguing deserve to be called mental disorders) fail or certainly appear to fail to emerge in a law-of-nature-like fashion or in whole cloth from causal mechanisms (or through the operation of unified causal essences, to use an expression of Richard Samuels [2009]). Natural kinds like lead and gold, by comparison, do tend to emerge in such a fashion. My reluctance also stems from the fact (a second fact) that violations of norms or evaluative standards are presupposed in the attribution or notion of disorder. Disorders badly gum up or incapacitate the works of mind and behavior. Disorders have (what may be called) a normative mode of being (they are bad for a person) and not just or only an empirical one (they affect a person). Natural kinds have an empirical mode of being only. There is nothing essentially bad (or good) about them. Natural kinds are not normatively-infused or value-laden. One can evaluate or assess them, depending perhaps on how one intends to use them. If I plan to use a three-legged horse to plow a field, I may be disappointed. I may dub it a bad 'natural kind'. But value-laden norms are not essential to their identity or being. Disorders (unlike paradigmatic natural kinds) are invariably bad. Just how bad depends upon a disorder's degree of severity or undesirability and context of emergence and progression.

I need to clarify my reference to norms. Talk of norms in discussions of mental disorder appears in at least three guises or distinct senses: "statistical", "biological design" and "value-preference laden". Only the third sense is germane to what I am calling a mental disorder's 'bad' or 'disorder' nature.

In a statistical sense something is normal on frequency of occurrence grounds. Normally, human beings secure and digest food, attract mates, walk and talk, sleep and so on. When a person cannot engage in one or more these otherwise frequent and perhaps, at times, needed activities, this 'cannot' or inability qualifies as something infrequent or statistically abnormal. It may also be bad for a person, but it does not have to be. Infrequency may be an aspect of being successful. Frequent failure to perform successful activities is utterly common for many biological organisms, structures, and activities. A predator goes hunting once, twice, six times before on the seventh it catches its prey. Getting perfect scores on a law or medical school admission test may be statistically infrequent but hardly a harbinger of professional failure.

In the biological design or adaptational sense, something is normal on grounds of whether it makes a contribution to reproductive success or inclusive genetic fitness. This sense of normal is an historical or evolutionary one. It requires reference to a creature's ancestors. A trait or capacity is biologically adaptational or the product of natural design if and only if it arose due to selection pressures for it.

In a value-preference laden sense, something is normatively proper or 'normal' on grounds of its conformity to standards, preferences, values or interests that may be personal, moral, social, medical or of some other sort. Normative impropriety ("abnormality" in this third sense or sense of "badness") attaches to conditions or processes that violate specific values, preferences or interests. Mental illnesses or disorders are conditions of a value-laden normatively improper sort – conditions that are bad or hurtful for a person, given appropriate norms, preferences, values, or standards for a healthy and well ordered mind (of which discussions in Chapters 5 and 6). Mental disorders are not necessarily conditions of a statistically abnormal sort. Disorders (in epidemics) may be widely spread. Besides which, even if disorders were uncommon this would not itself make them disorders and undesirable. A disorder's norm violations are also not best understood in historical/evolutionary terms, as failures to contribute to inclusive fitness or as conditions that currently depart from their Pleistocene age contribution (see Chapter 5, Section 4 for detailed discussion).

Having a grip on the different meanings of normal and abnormal helps in understanding why mental disorders are not natural kinds. It may be rare (abnormal-infrequent) that a lump of sugar does not dissolve in a hot cup of tea. But it is one thing for a lump of sugar to fail to dissolve in a hot cup of Earl Grey. There is nothing value-wise untoward or pathological on the lump's part in such 'dissolute' behavior. It would be absurd to suggest that the lump is acting imprudently or unwisely, no matter how statistically infrequent or evolutionarily maladaptive (for lumps?) a failure to dissolve. We may call it a bad lump, but the grounds for this assessment are not part of the lump's nature. They stem from our desired uses or standards for the lump.

It is bad to be clinically depressed and to disengage from emotional and personal attachments once held near and dear. It is part of the very idea of clinical depression that such disruptive or distressful disengagement is how people ought *not* to feel and behave, evaluatively or rationally speaking. The reason-responsive operation of certain key features or capacities of human mentality (such as, in depression, the capacity for enduring emotional commitments; see Chapter 6) is impaired or truncated in depression as well as in other disorders. Not obliterated, as happens in some neurological disorders, but impaired – partially incapacitated, gummed up.

The inherent or essential value-laden normativity of the domain of mental disorder is the subject of much controversy and disagreement in the literature on mental disorder. I plan devote two whole chapters to it later in the book.

As for natural kinds, if I am right that mental disorders are not natural kinds, this does not mean that they are relegated to the metaphysically feeble status of socially constructed categories of activities like touch football games or TV shows that your cousin Bernice loves. If you are the subject of a disorder this is an objective fact about you. It is not dependent upon anyone's classification of you or your situation as one of a mental disorder. Your parents don't decide whether you are clinically depressed. Properly regimented canons of psychiatry determine standards for that.

Mental disorders are conditions that cannot occur without beings with minds or emotions and attitudes. Nobody can be clinically depressed or delusional without possessing thoughts, perceptions, feelings, and so on. But if we are metaphysical realists about mental disorder, as I believe that we should be, then although without minds we would harbor no mental disorders, with respect to the condition of being *mental disorder* there are objective facts of the matter as to whether someone is depressed, agoraphobic or deluded. Such disorder-facts are not fits of decisional or classificatory fiat or social judgments of mental illness and ill-being that anyone is entitled to make. Some judgments or determinations of the presence of a mental disorder deserve to be dismissed and brushed aside. Others deserve assent (of which more discussion later in the book).

We are not done yet with the question of whether mental disorders (still taking clinical depression as exemplary) are diseases. Two distinguishing features have been mentioned: symptoms and causes. I am claiming that neither the typical causes nor the typical symptoms of a mental disorder tend to be like those of a typical disease. Is there also perhaps a third distinguishing feature? Actually, there is. It is this.

Merely knowing that one is a victim or subject of, say, a disease like scurvy and knowing of its symptoms does not by itself affect the course or character of the condition. Knowing that scurvy is associated with bleeding gums and multiple purple spots on one's skin plays no direct role whatsoever in the occurrence or appearance of those symptoms. Scurvy is what it is regardless of how it is conceived or classified by its victim. It is caused by a prolonged deficiency of ascorbic acid (vitamin C), which the body cannot synthesize. It commonly occurs in the spring, perhaps in part because of the relative lack of fresh fruit and vegetables during winter months. Of course, receiving a diagnosis of scurvy may and should motivate a person to embark on vitamin therapy. But the mere fact of knowing that one is victim of scurvy and learning of its symptomatic expression does not by itself affect the course or character of the illness. By contrast, just such a knowledge-and-illness interplay or pragmatic symbiosis can and sometimes does occur in prototypical cases of mental disorder. To be told that one is clinically depressed, say, typically includes sharing predictions about how the person is expected to react to events or to feel about self and future. A person's knowledge of such expectations may push or pull them to feel or behave in ways that conform to the predictions or to absorb the contours of the condition. Ian Hacking calls this feature of a state of affairs in which knowledge of one's classifi- cation helps to affect the evidence base for the classification (and disorders are not alone in possessing it) an interactive or feedback *looping effect* (Hacking 1995: 105, 121).

Looping is not confined to disorders. Numerous non-medical and social role-occupying conditions of persons are heavily prone to interactive or looping effects. To dub someone before their ears as a 'musical genius', for instance, may affect their attitude towards their future capacity for achievement. It may elevate their personal standards or expectations. To dub another individual a juvenile delinquent may encourage them to engage in certain stereotypical behaviors of a juvenile delinquent. Human beings notoriously react to how they are classified and may modify or regulate their behavior in light of how they are classified. So, a depression or mental disorder is not simply *there* as it is in a chemical kind, such as water, salt, or sugar, with its character fixed independent of human observation, classification and interpretation. A person with a mental dis- order is not simply *there* with their feelings and behavior evolving independent of the depressed (or otherwise so-classified) patient's self-understanding of the category. A shared diagnosis with a patient far from being a stolid and impassive category may be a malleable and plastic predication.

Example: Imagine that you have failed an entrance exam to medical school, and that your life's dream is to become a doctor. Offhand you may explain your performance error to yourself in a number of non-self-critical ways. "The examiner gave incomplete instructions" or "Bad luck but I'll try again". Self confidence may remain secure. Circumstances, you think, were out of kilter. But now assume the following: You have been diagnosed as suffering from a depressive disorder. Learning of its symptoms, you recognize that you are expected to slink away and blame yourself for lack of conscientious preparation, rather than blame incomplete instructions or sheer bad luck for the exam failure. You are also expected to be unstable in self-esteem or self- confidence. Partly because of these pronouncements, you may go into an emotional freefall. You may interpret yourself as suffering from low self-esteem and easily humiliated. "It's pointless for me to take the test again." "I've not got what it takes." Such occurrences and attitudes would be instances of looping. It is not that you are prone to free fall just by virtue of the depression (although, of course, you may well be). But the fact is that your response to failure is affected by your beliefs about how, as a depressive, you are expected to behave. Classifying yourself a certain way can contribute to your being that way. The dynamics of the condition may be affected by diagnosis of the disorder. As Hacking remarks, the conditions susceptible to looping "change the ways in which individuals experience themselves – and may even lead people to evolve their feelings and behavior in part because they are so classified" (Hacking 1999: 104).

The nature and precise forms of looping as well as its modes of operation (voluntary, involuntary, etc.) in human psychology are neither completely transparent nor uniform across situations, conditions, and individuals. But at least in rough terms the phenomenon is widely recognized within psychiatry. As the psychiatrist John Sadler puts it: Many patients think of themselves in "DSM jargon" and live out their "self-identity in a diagnostic concept" at least partly because of their knowledge of it (2004a: 359, 358).

Not so with somatic diseases. The course of hepatitis or scurvy is not directly affected by a person's knowing or being told that they possess the disease, no matter how appreciative one's apprehension of its symptoms. Or more precisely. Not so with somatic diseases in their normal course or character. Anomalous or wayward causal connections or a-rational causal chains between knowledge of a diagnosis and the character of an illness may occur. Knowing that I suffer from a cardiovascular disease may make me so nervous and upset that it induces episodes of a dangerously irregular heart beat and the attendant disease may achieve heightened resonance because I think of myself as under the diagnosis. Wayward cases aside, however, the typical contour of a somatic disease that is under treatment is not directly affected by classification knowledge. The character of a mental disorder under clinical care often is.

So, are mental disorders diseases? My take-home point or conclusion about disorder and disease actually is two alternative take-home points. I am not sure which one is best. One is bold or categorical. The other is modest or conditional.

The bold one goes like this. What does the Biomedical Disease Model of Mental Disorder tend to encourage? It tends to encourage, I believe, a conception of a mental disorder that is committed to, or pushes us to try to identify, a narrow range of causes of a disorder, symptoms that are discontinuous with normal variations in human health and well-being, and a disorder-identity that is immune to looping effects. Such encouragements are inappropriate or ill suited for the category of disturbance to which a concept of mental disorder is best suited. Prototypical mental conditions that qualify as mental disorders don't satisfy or tend to comply with those demands. So, they are best understood as failing to be outright diseases. (They may help to cause or contribute to the occurrence of diseases, of course, but without themselves being diseases. The lifestyle of a gambling addict, for example, may substantially contribute to somatic ill-health.)

But I am not without misgivings about boldness and denying that mental disorders are diseases. I assume that diseases like malaria and scurvy are exemplary. But someone may retort: 'Why not count, say, hypertension as a disease exemplar?' No firm boundary between abnormal and normal variations in arterial health or function helps to distinguish hypertension from healthy states. Moreover, if influences behind the emergence of a disease that are less proximate and more distal (say, deleterious eating habits or stressful cultural circumstances) are counted as among its sources or propensity conditions, some diseases (again, such as hypertension) may look very much like mental disorders in their multitudinous and risky distal propensity conditions. One person's penchant for cheesy omelets may resemble in being distally influential another's six month ago loss of a job or experience of the death of a loved one. Still (and so here is the conditional or modest way of stating my take-home point) *if* diseases are understood as assuming that there is a clear dividing line between diseases and non-diseases, a narrow range of causes, and imperviousness to looping, than this is not a helpful way in which to understand the nature of a mental disorder. It is not the path through the woods of a mental disorder. Many diseases run in that direction; exemplary mental disorders do not.

(Analogous points may be made for whether the concept of a natural kind applies to a mental disorder. The literature in the philosophy of science on natural kinds is a rich and complex area of enquiry that I do not have time to discuss here. Some statements of what makes a natural kind a natural kind provide little conceptual content, so that something is said to constitute a natural kind merely if it emerges and progresses in natural ways and lends itself to scientific study [even allowing, say, looping and that the emergence and progression of some natural kinds may not be law-like]. Such a weak or modest concept of natural kind may well apply to a mental disorder. I have no grief with modesty. My misgivings about whether mental disorders are natural kinds are directed at the stronger or more ambitious notion discussed above.)

Carl Hempel (1905–97) was one among a group of distinguished philosophers from Central Europe who came to the United States in the 1930s. He is the author of one of the great introductions to any field of philosophy (in his case, the philosophy of science) and was a major figure in twentieth-century philosophy of science (Hempel 1966). In 1959 Hempel was invited by the British psychiatrist, Edwin Stengel, to present a paper on psychiatric classification at a conference in New York City under the auspices of the American Psychopathological Association. In that paper Hempel (1965a: 151–52) claimed that the following should be expected of a classificatory system such as a system that categorizes mental disorders.

> In scientific research [entities] are often found to resist a tidy pigeonholing of any kind ... [S]ome of the objects under study will present the investigator with borderline cases, which do not fit unequivocally into one or another of several neatly bounded compartments, but which exhibit to some degree the characteristics of *different* classes.

Scurvy and malaria possess tidy pigeonholes – one cause, symptoms discontinuous with normality, no looping. Depression does not. Depression is the upshot of propensity factors, harbors symptoms continuous with normality, and typically is vulnerable to looping. Such (remember: taking depression as representative of the set) is the fate of a mental disorder. Not nested in a pigeonhole but perched on a wide, bumpy and permeable plateau.

MENTAL DISORDER, BRAIN DISORDER AND DSM

Suppose you visit a doctor's office with whom you have made an appointment. She is an orthopedic surgeon. You tell her that you wish to have your left leg amputated. You tell her that it feels as if it is not yours. It feels strange and unfamiliar. "It is not overtly crippled," you say. "Or at least I can and do walk with it." "But it feels like something alien." "Even when I look at myself in the mirror, I don't perceive it really as mine." "I am not me with this leg." You ask her to remove it surgically and to arrange to have it replaced with a prosthetic limb.

The surgeon is astounded. She examines your leg and finds it to be perfectly healthy. No tumors, no apparent neuromuscular disease. "I cannot amputate a healthy limb," she says. "But I am in profound discomfort," you reply. "I have spoken to four different surgeons in the past year and none of you seem to understand my feelings." "Don't you have an obligation to relieve my suffering?"

Most certainly, this is no ordinary human behavior. You strike the doctor as in acute distress. She certainly appreciates the dramatic anomaly of your complaint. For better or worse, you impress her as possibly being ill, psychiatrically, or as suffering from a mental disorder. Being a surgeon, she is not sure just what this disorder may be, however. So, she asks you to wait in her outer office, while she makes a private professional phone call. While you are absent, she calls a former medical school classmate, who now is a senior professor in the psychiatric department of a distinguished university medical center. She describes your case to him. He tells her that you may be a sort of patient sometimes colloquially described as a 'wannabee'. A wannabee is someone who wants to have a healthy limb amputated and claims to be emotionally dissociated from the limb. He says that you may be suffering from a disorder that has come to be known, in some circles, more technically, as Body Integrity Identity Disorder (BIID). It's a disorder, he says, in which a person undergoes a chronically distressful mismatch between a part of their body and the part as they experience, feel or emotionally engage with it. "Whereas," he remarks, "some people who actually are missing a limb feel as if it is present, in, say, phantom limb pain, other individuals feel as if a body part that actually is present and functioning is, in some sense, also absent – not a proper part of them." "That's the essence of BIID."

Then, he warns her: "In the absence of access to surgery, some sufferers have deliberately injured the affected limb or body part." "Tourniquets, dry ice, and even chainsaws have been used." "The intent has been either to remove the limb or to injure it so badly that a surgeon has had to remove it."

Her former classmate has no particularly decisive advice to give. Unfortunately, too, he practices psychiatry in a distant city, for otherwise your surgeon would perhaps send you to him for a consult. But he does recommend a psychiatrist in your immediate area for that purpose. "You may consider sending your patient to him," he says. "Psychiatry may have a critical part to play here."

Where should your doctor turn? Resting in her bookshelf, but rarely consulted, since she is an orthopedic surgeon, is the most recent version of the American Psychiatric Association's (APA's) *Diagnostic and Statistical Manual of Mental Disorders*, first published in 1952, and now in its fourth edition (APA 1994 and 2000). (Hereafter I shall refer to the various editions of this book as DSM-I, DSM-II, and so on. I continue to use 'DSM' to refer to recent editions of DSM in general. DSM-5, with Roman numerals replaced by the APA, as the book now in your hands is being written, is in the works for publication in May of 2013. So, I am assuming that the doctor has in her bookshelf APA 2000.) In popularity and influence, DSM is the international Bible of psychiatric diagnosis. Other diagnostic manuals exist, written by psychiatrists, psychopathologists, clinical psychologists, and others. However, these guides or nosological tool-kits are either similarly organized, like the World Health Organization's *International Classification of Diseases* (now in its tenth edition and often referred to as ICD; see World Health Organization 1992), or fail to have as significant an impact on clinical practice as does DSM. That's an overgeneralization perhaps. Goodwin and Guze (1996) enjoys readership as well as do other texts. But DSM is the text of dominating influence.

The first two editions of DSM, published in 1952 (APA 1952) and 1968 (APA 1968), more or less reflected the popularity, at the time, of Freudian psychology. Many of Freud's patients suffered from disorders currently described as forms of anxiety disorder (such as obsessive-compulsive disorder, panic disorder, and so on). Freud offered explanations of these disorders that made appeal to what he regarded as the misdistribution and repression of unconscious psychic energy or dynamic forces in people. So, Freud's psychological theory came to be known as "dynamic" or "psychodynamic" psychology. As noted in the first chapter, dynamic psychology pictures mental disorders as symptom-unspecific operations of unconscious mechanisms, not as discrete symptom-specific disorders. Repression of normal sexual instincts, for instance, may lead one individual to a case of sexual perversion, but another to compose a raunchy novel. "The hysterical symptom," Freud wrote of one sort of symptom, "does not carry [any particular] meaning with it, but the meaning is lent to it, soldered to it, as it were; in every instance the meaning can be a different one, according to the nature of the suppressed thoughts which are struggling for expression" (Freud 1963 [1905]: 57). The third edition of DSM, viz. DSM-III, published in 1980 (APA 1980), departed quite drastically from its two predecessors. Here, briefly, is what led to that departure and to DSM-III's creation.

Multiple research studies had indicated that psychiatric diagnosis, even using DSM-I and DSM-II, tended to be unreliable and inconsistent, not just between different countries (such as the United States and Great Britain), but with respect to the same patients in the same hospital or institution when examined by different clinicians. Improving consensus between clinicians was taken to be the primary goal or desideratum of DSM-III. One of the intended fruits of consensus, *reliability* so-called, is the ability to classify large samples of patients in the same diagnostic category, so that they may be pooled in research studies, serve as pedagogical reference points in the education of mental health professionals, and meet the financial strictures of insurance companies and managed care organizations, which do not reimburse without reliable uniform diagnostic categories across distinct cases.

So, DSM-III was composed. It classified disorders through the description of syndromes or syndromal clusters (symptoms, in effect), quite regardless of surmises about possible underlying or antecedent proximate causes and in a manner that is more or less isolated or stripped away from the social or biographical contexts in which a disorder may arise (other than those that can perhaps be discovered by a clinician on interview or may be available through discussion with family members). For better or worse, this meant that DSM-III freed clinicians from the need to secure detailed knowledge or an informed understanding of a person's history or social context in order to diagnose. A clinician could rely on what is called clinical phenomenology or a patient's clinical presentation. (The use of the word 'phenomenology' in "clinical phenomenology" is not the same in meaning as its use in referring to the what-it-is-likeness of conscious experience. In a clinic the term is used to refer to how a patient presents themselves and responds to a clinical interview. In philosophy of mind, the term 'phenomenology' is used to refer to, say, what it is like to a person to undergo an experience.) As Nancy Andreasen puts it:

"DSM criteria encourage physicians to jump ... into inquiring about specific signs and symptoms without [getting] to know the patient as a unique individual" (Andreasen 1984: 184). Sadler adds: "The DSM has little to say about the biographical life histories of patients." "It offers no dramaturgy, no climax, no denouement" (Sadler 2004a: 358).

Although immensely influential in purport and impact within the mental health profession, the reliability or consensus orientated framework of DSM has elicited a robust share of skeptical apostates and vocal critics. Criticism takes two main general forms. One is moral or sociological. It charges collusion between economic and commercial interest groups (such as drug and insurance companies, for example) in promoting the DSM-like system of diagnostic categories, on the one hand, and the medical profession and its diagnostic and treatment practices, on the other. As one critic observes:

> Symptom-based logics generate inflated prevalence estimates. They also show how these estimates are created and perpetuated because a number of particular groups have distinct interests in demonstrating the presumed pervasiveness of mental illnesses in the community.
> (Horwitz 2002: 91)

Part of the evidence for claims of collusion between economic interests and medical practice consists of the substantial increase in psychiatric diagnosis and illness categories since the deployment of DSM-III and an associated proliferation in the production, prescription and use of psychotropic drugs. Concern about over-diagnosis and over-medicalization of mental disturbances and distresses is said to suggest a scientifically or medically unwarranted level of influence exercised by the pharmaceutical industry on the professional conferences, work groups, and mental health task forces that construct diagnostic criteria for mental disorder.

A second and related but philosophically deeper form of criticism concerns the scientific or empirical credentials of DSM. Many critics charge that DSM fails to satisfy the proper goals of a good psychiatric taxonomic system, which include not just reliable or consensual diagnosis, but providing a framework for prognosis, treatment, and ongoing scientific research. Mere consensus is not enough. In essence, designers of recent editions of DSM (as well as of ICD) more or less have determined their criteria for what counts as a psychiatric diagnostic category by seeking agreement or fit among the diagnostic judgments of fellow clinicians and by trying to systematize and codify trends in current mental health care practice. Not by aiming at additional and in some ways more important goals such as the legitimacy of different diagnoses (a desideratum known as diagnostic validity), descriptions of the typical social settings or causes of onset, characterizing the courses of and variations within different disorders, and learning whether the diagnostic categories themselves, in the words of Richard Bentall, "are useful in predicting either long-term outcome or response to particular treatment" (Bentall 2007: 131).

Jeffrey Poland, a philosopher and one of the most outspoken and articulate critics of DSM, summarizes his own critical attitude towards DSM's construction as follows:

> Empirical evidence is not used in many [taxonomic] decisions; rather, loosely constrained speculations regarding concepts, coherence with other systems [like ICD], face validity, and consensus of the field are taken to suffice for making a decision [as for what to count

as a disorder]. Even when empirical evidence is employed, it is often not clearly relevant, or, even when relevant, the decisions are only loosely connected to the evidence cited. Many of the [deliberations about accuracy of diagnosis] are quite meaningless.

(Poland 2013)

The social/biographical setting of the onset or appearance of a disorder, just for one example, should not be treated lightly. DSM tends to treat it lightly.

Certain cultural environments may help to produce, scaffold or make possible certain symptoms or their particular mode of expression. Symptoms of an eating disorder or anxiety disorder like anorexia nervosa, for instance, are rare outside of Western postindustrial societies, where the majority of cases are young white females from middle- to upper-middle-class families (see Brumberg 1988). A Navajo Indian with the disorder is an anomaly, which social fact may reasonably raise a caution flag in the diagnosis of that sort of case (among the Navajos) as an instance of anorexia.

The taxonomic categories deployed in DSM-III have proliferated with each successive edition or textual revision. The first edition of DSM was a small pamphlet-like book with a grey cover and roughly 100 labels for disorders and symptoms. DSM-IV-TR, the most recent edition, is as thick and about as heavy as a brick with more than 800 pages of definitions, criteria, glossaries and related materials (APA 2000). It purports to identify about 400 distinct conditions as disorders or symptom types. The hundreds of diagnostic categories that appear in DSM-IV-TR are a motley collection that includes social phobias, generalized anxieties, gender confusion, and attention deficit hyperactivity, among numerous other classifications, as types or categories of disorders. So, in effect, non-traditional disorder categories (e.g. gender confusion) are described within the covers of DSM alongside more traditional categories of disorder like major or clinical depression and schizophrenia. As Rutger's sociologist Allan Horwitz puts it, the fourth edition of DSM "categorizes an enormous diversity of human emotions, conduct, and relationships as distinct pathological entities" (Horwitz 2002: 2). Another and ironic observer estimated (as far back as the 1990s) that the upcoming fifth edition of DSM likely will have 1,256 pages and contain 1,800 diagnostic criteria (Blasfield 1996). From handbook through brick and into a super-imposing monument.

The general scientific and clinical weaknesses of DSM are not pursued as a specific topic in this book. Much has been said and continues to be written about them in other locations and by other authors (see Poland, Von Eckardt, and Spaulding 1994; Horwitz 2002; Bentall 2004; Murphy 2006; see also Caplan 1995, Nesse and Jackson 2011, and Poland 2013). But before I return to our hypothetical case, I wish to offer a few brief remarks about DSM-5 (previously referred to as DSM-V until the American Psychiatric Association [APA] decided to abandon the use of Roman numerals).

Judging from reports of the APA's planning work groups, various drafts of materials available on the web, and other public documents and sources, all of which make evident the likely future contours of DSM-5, scientific critics of this new edition of DSM will complain that it contains the same weaknesses as earlier versions. The criticisms?

DSM categories have never been shown to be strongly connected with identifiable propensity conditions or causal explanatory forces. The typical diagnostic interview of a patient is effectively screened off from etiological concerns and sometimes even from concerns about a disorder's more or less proximate or immediate genesis. The methodological premise that mental disorders can be identified in terms of syndrome clusters or without reference to either distal (etiological) or proximate (pathological) causal explanatory sources has been a central presupposition of the manual since the late 1970s. In addition, the DSM's categories of illness do not successfully predict clinical course or response to treatment or clinical outcome. DSM-5 promises to be more of the same, although added with several new diagnostic categories, such as perhaps Behavioral Addictions, Premenstrual Dysphoric Disorder, Temper Dysregulation and Dysphoria, and Sluggish Cognitive Tempo. (Just which of these labels or others appear in the book will be known once it appears.) It also promises to include something called 'dimensional assessments' to the proposed diagnostic criteria for a disorder. Dimensional assessment is a method of diagnosis that permits evaluating the severity of symptoms as well as the manner in which the symptoms of one disorder may cross-cut with symptoms of other categories of disorder as well as with normal behavior.

Given the persistent methodological weaknesses with DSM, it is perhaps no wonder that some scientists and mental health professionals prefer to think of mental disorders as a subtype of brain disorder or neurological impairment and propose that psychiatry should be considered a specialty within neurology. An intimate rapprochement between the category of mental disorder and the diagnostic classification of brain disorder sometimes is envied and sought after. The lack of success with DSM-based research casts serious doubt on its premise that "a-theoretical" criteria (i.e. terms not referring to either pathology or etiology) can serve as the basis for a sound and sensible diagnostic scheme. By comparison, the medical specialization or field of neurology rejects any such premise – at least in the field's more advanced stages of development.

Neurologists aim to develop categories or taxonomies for brain disorders, to predict the progression of symptoms of brain disorders, and to treat those symptoms and the underlying disorders (see Graham [2013b] for discussion from which the material immediately below is derived). In order to do all that, it is presupposed, a clinician must have at least some hypotheses about causally proximate and damaged or dysregulated neural origins or causal-explanatory foundations. Origins or causal foundations are constitutive parts or components of brain disorder types and categories. In the words of two advocates of the taxonomic tradition in brain science, mental activities and cognitive functions "break down selectively following a brain disorder, whether due to a focal injury such as a stroke, or more diffuse degeneration" (Kosslyn and Dror 1992: 49). "Some parts of the brain [may be] more severely [affected] than others", producing different clinical manifestations or symptoms of disorder (Ibid: 56).

Brain scientists working on brain disorders are guided by something like the following taxonomic principle and methodological assumption. To give it a fancy name, I like to call it the principle of the proximate *causal-explanatory sufficiency of the neural-physical domain*. It goes like this: If a condition qualifies as a brain disorder, it has to have proximate causes or causal foundations that admit of an exclusive and exhaustive neural-physical description. So, if the very idea of a brain disorder is to be applied to that of a mental disorder, if, that is, mental disorders constitute a subset of brain disorders, then the category of a mental disorder, too, must observe the very same principle. Mental disorders must be fully explainable in terms of brain processes or conditions. This taxonomic principle goes beyond requiring merely that a causal-explanatory understanding of a mental disorder is loosely consistent with or complemented by brain science. It requires that a brain science explanatory understanding applies to a mental disorder, if it genuinely qualifies as a brain disorder.

To be sure, the standards for satisfying the above mentioned principle currently available in neurology and related fields are neither stably fixed nor the product of uniform consensus among brain scientists. In its use, interpretation or application within neurology (neuropsychology and so on), the application of the concept of a brain disorder tends to rely on judgments, sometimes quite controversial, about such things as the functions or fitness enhancing purposes of various neural systems or activities in the brain. But despite contestability over the very idea of a brain disorder or about the normatively proper behavior of neural systems, certain conditions or processes of brain and behavior enjoy pride of place in the literature as examples of brain disorders. What unites the otherwise rather loose collection of conditions and taxonomic categories of brain disorder that derive from such judgments and are presumed to be brain disorders, when consensus obtains, is reference to exemplars or prototypes of brain disorder and to the manner in which exemplars are best understood. These include conditions such as Alzheimer's dementia, epilepsy, and Parkinson's, for examples. Conditions that unquestionably count as brain disorders. One feature held in common by them (aside, of course, from their harmfulness or undesirability) is that each and every condition receives or hopes to receive the best (fullest and most complete) description of its causal foundations and behavioral impact or power from within, and only from within, neuroscience/brain science and in a manner that conforms to the above mentioned sufficiency principle. No psychological non-neural vocabulary whatsoever is used in prototypical cases to identify the causal springs or immediate sources of a brain disorder's symptom manifestations and foundations. People harbor Parkinson's, for example, not, it is assumed, because of job related emotional distress or imprudent beliefs or desires, but because they suffer from "a degenerative disorder of the brain," to quote one text, that "is responsible for [the condition's] motor and cognitive disturbance" (Litvan 1999: 559). Damage to dopaminergic, serotoninergic and various other neurochemical pathways, in particular, may produce the condition's distinctive deficits.

To extrapolate from neurological theory and practice, a constraining assumption or norm, then, behind the very idea of a condition conceived as brain disorder goes something like this: If a condition's immediate causal foundations, sources and powers *cannot* be best described or understood in brain science terms, then the condition should not be categorized as a brain disorder. This methodological constraint, which may be called the *closed under brain science constraint*, seems to hold firm in current neurology and closely related medical health sciences (such as neuropsychology) in spite of repeated failure to find a crisp or universally acceptable formula for a damaged brain. Indeed, the constraint holds firm in spite of disagreement over the just which sciences should count as sciences of the brain. (The closer the logical or conceptual distance a science is to describing the brain/central nervous system and to the role of brain processes and states in behavior, the stronger the claim of a science to be a brain science. This means that neuroanatomy, neurophysiology, neurobiology, and neurochemistry are all brain sciences. I assume them to be such in this book.) In any case, with the closure *constraint* in taxonomic place for qualifying as a brain disorder, then if or when a condition truly is a brain disorder, there is no conceptual need or even elbow room to step outside of brain science to describe its foundations. Such a description is closed off from explanatory reference to forces or events conceived in non-neuroscientific, psychological, Intentionalistic, or mentalistic terms.

Back to DSM. The point I am making here is that DSM provides a flawed or at least seriously incomplete picture of a mental disorder, just as a comparable a-theoretical conception would be a flawed or seriously incomplete neurological picture of a brain disorder. Without consideration of possible causal foundations for any deficit or impairment that constitutes a disorder, a truly valid or insightful diagnostic framework or categorical scheme (for either a brain or mental disorder) cannot be constructed. Reference to symptoms alone is not enough. (And DSM-5 shows no serious signs of addressing that particular flaw.)

Let's turn back to your hypothetical case of BIID.

Your doctor's psychiatrist friend neglected to mention that BIID does not yet appear in DSM. Reading a description in the manual, she hopes, would help her to figure out what to do and whether it is wise to turn to the services of a consultant psychiatrist. She believes that the concept of a mental disorder is a considerable conceptual distance from normal forms of bodily injury or typical disease. So, she wonders what health norms are relevant in the situation that you are in. Is it that a person must *feel* their body as their own? If so, she does not know how surgery could restore or reconstruct that feeling. Perhaps the bizarre absence of felt ownership is transient and ephemeral. Perhaps it represents a mere passing fall in certain types of neurotransmitters. So, perhaps there is no need to do anything other than to see you again in a few months. "Is this really something that ought to be surgically corrected by removing a limb?", she asks herself.

The surgeon opens her copy of DSM-IV-TR (APA 2000). BIID, as just noted, is not mentioned in DSM-IV-TR. Dr. Michael First, a psychiatrist at Columbia University in New York, who coined the expression 'bodily integrity identity disorder', and has become something of a specialist in the condition (and he is also one of the central players in the project to create DSM-5). He is among medical professionals urging its inclusion in DSM-5 (First 2005). If First succeeds, and given his prominence he may, and DSM-5 appears in 2013, you in your hypothetical condition may be classified as a case of BIID. But formal DSM recognition must wait. In the meantime what should be done? What now? (We are supposing, again, of course, that your office visit is taking place before the appearance of DSM-5.)

Diagnostic indifference is not an option. The surgeon suspects she should categorize you. She just does not know how. She describes an alternative possible course of action. It's the one suggested by her former classmate. She phrases it as follows: "I need to be assured, before I can even begin to consider removing your limb, that you are emotionally and rationally of sound mind." "So, would you be willing to see a psychiatrist and to have their evaluation directed back to me?" "You and I can then meet again after you meet with them."

"I know what you are thinking," you reply. "In a world where people are born without limbs or lose arms or legs in war or to accident or disease, only a disturbed person would wish a healthy limb removed." "But my limb *really* is not healthy." "If it was, why would it make me suffer so?" "Besides which, I don't want to see a psychiatrist." "I just don't trust what they will say."

Not trust a psychiatrist? Given its checkered history and the moral dilemmas posed by labeling, overextended drug use, and so on, psychiatric diagnosis is not an uncontroversial specialty. Towards the end of his life and career, Karl Menninger (1893–1990), a distinguished psychiatrist and member of the family that founded the Menninger Clinic, wrote a letter to Thomas Szasz (1920–). Szasz, although a psychiatrist, is a famous (infamous?) arch-skeptic about the validity of the concept of mental disorder. One observer of Szasz's career as a psychiatry critic describes him as like a "musician who does not like music." On past occasions Szasz had been critical of Menninger. Menninger, however, graciously wrote a letter to Szasz with the following remark: "I am sorry that you and I have gotten apparently so far apart all these years." "You tried; you wanted me to come there, I remember. I demurred. Mea culpa" (see http://www.szasz.com/menninger.html).

Mea culpa? Why did Menninger ask, rhetorically perhaps, for forgiveness from an infamous disorder and anti-psychiatry skeptic?

I cannot speak of Menninger's reasons. They are not evident in the letter. But certainly neither he nor Szasz is alone in worrying about the legitimacy of the concept of a mental disorder or in harboring distrust of diagnostic psychiatry (although Szasz is an extreme case). The particular and specific vicissitudes, above mentioned, of DSM aside, the very idea of a mental disorder (no matter the particular taxonomic manual) has been the subject of controversy and criticism. Is the World Health Organization to be trusted when it claims that "450 million people suffer from mental disorders in both developed and developing countries" or that "one in every four people ... develops one or more mental disorders at some stage in life" (WHO 2002)? Not only, as noted earlier, has the presumed categorical domain of mental disorder historically been much smaller than it is now, but a whole new family of mental health professions (therapists, counselors, etc.) has propagated itself since the 1960s, each claiming to diagnose psychological distresses and prescribe remedies for mental disorders.

Is there perhaps something deeply wrong or categorically mistaken with the very idea of mental disorder or with the proposition that mentality is gummed up or partially incapacitated by something that deserves to be called a disorder or illness? Should psychiatric diagnosis and psychiatric medicine be distrusted? Not distrusted just in the composition of DSM, but distrusted period. Rather than worry about what a mental disorder is (disease? complaint? neural impairment?), or which manual to use in diagnosis (DSM?), shouldn't we wonder *if* it is? Are mental disorders real, honest-to-goodness conditions of people?

Some anti-psychiatry critics believe that the problem with the idea of mental disorder is not with this or that diagnostic criterion for illness, but with the very concept of mental illness or disorder period.

I want to get back, of course, to the topic of the proper meaning of the term 'disorder' in "mental disorder" later in the book (in Chapters 5 and 6 in particular), but before doing so I plan in the next chapter to examine radical skepticism concerning the very idea of a mental disorder and, with it, some of the metaphysical and values assumptions of both psychiatric and somatic medicine.

SUMMARY

When is a behavioral condition or mental disturbance worthy of diagnosis as a disorder? The answer that I propose in this chapter, and which is developed later in the book, consists of referring to mental disorders as gumming up or incapacitating the mental and reason-responsive works of a person, of their mind, as it were, and in a manner that is harmful, involuntary, and typically requires treatment or assistance from others. The need for treatment or assistance raises questions about the moral status and not just therapeutic effects of clinical care as well as about the self-respect and dignity of the person with a disorder. The dual dimensions of treatment as a therapeutic act and as a moral relationship with a patient may help to suggest that somatic diseases constitute a good model for mental disorder. If so, clinical diagnosis necessitates looking beneath or beyond the symptoms of a disorder to a disease process or entity that is responsible for the symptoms. Such a model is known as the Biomedical Disease Model of Mental Illness. Although advocacy of the model usually is combined with an attempt to understand mental disorders as instances of a broken, damaged or diseased brain, it does not have to be associated with that specific attempt. A mental disorder may be pictured as a disease process or entity without also being classified as a neurological disorder.

The biomedical model has been developed in different ways, depending upon the conditions that are taken as exemplars of bodily disease and as prototypes of mental disorder, respectively. By picking certain illnesses as exemplars, this chapter has argued that mental disorders probably are not best understood as disease-like processes. They don't have the same numerically limited range of causes that diseases normally or often do possess and they lack the relatively precise margins often available for somatic illness between health and illness. They are also susceptible to a looping effect that typically is absent in somatic disease. Looping effects, so-called, connect the diagnosis as known to its subject with a condition's course or progression.

One final detour was necessary in this chapter before finally turning to the role of DSM in contemporary psychiatric practice. In describing a mental disorder and wondering whether it is a disease, the chapter also asked if it is a natural kind. It pointed out that disorders unlike natural kinds in chemistry and biology are value-laden in their nature or identity. Disorders are not just contingently normatively assessable (as I might assess a good or bad lump of sugar or horse, depending upon how I wish to use it). When a person has a mental disorder, there is necessarily something wrong with them. The condition is invariably bad. Just how bad depends upon its severity. So, the empirical description we apply to a disorder depends upon assuming that whatever condition is picked out as disorder is something that is undesirable – something wrong (as I put it in this book) with the reason-responsiveness of a basic or fundamental psychological capacity and that represents a reduction in a person's well-being. This assumption poses an impediment to thinking of mental disorders as natural kinds.

The chapter concluded by painting a picture of some of the conceptual difficulties associated with DSM, a major diagnostic manual for mental disorders. At the heart of those difficulties are doubts about the scientific utility of the manual. The main difficulty is DSM's agnosticism about the causal foundations of disorders. This worry becomes even more worrisome when we recognize that standard practice with disease diagnosis including taxonomies of brain disease and neurological disorder is incompatible with it. Standard practice in neurology aims to undercover the causal foundations of a brain disorder. If the methods of neurology are to be followed, albeit without assuming that the domain of mental disorder is a sub-domain of brain disorder, then we really don't have a sound and sensible theory of a disorder if we fail to possess plausible hypotheses about the causal explanatory conditions of its emergence and progression.

SUGGESTING READING

Bayne, T. and Levy, N. (2005), "Amputees by choice: body integrity identity disorder and the ethics of amputation," *Journal of Applied Philosophy* 22: 75–86.

Broome, M. and Bortolotti, L. (eds) (2009). *Psychiatry as Cognitive Neuroscience: Philosophical Perspectives* (Oxford: Oxford University Press).

Horwitz, A. and Wakefield, J. (2007). *The Loss of Sadness: How Psychiatry Transformed Normal Sorrow into Depressive Disorder* (New York: Oxford University Press).

Jackson, H. and McGory, P. (2009). "Psychiatric diagnosis: purposes, limitations, and an alternative approach," in S. Wood, N. Allen, and C. Pantelis (eds) *The Neuropsychology of Mental Illness* (pp. 178–93) (Cambridge: Cambridge University Press).

Thagard, P. (1999). *How Scientists Explain Disease* (Princeton: Princeton University Press).

4 Skepticism about mental disorder

One of the most conceptually puzzling things about the phenomenon of mental disorder is that there are intelligent people who deny that it exists. Nothing is a mental disorder or illness, so they say. This may be a difficult claim to fathom, given everything said about mental disorder so far in the book and in the culture at large. But puzzles are puzzles and should not be neglected. Unscrambling this particular puzzle contains lessons for a theory of mental disorder.

Theorists who deny the existence of mental disorder are sometimes called "anti-realists" – in opposition to so-called "realists", who affirm the existence of mental disorder.

Isn't it wholly absurd to deny the existence of mental disorders? After all, we have diagnostic manuals to identify them, don't we? Psychiatrists seek to treat them. Doctors are not trying to trick people into believing in mental disorders. The anti-realist agrees, of course, that there are thick manuals as well as caring and well-intended psychiatrists. Anti-realists don't reject the existence of people who talk as if mental disorders are real or of books that purport to identify disorders. No, they reject the existence of mental disorder itself.

Is anti-realism warranted? What considerations may lead a person to be an anti-realist? Some intelligent people find various arguments compelling for an anti-realist position. In this chapter I plan to look at two varieties of anti-realist argument – two forms of radical skepticism about mental disorder. One I call *metaphysical anti-realism*, and the other *moral anti-realism*. First, just below I offer a very brief sketch of each form.

Metaphysical anti-realism/skepticism: Very briefly, and leaving out details, some medical scientists and others believe, on broadly empirical and philosophical or metaphysical grounds, that reference to the mind or mentality of a 'mental' disorder can and should be eliminated or superseded and displaced by a brain-centered or physicalistic/materialistic and non-mentalistic understanding of a mental disorder. Given such displacement or replacement, no condition deserves or should deserve, they believe, to be classified as a mental disorder. The number of mental disorders, just like the number of unicorns and goblins, is zero.

Moral anti-realism/skepticism: Very briefly, and leaving out details, some critics of the very existence of a mental disorder charge that the attribution or ascription of mental disorders to people is a morally unacceptable or ethically misbegotten practice. It is morally unacceptable or ethically misbegotten because it is a human dignity violating or respect for persons under-mining process. If we truly, it is said, wish to help people who suffer from mental disturbance or distress, we must jettison the concept of a mental disorder or illness and re-describe the condition. We must replace the concept with morally alternative concepts or ways of thinking. These alternative ways should help us to understand and treat people who are mentally disturbed or troubled as compromised, although still fully responsible and not-ill agents. No condition should, they think, be labeled as a mental disorder. Re-describe it as an unwelcome condition, often requiring outside help perhaps, but not as a disorder or illness.

Though not enamored of either form of skepticism or anti-realism about mental disorder, I am convinced that each harbors important and useful lessons for a theory of mental disorder. The main lesson of metaphysical skepticism is that the category of mental disorder has important implications for our understanding of the causal-explanatory power of mind and mentality in the physical world. These implications must be properly understood and addressed, if a concept of mental disorder soundly and sensibly is to apply to persons. The main lesson of moral skepticism is that a diagnosis of mental disorder is morally contestable territory. Recognizing that the attribution of mental disorder is morally contestable territory is not the same thing as main-taining that the medical or psychiatric norms or standards for mental disorder cannot be objective or warranted or that the assessment of a mental disorder necessarily produces wholly intractable moral quandaries. But it does mean that protection or preservation of a person's dignity and self-respect must be a moral constraint on diagnosis and treatment. Ethically demanding standards for diagnostic labeling and care should be observed. If or when the social power of psychiatric diagnosis is overlooked, "we risk overlooking the moral impact diagnosis has on people's lives" (Sadler 2004b: 175).

In this chapter the lessons of each form of anti-realism develop over the course of examining each type of skeptical argument. In the first section of this chapter I plan to examine metaphysical anti-realism about mental disorder.

MENTAL DISORDER AND THE MIND/BODY PROBLEM

One of the most famous problems in the philosophy of mind is the mind/body problem. This is the question of the place of consciousness and Intentionality or of mind in the physical world. The general form of the problem, which has occupied the attention of philosophers and others since ancient times, is represented by two facts about human beings that seem not just distinct but separable in kind or nature: Physical facts, such as that I am six feet tall, with my feet planted firmly on the ground, my head held high, and mental facts, such as that I *believe* I am six feet tall, *want* to keep my feet planted firmly on the ground, and *consciously decide* to hold my head high. These seem like two categorically separable facts, expressive of two very different sorts of features or aspects of persons. For one thing, the mode of existence of the first sort of fact (the physical one) has nothing to do with the conscious feelings or Intentionality-infused attitudes (beliefs, desires, decisions, etc.) of people. The truth of a proposition like that of "Graham is six feet tall" has nothing to do with my or anyone else's state of mind. It is true no matter what I or anyone else thinks, feels or believes. It possesses what philosophers call mind-independent truth conditions. Contrastingly, the truth of a proposition like that of "Graham believes that he is six feet tall" is utterly dependent upon what someone thinks or believes. It's mode of existence (as a mental fact) depends upon a state of mind. Indeed, it *is* a state of mind. A state of *my* mind. So, it possesses mind-dependent truth conditions. Just what is the relation between these two sorts of facts and features? The one mind-independent in its truth conditions, the other mind-dependent.

It hardly needs saying that this is a difficult question. There is no general consensus about the correct answer. This is not an uncommon occurrence in the discipline of philosophy, of course. In debates about prominent philosophical topics, especially of a metaphysical variety like the mind-body problem, there are no "knock-down, iron-clad, settled once-and-for all arguments for, or against" a proposed resolution of a topic (Swoyer 2008: 18). "No recipe that forces a uniquely correct answer" (ibid.). There are famous attempts to answer the question of what is the relation, say, between mental and physical facts, mind and body (including brain), and, just as in philosophical debates about other topics, one must weigh the costs and benefits of each proposed answer before deciding which one is or may be the best. There may be no utterly decisive winner.

I plan to restrict myself to outlining and examining two of the most famous attempts to solve the mind/body problem. (For reasons of space, I do not consider all of the pros/benefits and cons/costs that attach to each position.) One position is known as *dualism*. The other is known as *physicalism* or *materialism.* I am taking special interest in these two positions in this chapter because they are especially relevant, as we will see, to an evaluation of the case for and against metaphysical skepticism or anti-realism about mental disorder.

Each of the two metaphysical positions just mentioned comes in different forms. One form of dualism is known as substance dualism. Another form is known as property dualism.

Substance dualism was famously defended by René Descartes (1596–1650). Descartes' idea is that the world divides into two different kinds of entities, objects or substances. Each substance can exist on its own and is dramatically different in nature from the other. Physical substances (like rocks, statues, and brains) are divisible and in space. Minds, on the other hand, are indivisible. They are not in space and cannot be divided into smaller pieces or segments. Minds serve as the basis of mental facts (such as that I believe I am six feet tall). Physical substances serve as the basis of mental facts (such as that I am six feet tall).

Property dualism is a less dramatic form of dualism. The idea is this: Although there are not two kinds of substances in the world, there are two kinds of properties or features that an object or entity (such as a human being) may have. Physical properties (like weight, mass, solidity, liquidity and so on). Mental properties (like consciousness, thought, belief, and desire). My belief that I weigh 175 lb. is a different sort of property or feature of me than my objective weight of 175 lb. Believing is one kind of feature; weight (or being a certain height, and so on) is another kind of feature.

Physicalism or materialism, as the name suggests, is the position that an individual person, me or you, or whatever we refer to when we use first-person-singular pronouns (like 'I', 'me', 'moi' …), is a physical object made up entirely of physical stuff (organs, cells, particles and the like). Just as a clay statue is composed entirely of clay particles that are arranged in statue-like form, and has properties such as mass, weight and a position in space, persons are composed entirely of biochemical or physical particles organized in a person-like form, and possess such properties as mass, weight and a position in space. There is no non-physical entity or substance in or associated with a person; no non-physical characteristics or properties of persons. Only matter makes up persons. So, physicalism is a type of denial of dualism.

Physicalists, of course, recognize that persons think and feel. However, physicalists claim that the mental facts that hold true of a person actually are a particular type or species of physical fact. It may not be obvious that they are physical facts, but they are. Minds themselves are something physical.

The most popular version of physicalism is the thesis that the thoughts and feelings of a person are identical to states of or processes in a person's brain. The brain is the mind, the organ of thought and feeling. It is the very thing or 'substance' that thinks and feels. And all mental states or activities should be identified with neural states or activities. This particular version of physicalism is known as the psychoneural *identity theory*. Psychoneural identity theory says that the characteristics of mind that are ordinarily described in mental or psychological terms (in the language of thought, belief, desire, decision, and so on) should literally be understood as physical or brain states or processes. Just as lightning is a form of electrical discharge, so my believing that I am six feet tall or am thinking that snow is white is a type of neural or brain activity.

Metaphysical skepticism about mental disorder, of the sort that I am about to describe, takes physicalism and anti-dualism about the mind-body/brain seriously. It sides with physicalism against dualism and supposes that dualism should be rejected. It also supposes that rejecting dualism and embracing physicalism is equivalent to claiming that mental disorders are not, strictly speaking, real. Literally speaking, they fail to exist. They are fictions – perhaps at times useful or convenient fictions – but fictions nonetheless. The reasoning behind metaphysical skepticism about mental disorder goes like this.

Why do we say that people have minds (beliefs, desires, thoughts, and so on)? We say these things because we wish to explain and understand human behavior. We appeal to people's states of mind or attitudes in describing what they say, do and why. Simple examples: Why do I take an umbrella with me to work? Because I believe it will rain today and desire not to get wet. Or: why is my next door neighbor running to the drug store? This is explained by reference to his belief that his infant daughter would otherwise suffer (without immediately needed medicine) and to his desire to preserve the health of a beloved child. But the postulation of minds and states of mind (such as beliefs, desires, love and so on) is part of an obsolete theory of behavior, so says the metaphysical skeptic. Dualism is an historical and unscientific anachronism. It is like the chemical theory of late seventeenth century science that proposed that the burning of an object consists in the release of a special substance called "phlogiston". Chemistry no longer talks of phlogiston. We no longer understand burning in terms of it. So analogously: We should no longer talk of minds. We should no longer understand behavior in terms of beliefs, desires, and other attitudes. We should replace talk of minds with talk of brains. We should explain behavior by reference to neurological mechanisms.

The metaphysically skeptical argument continues as follows.

Meanwhile: Talk of *mental* disorders (or of a distinct domain of illnesses classified as mental disorder) unfortunately presupposes that unlike non-mental physical or somatic disorders or bodily diseases (such as scurvy, cancer and so on), the class of mental disorders are disorders of a non-physical thing, substance, or entity, viz. the mind. Associated with this allegedly non-physical thing are certain purported defining features (such as non-extension in space and weightlessness) that are unshared with anything physical. But, so this metaphysical form of skepticism about mental disorder continues, there are no non-physical things (or properties). The assumption that non-physical minds exist and that dualism is true just doesn't mesh with a sound and sensible medico-scientific picture of the world or cohere with a properly informed understanding of the role of the brain in the behavior of persons. Mind is nothing but brain. Mental activity is neural activity. It is part of what brain does. It often operates or functions as a mind. In so doing its states or activities *really* are nothing but brain states. So, any so-called 'mental' disorder, if it qualifies as some sort of disorder, must be a disorder in a physical thing, viz. the brain. Calling it 'mental' is a metaphysically misleading and scientifically naive misnomer.

Spelled out schematically, the argument looks like this:

1   Suppose a psychiatrist diagnoses a person's disturbance or illness as a mental disorder or illness rather than as some other sort of illness entirely. Then *either* (a) the diagnosis is right because the person actually does have a mental disorder or illness as opposed to some other sort of illness *or* (b) the diagnosis is wrong because the person fails to have a mental disorder or illness, although they may have some other sort of illness.
2   But if we take option (a), then some disorders qualify as mental; moreover mental disorders are not some other sort of disorder or illness.
3   If we take option (b), then we have not admitted to the existence of a mental disorder and we have permitted a person to be diagnosed with another sort of disorder entirely.
4   If mental disorders exist or are real, and are not some other sort of disorder entirely, then dualism about mind/body must be true. The truth of dualism is presupposed by the very existence and distinctness of the category or domain of mental disorder.
5   However: dualism is false. Physicalism is true. No thing or entity is a non-physical entity. There are no non-physical things (or non-physical properties). Non-physical things (or properties) play no role whatsoever in human behavior. The idea that non-physical things (such as minds) exist is a non-scientific residue of a misbegotten picture of the world. Minds are nothing but brains.
6   So, there are no *mental* disorders. No type of disorder should be called a mental disorder. No person *mentally* can be ill.
7   Therefore, if the person mentioned above really has a disorder, their disorder must be some other sort of disorder entirely – a disorder in (and of) the brain.

The main idea behind the metaphysically skeptical argument just outlined is that the concept of a mental disorder has no application to anything real or that exists in the world. Minds as such are not real, strictly speaking. Brains are real, of course, but minds as minds or as something distinct from physical brains are not. Strictly speaking, therefore, there are no mental disorders or illnesses.

Perhaps unexpectedly self-critically, given the identity of its authors and its audience of mental health professionals, DSM-IV expresses sympathy for this anti-dualist position. It says the following: "Although this book is titled the *Diagnostic and Statistical Manual of Mental Disorders*, the term *mental disorder* unfortunately implies a distinction between 'mental' and 'physical' disorders that is [an] ... anachronism of mind/body dualism" (APA 1994: xxi). However, this has not stopped the manual from containing a nosology or botany of mental disorders (and arguably for none of which have brain disorders been found; see Poland 2013).

Anti-dualist/pro-physicalist sentiment appears in a wide variety of guises in the literature on mental disorder. Michael Allen Taylor (1999: viii), for instance, affirms it in a popular textbook on clinical neurology. Taylor writes:

> Psychiatry and neurology [is] one field. [M]ental illness is not 'mental' at all, but the behavioral disturbance associated with brain dysfunction and disease.

Not mental at all? This is because, so Taylor assumes (note also his talk of brain dysfunction and disease), no mental things exist. Brains exist; minds don't.

Many thinkers (this author included, of course) continue to believe that mental disorders are real, honest-to-goodness conditions of people and that the category or concept *mental disorder* applies to a certain general type of disturbance or distress in persons. The expression 'mental disorder' is not a misnomer. It is not an anachronism. It is not unscientific. It is not a term for a fiction. So, the conclusion that there are no mental disorders is unacceptable. How so, though? How can one defend mental illness realism against metaphysical skepticism?

In retort to metaphysical skepticism, two general lines of defense may be offered. One consists in defending dualism. It rejects the fifth premise, which means, in effect, that the defense also rejects physicalism viz. the proposition that mind is nothing other than something physical or the brain. The defense may be outlined as follows.

PRO-DUALISM: THE FIRST LINE OF DEFENSE

Dualism depicts mental disorders as separable from physical states or conditions, although causally interacting with them. It claims that mental disorders can be, and sometimes are, causes and effects of physical activities in the brain, body and physical environment. But dualism insists that any theory of a mental disorder must include reference to non-physical facts as essential pieces of information about a mental disorder. So, a theory of mental disorder must not just employ talk of conscious experiences and Intentional states or attitudes (such as beliefs, desires, decisions, and so on), but must be interpreted as referring to properties or features of a non-physical, weightless and intangible entity – the mind – or to non-physical properties.

So, one line of defense against the metaphysically skeptical criticism is to defend dualism about mind/body and a dualist depiction of a mental disorder. It consists in attacking the fifth premise mentioned above viz. that nothing is non-physical. It argues that the mind is both real and non-physical. Separable from the brain. The brain is implicated in both the origin and treatment of a mental disorder. Mind and brain interact, no doubt. But the mental is not something neural. The mental of a mental disorder inheres in a special non-physical substance. (Or: To put this in property dualist terms, the mental properties of a mental disorder are categorically distinct from physical properties of the person with the disorder, though the two sets of properties causally interact.)

There is, dualists or most dualists maintain, a very special and intimate way in which the mind both affects and is affected by the body/brain. The mind of a person *immediately* or *directly* causes changes in their body/brain without directly causing changes in any other organism or individual. Conversely, the body/brain directly causes changes in a person's mind without directly causing changes in any other mind. Call this mind/body or mental/physical mode of bidirectional causation *direct interaction*.

Consider an episode of mental disorder. Suppose a person is suffering from a panic attack. Suppose anxiety (a mental state) immediately produces changes in various neurochemicals in a person's brain (say, in its noradrenalin). Suppose these changes in turn bring about further changes in the anxious mood of the person, perhaps adding generalized and excessive fear to the anxiety. Each sort of change is directly caused in the person. The occurrence of anxiety immediately affects no one's brain but that of the person with the disorder. The neurochemical changes immediately affect no one's mood but that of the very same person.

All of this raises the following Big Question, of course. Does or can dualism offer a truly promising or perspicuous approach to matters mental including the topic of mental disorder? It may be thought that there is a sound sociological reason for dismissing dualism. This is that it is unpopular among scientists. "Today, most scientists do not accept dualism" (Frith and Rees 2007: 9). But dismissal on grounds just of scientific or medical unpopularity really isn't sensible, for, as Christopher Frith and Geraint Rees (each scientists), just quoted, aptly note, dualism does appreciate that "the brain [has] a key role in linking matter and mind" (Frith and Rees 2007: 9). Dismissals of dualism sometimes rest on simplistic caricatures of the dualist position, as if, for example, it is anti-brain. But insofar as dualism (in the form being described here) insists that there are direct causal interactions between neural and mental activity, it offers prominence to the brain, albeit not the referential (reverential?) throne offered by physicalism/anti-dualism or by the psychoneural identity theory. Dualism respects the physical domain in certain ways. However, dualism denies its causally-explanatorily unbridled range over questions about the behavior of persons. A neighbor's running to the drug store is not best explained by reference to his neural activity. A non-physical mind possessed of mental states is behind the sprint.

From the perspective of developing a concept or theory of mental disorder, a dualist conception of mental disorder has two possibly appealing features. For one, it helps to explain why neuroscience is an incomplete explanatory instrument for addressing many of the questions that we wish to answer about a mental disorder. On a dualist conception of a mental disorder, neuroscientists may inform us about neurotransmitters, the activity of cells, and so on. This information may be useful in helping to understand the sources and treatment of a mental disorder. In addition, however, to considering disorders in neural or neurological terms, there are disturbances of consciousness and Intentionality in a mental disorder, which, as I am arguing in this book, are distinctive of a mental disorder and part of its foundations. So, on a dualist conception, if a disorder is a mental as opposed to a brute somatic or body/brain disorder, reference should be made to consciousness and Intentionality as features or aspects, not just of the foundations of the disorder, but also (adds the dualist) of something non-physical. The mind. That is why (again, says the dualist) neuroscience is an incomplete explanatory instrument. It fails to make the necessary reference to the non-physicality of the vehicle of consciousness and Intentionality viz. the mind.

Dualism's second possibly appealing feature is that it offers a ready answer to the question of why medical science ought to contain a specialization in psychiatry. Why not just clinical neurology, as Michael Alan Taylor recommends? If mental disorders are not physical and not neurological, they are not disorders in the brain. Medicine needs a specialty that is uniquely devoted to the health and illness of a non-physical mind, viz. the personal subject of experience, albeit in a manner that also attends, as neurology does (for a dualist), to neural causes and effects of mental activity. A dualistically informed psychiatry may fit the bill.

Are dualism's possible appeals truly appealing? We cannot adequately assess the possible appeal of a dualist theory of mental disorder until we have a well worked out theory of mental disorder of a dualist type to examine and assess. I, for one, don't know of any such a theory. But still it should be pointed out that dualism possesses arguments intended to be in its favor that are totally independent of the topic of mental disorder. These arguments are based on a number of claims about consciousness and Intentionality. I outline one such argument just below, although for reasons of space, I do not discuss it in detail here.

It goes like this: Does what we consciously think, believe or desire ever effect what we do? Does the content or Intentionality of our thoughts affect our behavior? If the answer is yes, as certainly seems to be the case, can the Intentionality of thoughts or what thoughts are about (their content) and their causal powers be described in physical terms? The *limit of physical description argument* (as the following line of argument may be called) charges that we cannot describe the causal role of thought or of the contents of thoughts (and other conscious attitudes) in behavior in physical or physically scientific terms. This is because thought contents (viz. what thoughts are about, their Intentional contents) are fundamentally private, subjective or personal. The content of a thought can be appreciated (introspected, recognized) by and only by the person or thinker who has the thought. For physicalism, however, no features of or facts about a mind can be appreciable by, and only by, just one person. There may be physical situations that contingently enable one person to know something that other persons do not know, viz. circumstances that put one individual in touch with facts with which other people are not in touch. For example, I may be on one side of a street, you on the other, and I can therein notice facts on my side that you do not – unless you move to my side (which you can). But for physicalism there can be no one-person-alone appreciable facts. Facts for one person and one person only. For physicalism facts are physical facts and physical facts are facts about phenomena with spatial extension, weight, and so on; nothing private about that.

When it comes to physical facts, you can always move to my side of the street and I to yours, so to speak. However, so this dualist-like argument continues, no matter how widely or deeply we examine the physical character of the brain and transactions that occur when it interacts with the environment, no matter 'the side of the street', we inevitably miss whatever the other person is thinking of. This left out fact is that when any particular thought, viz. *this* or *that* thought (with this or that particular content), occurs to a person, then the person and only this person can know of what they are thinking. Of what their thoughts are about. My thought contents are experienced by and only by me. The estimations or hypotheses of other persons about whatever I am thinking of, arrives through and only through inferences from my speech and bodily behavior (hypotheses that may be profoundly mistaken). So: Between the two, viz. neural activity and thinking, there is an "explanatory gap" (Levine 2009: 284). Physical descriptions alone cannot account for, cannot identify, the contents of thought.

So goes the limit argument. To illustrate.

Suppose I am thinking of frogs and toads. I am having frog and toad thoughts. You may guess that I am thinking of cats and dogs. But you are wrong, let's assume. You may guess this because you see that my eyes are fixated on cats and dogs as we walk along the street. But my eyes may be fixated on cats and dogs, all the while as I am thinking of frogs and toads. Or perhaps you assume that I am thinking of cats and dogs because you are a neuroscientist. You have studied my brain when, in the past, I have said that I am having thoughts of cats and dogs, and you have good reason to believe that the brain states that now I am in are the very same sorts of brain states that occurred when I reported to you that I was thinking of cats and dogs. But still it is possible, of course, for your assumption about what I am thinking to be wrong. The assumption may be wrong because my earlier reports about my thoughts may have been deceptive or insincere. Or your assumption may be wrong because, although I am in the same sorts of brain states as did occur when I was thinking of cats and dogs, the states themselves have since come to assume very different functional or operational roles. A neural network that once implemented my thinking of cats and dogs may now have come to implement or assume the functional role of implementing frog and toad thoughts. Given the privacy of thought or of the contents of thought, we cannot decisively rule against just such empirical possibilities.

If the contents of thought are inescapably private or subjective and do not lend themselves to impersonal physical or brain science description, this (seems to some philosophers) to favor some form of mind/body dualism. Perhaps not substance dualism, but some form of dualism. Perhaps property dualism – a dualism of literal Private Property, as it were. If we are physicalists, however, it is assumed (by most philosophers who favor physicalism) that then we must ultimately employ nothing but physical descriptions of mentality. Nothing irreducibly or intractably private or subjective can be allowed. As Fred Dreske, a philosopher of physicalist or materialist persuasions puts it, "subjectivity [must become] part of the objective [or public] order" (Dretske 1997: 65). If not, if some mental facts just are not knowable or appreciable by more than one person, dualism of some sort, it is believed, may well be the only explanation for how this is possible. My 'mental' street is private; your 'mental' street is private. Mine is "in" me. Yours is "in" you. And never the two can meet or metaphysically intersect.

I don't wish to explore here whether privacy considerations favor dualism. (I and legions of other philosophers have spilled a lot of ink over issues involved in arguments such as the limit argument above. See, for example, Graham and Horgan 2002.) But, for what it is worth, I shall lay my cards on the table by stating that if there is anything to privacy of thought arguments, and I believe that there is, it does not lie in supporting dualism. It lies in the fact that the privacy or subjectivity of conscious mental phenomena poses problems for the metaphysical understanding of mind/body *period*, whether it is dualism or physicalism. It is no more manageable to understand how a non-physical entity (a brainless mind) can harbor private conscious thoughts or thought contents than it is to understand how a brain harbors them. Either metaphysical possibility is immensely puzzling. As Eric Olson puts it: "It is no easier to explain a thing's ability to think on the assumption that it is immaterial than it is on the assumption that it is material" (Olson 2007b: 153; see also van Inwagen 2009: 221). So, if the subjectivity or personal privacy of consciousness poses problems for the physicalist thesis that thinking is a brain process, then why should it be assumed that the subjectivity or personal privacy of experience is less of a problem for a mind if it is not physically extended but some-how interacts with the brain – as dualism says? The fact that I am thinking of frogs and toads and not of cats and dogs may not be understandable in strict physical terms, but is it any more intelligible if we assume that there is something non-physical or immaterial 'inside' of me that harbors thoughts? I should say not. Dualism seems perhaps only to mystify the puzzle.

Suppose, however, that, for whatever reason, dualism somehow still enjoys warrant, not deci-sive warrant (whatever may mean), but warrant enough to be taken seriously as a contender for solving the metaphysical mind/body problem. If some warrant is possessed by dualism, then one way of proceeding would be to learn if a dualistic theory of mental disorder can be devel-oped that combines the best interpretations and defenses of the just mentioned limit argument and related others while, at the same time, can help to make plausible sense of a mental disorder. Of course, this would be an immensely ambitious or proto-Herculean project: a dualist theory of mental disorder. It would occupy a huge book all by itself. The nature and variants of dualism are complex and various. Work would also have to be done to defend a dualist theory of a mental disorder in light of contemporary attitudes and practices in science and mental health medicine, wherein so much attention is being given to the role of the brain and central nervous system and wherein numerous medical scientists favor neuroscientific theories of mental disorder. Adding an account of just how dualism can accommodate neuroscience in a theory of mental disorder would add still another chapter to a dualistic theory.

Taking on a complex and ambitious project like that of a dualist theory of mental disorder may be a worthy task (although, as said, I know of no serious and systematic attempt to do so), but only if we concede, at the outset, that certain characteristic features of a mental disorder should be interpreted as properties of a non-physical thing (or in some other pro-dualist, say, property dualist, manner). But do we really need to be dualists in order to be *realists* about mental disorder i.e. in order to maintain that mental disorders are a distinct category of ill-health from somatic or bodily illnesses? Do we really need to be dualists to defeat metaphysical skepticism about disorder? I think not.

The assumption behind any such perceived need for dualism is false. The class of mental dis-orders does not need to be demarcated in a manner that is metaphysically independent of the possible materiality or physical basis of mind. The assumption that it does need to be independent of the truth of some form of physicalism reflects a less than fully conceptually resourceful view of the relation between theories of mental illness or disorder and the metaphysics of mind/body.

In short, there is a second and alternative means of deflecting metaphysical skepticism about the very idea of a mental disorder. The first line of defense against metaphysical skepticism about mental disorder, as noted above, attacks the fifth premise that there are no non-physical entities. It defends dualism. But a second line focuses on the fourth premise. This is the claim that if a mental disorder qualifies as a real, honest-to-goodness disorder, then it must be a disorder in a non-physical entity or thing. The second line argues that mental disorders can be distinct disorders and distinct from somatic illnesses or disorders *even if* mental disorders are not disorders in some non-physical thing, and, indeed, even if the brain is the physical existential base of mental disorder. Physicalism (at least in some loose form) may be true and yet mental disorders may still qualify as a special class of disorders.

METAPHYSICAL ECUMENISM AND PHYSICALISM: THE SECOND LINE OF DEFENSE

In describing the second line, some preliminary stage setting is required. We should remind ourselves that, despite the unpopularity of dualism in mental health science, a distinction between mental and non-mental somatic or physical disorders is widely accepted within medicine. There is a medical specialty that deals with mental disorders (psychiatry). There is an institute of the U.S. Federal Government that supports research into mental disorder (National Institute of Mental Health). There is a branch of the British National Health Service (Mental Health Services) that deals with mental illness. There are specially trained personnel or mental health professionals who deal with people who are subjects with mental disorders, and there are special treatments (e.g. psychotherapy) and medications (e.g. anti-depressants) that are regarded as appropriate and effective for those disorders. Fully accredited medical schools, doctoral programs, and other institutions provide training for mental health professionals and support research designed to understand and ameliorate mental disorder. Each year many thousands of people are diagnosed as suffering from some type of mental illness or disorder. The validity or legitimacy of these diagnoses is accepted by both the lay public and medical professionals alike and, frequently, of course, by those who have been diagnosed.

Does all that presuppose dualism? Does it imply that the mental is something non-physical? No, it does not. Here's why.

It must be recognized that not every distinction is a dichotomy i.e. is a separation between two categorical types of features or entities. Some distinctions are dichotomies. Some are not. The distinction between being, say, dead and alive is a dichotomy. One and the same person cannot be both dead and alive. However, a distinction like that between standing, say, 6 feet tall and weighing 175 pounds is not a dichotomy. One and the same person can be both 6 feet tall and weigh 175 pounds. So, likewise, one and the same condition of a person may be (absent argument to the contrary) a physical condition or process, in some sense, as well as a mental disorder. The contrast pair 'physical/mental' when applied to a physical condition versus a mental disorder may be a distinction that is not a dichotomy. A non-dichotomous distinction would be the case if, say, the mental somehow is a distinguishable form or variety of the physical, just as height is a distinguishable physical feature from that of weight. The mental is (so one line of reasoning goes) a particular species of physicality. A variety that is best described in mental or psychological terms i.e. in the language of consciousness and Intentionality or the vocabulary of psychology. The somatic or bodily, by contrast, is a type of physicality that is best described in straightforward physical terms i.e. in terms, say, of the natural or physical sciences (and without psychologically linguistic reference to consciousness or Intentionality). If one wants to refer to, say, the Intentional content of a state or condition or to the what-it's-likeness of a phenomenal experience, the language of mind is the most appropriate, indeed the inescapable language. Whereas to talk of ion channels the language of neuroscience should be used.

Does such an approach to the mental disorder/somatic illness distinction make sense? Is there empirical applicability and metaphysical traction to it? First off, there are reasons to believe that conscious and Intentional states (beliefs, desires, and so on) are part of the physical world. But then, as paradoxical as this may seem, when first stated, there also is reason to describe conscious and Intentional states in mental (conscious and Intentional) rather than brain science terms. This is not because describing conscious or Intentional states in the language of brain science is dreary or unaesthetic. It is because mental descriptions are the best or perhaps even the only terms in which to understand certain forms or features of the foundations of human behavior – including the foundations of mental disorder. Just as, in certain cases, I need to refer to a person's weight rather than to their height, so in some cases I need to refer, for example, to a person's thoughts of frogs and toads rather than to cellular and molecular networks in their hippocampus that may help (along with other areas of the brain) to implement or existentially realize such thoughts.

So, what reasons are there for believing that mental states are physical states? Two lines of reasoning stand out.

The beginning of the first line of reasoning of has been hinted at just above. Remember that a dualist claims that the content of thinking itself makes it hard to imagine how to classify a physical thing (like the brain) as thinking. The notion of the content of thought is essentially the notion of something that is personally perspectival or subjective. Only I can know of what I am thinking. Only you can know of what you are thinking. Whereas the notion of physicality is essentially, it would seem, of something in the objective or public world (of tables, rocks, ion channels and snowflakes). But I claimed that the notion of a non-physical thing that thinks is equally mysterious to that of a material thing that thinks. Actually, as suggested, it's more mysterious. If a dualist can tell us nothing more about how a non-physical thing is supposed to harbor or house a thought (other than that it is a non-physical thing), dualism gains no advantage over anti-dualistic physicalism, and dualism also possesses the disadvantage of our being unable to form a mental image or picture of where a thought is supposed to occur. If thoughts and feelings could be features of physical organisms, we would at least know, in some broad sense, where to locate them. Wherever the organism is, their thoughts and feelings are. But if thoughts and feelings are supposed to occur in a non-physical thing, where are we supposed to locate them, even in the broadest outline (see van Inwagen 2009: 223–26)? Isn't it quite unhelpful to locate then in something non-physical? Simply put, if something isn't physical, it has no location.

These rhetorical queries do not necessarily favor physicalism, but taken along with the following picture of the natural world, some sort of physicalism may well be favored over dualism. The picture is what may be called a *Hierarchical Conception* of the natural world. It is based on the inspiration that there are levels of reality, and that higher or more abstract levels are existentially based in or on, but not descriptively or linguistically reducible to, lower levels.

Imagine the following picture of the relation between a clay statue and the particles that make it up. The particles stand in a special relation to the statue. The relation may be called an *existential base* relation. And this relation is, as a logician would say, an asymmetric relation. Meaning: Just because the particles have it to the statue, does not mean that the statue has it to the particles. The particles are the existential base of the statue. The statue cannot exist without the particles or without some quantity of particles serving as its base. But the particles existentially base the statue without the statue existentially basing the particles.

You might re-describe this basal relation by thinking of the statue as a more 'abstract' object than a particle, and as existing at a higher level of reality. Here are four descriptions of a statue: *statue*, *clay statue*, *clay statue in a museum*, and *clay statue in the Brooklyn Museum of Art* (the 'BMA'). A statue (a generic statue) must be existentially based in some quantity of particles, but a clay statue must be based in a quantity of particles that bases clay (and not that bases bronze), and a clay statue in the BMA must be based on a quantity of particles that both bases clay and is located in Brooklyn.

Shift now from thinking of statues and particles to persons and particles. It may be argued as follows: The world in which we live in is a hierarchically layered or multi-leveled world. It has lower and less abstract levels and higher or more abstract levels of entities, processes, and phenomena. The levels are associated with and described by different sciences, languages or descriptive disciplines. Physics describes the most basic or general level (of particles or sub-atomic particles), chemistry a level above that, and biology, psychology, and sociology each describe successively higher and more abstract and specialized levels.

Physics describes the most basic or lowest level of phenomena, because it describes both the broadest or most general range of entities, from the smallest (such as particles), to the largest (such as galaxies), as well as the most universal processes or forces in the natural world (such as gravitational forces). Not just those of clay or in Brooklyn, but those all over the known universe or natural world. These lowest level objects or forces are the physically existential or realization bases in the natural world of any and all higher level entities. Or equivalently: The physical level provides particular material substrata for any and all higher level entities. Some such higher level entities include organs and organisms; others include statues, aluminum cans, persons, museums, street corner societies, economic systems, and cultures.

We persons are special or distinct in our detailed multi-level complexity or layered character. But otherwise we are physically based, like statues, in particles. We, too, like statues, require a physical existential basis. So to be us (the hierarchical conception continues) ultimately is to be physically based or realized. This does not mean, however, that each and every activity, state, aspect or component of us can be exhaustively or completely described in lower level physical scientific terms – such as in terms of physics or neuroscience, for example. We are, after all, higher level entities. And if this (a complete description in lower level terms) cannot be done for statues (assuming that it cannot), it certainly cannot be done for us. Although our nature or identity *ultimately* is physical or physically based or realized, when we ask why we think, feel, and act as we do, descriptions of ourselves available in the lower level natural sciences (of physics, chemistry, and biology) are incomplete or inadequate. In discussing why we think as we do, believe as we do, and so on, we need to appeal to upper level psychological or mentalistic descriptions of ourselves and our behavior. Psychological language is language that cannot be reduced or translated into physical terms. It is a type of thought or talk that refers to mental states as mental states (as possessed of Intentionality and/or as conscious).

Robert McCauley neatly summarizes the oftentimes need for a hierarchically upper level of theory (such as that available in psychology) of human behavior to offset the incompleteness of a lower level of talk or analysis (such as that available in the neurosciences):

> [T]he upper-level of theory lays out regularities about a subset of the phenomena that the lower-level theory encompasses but for which it has neither the resources nor the motivation to highlight. That is the price of the lower-level theory's generality and ... grain.
>
> (McCauley 1996: 31)

If, for example, we want to know why a man is running to a drug store, we don't explain his behavior by referring to the motions of his particles. We refer to why this person desires medicine for his child and believes that he needs to run to a drug store to get it. His particles, as it were, come along for the ride, although without them the man would never make it to the store or place his feet on the street. They base him physically in the natural world.

This hierarchical picture of us as metaphysical citizens in a multi-leveled world sometimes is described as a non-reductionistic version of a Naturalistic World View or Naturalistic Metaphysic. (Naturalism comes in reductionistic varieties as well, in which a person is treated not just as physically based, but as itself a physical system that is, ideally, completely and utterly physically describable.) The wisdom or plausibility of the picture requires a method of ordering levels and talking of the relationships between them (see Craver 2007: 163–95). But if warranted, it helps to make it plausible to believe in a broad, basal or generic physicalism about mind/body. A physicalism that claims that mentality possesses a physical base. No mental states without basal physical states (such as brain states). (Not a specific and more explanatorily ambitious form of physicalism that demands physical descriptions of our psychological states or properties at the level of cells, particles, or neurobiological/neurochemical activities.)

What follows from this particular brand of physicalism – a physicalism that says that each and everything that exists in the natural world has a physical base? Well, it's an "ism" that rules out dualism, or any view that says or implies that persons or minds are not physically based. Physicality of a lower level sort is required of our existence. On this view, however, basal physical necessity does not mean the attainability or presence of descriptions of all levels (minds, persons, or cultures) in physical-thing languages – in the languages of brain science or whatever.

A second line of reasoning for the physicality or (at least) physical basis of mind and mentality derives from a related serious difficulty for dualism to the difficulty of locating thought. It is a problem about causality. It is known as the *problem of mental causation*. It may be described like this.

Imagine that one morning you are faced with the choice of either staying in or getting up out of bed, and then washing, dressing, eating breakfast and going to work. Suppose you decide to get out of bed, make the effort to get out, and lo and behold, succeed. You then dress and head off to work. It takes, we may suppose, considerable effort on your part to rise up out of bed and to prepare for the workday. You have to combat a strong impulse to remain in bed – an impulse grounded perhaps in a fatigued or unenthused mood.

The decision and movement (of getting out of bed) must be causally linked together in an appropriate manner for the decision and its content to produce the effect viz. getting out of bed. Note, however, that if minds are non-physical (if dualism is true) then the mental or decisional causation of something physical (e.g. like the movement of a body out of bed) fails to appear up to the motor task. Non-physical minds and the decisions that they make seem too weight-less, ethereal or 'soulful' ever to move limbs or to be linked together with getting out of bed. Your mood explains why it is difficult to get out of bed, but dualism appears to transform a difficult effort into an explanatory miracle. How can something non-physical, like a decision, move, actually move, something physical?

Princess Elizabeth of Bohemia (1618–80) worried that dualism could not account for the actions of mind on body or in the physical world. She wrote to Descartes about it. "How [can] a man's soul," she asked, "being only a thinking substance ... determine animal spirits so as to cause voluntary action" (see Kim 2003: 66). The philosopher Jaegwon Kim has recently offered a 'bohemian' variation, one of numerous in the literature, on Elizabeth's critical query.

Kim writes: "The radical non-spatiality of mental substances rules out the possibility of invoking any spatial relationship for cause-effect pairing" (Kim 2003: 71). Kim adds: "Temporal order alone will not be sufficient to provide us with such a basis." In order for causes and effects to be paired or linked, Kim claims, "we need a full space-time framework" (2003: 74). The trouble, says Kim, with mere temporal order (say, the fact that an alleged mental cause occurs just before its effect but not in physical space) serving to pair cause with effect is that temporal order alone cannot pair or link a cause with *its* effect. Causal relations must be more "selective and discriminating, in the sense that there can be two [events] with identical [temporal] properties" and only one, but not the other, causally produces the effect (2003: 73). Which event is the producer? This is the one, says Kim, with the right linkage in space to the effect viz. an event with the right spatial properties. So, it is spatial relations, such features as dis-tance, orientation, etc., and not just temporal relations (such as occurring before or after), that are required to pair or link causes with their particular effects.

Descartes himself puzzled over how non-physical minds could possibly interact causally with physical objects in space. "At one point," notes William Lycan, "he suggested gravity as a model for the action of something immaterial on a physical body; but gravity is spatial even though it is not tangible in the way that bodies are" (Lycan 2003: 48).

What goes for causes goes also for people in beds. No non-physical thought can move a body out of bed. Only something spatial or something perhaps with a physical base can. Or so the anti-dualist mental causation line of criticism goes.

Let's return to the example of the bed. Suppose you are trying to decide whether to get out of bed and there is a 'moving particle' (a neural or neuromuscular process) in you that is active just before you start to rise and (at the exact same moment) a decision of the form 'I shall now get out of bed'. Suppose that this decision takes place 'in' a non-physical substance or thing. We, if Kim is right, cannot use the mere temporal proximities of these two events (the neural process and the decision) to the movement of getting out of bed to identify which one of them, and not the other, is responsible for rising. Each bears the same temporal relation or proximity to the rising. We need, Kim would urge, a space-time framework to individuate or specify the actual cause. We need to refer to the spatial connectivity of the neural process with the activity of rising. Only by referring to neural events or processes are we able pair the rising from the bed with its cause. A non-physical decision lacks the proper pair-wise connection or clout.

As it happens, the physicalist identity thesis offers one manner in which to explain how decisions may cause movements of the body. Prima facie, at least, if a decision and its content are one and the same as a brain process, than it is a real physical process (in the brain and neuromuscular system) and may therein be responsible for getting out of bed. But there may be other more broadly physical manners in which to explain how a mental event can produce effects in the physical world. A physical existential base (say, in the brain) for a decision may also solve the pairing problem. Perhaps reference to the neural base of the causally responsible decision may help to explain how *this* decision caused *that* getting up, insofar as the base is describable as being in a full space-time framework. It pairs the decision-as-cause with a getting out of bed-as-effect. It distinguishes, say, this particular decision as the cause rather than some other event. And it does so without requiring, as the identity thesis does, at least in some of its forms, the content of the decision to be described in physical terms.

The details of just how mental events (like decisions) can cause physical changes or activities and in a manner that is compatible with some form of physicalism present all manner of technical difficulties in the metaphysics of mind. A flood of philosophical projects over the last thirty or forty years have attempted to describe how mental causation can fit into the physical world. I have no intention here of allowing us to be swept up into its metaphysical waters. I want to quickly extract two morals or lessons about the metaphysics of the mind/body problem from the problem of mental causation and from our discussion of dualism and physicalism.

One lesson of taking the problem of mental causation (or, for that matter, the symmetric problem of physical causation of the mental or the problem of locating thought) seriously and of worrying about what it means for the topic of mental illness is that dualism should not be regarded as the option of *sole metaphysical* choice for appreciating the foundational nature or categorical distinctiveness of a mental disorder. If the problem of mental causation is to be solved, we need also to possess a non-dualistic and at least broadly physicalistic metaphysical alternative for understanding disorder.

The second lesson is about how we ourselves should now proceed. We have reason, I believe, for believing that there is a class of disturbances or disorders (viz. mental disorders) to which explanations in psychological or mentalistic terms contribute alongside explanations in brute a-rational causal terms. A metaphysician may wish for a "well-founded understanding of [just] how these explanations, and their subject matters, relate to one another" (Burge 1993: 117). Relate to one another metaphysically, that is. But we should agree with the philosopher Tyler Burge, just quoted, when he adds that it serves no useful explanatory purpose to "over-dramatize the conflict between different ontological [/metaphysical] approaches" to the mind/body problem (ibid.) "What matters is that our mentalistic explanations do not [necessarily] conflict with our physicalistic explanations" (117). Each may somehow complement the other (of which more discussion later in the book).

So, I urge that we not endorse a particular metaphysics of mind/body in this book or, for that matter, in our concept or theory of mental disorder. I suggest that we help ourselves to a metaphysically agnostic or ecumenical strategy in understanding the metaphysics of mind/body. This is a strategy, which, as I suggested just above, should be compatible with physicalism (in some form) and perhaps also with dualism (assuming that somehow a dualist can dissolve the problem of mental causation and other problems). Here is a brief sketch of how such ecumenism might work.

First a short background anecdote, which is adapted from an example of Dretske (Dretske 1988). Suppose a talented soprano in an opera by Puccini sings an aria, and this is followed by a glass on stage shattering. What her song is about or its Intentional content viz. unrequited love plays no role in causing the glass to break. If the aria had not been about love but about something else (say, waffles or sea salt), or if it consisted of nothing but nonsense syllables, as long as she hit the high notes, the glass would have shattered. An idea owed to the philosopher James Woodward helps us to understand the causal relation between singing and shattering at work here (Woodward 2003).

Hitting the high notes (HH) caused the glass to shatter (GS). On Woodward's account, a causal relation is a relation between two variables (such as HH and GS) that can take on different values (such as, either hitting or not hitting the high notes), and HH causes GS just in case the value of GS would change under some intervention or manipulation on HH. For example, if a crazed opera fan was to have jumped onto the stage and vigorously hugged the singer, thus preventing her from hitting the high notes, no shattering would have been produced by her voice. Or, if the singer had only hit notes lower in pitch, a vibration or two might have been produced in the glass, but it would not have broken.

Now compare. Here is a case of mental causation. Suppose in singing about unrequited love, the soprano's singing, in addition to shattering the glass by virtue of its high notes, is accompanied by people in the audience sobbing and breaking into tears. Is the Intentional content of the song (what it is about, unrequited love, UL) causally efficacious in producing the sobbing and tearing (ST)? Again, on Woodward's account, UL is the cause of ST if and only if the value of ST would change under some intervention on UL. If the audience would not have sobbed and become teary had the soprano sung about waffles or sea salt, but only given its expression of unrequited love, this gives us reason to believe that the fact that her aria was about unrequited love caused the audience to sob. Content is not efficacious in causing the glass to shatter, because the aria could have been about waffles or sea salt and the glass would still have shattered had the singer hit the high notes. But in singing about unrequited love the audience sobbed.

This may seem like a neat and nifty approach to uncovering causation in general and mental causation in particular, and it truly is, I believe. Simply intervene in a process and see what happens. In, say, a case like that of a major panic attack, one of which will be discussed in the next chapter, accounting for the onset of an episode of a major panic attack by explanatory reference to a person's fear of crowds suggests that had the fear been interfered with, then panic may not have occurred. Given the fear of crowds, therein panic. But we are not always in a position to intervene, so we may have to manipulate variables hypothetically in the imagination. Associations between events are not always invariant or necessitating (oftentimes they are probabilistic or propensity-like), and background conditions though causally relevant are sometimes difficult to specify with precision. The beauty of Puccini's music and the text of the opera may also have contributed to the audience's tearful reaction. And so, while it is helpful to conceive of interventions or manipulations as well designed experimental interventions (hypothetical or otherwise), we must not picture them as exclusively the products of human agency. If a brick falls on the glass on stage, this, too, counts as an intervention in the glass's integrity.

All that granted, what is the anecdote's lesson for how to avoid taking sides in the physicalism/dualism metaphysical debate if we are to understand a mental disorder? A particular kind of causal efficacy is definitive of mental causation. This is Intentional content efficacy i.e. the power or potency of states or attitudes with Intentionality to bring about changes in a person's activity and states of mind. Provided it is possible for the existential basis of mentality (if some version of physicalism is true) or for a person's non-physical mental states (if dualism is true) to possess Intentional content, and also possible for the content of such states (what they are about) to play a causal role in the sources of a disorder, no choice between the two metaphysical positions (either physicalism or dualism) with respect to understanding the causal foundations of a disorder has to be made in order to satisfy the demands of a theory of mental disorder. We may be physicalists of some sort and still admit to a role for mental causation in mental disorder. Or we may be dualists and, by way of the dualistic bifurcation, distinguish between somatic and mental disorders. A metaphysical choice between dualism and physicalism may perhaps need be made on other grounds (parsimony, compatibility with science, or whatever), but we ourselves can attempt to explanatorily understand the nature and foundations of a mental disorder without making such a metaphysical commitment. All we need, metaphysically or mind/body-wise speaking, is commitment to the power or efficacy of states or attitudes with Intentional content and to the real existence of such states or attitudes as well to their specific explanatory roles in a mental disorder.

Or more exactly, all we need is such a commitment together with commitment to whatever more or else is required in association with the causal efficacy of attitudes, if we are to understand the origins of a mental disorder. This is an important 'whatever more' proviso. One other commitment also is needed, I believe, as I describe in the next chapter. This is the recognition that, in the words of John Searle, "Intentional phenomena are subject to constraints of rationality" (Searle 2001: 108). It is constitutive or partially definitive of Intentional content and of the causal efficacy of Intentional content (the contents of beliefs, fears, desires, and so on) that contents are subject to rationality norms or to standards of reason and reason-responsiveness. So, for example, it is part of the explanation for why the audience sobbed and became teary on listening to the aria about unrequited love that this was a sensible reaction for them to have, given the background text or story of the opera. If they had had an irrational obsession to remain stoical or if the content of the aria had been about waffles, the aria would not have been effective in eliciting tears or sobbing. If things had been so different, then there would have been no tears and nary a sob. It would have been unreasonable to weep in such circumstances.

So, here is what I shall assume about the metaphysics of the mind/body problem in what follows in this book. I shall assume what I call the perspective or way of *metaphysical ecumenism* (or as called in the first edition of this book, the way of metaphysical cohabitation). The physicalist says: mind ultimately is based in matter. The dualist says: mind is not based in matter, although it matters in the physical world. I shall refuse to choose. A presumption of dualism may perhaps cohere with an understanding of mental disorder. A commitment to physicalism (of at least some sort) may fit with an understanding of mental disorder. Or so I shall assume. Dualism may be more vulnerable to metaphysical worry or empirical irrelevance than some sort of physicalism (which is my view viz. dualism is less attractive than physicalism). But the ecumenical assumption or hope is that our ability to explain and to understand a mental disorder has nothing directly or immediately to do with the truth or falsity of dualism and it is not threatened by the truth of physicalism, provided that physical stuff (complexes of particles, as it were) can be bases of causally effective Intentional content. This last proviso, by the way, is consistent with what Dretske himself says (Dretske 1988). Mentality is causally effective in the physical world insofar as Intentional content is effective and also if Intentional content is supportable by physical states or processes.

Now let's turn to the second criticism of the idea of mental disorder. It's a criticism with a moral purpose, albeit with hefty metaphysical underpinnings (not to be discussed in detail here).

MENTAL DISORDER AND RESPECT FOR PERSONS

In this section of the chapter I plan to combine a number of different critical claims that have been leveled against the category of mental disorder, all of which share the following assumption. Characterizing a person as the subject of a mental disorder is a form of disrespect or an indignity to them as a person. I call this the *respect-for-persons* argument for anti-realism about mental disorder. It needs some stage setting. I am going to begin with something hypothetical and imaginary.

Suppose we discover that a number of college and university students are dramatically and unhappily concerned with grades. Suppose this concern leads to imprudent and reckless behavior (e.g. pulling 'all-nighters' which cause sleep deprived students to do poorly on tests and to risk somatic ill-health) and needlessly redundant activity (e.g. repeating class note reviews on too numerous occasions); that these students are temperamentally predisposed to be more concerned about status orientated intellectual performance than their classmates; and that their states of grade anxiety are accompanied by statistically abnormal activity in the verbally dominant left hemisphere of the brain.

Suppose a psychiatrist, who has helped to make these discoveries, joins the team composing DSM-5 and argues that disturbances and behaviors distinctive of grade hyper-concern deserve their own classificatory status in DSM-5. Systematically preparing notes, updating class files, and reviewing assignments before exams are good work study habits, the psychiatrist argues. However, repeating these activities, when they already have been conscientiously performed, and doing so in redundant and oftentimes ritualistic ways; and, then, failing to gain rest or sleep, so that concern with grades occupies the waking day and causes sleepless nights, is, the psychiatrist claims, a special sort of disorder. The psychiatrist has a name for it – Grade Obsessive Disorder, GOD, for short. In a respected professional publication the case for GOD as a special disorder is summarized as follows:

> Grade Obsessive Disorder meets all the reasonable criteria for being a mental disorder. It consists of a syndrome of behaviors. There is evidence that it reflects the bothersome activation of the central nervous system. It is associated with sleep disturbance and with various cognitive dysfunctions – in particular, the inability to do well in academic

performance despite being intelligent and well prepared. It should be regarded as a special and distinctive type of disorder.

What sort of argument would be mounted *against* classifying GOD as a disorder? One general answer is what I am calling the Respect for Persons Criticism. It goes like this (and will take the next three paragraphs to describe).

What does it mean to respect persons? To respect persons is, in part, to treat them as responsible for their own conduct and behavior. When we scold a dog for chewing on a rug, for instance, we are trying to train him. We do not hold the dog responsible for his conduct. We try to correct him. (We may hold the dog's owner accountable for correcting or failing to correct the dog. But we don't charge the dog with correcting itself.) People, however, unlike dogs, should be treated as capable of being reasoned with about their conduct, and as deciding to behave as they do, selecting their goals, and directing their own behavior. We should respect their rationality and reason-responsiveness and treat them as responsible agents. If a person were, say, to obsessively chew on a rug, we should not aim to train them. We should help them to modify their own behavior and to become better at reasoning about how to behave.

Some people have unusual preferences, unshared by others, or imprudent desires, harmful to themselves (wishing to chew on rugs, for example). But an unusual or imprudent desire just is another desire or preference. There is no good reason for believing that it needs to be 'cured' by classifying a person as mentally ill. Some people like to gamble, whereas others have a taste for saving money. Some people become listless and despondent in response to life's misfortunes, whereas others respond to setbacks as challenges that they are eager to overcome. Some folks chew on candy, others chew on rugs. To refer to people as mentally ill, as the philosopher Eric Matthews puts it in a recent paraphrase of a notorious advocate of respect for persons criticism, viz. the psychiatrist Thomas Szasz, "is to deny the human dignity of the 'mentally ill' by denying them their ... power to choose how they will behave" (Matthews 2007: 311–12). Some people like to risk their lives in extreme sports, whereas others like to sit on a couch with an electronic remote control for their television and watch soap operas. If some people have the bad luck to be born with temperaments that lead them to 'stress out' with poor academic performances, we should expect them to recognize that this reaction is not conducive to their own welfare. We should expect them to take whatever steps are necessary to combat this source of distress or unhappiness. If they fail in that expectation, the responsibility to change ultimately is their own. Their mental welfare is their business, not that of the medical profession.

To continue with the criticism: Focusing on the anxious or obsessive behavior of students and classifying it as a disorder, dehumanizes a young person and pictures them as non-autonomous, non-responsible objects of medical manipulation in need of therapeutic assistance. To categorize someone as a victim, in particular, of GOD is to discourage them from taking responsibility for their emotional and behavioral academic problems. Each and every student needs to learn to manage their own desires and to cope when academic achievement falls below a desired baseline. Worrisome socially, a classification such as GOD may also serve as a legal basis for exclusion of certain people from normal or desirable patterns of student social life – an exclusion that is a violation of their civil liberties. Individuals diagnosed as victims of GOD may be stigmatized or discriminated against when seeking to join a fraternity, sorority or social club. Labeling them as disordered also allows psychiatrists and other mental health professionals to assume a position of unwarranted judgmental authority over otherwise socially intimidated and medically poorly informed non-psychiatric educational professionals of a college or university. A medically uneducated dean of students, for example, having read of the alleged disorder in *Time* or *Psychology Today*, may require either that (a) students diagnosed with GOD take plenty of extra-time with exams, which would be unfair to un-GOD-like students, or (b) refrain from enrolling in certain courses (which would be unfair to the anxious students themselves) on grounds that it would acerbate GOD's symptoms. Meanwhile, parents conscientiously shepherding their children's applications to colleges and universities may turn to psychiatrists for advice on whether their son or daughter is a potential victim of GOD, thus enhancing the power and expanding the scope of mental health professionals into what otherwise should be the private lives of individuals. "The judges of normality are present everywhere," wrote the French philosopher-historian, Michel Foucault (1926–84). "We are in a society of the teacher-judge, the doctor-judge, the educator-judge, the social-worker judge" (Foucault 1977: 304). Do we also want physicians to be the student-judge? Indeed, we do not.

The above critical claims are offered here, for illustrative purposes, against counting GOD as a mental disorder. GOD as a classification is a construction of my imagination, of course. But I mention a full set of critical claims and wage it against GOD, because it includes the moral charges that various critics level against the very idea of a mental disorder, no matter the alleged type of condition. Addiction. Depression. Obsession. Even schizophrenia. It is said: People's minds or reasoning capacities are not to be treated, clinically re-trained or "fixed". People ought to be regarded as responsible individuals who, in the final analysis, have control over their own behavior and can be reasoned with. Granted, some people may need or welcome help from others to cope with emotional and behavioral problems. But non-medical assistance is one thing (especially when requested); medical labeling and involuntary treatment or intervention is another. In brief: labeling and involuntary treatment is morally inconsistent with human dignity, with respect for persons.

Each claim within the set above represents its own cluster of potentially distinct issues. Also, although the set is not intended as an explicitly metaphysical criticism, it does, of course, harbor contentious metaphysical assumptions about human agency and the powers of reason and self-control especially for people who are distressed and disturbed.

Disorder and respect

When the various claims in the respect for persons argument are put together and used as an objection to the very idea of a mental disorder (and not just to the proposition that GOD, alcoholism, etc. is a disorder), what should happen? Is the category of mental disorder somehow in and of itself disrespectful? Undignifying? Surely, classifying someone as a victim of cancer, diabetes or scurvy does not disrespect them as persons. So, then, why believe that there is something inherently disrespectful or morally unacceptable about describing a person as a subject of a mental disorder?

For disorder skeptics or anti-realists of the respect-for-persons type, the difference in moral attitudes towards persons which is reflected in the ascription of a somatic as opposed to a mental disorder is that, in the second case, it's the mental powers and faculties of a person that are the object of categorization, whereas in the first it's 'merely' the body. That difference, say skeptics, makes a big moral difference. How so? Well, consider, for the most famous description of the nature and importance of this difference, Thomas Szasz's attack on the idea of mental illness (Szasz 1960, 1972, 1974, 1982 and 2001).

Szasz charges that ascribing a mental disorder to a person, unlike the ascription of a somatic or physical illness, reflects essentially contestable value judgments that often are moral and socio-political in character, rather than (what he assumes to be) the well-defined and more or less value free somatic or biological illness categories. Being depressed, anxious, and so on, are problematic disturbances, certainly, but they are not illnesses, not disorder classes. Or so Szasz claims. To call them illnesses or disorders, says Szasz, confuses what is sickness with what is difficulty, medicine with morals, mechanistic conditions that need to be fixed or repaired with reason-responsive attitudes that may need to be deliberated about, re-examined and altered. When persons are treated as patients with a mental illness, Szasz claims, the door is wide open to disrespect and indignity: for giving people less credit (or discredit) for their behavior than they deserve: for manipulating them: for failing to respect their powers of reason and personal preference. In the case of a somatic ailment, by contrast, that particular door to disrespect is closed. The very idea of a physical illness is value free. Or at least it is free of reference to or assumptions about essentially contestable values. Saying that a person has cancer poses no affront to them as a person. But saying that a person is addicted to alcohol or beleaguered by GOD does.

Is Szasz correct? Whether he is correct that the very idea of a mental illness presupposes essentially contestable values is not the issue I plan to address here in this particular chapter. (The value presuppositions or norms for mental disorder are examined later in the book, primarily in the next two chapters.) But is Szasz correct about the notion of *bodily* or somatic illness? Is the very idea of a somatic illness truly value free? Or at least contestability free? If it is not, then it is irrelevant whether the concept of mental illness presupposes contestable or unsettled values. Evaluative asymmetry between somatic and mental disorder vanishes. Moreover: if the very idea of a somatic illness, although not value free, is sound and sensible, then so, too, may be the very idea of a mental disorder. It's not as if the latter presupposes value or valuation, whereas the former does not.

Attempts have been made to define bodily disease or somatic illness in value-free terms and therein in terms that do not reflect contestable values. One widely discussed means of doing so is owed to the philosopher Christopher Boorse (see Boorse 1975, 1976 and 1977). Although Boorse would not describe his particular means precisely as I do below, on reconstruction it goes something like this.

Bodily illnesses or diseases are illnesses or diseases that are normatively assessable or evaluable. They are bad or wrongful conditions of the body. What norms or standards are bodily illnesses subject to? There are two theoretical possibilities. One consists of referring to medical or scientific norms and the other consists of referring to norms of personal and social desirability or preference – to (what may be called) human values. Medical or scientific norms are not as such (on Boorse's picture) best understood as human values, personal or otherwise. They are impersonal. They are standards of nature or natural design, not reflective of human judgment or preference. Impersonal medical or scientific norms determine whether something in or about the body is sick, ill or diseased. Human values have or should have nothing to do with such determinations.

Suppose, for example, someone is coughing or shivering uncontrollably. Are they sick, ill or diseased? This is not for persons to decide. Persons decide only whether if the person is sick, ill or diseased, they should be treated or assisted medically. But whether their cough or shiver is a sign of illness is up to Mother Mature. Nature says, by proxy, what is broken; humankind decides whether it merits repair.

Let us now consider the proposed impersonal medical or scientific norms for a disease or illness in the body. Nature's norms. Boorse and others who press for the value neutrality of biological illness or disease argue that our bodies consist of biologically evolved and adaptationally functioning components and that breakdowns in these components are the constituents of somatic disease or bodily illness. This means that medical norms of illness or disease must be interpreted very narrowly. Only failures of evolved or adaptational (and selected for) function qualify as diseased organs or organ systems. It is not just that the body has evolved, but that reference to adaptation or maladaptation *alone* explains when the body has gone wrong, scientifically or medically. Our preferences or values as persons have nothing whatsoever to do with this activity of assessment.

How are we to know when or how an organ or organ system is an adaptation or functioning so as to improve genetic fitness? These details depend, Boorse and others claim, on the connection between biological data and the interpretation and analysis of that data by evolutionary biologists. The assumption is that the body is an assemblage of special purpose mechanisms (kidney, liver, lungs, and so on), rather than a general purpose machine, and that it is organized around the different adaptational purposes or functions that these mechanisms are impersonally designed to serve. Perhaps we can often rely on common sense to simply assume how these mechanisms are supposed to work, but in difficult medical cases identifying how systems (organs and so on) are supposed to work is a more serious and oftentimes challenging empirical and investigatory issue. If we could know the evolutionary problems that our ancestors faced, and if we assume special purpose designs for the body's organs and organ systems (sometimes called an assumption about Modular Design or biologically modular organization), then we can know when or if specific organ systems fail or are ill. An eye that fails to see is a bad eye. An ear that fails to hear is a bad ear. Whether we like it or not.

Suppose that this Boorse-like line about the impersonality of illness is correct, does it mean that the very idea of somatic illness or disease is value free or neutral? Yes, if medical norms are totally free of personal or social values or standards of desirability. As far as I can tell, however, there is no good reason to suppose that the medical norms for illness or disorder are free of values of those sorts. In asserting this, I do not deny, of course, that properly described bodily illnesses are sometimes classified on grounds of being biologically maladaptive. Perhaps the intuitions that we sometimes have about somatic illnesses are that they violate standards for their evolutionary design and our own genetic fitness. But the fact that design violations or assumptions about them, on occasion, may be part of the diagnoses that we sometimes associate with somatic illnesses does not entail that adaptational malfunction is the defining or essential property of a somatic illness.

There is a way that bodies or the parts of bodies of persons and animals are supposed to be in order to be genetically fit, but the concept of a somatic illness or disease has nothing directly or invariably to do with the failure of a body or part of a body to contribute to genetic fitness. In order to determine whether the function of an organ or system is biologically adaptational, we must know not only its current powers, properties and behavioral dispositions, but also its evolutionary history. Typically, however, we have no access to that history. We can often only guess at (what may be called) Mother Nature's intentions by proxy. On the above Boorse-like argument, value freeness in the attribution of somatic disease or illness requires not only that our body and its parts possess biologically adaptational functions or utilities, but that normally we can identify and recognize them in order to insure a proper medical diagnosis. Alas, often we cannot specify them or at least we cannot identify them without contention and disagreement among evolutionary biologists. And for this and other reasons, violations of evolutionary design are not what a medical diagnostician or physician thinks of, needs to think of or even can think of each and every time he or she applies the concept of a somatic illness, disorder or disease to a patient or person. What he or she thinks of (and often only can or should think of) in many cases is, "Is this person's condition painful, does it cause suffering, or is it going to cause them to die if untreated?" "Is it undesirable in a medically relevant sort of way?" "Is it producing behavior that reflects an involuntary deficit in the desired activity of the body or part of the body of the person?" Not undesirable by or only by evolutionary standards, though the two domains of norms, the one relative to Mother Nature, the other relative to a mother or person herself, may overlap or intersect on occasion. (Premature death, for example, may be bad both for young individual mothers and for the whole species as well.) But 'undesirable' relative to other personal or medical values or norms. In the case of our kidneys, for example, the primary reason we worry and should worry about their health is not for fear of decrements in genetic fitness, but because without (as they do) filtering the blood of metabolic wastes for excretion, we individuals (patients in the office, as it were) die.

Examples of our evolutionary ignorance abound in clinical practice. How immobile does a person have to be before his motor impairment is a violation of evolutionary standards? Or: How filled with un-discharged feces does a person need to be before there is a malfunction in Mother Nature's design of the human gastro-intestinal tract? It's enough for a physician, and often in the clinical coal face has to be enough, just to think in terms of current malfunctions and personal dangers. The relevance of evolutionary theory to the attribution of bodily illness or disease is clinically only loosely and occasionally germane. The relevance and utility of human values and preferences, however, is inescapable for a concept of illness or disease.

R. E. Kendall is the former President of the Royal College of Psychiatrists in the U.K. and is the author of a number of influential pieces on whether mental illness is a genuine illness (Kendall 1975, 1985 and 2001). Kendall, although critical of Szasz's dismissal of the category of mental illness, accepts (or appears to accept) the assumption shared with Szasz that if a condition is to qualify as a genuine illness, then it must be described in value-free scientific or bio-medical terms. Contrary, however, to Szasz and Kendall, the very idea of bodily illness or disease cannot achieve a normatively disinterested or impersonal value neutral standard.

The attribution of bodily illness and disease presupposes norms and values, personally and socially salient (and not just evolutionary) standards of efficient and desirable functioning of the body's organs and of its other systems (cellular and so on). This is not just because the purpose of medicine is premised on the disvalue of pain and reduced life expectancy (as Szasz himself admits). But it is due to the fact that the notions of bodily health and physical well-being are evaluative or normative through and through. The back jacket to a recent book on human vulnerability to illness warns, "The next time you get sick, consider this before you pick up aspirin: your body may be doing exactly what it's supposed to do" (Nesse and Williams, 1996). But who is to say what the body is supposed to do? Supposed to do by what standards, which norms? For whom exactly? For you, our species, your genes? Drug manufacturers who believe you should never get headaches or run fevers but should take their medication?

Suppose you are an obstetrician-gynecologist. Suppose one of your pregnant patients complains of severe morning sickness. Is this a hormonal dysfunction? A mark of poor somatic health? It's called a sickness isn't it? If pregnancy itself was a disease, we might think of morning sickness as a symptom and be committed to its diminution. However, of course, we don't think of pregnancy as a disease. But why is that? Appreciation for its utility during, say, the Stone Age, as an instrument of needed population growth, is irrelevant today. Humankind may well profit from a dramatic decline in growth of population. More of the world's limited resources would be available to distribute to the poor and needy. And, goodness knows, a woman with the condition may appreciate ameliorating the condition. So, what about a drug for *eliminating* morning sickness? Is that a good thing? A bad thing? Such a drug, if pregnancy is a good thing and not an illness, might actually be bad, depending upon how it is used. Nausea and associated food aversions during pregnancy may help a woman to avoid spicy plant toxins or foods produced by bacterial and fungal decomposition, thus contributing to lowering her miscarriage rate and mothering a healthier, heavier neonate.

My neighbor is allergic to cats. Is this a dysfunction? Something bad? Could it be an allergy that protects them from a dangerous toxin? Should they take drugs to suppress the allergic reaction and restore them to 'proper bodily well-being'? But suppose it is shown that eighteen out of twenty people with untreated cat allergies are less likely to develop blindness than those who take medication for them. How is this to be understood? Are those with the allergies in a healthy somatic condition? Or suppose that some adolescents possess abnormally heightened vulnerability to physical injury when playing high school or intramural sports, and that this decreases their reproductive fitness. Suppose, also, however, on a personal plus side, the vulnerability condition makes for greater academic success, superior performance on I.Q. tests, temperance in the consumption of alcohol, and dramatically reduced visual impairment rates. Who's to say whether these pre-adults are physically ill rather than that their body is behaving precisely as it should?

Much of what passes for the value-freeness and incontestability of the category of physical illness or somatic disease rests upon two facts about values or norms presupposed by physical illness diagnosis. One is that the values often are not obvious, but hidden behind social practices and conventions. The other is that even when obvious, such values typically are not questioned or debated because they are widely shared. Physical illness classification often rests on near universal human aversions to injury, pain, and death. Even so, considerable elbow room for contestation and critical scrutiny may be present in somatic illness attribution, even if few people have the stomach for it. Especially if or when social and environmental conditions change or the cost of health care rises sharply, then contestation about norms of bodily health previously unquestioned may abruptly bubble up to the social and discordant surface.

Lawrie Reznek writes as follows: "Diseases are so classified because they ... make us worse off" (Reznek 1987: 159). But if the world were suddenly to change so that it is "filled with useless noise", something that once was a disease, such as osteosclerosis leading to deafness, might not be classified as a disease. This is because "it would not make us worse off" (Reznek 1987: 160).

Let me try to clarify and defend the proposition that the very idea of physical illness is vulnerable to value contestation with a distinction between two types of human goods or values. I have in mind the distinction between instrumental values, that is, things valued as means to other things that are valued, and categorical values, that is, things valued for their own sake.

Some health/illness values are instrumental. Others, at least in a broad or general human context, are categorical. By way of illustration, consider, again, the value of pregnancy. Suppose that medical scientific research establishes that the experience of morning sickness protects fetuses from deadly food toxins. Morning sickness helps to insure that more healthy fetuses survive until birth. Would not medicine, then, have shown objectively or scientifically that morning sickness is a value-free proper or evolutionary adaptational function of, say, the hormonal system of pregnant women and not a genuine sickness or illness? Despite the proposition's Boorsian credentials, not quite. All that would have been shown is that a type of *instrumental* value is possessed by morning sickness; namely, if pregnancy categorically is good and morning sickness is the only, best or most reliable means in which to avoid ingesting certain harmful toxins, then it is better to undergo morning sickness than to eliminate its occurrence by, say, taking symptom dissolving medication. Morning sickness allows more fetuses to crossover healthily through the threshold of neonatal life.

The instrumental value of morning sickness does not settle whether morning sickness is categorically valuable or good. For that proposition to be true, it needs to be decided whether pregnancy itself is good, categorically. And warranting a decision like that requires debating the merits and demerits of pregnancy and the comparative reliability of morning sickness as a gatekeeper against toxicity.

Generally, if a decision is to be reached as to whether this, that, or another condition of the body, its organs or systems, is healthy and well rather than unhealthy and unwell, we have to accept some categorical evaluative or categorically normative standards for what counts as good or bad states of affairs for persons and their bodies (pregnant or not pregnant, with or without cat allergies, with or without deafness or blindness, and so on). In some cases of some illnesses we may decide to take biological adaptational utility as a proper norm. (We might do this, for example, in trying to decide whether this, that, or another case of neural behavior or processing is damaged or diseased.) But the necessity or wisdom of such a decision is not written in factual stone. Categorical standards may be anything but incontestable and immune to critical scrutiny especially when contexts change or environmental situations shift. The question of which conditions of the body to treat categorically (pregnancy good, pregnancy bad) calls for, as Carl Hempel has put it, "standards which are not objectively determined by empirical facts" (Hempel 1965b: 89). Even the most pedestrian sureties about the value of certain somatic conditions may be disrupted if our environment shifts, and with it the value or disvalue of certain bodily states. Reznek offers a clever if chilling example:

> Albinism – the failure to produce the pigment melanin – is a pathological condition because it fails to protect the skin from the sun's rays. But suppose that the amount of light in our world was greatly reduced (in a nuclear freeze), so albinism would be valuable because it would enable the skin to synthesize vitamin D from the small amount of light available.
>
> (Reznek 1987: 86)

The moral of Reznek's little thought experiment? The value-laden character of the very idea of somatic illness often is deep beneath the skin of alternative possibilities, environmental contexts or situations. Evaluative assumptions may rest buried within the taxonomic conventions of the ascription of somatic illness.

It is worth noting that once we accept the proposition that the concept of a somatic disease is normatively evaluative through and through, and that such norms or values may be or become contestable, we may reflectively appraise standards for bodily disease on normative grounds, debate their wisdom and then proceed to conduct medical science accordingly (see Levy 2007: 94–103). (I will make an analogous point for the concept of mental disorder later in the book.) Acting as if standards for physical health are objectively biologically neutral and value free ultimately hurts the cause of physical medicine just as much, if perhaps not more, than it does the case for mental disorder. It is impossible to define standards of physical health and somatic well-being without appealing to potentially contestable norms.

Attributions of somatic illness or disease are thus always hostage, potentially if not actually, to background categorical values or value judgments, and these can prove to be muddled, confused, imprudent, immoral, or just plain wrong. If they are so hobbled, then we may have to rethink whatever categorical values we take for granted or how we should derive them.

Now back to the category of a mental disorder. Part of what worries Szasz and others about the values that underpin the notion of a mental disorder is legitimate anxiety about some of the norms or evaluations that, over history or in different cultures, have supported the attribution of mental disorder. During the Renaissance and through to the conclusion of the eighteenth century, for example, there was a marked tension and disjunction between treating individuals with mental illnesses as suffering from natural ailments or as possessed by malign spiritual forces. Demonology, witch-hunts, and the torture and execution of the mentally troubled were not uncommon. Contestable or worse, utterly despicable cultural, political, and moral values at particular times and in particular places, have characterized our explanatory understanding and treatment of mental illness. (The category of somatic illness has also had its share of witch hunts, of course.) Wise and compassionate apprehension about abhorrent social possibilities repeating themselves helps to motivate some critics to polarize the distinction between mental and non-mental physical illness and to dismiss the first as controversially value-laden and misjudge the second as value or contestability free. But history, in this case, should make only for a cautionary tale. Not a dismissive one.

So, what about *mental disorder*? May this still be a personally disrespectful category even if the category of physical illness possesses its own zones of value contestability? True, the attribution of a mental disorder does not always serve the interests of those who are diagnosed. (Certainly attributing a pseudo-disorder like that of GOD would not!) Attribution of a mental disorder, depending upon how this is understood, conducted or implemented, may inhibit recovery and an effective return of personal well-being. As one 18-year-old with a diagnosis of schizophrenia puts it: "The belief held by hospital staff was that I would be powerless to influence the return of psychotic symptoms that could at any moment strike again" (May 2004: 246). Another person, diagnosed with a mental illness, writes of his being labeled as follows: "[I was] placed in the category of persons whose experience is devalued ... simply because at a certain time or times I lost contact with the ... view of reality agreed upon by my peers" (P. Campbell 1996: 57).

Fortunately, safeguards against the misuse and misapplication of the category of mental disorder have been and are being imposed on psychiatric practice. Fortunately, too, a number of counter-judgmental and anti-discriminatory responsibility themes have been absorbed into current mental health care practice, in movements like those of patient power and of user services and user-led research, in the popularity and selling power of anti-psychiatric medication literature, and in the organization of mental health services along multi-disciplinary and patient-as-person centered lines (see Bracken and Thomas 2005).

Alas, it is true, too, that with the ever-swelling nomenclature of DSM, more and more forms of human behavior are classified as disorders and 'medicalized', and the sad day may come when a bizarre category like that of GOD may push its way into the pages of our diagnostic manuals. Fortunately, however, both the idea and extended range of the concept of mental disorder are under constant critique, vigilance and modification (see Horwitz and Wakefield 2007). Likewise, just as there are situations in which people are disrespected when classified or treated as mentally ill, so there are numerous cases in which people's lives are transformed or reconstructed much for the better by receiving a mental disorder diagnosis, along with the care and medical attention that they need. The mental illness memoirs of Styron (1990) and Jamison (1995) offer vivid personal testimonials of the invaluable help which is often received by mental illness patients.

Anyone who has lived through what Bentall calls, referring to their commonness, not blandness, for certainly they are not bland, "the ordinary tragedies of life" will appreciate that many challenges and disappointments in life provoke profound psychological disturbance and scars – the death of a beloved spouse, a humiliating embarrassment in the eyes of one's colleagues, friends, or family, the inability to care for one's children, and so on (Bentall 2004: 239). Some people adjust to such events. Some persons manage to manage, so to speak. It's tough but they survive more or less intact. However, other persons come apart and become destabilized, if only for a time. Some seek or need assistance. Some need medical assistance. In fact, sometimes, the very same sort of grief, humiliation or sadness that moves, in the words of Karl Jaspers (1883–1969), "one individual to the psychiatrist as a sick person ... will take another to the confessional as one suffering from sin and guilt" (Jaspers 1963: 780).

What should the profession of medicine do? Should the profession insist that no such difficulty deserves to be classified as a disorder and treated in medical terms? When people behave in a manner that surely does seem to require medical help, when they profoundly or profusely complain or are troubled, then the clinical responsibilities of psychiatry appear clear, urgent and demanding. A physician must ascertain the content of a patient's complaint, symptoms or behavioral signs and then try to do something about them – based on the common sense assumption that for most people what is wanted is absence of pain and suffering, some measure of pleasure in existence, a range of opportunities to engage productively with other people, to work, to complete normal human tasks, to live a decent life.

I am a philosopher and not a clinician, although as a young man in my twenties I spent an informative lessons-filled year as an aide in the psychiatric unit of a Harvard teaching hospital in Boston. As I see matters, the clinically compassionate 'coal-face' of mental disorder has always been the problem of relieving suffering and helping to build or restore psychological well-being. So, even though the respect for persons critique of the category of mental disorder has important lessons that need to be assimilated into mental health professional practice, ultimately it presses for an unhelpful and overly dismissive agenda. It is one thing to build respect for persons into psychiatric practice (no small or uncomplicated order). It is another to dismiss the whole enterprise of disorder attribution and treatment as morally misbegotten. The first task, namely incorporating respectful safeguards is necessary. The second, namely dismissal of the very idea of mental disorder on respect for person grounds is overbearing and uncompassionate. Besides which, as we will see in the chapters to follow, there are honest-to-goodness disorders of mind. Persons do, mentally, breakdown or destabilize.

SUMMARY

Some observers are skeptical about whether mental disorders or illnesses truly exist or are genuine and distinct disorders or should be thought of as such. They deny that mental disorders are real. This chapter examined two grounds for skepticism or anti-realism about the existence of mental disorder and about attribution of the concept of a mental disorder. Each form of skepticism offers lessons concerning the proper or properly regimented idea of a mental disorder. Neither warrants dismissal of the category. But the relevant lessons are important.

A plausible and familiar reason for thinking that mental disorders are real or exist is because reference to them helps to explain certain forms of human behavior. Why does so and so spend so much time at the local casino? Because he is addicted to gambling. Why does so and so never get out of bed in the morning? Because she is clinically depressed. That referential explanatory role is as sound a reason as any for thinking that mental disorders exist, but it is not good enough, say metaphysical skeptics, if we get better theories of human behavior from brain science and if mind or mentality is nothing other than something neuro-physical. In this chapter I tried to untangle the physicalistic assumptions of metaphysical skepticism – which, given its fear of mind-body dualism, refuses to acknowledge the distinctive and important role of psychological explanations of behavior including the behavior of those who are mentally ill. The chapter argued that if mental disorders are real – that is, real disorders of people – there must be ways of construing or describing the causes of behavior in mentalistic or psychological terms even if or though mental disorders are physically based. Mental disorder realism certainly does not require dualism (which may be incompatible with mental/psychological causation). However, it does require the possession of Intentional content by those causes. What a person thinks about (or desires or believes) affects what they do about the things that they think about (or desire or believe).

The category of mental disorder is often viewed as normatively and in particular morally prob-lematic in its diagnosis and in a manner that differs from the diagnosis of a bodily or somatic disorder. The idea goes like this: When an individual is somatically ill (say, with bone cancer or malaria), there is necessarily nothing morally suspect or demeaning in the condition. The rel-evant norms for somatic illness are purely scientific or biological norms. No slight to the person as a person or rational and responsible agent is involved. But the moral skeptic charges: the relevant norms for mental illness or disorder are moral or moral-social norms. They are norms that depend upon moral values as well as perceptions or assessments of whether people are morally responsible agents. On Thomas Szasz's construal mental illness is a 'myth' masquer-ading as a proper medical category. An individual with problems in living may reasonably seek help, if they wish, but he or she should not be classified as a patient – as somehow mentally ill – lest they are mistreated as persons or lest morally unjustified stress be placed on their dignity as a responsible agent.

In order to fully respond to moral skepticism about mental disorder, we need to system-atically consider the norms for mental illness or disorder: What norms are or should mental disorders be subject to? Are norms involved in the assessment of a mental illness essentially demeaning to persons as persons? Only if attributions of mental disorder are essentially morally suspect or demeaning should we suppose that moral skepticism about the category of mental disorder is justified.

Consideration of the proper norms for mental disorder is not discussed in direct detail in the current chapter. It is a too big a topic for part of one chapter and is discussed in the next two chapters. Special attention is given to the moral dimensions of such norms in the last section of Chapter 6.

Moral skepticism about mental disorder is also committed to the claim that somatic illness norms are different sorts of norms than mental disorder norms. Should we suppose that that claim is true? Should we suppose, in particular, that somatic illness norms are value free and hence not contestable, whereas mental disorder norms are value laden and essentially contestable (and therein also open to moral criticism)?

Perhaps the assessment that physicians make of bodily illnesses may appear to be value free and scientifically impersonal, but any such appearance is, as the chapter argued, misleading. The assessments or norms of somatic illness are constituted by social or personal values and harbor the possibility of contestation (especially when the environmental contexts of bodily function change). As for assessments of mental illnesses, if they somehow harbor the possi-bility of contestation this is no mark unshared by somatic illness norms. Quite apparently, there also is nothing inherently disrespectful about the attribution of mental illness any more than there is something inherently undignified about the ascription of a somatic or bodily illness – although the content of the book's discussion of mental illness norms awaits time on stage.

Metaphysical skepticism raises a fundamental explanatory challenge for any approach to mental disorder or illness that requires mental disorders or illnesses to have their own dis-tinctive (if partial causes of this type) psychological causes – causes that are themselves best described as non-mechanisms. Moral skepticism raises a fundamental normative constraint on any assessment of mental disorder or illness – the constraint of respect and dignity preservation. These are the lessons of skepticism or anti-realism about mental disorder. No mental disorder without an explanatory role for the psychological. No attributions of mental disorder without respect for persons.

SUGGESTED READING

Dretske, F. (1988). *Explaining Behavior: Reasons in a World of Causes* (Cambridge, MA: MIT Press).

Graham, G. and Horgan, T. (2002). "Sensations and grain processes" in J. Fetzer (ed.) *Consciousness Evolving*, pp. 63–86 (Amsterdam: John Benjamins).

Heil, J. and Mele, A. (eds) (1993). *Mental Causation* (Oxford: Oxford University Press).

O'Connor, T. and Robb, D. (eds) (2003). *Philosophy of Mind: Contemporary Readings* (London: Routledge).

Szasz, T. (2007). *The Medicalization of Everyday Life* (Syracuse: Syracuse University Press).

5 Seeking norms for mental disorder

The disturbances or conditions that are mental disorders are not best understood as brain disorders. Or more exactly: If a disorder has a causal explanatory foundation whose description requires referring to its psychology (Intentional content and so on) and not just or only to its underlying neural mechanisms, then it qualifies as a mental disorder and not as a disorder of the brain. Or so I have argued. This is true, I have claimed, even if or though mental disorders are based existentially in the brain and central nervous system.

The disorderliness of a mental disorder is connected, in part, with its being undesirable and its undesirability is constituted, again, in part, by the fact that a disorder makes a person worse off and does so involuntarily. Diseases do that too, of course. They unwillingly make persons worse off. But mental disorders may not best be understood as forms of disease. I have argued for those claims as well.

I am not finished examining what makes a mental disorder a disorder or undesirable for a person. In this and the next chapter I hope to complete the task. Here, in this chapter, I plan to examine three candidate norms or standards that may be relevant to negative judgments or appraisals of a person's mental condition and could help to warrant the clinical attribution of a disorder to the condition of a person.

The chapter addresses a tough issue. Norms for disorder. What are they? Many controversies associated with the topic of mental illness or disorder stem from disagreement over which standards or norms are germane to a disorder. A little saintly assistance should help.

DESPAIR, DEPRESSION AND DISORDER

St. Augustine (354–430) was born in Tagaste in the North African province of Numidia in AD 354. Augustine's *Confessions* is one of the literary and autobiographical masterworks of western literature. In it he describes his quest to find a meaning or purpose to life and his deliberate and dramatic conversion to Christianity. To him, for him and in him, purpose meant Christian purpose. Without it, he says, he suffered from intellectual confusion and emotional turmoil.

Augustine reports that his mother once "found me in a dangerous state of depression" (Augustine 1992: 90). So: Was he ever subject to episodes of a mental illness? Clinical or major depression? Nancy Andreasen says yes. She writes:

> No medical texts are extant from the early medical period, but literary and historical evidence indicates that the absence of texts does not bespeak the absence of illness. St. Augustine has confessed to his struggles with the hopelessness and despair of depression.
>
> (Andreasen 1984: 144.)

Confession to depression? Is Augustine's autobiography a tale, in part, of his personal struggle with a mental disorder? If given a chance and fast forward to current times, would the venerable but often unhappy saint consult a cognitive-behavioral therapist or embrace a drug regimen of a selective serotonin reuptake inhibitor (Prozac)? True, Augustine does speak of periods, one just noted, of depression and unhappiness. Here, for a second instance, is how he describes his grief on the loss of a friend in death:

> Everything on which I set my gaze was death. My home town became a torture to me; my father's house a strange world of unhappiness; all that I had shared with him was without him transformed into a cruel torture. My eyes looked for him everywhere, and he was not there. I hated everything because they did not have him, nor could they now tell me 'look, he is on the way', as used to be the case when he was alive and absent from me. I had become to myself a vast problem.
>
> (Augustine 1992: 57)

But was, in this 'vast problem', Augustine suffering from a clinical depression? The mental disorder? Augustine?

Imagine that a psychiatrist enamored of medication says to him, "No, unhappiness over finding a purpose to life or even over the death of a friend is completely and utterly unwarranted." "Yours is a chemical problem." "Likely, it is located in your endocrine or stress response system." "Your autoregulatory mechanism for cortisol production probably is impaired or dysregulated."

Nomy Arpaly remarks that "being told that one's cherished beliefs or emotions are symptoms of a ... disorder ... can be insulting, however ... compassionate" may be the intention (Arpaly 2005: 285). Augustine, no doubt, would be insulted. "My problem is not with life's purpose?" So he may exclaim. "It's with my hormones?"

Augustine, I believe, does not confess to clinical depression.

Part of the problem in describing emotions like that reported by Augustine is that a word like 'depression' may be used for different purposes in different settings. It is one word with more than one meaning or use, and referring to clinical depression (or to the disorder of depression) is only one of them.

I believe that what Augustine confesses to in bemoaning the absence of purpose in his life is what the philosopher Richard Garrett aptly refers to as philosophical despair. Garrett writes: "When an individual comes to the ... conclusion that not simply their own life but everyone's life is, as a whole futile, then we have ... philosophical despair" (1994: 74). For Augustine the struggle to overcome fear of life's essential futility, aggravated perhaps by the death of his friend, took a religious or spiritual turn. He describes himself as having searched for a transcendent or overarching purpose to human existence. Augustine discovered this purpose, he reports, only in belief in the God of Christianity. When, for example, his mother once had discovered him in a philosophically despairing state, "I had lost all hope of discovering the truth" (1992: 90). But later after conversion Augustine reports that he prayed to God as follows: "Late have I loved you, beauty so old and so new, late have I loved you" (1992: 201). "I feel but hunger and thirst for you ... to attain the peace which is yours" (1992: 201). Peace. No longer despair.

Of course, Augustine's unhappiness ('depression', hopelessness) may be based in part on hormonal activity. But although saying that his unhappiness may be grounded, in part, in hormone levels is perhaps saying something that is true, it is not saying much, for we still may ask about its Intentionality. It's conceptual content. It's focus or direction. What, if anything, is the unhappiness about? If the answer is the meaningless of life, may it not also be reasonable or sensible, depending upon background conditions, for a person to be unhappy about a life that they believe to be utterly meaningless or purposeless and to speak of themselves as being hopeless or depressed?

If so, if purposelessness is a focus, then it must be no mere hormones that are responsible for the negativity of mood or emotion that may be part of a philosophical despair. A person who was not unhappy over human purposelessness, it may be surmised, must either be 'in denial' or have achieved some sort of countervailing stoical or ironic affect-less detachment over their circumstances of life, complementary reference to hormone levels notwithstanding.

Compare and contrast: Consider a person made sad or negative in mood because they suffer from an illness such as Addison's disease in which the adrenal glands no longer produce cortisol, and wherein sadness may occur no matter what the person thinks or believes. A person with Addison's may believe, in fact, that life is immensely purposeful and yet still feel forlorn. Unlike Augustine's unhappiness, which was rooted in the attitude that life is not worth living, and arose in his frustrated search for meaning and direction, unhappiness when a part of Addison's disease is neurochemically fastened onto the somatic illness. It is not focused on some particular Intentional content. Content or Intentionality has nothing to do with its causation. The unhappiness is not the product of philosophical reasoning or argumentation. Commitment to Christianity is no antidote for Addison's.

Carl Elliott complains of the tendency of contemporary psychiatric culture to categorize too wide and motley a variety of human distresses as "scientific problems defined by the language and techniques of psychiatry" (Elliott 2003: 157). A recent book laments that the extreme popularity of antidepressant medication is making Americans "comfortably numb" (Barber 2008). Be numb, not disturbed, not writing confessions in North Africa.

Complaints about over-medicalizing human distresses like sadness or depression are apt even if their purport is imprecise or unclear. Over-medicalization "violates," in the words of Jennifer Radden, "our intuitive sense that [various] forms of suffering are importantly different"

(Radden 2009: 102). Not every 'disorderly' or distressful mental condition qualifies as a mental disorder. Some conditions do, of course. But others do not. Moreover, the distinction between forms of suffering that are and are not mental disorders is of critical personal and public policy importance. How this distinction is interpreted not only influences people's interpretations of life and circumstance, but helps to legitimate psychiatric intervention and mental health medical practice.

Andreasen, I believe, over-medicalizes Augustine. Augustine, the saint, sought God and Meaning. A student at Princeton or Cambridge may try to escape from the clutches of GOD. The behavior neither of Augustine nor a grade obsessed Princeton sophomore is, taken just by itself, truly indicative of a mental disorder. Each person is in a distressed and undesirable condition, to be sure. But that is not enough, certainly, to qualify for a mental disorder.

What then is? When is enough actually enough? Which norms or standards of assessment help to divide the threshold between order and disorder, mental health and mental illness?

ANXIETY, DSM AND ASSESSING NORMS

Let's look at a real case of mental disorder. An exemplary one. A case with specifics.

The case to be examined is adapted from a clinical case, discussed by Kraepelin, who, as noted in the first chapter, helped to provide the conceptual foundations for the modern style of classification of mental disorders of which DSM is the most prominent example. The real case was discussed in 1904 in Kraepelin's *Lectures in Clinical Psychiatry* (translated by Thomas P. Johnstone, New York: Hafner, 1968: 262). Assume that the context for offering the case is Grand Rounds of a Department of Psychiatry of a distinguished university hospital and medical center.

> Arthur A., a school teacher, has been in the hospital two weeks. He is thirty-six years old and entered the hospital of his own accord in order to be treated here. He is reluctant to be part of today's Grand Rounds. When told that he would be presented at Rounds, he became agitated and said that being paraded in front of so many strangers all at once might cost him his life. He did not explain what he meant by that remark, but he begged to sit in the corridor before the presentation so that he could see the audience enter gradually before him. "I just cannot face so many people all at once," he said.
>
> Arthur says that one of his sisters suffers as does he from fear of public places. He also says that his fearful condition began when he had to study for entry exams to graduate school. He became intensely afraid that he would fail. He became short of breath and dizzy. He felt his heart pounding rapidly. Sweat poured down his face. Because of these physical reactions he feared that he had a serious heart disease. His internist tried to assure him that he was in good cardiac health, but assurances fell on deaf ears. For this reason, Arthur sought out cardiac specialists and visited several heart clinics, his fears about his heart increasing steadily. Again, despite receiving optimistic assessments, he persisted in believing that he had a bad heart. He found that he could not cross public plazas or walk into busy stores. He stopped taking buses because of apprehension about

accidents and crashes. He had an opportunity for an ocean cruise and vacation, which he declined, fearing that the boat might capsize. The fears, he says, aggravated his heart condition, which he says make public concourse an emotional bridge that he cannot cross.

His wife describes him as "chicken-hearted", afraid of all sorts of diseases and of crowds. Arthur himself admits that his fears and anxieties feel morbid, and that they keep him from leading a normal life, yet he cannot free himself from them. He walks in the hospital garden, by himself, retreating to his room if other patients enter the garden while he is there. He asks for "pills" to give him the energy to address audiences of parents of schoolchildren, a chore that he has to perform several times a year. He is scheduled to make one such address next month. He doubts he will be able to do it.

Arthur says that sometimes he feels his heart violently palpitate, when he is forced to be in a crowd. This morning, he says, small acne spots have begun to appear on his face, and he believes that this is evidence that he stands visibly out in the hospital and is likely to be treated in unwelcome terms. He wonders, too, if the acne has something to do with his heart condition. A dermatology resident examined Arthur later this morning and found no unusual spots, acne or otherwise. Arthur, however, is not persuaded.

Arthur A's case has four clinically prominent features among others.

1. Arthur has disturbances or interferences in his conscious experience – in his (as it may be put) Intentionality of self and world.
2. Because of these disturbances, Arthur struggles with one or more necessary activities of daily living, and is impaired or disabled in their performance.
3. The disturbances are characterized by a variety of negative and imprudent thoughts, feelings and behaviors.
4. If Arthur is not helped or treated, he may suffer important and continued losses of freedom and social functionality. His condition seems to be worsening.

Given its particular symptoms Arthur's case would be diagnosed using DSM as Agoraphobia (i.e. acute anxiety associated with being in public places or situations with other people, strangers foremost, and in which escape may be difficult) with Panic Attacks or Disorder (APA 1980: 226; APA 1987: 235f). This diagnosis would be supplemented with a diagnosis of Hypochondriasis [APA 1980: 249]. Arthur A.'s heart is healthy, but he is convinced that he has an infirm heart. He has no acne either.

But why should Arthur A's condition be classified as a mental disorder in the first place? What sort of assessment of his condition or rationale is there for the DSM assumption that someone like Arthur is ill or disordered, psychiatrically? Let's focus on his acute anxiety about crowds with the proclivity to panic and not on his hypochondriasis.

No doubt, Arthur's emotional response is a deeply upsetting disturbance in his experience of self and world, broadly understood. This does not mean that strictly neurobiological/neurochemical or brute mechanical processes play no role in Arthur's unfortunate behavior. Of course they play roles. Nor does it mean that the specific source of his acute anxiety is obvious to him or that it stems, as he believes, from an incident in which he was afraid of failing an exam. But it does mean, as Karl Jaspers (1883–1969) puts it in his *General Psychopathology*, "psychopathology has, *as its subject matter*, actual … psychic events" (Jaspers 1963: 2). The content, character and consequences of Arthur's experience help to explain both why his 'psychic' or mental condition is a disorder and why this particular disorder is of the type that it is – anxiety as opposed to, say, depression or delusional disorder.

In mentioning Jaspers, it should be noted that although some disorders in DSM's all-too-hefty catalogue are compatible with Jaspers's proposition that psychopathologies (mental illnesses/ disorders) are disorders in a person's conscious experience, DSM is not in complete and uniform accord with Jaspers on this score. Some conditions mentioned in the manual are not disturbances in experience or conscious Intentionality and behavior, although they are classified as mental disorders. This fact is worth a brief digression since it is associated with the topic of anti-dualism, considered in the last chapter.

DSM counts or appears to count Down's Syndrome as a mental disorder (see e.g. APA 1987: 28ff). If Down's is a mental disorder, then an IQ of 55, depending upon its chemical cause, may qualify for DSM as a mental disorder irrespective of the presence of conscious distress or behavioral disturbance. Down's can even be diagnosed prior to birth and actual behavior by identifying a chromosomal abnormality that is its cause in samples of fetal cells taken from amniotic fluid. The presence of an extra twenty-first chromosome is the source of mental retardation in Down's. But, then, why classify Down's as a *mental* disorder?

The inclusion of Down's Syndrome in DSM may stem from the following two facts: (i) Down's is a neural-developmental disorder and (ii) the distinction between neurological or brain disorders and mental disorders is arbitrary from DSM's perspective given its worry that the category of mental disorder must somehow be pruned of dualist presuppositions.

Taxonomists are mistaken, however, or so I have argued and shall to continue to argue, to absorb mental disorders into the category of a neurological disorder, even if it is sensible to assume that mental disorders are based (like brain disorders, although in different causal explanatory ways) in neuro-physical reality. The authors of DSM may classify certain brute brain or neurodevelopmental disorders (like Down's) as mental disorders, in part, to demonstrate that dualism has been excised from the manual's conceptual or metaphysical foundations. It's odd, however, regardless of the wrongness of the classification, for something like Down's to be listed as a mental disorder, whereas another neurological condition like, say, Parkinsonism, which is a basal ganglia disorder, characterized by tremor, muscular rigidity and loss of postural reflexes, and which may be much more disturbing consciously for a subject, does not appear in DSM. This is despite the fact that some of Parkinsonism's symptoms may be ameliorated with psychological treatments. (Psychotherapy may reduce the anxiety persons often feel over the condition.) No manner of psychotherapy is able to build up a Down's patient's IQ.

Down's is no *mental* disorder by the standards of the theory of mental disorder being developed in this book. Down's is not associated with distress or disturbance in a victim's experience, except indirectly through personal adjustment problems that may stem from social circumstances of the condition. Nor do states with Intentionality/Intentional content figure in its propensity or onset conditions. Down's is, however, the sort of condition that some disease oriented psychiatrists wish to count as a mental disorder. Perhaps this is because if Down's qualifies as a mental disorder, then it stands not only as emblematic of DSM's commitment to anti-dualism, but as a case of disorder that is both a disease (with one or few causes, etc.) and an instance of a broken brain. So, classifying Down's as a mental disorder is an application of the biomedical model of mental illness in full aspiration. If all mental disorders could, like forms of mental retardation, be "linked to specific biological abnormalities," writes George Heninger, a psychiatrist at Yale University, "it would greatly simplify matters" (Heninger 1999: 89). "As the biology of a disease becomes more clear [then] so does our understanding of specific dimensions of clinical data" (ibid: 97). (Note that Heninger speaks of mental disorders as diseases.)

Of course, we do not need to endorse either a disease or a broken brain conception of mental disorder to urge *treating* Down's as at least somewhat like a mental disorder. Down's children have a general impairment in intellectual function that pervades all aspects of learning – reading, writing, mathematical computation. Education or training in the skills necessary to compensate for these impairments, such as self-help skills, communication skills, and so on, often fall within the province of the mental health profession. Likewise, social adjustment problems faced by certain victims of Down's, which may be exhibited in aggressive, self-injurious or withdrawal behavior, may stem from trying to lead a life in an environment where a person is unable appropriately to adjust without outside direction and assistance. The mental health profession possesses valuable assistance tools and services for people in distress in different walks of life, even if they are not subjects of a mental illness or disorder. Victims of Down's sometimes are among them.

Let us return to Arthur A. What about his case? Where is the disorder, the psychiatric condition or mental illness, behind his complaint or symptoms? This is not a question about the particulars of Arthur's diagnosis (of panic attacks), but about his being classified as the subject of a mental disorder period. What makes his case an example of a mental disorder according to DSM?

For DSM a mental disorder is described as a "clinically significant behavioral or psychological syndrome" of a sort that "occurs in a person and that is associated with present distress … or disability (impairment in one or more important areas of functioning) or with a significantly increased risk of suffering death, pain, disability, or an important loss of freedom" (APA 1994: xxi). In Arthur's case the elements of disability and loss of freedom are parts of the second, third, and fourth features of his condition; distress is a first feature. The disorder also is *in* him in the form of the first feature, namely in his distressful or disturbed experience of self and world.

Clearly, the DSM description is not intended to identify a readily or empirically tractable set of necessary and sufficient conditions for qualifying as a mental disorder. That's all in line with the unavoidable, given prototype semantics for the very idea of a mental disorder. Prototypes, it may be remembered, don't possess necessary and sufficient conditions. Not that other features of the DSM theoretical framework for understanding mental disorder also are unavoidable. Certainly DSM's a-theoreticity (or silence about proximate causes) is avoidable (and undesirable). But DSM's description also contains a gerrymandered collection of terms, referring to distress, disability, impairment, pain, and so on. So, if one is looking for a regimented or even modestly clear and precise characterization of what makes a disorder a disorder, DSM fails to provide it.

DSM's gerrymandered characterization of disorder aside, what I wish focus on in DSM's description is the following feature. For DSM if a mental or psychological condition consists *merely* of distress, loss of freedom, and so on, it fails to qualify as a disorder. Remember: Augustine was distressed, but not for that reason clinically depressed. To qualify as a disorder for DSM, a distress or loss must also stem from a so-called clinically *significant* disability or impairment. This means (among other things) that the condition is neither the product of reasoned argumentation, as is the case of the philosophical despair of Augustine, assuming his despair stemmed from no disability, nor a mere performance lapse or error.

So what then is it? A clinically significant disability or impairment? It is one thing if I am distressed because I voluntarily expose myself to distress (say, by bungee jumping). It's another if my distress indicates a clinically significant disability or impairment. It is one thing if I am distressed because I am trying to learn to perform a Beethoven piano sonata and suffer from a lack of self-confidence. It is another if I am distressed because no matter how hard I try I cannot get myself to interact with strangers or to calm myself down from episodes of florid mania.

All that makes good intuitive sense, doesn't it? Even without knowing just what it may mean in theoretical detail to refer to a *clinically significant* disability or impairment? In order to appreciate the wisdom of the demand for clinical significance for any condition that qualifies as a disorder, consider GOD. Students in this hypothetical condition are precluded because of their grade anxiety from doing as well as they wish on graded academic performances. But although grade anxiety is disturbing, doing extremely well academically is not *that* clinically important or significant. Besides which, it is not a capacity that most human beings share. We are not all above average academically. If I am failing to get top scores, I am missing out on Phi Beta Kappa or academic honors. Life, however, is filled with an immense range of other satisfactions and opportunities, including intellectual challenges, through which to develop and express talents that do not require acing calculus tests or getting top grades on term papers on European history.

It's hard for certain people, especially perhaps for certain students at highly selective colleges or competitive universities to appreciate all that. In an academic culture that is meritocratic, to quote Erik Erikson (1902–94), from a book musty on my shelf but a must-read when I was a student, many "young men and women [are] forced by a compulsion to excel fast, before enough of a sense of being [has been] secured" (Erikson 1968: 151.) However, in order to be truly secure and healthy, a person must learn how to moderate their desires or expectations and cope with personal failure. A prudent and mature person realizes that sometimes they should seek satisfaction down other avenues or through alternative opportunities. Not in nailing honors or other short-lived classroom successes.

No such admonition to seek satisfaction elsewhere or to learn to adjust to failure is appropriate for the likes of an Arthur. Part of what helps to distinguish his fear or anxiety over being in public from the grade anxiety of students in the grip of GOD, is that avoiding contact with strangers or people in crowded places just is not feasible in normal social environments. Public concourse and interaction with other people is necessary for a vast variety and majority of activities and normal forms of human satisfaction. One cannot simply switch majors or decide to become a lighthouse keeper.

So, although DSM's description of the disorder of a mental disorder is complex as well as disjointed, one aspect of it is both direct and, I believe, sound. According to DSM to attribute a mental disorder to someone requires evaluating not just the person's capacity (or incapacity) to avoid harms or losses of freedom, but also the 'clinical' importance or nature of those losses as well as of the capacities or competencies that are impaired or incapacitated. And this raises the following question: Where do we get standards or norms for such clinical judgments or evaluative appraisals? Absent countervailing considerations, "rational persons in all societies" agree that "death, pain, disability and loss of freedom" are undesirable (Gert and Culver 2004: 421). No one denies that. But for DSM an incapacity or impairment does not count as a disorder just because it is painful, risks death, and so on. One can imagine, for instance, being incapable of climbing a mountain in the winter or wrestling with a bear in the woods and this may cause losses for a person (and risk death) if they are in a situation in which they must do these things but can't. But such events for DSM would not mean that the relevant incapacities or inabilities qualify as mental disorders. For a disorder, for DSM, an incapacity or impairment must ascend to a clinical standard or level of significance. Pain stemming from a significant incapacity? Impairment in avoiding a serious loss? What's that? No psychiatrist should be asked to help you to learn how to wrestle with a bear in the woods.

The necessity or need for identifying when psychological disabilities or impairments are serious enough, clinically speaking, or of sufficient clinical or medical import or relevance, to qualify as disorders arises inevitably, I believe, for any effort to appraise what makes a mental disorder a disorder. Not just for DSM, but for any genuinely normative or values-based concept of disorder. So, it is no surprise to find that the history of psychopathology has traditionally been concerned simultaneously both with the study of impairments and disabilities and with their degree, nature or type of evaluative significance. A list of impairments would not be of much interest to psychopathology without consideration of standards or norms.

We could, of course, try to decide on the clinical significance of a disability in a normatively flatfooted and unsophisticated way. Social scientists spend a great deal of time gathering statistics. We may try to use statistics to try to identify statistical norms of human psychological functioning. The evaluative seriousness of a psychological incapacity may then just be understood as statistically deviant or abnormal functioning. Being unable to do calculus and therein losing honors would not count, assuming that most people cannot do well at calculus. Whereas being unable to know where one is or what one is doing would qualify. Knowing where one is and what one is doing is quite normal. But we need to ask ourselves (again, for remember our earlier discussion of this topic) whether statistical infrequency should be encoded in a concept of mental illness. Descartes was statistically aberrant, a genius at both science and philosophy. He found himself accepting, imprudently, an invitation to go to Stockholm to give philosophical tutelage to Queen Christina of Sweden, where he behaved foolishly. Christina hoped for instruction in the royal palace in the cold hours of pre-dawn. Descartes assented but it killed him. He caught pneumonia and died just shy of his fifty-fourth birthday. Does this mean he was mentally ill? With Augustine already on the taxonomic cutting block and perhaps now adding Descartes, one may wonder whether any philosopher can escape a diagnosis of mental illness.

Suppose we discover that human beings suffer from all sorts of decision-making errors and cognitive biases. Here is a partial list of potential candidates with their standard names: An outgroup homogeneity bias, in which persons describe people in their own group as being relatively more varied in personality and behavior than members of other groups; a fundamental attribution error, in which persons over-emphasize the causal role of personality traits in controlling behavior and downplay the power of situational influences on the same behavior; the neglect of prior base rates, in which people fail to incorporate prior known frequencies that are pertinent to a current decision made under conditions of uncertainty; the gambler's fallacy, in which a person assumes that series of individual random events are influenced by previous random events ("I've flown so many times without accident, that my plane is bound to crash sooner or later."); and hyperbolic discounting, in which people tend to more strongly prefer smaller payoffs or rewards for their behavior than larger payoffs if the smaller payoff is closer in time.

Are any of these biases or errors, which may be quite harmful, mental disorders or symptoms of mental disorder? Not both if they are statistically frequent and if statistical infrequency is necessary for a mental disorder. But that hardly seems right. In somatic medicine, during a massive epidemic (in which a deadly virus is spread) nearly everyone has the relevant illness. Frequency does not count against being ill. As for biases, a good concept of mental disorder should spell out just which, if any, biases (assuming that they deserve such a label) are significant. Perhaps none. Perhaps all. Perhaps some. Or perhaps when and only when associated with certain other impairments or disabilities.

It is one thing to be biased in reasoning or decision making. It is another for bias to be due to impairment in reasoning as well as clinically significant. Important or significant enough, that is, to qualify as a mental disorder or symptom of a disorder. When is 'enough' enough and clinical significance achieved? Infrequency is a poor norm. So perhaps, for an answer to this enough-question, we should simply leave the relevant standards of importance and significance at a subjective and intuitive level? Forget statistics. Let's just rely on psychiatrists' judgments of importance, hoping perhaps that they will reach some measure of reliability, unprejudiced by economic and non-medical considerations. "All this," as one theorist of clinical assessment puts the matter in a related context, "is a question of judgment rather than pure tests results" (Powell 2000: 100).

The clinical coal-face of mental disorder is human suffering and the need to ameliorate it. Educated compassionate judgment when addressing the needs of particular people with possible disorders may be, in certain instances, not just unavoidable but desirable. Other things being equal, however, if we can find at least a rough-n-ready principled means to make the judgments of importance or significance we need, we should embrace it. Not statistics or infrequencies. Not subjective guesswork. But then what? Let us look at some hypotheses for explicit standards of clinical importance or significance.

This brings me, then, to an examination of candidate norms or standards of clinical seriousness or importance – which I am equating with norms for mental disorders or illnesses as disorders or illnesses. As mentioned earlier, I plan to look at three. One is tied to culture. One relies on evolutionary speculation. One (and the one that we should prefer, I believe) is rooted in appreciation and understanding of a special feature of Intentionality and of the Intentional attitudes (beliefs, desires, and so on) of persons. This feature is the rationality and the environmental or contextual situatedness of the reason-responsiveness of persons, broadly understood.

CULTURAL CONVENTIONALISM

Suppose the following is true: Different cultures and sub-cultures possess different standards or conventions for the seriousness or importance of psychological impairments and disabilities and therein for whether a condition is a disorder. In the context of, say, a tribe of Ivy League Phi Beta Kappa scholars, GOD may be classified as a significant disability and count as a disorder.

Whereas when in a tribe of general educational malcontents, a syndrome like GOD may have no perceived significance whatsoever. Certainly not that of a mental disorder.

In 1940 in the United States homosexuality was thought to be a "disease" of sexuality or sexual behavior. Today unless it is believed to be accompanied by a "persistent and marked distress about sexual orientation" it is no longer mentioned as a diagnostic category (Soble 2004: 54–55).

Is clinical seriousness or significance just a matter of social or cultural conventions or norms? The idea that the norms or standards for disorders are nothing but a matter of social conventions may seem appealing. It is appealing if for no other reason than that if conventions say that a particular disability is serious or significant enough to qualify as a mental disorder, then, in a sense, there is a determinate and discoverable fact of the matter as to whether the disability is a disorder. A form of distress is a disorder just in case a relevant disorder determining cultural convention is in place and says it's a disorder.

Let's put the cultural criterion of seriousness as follows. The possession of the property of being thought, judged, or otherwise treated as serious by a culture both makes a disability important or qualifies it as a disorder, and enables us to recognize it as such. On such a view, for example, "Arthur's A's panic attacks are a symptom of a mental disorder" means "The attacks are symptoms of a disability that is thought serious by Arthur's culture and qualify in that culture as a disorder." Insofar and only insofar as we can identify psychological disabilities thought serious by a culture, we can identify what counts, or should count, as a mental disorder. The cultural criterion, which may be referred to as *cultural conventionalism* about disorder, implies that a disability is not a disorder if a culture fails to judge it as sufficiently serious.

There are different versions of cultural conventionalism about disorder and associated standards of clinical significance. There is also indeterminacy in the concepts of culture and convention, enough, at least, to make it difficult to know, in some cases, whether to count a criterion as a culture's criterion. But these facts do not upset the cultural criterion. Indeed, what most unnerves those who may wish to defend the criterion is when critics misread it.

Consider the statement:

1. An uncontrollable proclivity to panic attacks is a mental disorder.

Is this statement true, or is it false? For the conventionalist, it is neither true nor false. It is semantically elliptical. It's like saying that 'Boston is next to', but not saying next-to-what. Or saying that 'Sam is tall' but not saying as compared to whom. The truth is, says the conventionalist, that a proclivity to panic attacks is a mental disorder just in those places or situations in which it culturally is judged to be a mental disorder or clinically serious, but not in situations in which it is not. Or consider the statement:

2. An uncontrollable proclivity to panic attacks in the judgment of Arthur's culture is a mental disorder.

Is that statement true, or is it false? It is true, but not truly a perspicuous expression of the conventionalist criterion. Conventionalism as such is not saying that cultures make judgments about (or have conventions with respect to) mental disorder, which, of course, they do, but that,

3. An uncontrollable proclivity to panic attacks is a mental disorder in those cultures (like Arthur's) in whose judgment or according to whose conventions it is a mental disorder.

The third claim is a very different claim from the second. The second merely reports a social convention. The third identifies the convention as *the* criterion of a disorder. (The logical or clarifying points I am making here are analogous to some made in defense of moral conventionalism and relativism. See Hocutt 2000 for discussion).

But is a cultural judgment or convention a sound and sensible criterion of disorder – of clinical seriousness or importance? Suppose we take the criterion to theoretical heart. What are some of the implications?

Reasoning about whether something is a serious impairment and genuine mental disorder terminates when we reach facts about cultural conventions

Suppose we know that in Culture C slaves who attempt to flee from their owners are treated as suffering from an illness known as "drapetomania". Or that gays and lesbians in Culture C* are said to be disabled and in need of a clinical intervention. How do we know this? It may be hard in some cases, but with the aid of anthropologists and sociologists such facts, if they are facts, are discoverable. However, is that where concern about whether a distress or impairment is serious or behavior a disorder should terminate? Is that the end of the investigatory line? Not in psychiatry but in cultural anthropology? One should think not.

We would lose our notion of cross-cultural medical scientific progress in the study of mental disorder

Psychiatric medicine has long suffered from what seems to some prominent observers to be an unflattering contrast with somatic illness medical specialties. This is that while advances in somatic medicine tell us more about heart disease, cancer, and obesity, medical science is stymied when it comes to understanding an unhealthy mind. Who's to say what constitutes an advance in psychiatry? This alleged unflattering contrast between somatic medicine and psychiatry has tended to provoke either one of two responses. One is to put the very idea of mental disorder (in the manner argued for by Thomas Szasz) into a dismissive category, wherein debates over what counts as a disorder become contests of value judgments rather than inquiries into health and illness facts. The other is to identify psychiatric progress with a slower and more complicated history of scientific development than is available for other areas of medicine. This second line of response goes as follows: A psychiatric pathology is, in some ways, a more complicated phenomenon than, say, a malfunctioning heart or diseased kidney. Thus, to take this chapter's example, Arthur's seeking to escape from crowds is distressful for him, but, so the tale goes, just which of his capacities are disabled is open to doubt and debate. There is no clear sense in psychiatry, as there often is in somatic medicine, of just where an impaired performance or symptom has its source. So the line of thought goes.

Cultural conventionalism about disorder would contribute conceptual ammunition to the picture of an unflattering contrast between somatic and psychiatric medicine. For if we adopted the perspective of conventionalism, we would have to admit that one culture could not criticize another for its inferior explanatory understanding of a mental disorder. On the contrary, if one culture condemns masturbation as, say, a mental disorder, this isn't an empirical mistake. The act of judgmental condemnation by a culture makes it a mental disorder in that culture.

Genuine scientific progress means replacing inferior ways of understanding a phenomenon with superior modes of comprehension. Breakthroughs in AIDS research would be one thing; breakthroughs in clinical depression research, if conventionalism is right, would be an oxymoron. A breakthrough? For by what criterion do we judge a new understanding of an illness to be superior? In nineteenth century Anglo-American culture, masturbation was said to be a serious sign of mental illness, which was "characterized by intense self-feeling and conceit ... derangement of thought [and] nocturnal hallucinations" (Maudsley 1867: 452). One unfortunate man in Texas had his penis amputated for treatment of the condition. Two British physicians blistered the prepuce as treatment. A large number of female cases in the office of a London physician were subjected to clitoridectomies (see Reznek 1987). To say that we have made progress in no longer thinking of masturbation as a disorder is precisely the sort of trans-cultural trans-conventional judgment that, according to disorder conventionalism, is illegitimate or without a supportive evidential foundation. It is too non-cultural.

Suppose, contrary to fact of course, that Texans still classify masturbation as a sign of a mental illness or disorder. But natives of California do not. If conventionalism is right, Californians cannot criticize Texans on grounds that they misunderstand the psychiatric status or unhealthy seriousness of masturbation. For conventionalism it matters decisively what a society or culture thinks and, when it comes to a mental disorder, no society is more backwards or forwards in its thinking than any another. Assuming that the same criterion of social mattering (namely, conventionalism) does not hold true for somatic medicine, cardiovascular medicine makes cross-cultural progress. Masturbation still is stuck, by contrast, hypothetically, in Texas.

We could make a mental disturbance a mental disorder just by changing the judgmental practices of a culture

Alcohol abuse is described in DSM as a maladaptive pattern of consumption that leads to impairment and distress (APA 1994: 182–83). But the patterns allowed by DSM to count as maladaptive in a case of alcohol abuse may consist in nothing but censorious cultural/social judgments aimed at an alcohol abuser. So, if you drink heavily, "your spouse [if deemed culturally representative] can give you a mental disorder simply by arguing with you about it," causing you distress and besieging you with marital problems. Then, your spouse [culture] also can "cure you by becoming more tolerant" (Wakefield 1997: 640; see also Horwitz 2002: 102).

Consider, in a related connection, the clinical fate of homosexuality. Homosexuality was listed as a disorder in DSM-II, but following the emergence of the gay rights movement in the late 1960s, and of gay activists lobbying at meetings of the American Psychiatric Association, support shifted in 1974 from saying that it is a disorder to seeing it as a human sexual preference variation. Homosexuality itself hadn't changed, of course, but what did change were social and cultural judgments about being gay. (Or rather, such judgments changed more or less. Bias against gays has not disappeared entirely from within the psychiatric profession. See Sobel 2004.) If there is little or no significant distress, as it were, associated with a condition, so that whatever significant disturbance is associated with it stems more or less exclusively from a culture's untutored assessment of individuals in the condition, it surely is a mistake, say critics of conventionalism, to classify the condition as a mental disorder. Culturally frowned upon, yes. Socially awkward, no doubt. Serious impairment or form of mental disorder? No. My culture's judgment of my behavior may cause me distress, but should not itself constitute the fact that I am the subject of a mental disorder. Saying so does not make it so.

True, some symptoms of a disorder may be culturally or historically unique, occupying niches not replicable across cultures. However, the cultural uniqueness of symptoms is one thing; cultural conventionalism about a disorder is another. Certain disorders may also express unstable historical conditions only to disappear when conditions dissolve. In somatic medicine transient biochemical conditions may cause illnesses to occur for a period but only for a period. (Imagine that diabetes somehow disappears.) The same may wisely be expected of at least some mental disorders. Dissociative fugues or 'travelers' syndrome', in which sufferers wander roads in trance-like states for months, and which flowered in France at the end of the 19th century, seems to have evaporated (see Hacking 1998). But the transience or cultural instability of a condition is not the same phenomenon as the cultural conventionality of standards of disorder. When a disorder is transient or unstable this should make us wonder why it has disappeared or whether it merely is a passing symptom of some more general condition. Conventionalism, by contrast, should make us worry that we may construct or produce disorders just by adopting certain normatively negative conventions towards persons or merely by classifying them as disordered.

The above three italicized consequences plus the actual existence (noted earlier) of exemplars or prototypes of mental illness should lead us, I believe, to reject cultural conventionalism about disorder. It makes sound sense, I claim, to think of some conditions of mind and behavior as disorders wherever they appear. (It also makes sound sense to charge DSM with containing some disorder categories that fail to qualify as disorders because they reflect culturally biased or uninformed conventions, though I do not explore that topic here.) And it also makes sound sense to believe that psychiatric medicine has made and hopefully will continue to make scientific progress or strides in the study of mental disorder.

Caution though. Dismissing cultural conventionalism as the criterion for the seriousness or disorder-nature of a psychological incapacity or form of involuntary distress by no means implies that we turn a blind eye or deaf ear to other ways in which social and cultural factors are germane to the presence of mental disorder. Conventionalism says that culture and context matter to disorder. The problem with conventionalism is not with taking culture seriously. Culture *should* be taken seriously. The problem is that conventionalism ends up saying falsely that the cultural conventions for disorders are apt *criteria* for disorders.

How should culture and context be taken seriously? This is a big topic. I can only speak to it briefly here.

Culture and social context are relevant to the presence or absence of disorders in personal welfare impacting ways. The harms or risks with which disorders are associated are socially or culturally situated. A job lost because of an addiction. A family shattered by a parent's depression. No person is a solipsistic island.

Social/cultural or contextual factors also contribute to a condition's distinctive complaints or symptoms, vulnerability or propensity conditions, appropriate forms of treatment, and dynamics of recovery and self-reclamation. Eating disorders (like anorexia), for example, surely have something to do with exposure to Westernized norms of thin beautiful women and the fear of being socially disapproved because of being fat. Western norms help to scaffold such a disorder. Or (for another example) as Julian Leff, a professor of social and cultural psychiatry at the Institute of Psychiatry, King's College, London, notes, a disorder diagnosed as conversion hysteria and which used to be common in Europe has now "become a rarity" in Europe, even though it persists in places like Libya and North India (Leff 2000: 13). Why is that? How has the disorder become a rarity in Europe? We don't really know, but perhaps, surmises Leff, patient complaints once interpreted as signs of hysteria have metamorphosed in European cultures into complaints associated with "more cognitive forms of depression and anxiety" (Leff 2000: 13). Cultures also offer different ways of complaining about distress – of, say, describing being depressed. William Styron writes a memoir about depression, whereas a farmer in rural Asia visits a local medical practitioner and complains of sexual impotence.

I like to sum up the above just mentioned points by saying that mental disorder is culturally situated or embedded, but without being culturally defined or constituted by cultural judgments. There are no contextually or culturally disembodied disorders. The reason for this is simple. Human mental activity is always situated. It is existentially based in a body/brain. Meanwhile the body/brain is situated in a natural and social environment. However (and this is the main lesson I wish the current section of this chapter to offer) it does not follow from the situatedness of disorder that cultural judgments or conventions determine whether a condition is a disorder.

One final point should be mentioned about culture and disorder before leaving the topic in this section (although more will be said about it later). The main reason we find disorders undesirable is not that they are undesirable for us as Americans, Asians, or Africans or just when or if they are contrary to the disorder standards or conventions of the cultures in which we live. The main reason we find disorders undesirable is that they are, in some sense, undesirable for us as human beings period – harmful in any or virtually any context or cultural environment. They make us worse off when we have them: seriously worse off, no matter where we are. They incapacitate us or gum us up.

Even a lonely hermit can suffer from obsessive-compulsive disorder. Even a solitary monk can be profoundly depressed. But a hermit may be obsessing over cleaning roaches in a cave. A monk may be sleeping in a painful and self-imposed hair-shirt in a monastery. Each is somewhere at some time. Their disorders are not so self-contained as to be untouched by their dwellings – or harmful or incapacitating therein.

MIND MALADAPTED

Evolutionary speculation is a prominent feature of interdisciplinary cognitive science as well as of medicine. I myself engage in a bit of it in this book, when talking about neurological or brain disorders and candidate hypotheses for standards of proper or normatively normal brain function. So, too, as earlier noted, does the philosopher Christopher Boorse in talking of supposed impersonal adaptational standards for biological disease or illness. Even self-help books about somatic health and well-being now are beginning to employ evolutionarily inspired theorizing about standards of personal well-being. Here, for example, are some remarks of a physician on the clinical faculty of Columbia University's College of Physicians and Surgeons, admonishing 50, 60, and 70 year olds to exercise six days per week and to remain physically active. It's offered as a Darwinian nudge to physical activity and dietary prudence.

> Being sedentary is the most important signal for decay ... In nature, there is no reason to be sedentary except lack of food. Remember we grew up in Africa. No matter how plentiful the game, it rotted in hours ... You had to get up and hunt for hours every single day ... [In order to rot] store every scrap of excess food as fat, dump the immune system, melt off the muscle and let the joints decay. Time to find a cave, huddle in the corner and start shivering. ... Our ancestors ran for their lives.
>
> (Crowley and Lodge 2004: 39, 46)

Our taste for sweet and fatty foods may have been adaptive and contributive to inclusive genetic fitness in the nutritional challenges posed by the Pleistocene environment, but it has since been rendered unhealthy and maladaptive by the mass availability of ice cream, burgers and fries. Unfortunately, however, selection pressures haven't had time to select for tastes for other more healthy cuisine.

Given the scientific prominence and bookstore popularity of evolutionary theorizing and speculation, it may appeal somehow or in some manner to derive judgments about the importance and clinical seriousness of a mental incapacity or impairment from results of the theory of evolution. If so, then evolutionary norms can determine whether or not a given condition is a disorder: whether or not there is something clinically or medically wrong and undesirable in the mind and behavior of an individual person.

One general method for an evolutionarily inspired derivation of a judgment of clinical seriousness goes something like this: Begin by assuming that the human mind possesses various psychological faculties and capacities that have been acquired through the mechanisms of natural selection. We human beings possess, at least in part, an evolved psychology. Then, argue that a disability or impairment is important, a loss of freedom clinically significant, an impairment serious enough for medical attention, and so on, just when it stems from a circumstantial mismatch between the activation of an evolved or selected for psychological faculty or capacity and the novel demands of a current environment. Randolf Nesse of the University of Michigan, and the promoter of an approach to medicine known as Darwinian Medicine, has this to say about such a method of warranting a judgment or assessment of mental disorder: Much disorder "results from differences between the environment in which we live and the environment in which we evolve." "Natural selection simply has not had the time to adopt [us] to the change in circumstances" (Nesse 2001: 187; see also Nesse and Jackson 2011).

Here is an example or illustrative case for what Nesse seems to have in mind: Flight-inducing anxiety among strangers. Suppose it was adaptationally or biologically functionally useful in ancestral environments for human beings to quickly decide whether to circulate among strangers in a comparatively public or social space or whether to run and flee. Quick decision making may have been especially useful if a person was confronted with serious behavioral challenges that required them to rapidly determine whether to trust or rely upon utter strangers. Should one hunt or gather food with them? Perceptually simple stimuli like a certain noise level combined perhaps with certain threatening facial expressions in strangers may have served as immediate prompts to avoid contact or to remove oneself from the social space. Such signs or situations may have issued in anxiety – and then produced flight.

Compare the anxiety of Stone Age Hunter/Gatherers with the sort that plagues Arthur. It may be surmised that certain features of current situations that cause some people (like Arthur) to become anxious may sometimes be similar to those in once dangerous ancestral environments – e.g. facial expressions; noises. The differences being though that today those facial expressions or noises don't signal real threats. They may merely mean that shoppers are intensely or fretfully foraging for goods in a mall. If so, if that is true, then becoming anxious or fearful among strangers, for example, may be an inbuilt emotional response that once guarded "against the many dangers encountered outside the home range" of tribe or family (Marks and Nesse 1994: 251). But in modern urban environments, people who become anxious away from their home turf and in noisy spaces among strangers likely will "find it all but impossible to lead a normal life" (Murphy 2006: 284). They may respond to a current environment as if, in matters of public or social intercourse, it is, in effect, similar to ancestral environments and perhaps filled with untrustworthy people, when, in fact or reality, it is not. It may be a mere shopping mall in Birmingham or high school auditorium filled with parents for a PTA meeting in Boston. Then, when unwarranted anxiety occurs, such anxiety responses in the current environment may represent a serious impairment or disability, not a minor quirk or handicap. Fear and anxiety in a shopping mall may express a misalignment of an old mental or emotional mechanism or response pattern in a new environment. The anxiety-response is no longer a reliable guide to inter-tribal danger or hostility. It is (so this line of thought continues) clinically significant and therein a mental disorder.

Can evolutionary mismatch explanations like one just sketched above stand up as a warrant basis for the attribution of clinical significance to a condition of impairment? Can it capture the pathology of a condition? Can evolutionary theory be 'adapted' to help to determine the clinical resonance of Arthur's inability to shop or attend parent-teacher association meetings? The disorder of his disorder?

Responses in the literature to these questions vary in a number of different ways. One unsympathetic response argues that evolutionary theorizing is all very intriguing and imaginative, but has little or nothing empirically verifiable or genuinely scientific to contribute to the project in psychiatry of plotting the normative contours of a mental disorder. The anxiety-picture of hunter/gatherers sketched above is highly speculative, to say the least, and is a type of explanation that "is often unverifiable" (Gert and Culver 2004: 420). Our evidence about the details of the environments, social structures, and character of human psychology and affect or emotion in ancestral time periods is so meager that any hypothesis about fear or anxiety being an adaptive emotional response in specific ancestral circumstances (say, among strangers with various facial expressions) is likely to be massively underdetermined by available evidence. True, this does not mean, as the philosopher Robert Richardson aptly notes, that we should "peddle some fatuous form of philosophical skepticism" about evolutionary psychology (Richardson 2007: 381). We plausibly may assume, for instance, that there were situations that "put our evolutionary ancestors in danger" and that "fear is the emotion that motivated our ancestors to cope with the dangers that they were likely to face" (Pinker 1997: 386; see also Nesse 1990). In a fit of being too finicky, we should not demand the end to any and all evolutionary speculation about human psychology. But it is a speculation. Sheer speculation. So, we must be cautious in evolutionary hypothesis formation. Immensely cautious. The bands of hunter-gatherers who were our Pleistocene ancestors did not leave behind tools and bones that reveal the function-ality of avoiding strangers or which pinpoint the particular features of conspecifics that set off flight alarms.

Another sort of response is more accommodating or sympathetic (for discussion see Murphy 2006: 281–305). It maintains that evolutionary speculation can be interwoven with questions about the warranted grounds for speaking of a condition as a mental disorder and of clinical significance, if it is wedded to references to what we have independently determined is good reason (independent of concern with the topic of mental illness) to believe is the adaptational utility and biological functionality of traits and response patterns. "There exists a deep ancestry to our basic emotional feelings", writes one neuroscientist, and the "instinctual emotional action apparatus of the brain may be the fundamental source of basic emotional affects and behaviors" especially when part of "psychiatric disorders" (Panksepp 2009: 399, 404). Just as fear of snakes or heights may have been implanted in us by natural selection, so apprehensiveness about strangers may have been selected for, and implemented in an anxiety producing brain mechanism that is triggered by stimuli that are not reflectively or straightforwardly deliberately self-controlled by a person.

Suppose then, throwing caution about sheer evolutionary speculation aside, we assume that fear of strangers and anxiety over traveling or being in crowds among strangers is an evolved trait, and that Arthur's emotional response is a mismatch between this implanted response pattern and one or more features of current circumstance. Would that make his disability serious or clinically significant? A disorder? As part of the mismatch, say, Arthur complains that when he performs or associates with others publicly he becomes hyper-aware of every gesture he makes. His voice becomes high-pitched and reedy, his forehead drips with sweat, and his heart beats rapidly with noticeable palpitations. Suppose that unbeknownst to him these are signs that his autonomic nervous system is preparing for a so-called 'fight or flight response' (apposite, we may assume, under certain ancestral circumstances). Suppose Arthur actually is in a fight/flight mode, just as our primeval ancestors were when confronting an alien tribe or a mysterious group of hunter-gatherers. Suppose, too, that he somehow misinterprets the activation of his body's fight/flight response as evidence of an impending somatic disaster (say, a heart attack). In support of this sort of supposition (namely, that Arthur misinterprets the activation of his autonomic nervous system) a large and independent body of empirical literature suggests that panic attack or disorder victims tend to be hyper-attentive to internal physiological cues of somatic distress [Barlow 1988: 108, 232]. As David Barlow and his co-authors write: "Clinical observations over the years have indicated that patients with anxiety disorders, particularly panic disorder, seem to evidence greater awareness of internal bodily states and are constantly vigilant for any somatic changes that might signal the beginning of the next panic attack"

(Barlow, Chorpita, and Turovsky 1996: 266). Such somatic states 'irrupt' into the experience of ourselves as embodied subjects or agents.

Now introduce medication into the story. Suppose that since his hospital admission, Arthur has been receiving treatment with Inderal, a trade name for a beta-blocker. The medication does not directly alter Arthur's conscious distress, but it does block somatic signals of the fight-or-flight response. It keeps the heart from pounding, sweat from dripping, and voice from trembling. The drug does not by itself make Arthur relax, but it strips his body of the felt signs that he otherwise misreads as signals of impending somatic disaster. The absence or suppression of such signals does, in turn, make him relax. The mode of the drug's action is indirect but effective.

With the help of our story of Arthur are we there yet? Have we identified a plausible source of norms for seriousness or clinical significance? Maladaptation of an evolved response mechanism (namely, a fight/flight response in a state of anxiety), which is unsuited to a current environment. Would an initially well-designed flight pattern left over from ancestral circumstances express too much of its disutility at current malls or social intersections – and do this over and over again? Preserving in a repetitive loop what now has become a harmful and clinically significant impairment?

A general presupposition of this imagined or hypothetical picture is plausible. Namely, past biological utility fails to insure adaptational functionality now or at times and places for which a trait or response pattern originally was not designed. My legs were designed presumably for getting around fields and forests, but not for walking up the steps of a skyscraper. Elevators may be needed. However, to make a mismatch explanation appeal as a criterion of clinical significance for a pattern of behavior, the reference to the mismatch must explain what makes the inappropriateness of the response pathological or a disorder i.e. something of clinical significance. Not a mere dysfunctional or disruptive mismatch, but a *particularly* bad, deleterious or harmful one. The problem with Arthur is that his response is not just one of anxiety or fear and contextually inappropriate, an ancestor-tethered mismatch perhaps, but a form of anxiety that is so extreme, so nakedly or dramatically out of place and imprudent, that it is incompatible with his personal responsibilities and welfare. His reaction is not merely a misplaced hair triggered response to avoid strangers, but an over-reaction, an *utter* panic. It is one thing for him to become anxious and to remove himself when he should not, but another to interpret shopping in a mall or attending a parent-teacher association meeting as an impending *catastrophe*. His reaction is not just an expression of an inappropriate or 'mismatched' sensitivity, but of anticipated *trauma*. And *this* feature of his response (a feature that helps to make it a mental disorder) so far is left unexplained by the evolutionary speculation alone (offered above). Something is not just misplaced and unhelpful in Arthur's response, but harmful in its severity, imprudent depth and dramatic resonance.

There is no doubt, as Dominic Murphy aptly puts it, that "breakdowns in [our] psychology" have something to do with "how evolved minds are organized" (Murphy 2006: 305). But the difficulty with reliance on evolutionary conjectures in such cases is that (if the hypothetical example of Arthur is representative) an alleged mismatch between responses that may have been adaptational in ancestral environments and corresponding imprudent responses in current environments has got to be used to pick out the clinical *seriousness* of an impairment (of a mismatch) – it's pathological, wrongness or badness character, as it were. Mismatches are not themselves candidates for pathologies or disorders unless the responses in the current environment are over-reactive, harmful or deleterious. Not mere mismatches with modestly negative consequences, but overly dramatic responses in current circumstances. It should be on the shoulders of current harmfulness and undesirability and not distal ancestry (or speculations about ancient pedigree) that a disorder's seriousness lurches.

Imagine: A person shivering or trembling when standing at a cliff's edge overlooking the Grand Canyon may fear that she is in danger. Fear of such heights may have been an apt response historically biologically for the species. If she avoids such heights in other modern environments unnecessarily, this may have only a small negative impact on her health and well-being. Her fear may be relatively benign. Arthur's anxiety is not. Arthur is off the normal population distribution scale with his degree of anxiety. Why so severe? Why so pathological?

Our brief discussion has landed us in the following conceptual terrain: For evolutionary hypotheses to be used as standards or parts of standards for a mental disorder, it needs to be the case that there must be information concerning the environments of our ancestors, their psychology, and behavioral response patterns, to reveal something about the strength and former adaptational utility of those patterns. We must also distinguish between mere mismatches with current environments and their degree or type of harmfulness or wrongfulness – their clinical seriousness. The speculative nature and uncertainty regarding ancestral environments and the ongoing need to assess the clinical seriousness of current behavior seems to leave appeal to evolutionary psychological speculation as a deficient or at least seriously incomplete theoretical framework in terms of which to identify norms or standards for a mental disorder. We need some more proximate standard of seriousness and of a disorder's disorderliness.

RATIONALITY AND INTENTIONALITY

Immanuel Kant (1724–1804) asked what distinguishes the harmful behavior of a foolish person or buffoon from that of the "the mentally disordered". He claimed that "they differ not merely in degree but in the distinctive quality of mental discord." What is the distinctive quality of mental discord? The subject of a mental disorder may need to be guided, controlled or directed, he said, "by someone else's reason". A fool or buffoon does not. The reasoning of such people remains intact. Not that of a victim of mental illness (Kant 1793/2000: 199).

I would not wish to defend Kant's account of disorder precisely in the form that he himself may have intended (which likely is too intellectualistic or logistic, knowing Kant). But, like him, I believe that the best standard or norm for the general sort of psychological inability or impairment that is distinctive of a mental disorder is that the subject behaves, and cannot help but behave, in a rationally impaired way. By this I mean a way in which such a person is comprised or incapacitated in their ability to rationally control their own behavior. They cannot prevent what they do or how they feel, think, or behave.

Unlike thousands of other persons who make unreasonable choices or behave in ways that are harmful or imprudent, the choices, behaviors, judgments, moods or thoughts of a subject of mental disorder are unreasonable or unwise in ways that they cannot manage or guide. Where they are presented with a sufficient reason to behave in a different way, or to refrain from behaving in a harmful way, they are not capable of recognizing and appreciating the reason's sufficiency. Or when they do recognize it, they cannot react or respond to it as they should. Perhaps they engage in patently inappropriate or deleterious means to try to achieve their purposes or ends, make grossly harmful and unwarranted inferences from their perceptual experiences, or unwisely disengage from otherwise deeply valued personal relationships or ideals. Their best interests are not represented by their behavior, but they themselves are too incapacitated or 'gummed up' to help it or to do anything directly about their thoughts or deeds. If I (not a subject of a mental disorder) act unreasonably although am capable of doing otherwise, then my behavior may be imputed to a flawed character trait or foolhardy temperament, or to transient vicissitudes of performance (such as simple bad luck, motivational distraction, emotional fatigue, or unusual circumstantial constraints). But when Arthur, for example, is unable to enter a mall or to attend a parent/teacher association meeting, as an individual with a mental disorder, his behavior is no mere performance lapse, mark of fatigue, or blemish of character. Insofar as he is the subject of a mental disorder his 'reason-unresponsiveness' is due to one or more psychological impairments that render him incapable of behaving otherwise. His behavior should be responsive or receptive to the sufficient reasons he has (and which he himself, in this case, recognizes that he has) for entering a mall or attending a public meeting. But if we appreciate that he is agoraphobic, then we must realize that he cannot enter the mall or attend the meeting, no matter how hard he tries and even though it is in his best interest to do so.

The notion that the subject of a mental disorder is impaired in one or more forms of the exercise of reason or reason-responsive self-control is capable of being developed in a number of different ways (on the very idea of reason-responsive self-control, see Fischer and Ravizza 1998). Care must be taken in how it is developed. In this section of the chapter I make some suggestions for how the notion may be used and described as a norm or standard for a mental disorder or for the clinical seriousness of an incapacitating condition of mind and behavior that qualifies as a mental disorder.

Descriptions of the nature of reason, rational control and reason-responsiveness vary along various dimensions. Towards one end of one of these dimensions is a position according to which the only aspects of human psychology that are amendable to assessments of rationality, quality of reasoning or reason-responsiveness are questions about the consistency or coherence of thought or belief. At the opposite end of this dimension is a position that claims that assessments of reason-responsiveness or rational control are not restricted to thought, or to questions of coherence and consistency, but may and should be extended and applied to the full spectrum of human mental states or attitudes (including not just beliefs but also desires, moods and emotions) as well as to the overall wisdom or prudence of a person's choices and behavior. These two classes of positions may be said to belong to a *narrow logicist* or intellectualist notion of reason and to a *broadly personal* or existentially situated notion, respectively.

The broadly personal or existentially situated notion is the notion of reason and rationality that I shall be adopting. It is one that, I shall argue, is most relevant to understanding and assessing the disorder of a mental disorder. Narrow logical forms of assessment are also relevant to understanding mental disorders, but far from most germane, most applicable or exhaustive. To gain some traction on the broadly personal notion and its application to a mental disorder, it is helpful to focus in more detail on how we should think of the Intentionality, aboutness or directedness of the mental.

I refrain from crossing streets at red lights, ride the subway to work, read the The Nation, and write books for reasons. These reasons are constituted by beliefs about the circumstances that I am in, desires about the circumstances I would like to be (or remain) in, and beliefs about how to get (or remain) in those circumstances. The attitudes of belief and desire as well as other attitudes are permeated with Intentionality. Their mental or Intentional content includes thoughts of streets, lights, subways, magazines, and much else besides. The role of reason, reason-responsiveness or rationality in Intentionality and Intentional content has been much discussed in recent philosophy of mind. The following observations are meant to clarify that role.

The view that I favor, and believe we should favor, owes much (in different ways) to philosophers like John Searle, Donald Davidson, and Daniel Dennett. It claims that the content of Intentional attitudes (what a belief or desire is about) has, as it may be put, rationality (reasoning, recognition and responsiveness to reasons) as one of its essential building blocks. Nothing is an attitude possessed of Intentionality or Intentional content (direction or aboutness) apart from its being able to function as a possible reason for you, me, or someone else to think or act in one way rather than another, and also as something that can figure in rational conduct and in the normative assessment and evaluation of conduct. Thus, to have a desire to write a book is not (or not merely) to tend to write a book. It is to be disposed to write a book because the desire gives one a reason to write it. Writing is the content of the desire. It is what the desire is about.

Rationality is essential to Intentionality. The philosopher John Searle writes: "Once you have [I]ntentionality ... you already have the phenomena that internally and constitutively possess ... rationality" (Searle 2001: 23). "Rationality," he says, is a "constitutive structural feature of ... Intentionality." "When I say that it is constitutive and structural, I do not mean that we always ... think rationally, but rather that ... constraints set by rationality are built in as intrinsic features of intentional states" (Searle 2007: 15). Rationality is not "something added to ... mind" (Ibid: 9). Rather: "You cannot have ... Intentionality" without it. (Ibid: 16).

Donald Davidson (1917–2003) writes: "When thought takes thought as its subject matter, the observer can only identify what he is studying by finding it rational" (Davidson 2004: 98). The ascription of thinking, believing, intending, and other attitudes (with Intentionality or Intentional content) to another person depends on assuming the presence in the person of a broad or personal level of rationality. Ascribing beliefs, desires, and so on is a way of making sense of a person's behavior and it requires, claims Davidson, discerning a background of rationality and reason-responsiveness in the person.

None of this (in either Searle's view or Davidson's) is meant to require an ideal level of rationality or of rich and elegantly nuanced powers of reasoning in people. But it does mean (among other things) not ascribing beliefs, desires, and so on, to an object (like a stone) that is completely and utterly devoid of reason or reason-responsiveness.

Consider a No. 2 Office Depot pencil, which you are holding in your hand as you read this book. Suppose you place it down on your desk, as you finish reading this page. Suppose once on the desk, it starts to move across the surface. The surface is neither tilted nor slippery. You pick the pencil up to examine it, to learn why it moved, but when you put it back down, it begins to move across the desk again. You want to account for why it moves, but are unable to decipher a cause. You know that reason-responsiveness is a kind of cause or propensity condition (remember: propensity conditions increase the likelihood of certain events or behaviors). So, perhaps being fatigued or in search of a quick explanatory fix, you may be tempted to ascribe beliefs, desires, and other attitudes to the pencil. "Perhaps", you say to yourself in a moment of anthropomorphic weakness, "the pencil is revealing that it does not like to be put down until it has been sharpened." "It finds me a disrespectful pencil handler." If so, the pencil is doing what it is doing (sliding across the desk) for a reason (because of its attitudes and contents of those attitudes).

You resist the attribution of attitudes and reasons to the pencil, of course. Why is that? This is because you believe that although you don't now know just what the explanation is, you assume that there is a physical mechanical explanation for why the pencil moves. Perhaps a local seismologist will stumble upon discovery of a mild local earthquake whose perturbations, although otherwise unnoticed, account for why the pencil and certain other light and inanimate objects on other neighborhood desks moved. You therein appreciate (Searle-wise, Davidson-wise) that there just is no "background of rationality" in the behavior of the pencil. There is no coherent or reason-responsive pattern of beliefs, attitudes, emotions, intentions, operative in its movements, not just on the desk but elsewhere. It is a mindless, Intentional content-less artifact.

There are a number of ways of explaining why both the presence (as Searle puts matters) and attribution or ascription (as Davidson puts matters) of Intentionality or of states with Intentional content presuppose rationality – presuppose reason-responsiveness. I will be brief and confine myself to two sorts of explanation.

One has to do with the very idea of Intentional content or with what an attitude (thought, belief, etc.) is about. So, for example, if I believe that it is raining in Boston, Massachusetts, I sincerely take it to be true that it is raining in Boston, Massachusetts. What is taken to be true or believed (e.g. that it is raining in Boston) is the Intentional or mental content of the belief.

Something possessing Intentional content, or having aboutness, can be a cause of or propensity condition for events without the fact that it harbors aboutness being germane to its causal powers. The soprano's song may be about unrequited love, but the explanation for how she shattered a glass on stage during a performance may be offered just in terms of the high note that she hit. Acoustic mechanisms and the molecular structure of the glass account for the shattering. But mental or Intentional content is germane to the *reasons* had for behavior and enters into the causation of behavior performed for a reason. I take the subway rather than walk to work insofar as I believe that the subway is less time consuming and more convenient. I read *The Nation* rather than *Commentary* or *The National Review*, because I favor its editorial politics over those of the other two magazines. Differences in content also have different behavioral effects. I buy the one magazine rather than others, take the Red Line rather than walk along Peachtree Street, because I guide and control my behavior in terms of attitudes possessed of one set of contents rather than some other set. Attitudes acquire their causal responsibility or power over behavior as a consequence of their Intentional contents.

Contents of beliefs and other attitudes require a medium in which to mean just what they do mean. An Intentional content identity or individuation medium, as it may be called. The medium consists of concepts.

What is a concept? One of the most fascinating experiments in the literature on concepts was conducted in the 1960s with pigeons. It deployed what is known as a discrimination learning paradigm to demonstrate that pigeons (yes, that's right pigeons) are able distinguish or discriminate between pictures that have human beings in them and pictures that do not (Herrnstein and Loveland 1964). The images varied so widely from picture to picture (people of different ages, gender, and dress, pictured in many different settings and positions), that the experimenters claimed that pigeons have a concept of human being. How so? On some accounts having a concept requires that a person or subject has the ability to use so-called general terms correctly. General terms are linguistic terms that classify types, kinds or categories of things (like human beings, apples, numbers and oranges). Nothing like this requirement was met by the language-less pigeons, of course. But on other more generous or ecumenical accounts having a concept means being able to make relevant discriminations and to re-identify individual things (or one and the same type of thing) on separate occasions or instances. Language or linguistic symbol systems may help in some of these tasks or even be required for some concepts (such as theoretical concepts in physics, like mass and energy), but mere concept possession itself is not contingent on linguistic competence. As perceptual discriminators of figures in photos the pigeons shined. As quantum mechanists or historians of Russian history they could not even get off the ground.

Pigeons aside, how is that human beings are able to possess beliefs about things or states of affairs which are very far away in time or space (like Abraham Lincoln's assassination, planets) or things that fail to exist (like Santa Claus, unicorns) as well as things close at hand or that do currently exist (like a bachelor who lives next door, a pepper shaker on the dining room table)? The simple and intuitive idea is that belief (or other Intentional attitude) contents are concepts or conceptual contents. They are *conceptual* Intentional contents. I can believe that Lincoln was assassinated, because I have concepts of Lincoln as well as of assassination. (I can discriminate between the two – Lincoln and assassinations.) I can believe that the bachelor who is living next door is dating my cousin, because I have concepts of bachelor, living next door, dating, and cousin. (I can distinguish between all four.) Inside a conceptual medium all kinds of other beliefs or 'contented' attitudes are possible as well. If I believe that a bachelor is dating my cousin, I can also believe that my cousin is dating a bachelor. If I can believe that President Lincoln was assassinated, and that Mars is a planet, I can believe that Lincoln was assassinated but not on Mars.

The conceptual media of contents of attitudes help to distinguish or individuate one Intentional content or attitude from another of the same type. Suppose that Lois Lane believes that she kissed Clark Kent. Clark Kent is Superman. Does this mean that she also believes that she kissed Superman? No, not if she fails to apply the concept of Superman to Clark. Intentional content is distinctive or differential in its conceptual character. (The distinctiveness or individuality of concepts is to be expected, since contents/concepts are discriminatory. Remember the pigeons.) So, there is a difference between, for example, Lois believing that she kissed Clark and believing that she kissed Superman (even though Clark is Superman) or my believing that I am attending a parent/teacher association meeting and my believing that I am attending a meeting in a local high school auditorium (even though the meeting is in an auditorium). She or I may believe the one proposition, which harbors one sort of conceptual content, without believing the other (harboring a different content).

Conceptual media harbor or make possible a property of intimate connectivity or rational relevance of one concept to another. Possession of conceptual content by a belief or attitude presupposes the presence of other relevant concepts and germane beliefs in a person's possession or range of attitudinal competence. In believing that it is raining, I also believe things like rain falls from the sky, is wet, and makes the ground slippery. In believing that a runner stole second base in a baseball game, I also believe such things as that a baseball game is being played, the runner is in scoring position, and he touched the base before a fielder could tag him out with a ball. Stripped of such connections and the concepts at work in them (e.g. of sky, wetness, running, fielder, etc.), the conceptual contents at work in attitudes lose their distinctive identity and their ability to figure as reasons for thought and behavior.

Pigeons, I assume, can learn to identify human beings in photographs. Other than being of people, the photos (mentioned above) did not have much else in common. But can pigeons also believe that the object or place in which a person is pictured is a car or garden? Do they have concepts of car and of garden? (Or: of a runner stealing second base? Or: of rain falling from the sky? Or even, if the final investigatory truth be told, of personhood itself?) Small children may not be as good as pigeons in recognizing persons in photographs, but with conceptual development or maturity in their powers of reason and reasoning, they acquire (as pigeons, I assume, do not) concepts of cars and gardens, games and rain. They may come to expect to ride in cars or to walk in gardens. They may also come to harbor desires about bases or about tulips and roses. What changes in children as they mature conceptually, but not in pigeons, is that their powers of discrimination and re-identification dramatically expand to include new concepts (or forms of discrimination) and secure novel links between concepts or discriminatory powers they already possessed. Concepts cluster or fold into intimate conceptual networks. A concept that, as it metaphorically may be put, began its career as a solo monk in a cell, may forge semantically gregarious relationships with various conceptual neighbors or apposite kin. It may take on a holistic or global character and become positioned in a network or neighborhood of surrounding concepts. A person's attitudes (beliefs, desires, and so on) follow suit. One day I could not believe that a runner stole a base. I knew nothing of baseball. I had no concepts for it; no range of relevant discriminatory experiences. Now I have a picture on my office wall of Jackie Robinson stealing home plate in May of 1952.

Alas, concepts or discriminations can be torn from their neighborhood medium and stripped of their individuating connections with other concepts. Suppose when I say "President Lincoln was assassinated", I have grown senile and now suffer from a serious neurological disorder evidenced by unusual memory loss (Stich 1983: 55–56). So if, for example, you ask me whether Lincoln is dead, I reply that I do not know. If asked whether the Vice President took office after the assassination, I ask "Vice President? What's a vice president?" In brief, suppose I possess no reasonable or rational grasp of the notions or concepts of either assassination or presidency (or related notions), although I apparently claim that Lincoln was assassinated. How should we understand this? What is going on in me? What does my noise making (or thinking?) 'President Lincoln was assassinated' mean to me? Do I, can I, really believe that Lincoln was assassinated in so conceptually barren a medium of connectivity? Is there an attitude of my mind that contains the Intentional conceptual content *Lincoln was assassinated*?

Intuitively, it seems that I can mean or think no such thing. A background of rationality – of network of conceptual coherence, a neighborhood of some semantically apposite sort – is presupposed by competence with notions of assassination and presidency. Assuming that this relevant background is absent in me, I do not and really cannot believe that Lincoln was assassinated. I may make concept-like sounds, but they are content-less speech acts.

Again: As Searle puts it, there is no Intentionality without rationality. Or as I like to put it in light of my discussion above of concepts as contents, there is no Intentional content on the part of a believer or agent without reasonable connections between contents (or conceptual contents). When there is no evidence of "rational connectivity" in such cases (think of the example of assassination), there is no evidence of (identifiable or present) Intentional content. No content. No Intentionality. So Searle is right: no Intentionality without rationality.

There are other and related ways of explaining why Intentionality presupposes rationality. I said I would mention two. Here is the second.

Thinking of Intentional attitudes (beliefs, desires, and so on) as presupposing the rationality and reason-responsiveness of persons makes it clear that we persons often are purposive or goal directed in our behavior. How we act or behave often depends upon our purposes or reasons for acting. So, for example, suppose I am crossing a busy street, with eyes wide open, and a truck is barreling down towards me. I spot it. Suppose I scurry away from its path. Why do I do so? Here is an explanation: Because I believe that if the truck hits me I will get hurt or killed. I desire not to be hurt or killed. Being rational, I move away from its path. I have good reason to move, given my premises.

Much of human purposive behavior is, as Daniel Dennett puts it, "simply not interpretable except as being in the rational service of some beliefs and desires or other" (Dennett 2009: 348). So, one role or function (a definitive or constitutive function) of Intentional states and attitudes is their serving as a *basis for reason-responsive* or purposive or goal directed behavior. Absent seeing the truck or desiring not to get hurt, I would not have scurried. I would have had no reason to move. There would have been no purpose to scurrying. To understand my scurrying, an observer only needs to recognize the 'logic' that governs my response. I don't want to get hurt.

As Searle may put it, rationality is not something added to beliefs and desires (or Intentional attitudes). It is central to their role in helping to govern and control purposive or reason-responsive behavior.

These explanations of the connectivity between Intentionality and rationality are brief. They raise questions I cannot pursue here. But they at least give, I trust, the flavor of warrant for the position that Searle and numerous other theorists (including, in different ways, Davidson and Dennett) favor. Wherever there is Intentionality, there is rationality.

Of course, the claim that wherever there is Intentionality, there also is rationality, this claim, is not without critics or skeptics. It is sometimes charged that the idea or thesis that Intentional states or attitudes are in their nature or character rational (hereafter the *Rationality Intentionality Thesis* or 'RIT' for short) is defeated by counterexamples. For example, it is said, I may sincerely deny some proposition that I report believing to be true. I may deny that I have a brother in Cleveland, all the while saying that I believe my brother lives in Cleveland. So, the charge goes, it is false that rationality norms are built into the presence, assumption, or concept of Intentionality (see Bortolotti 2004).

If the type of counterexample sketched above is taken as intended, our ability to recognize Intentionality in behavior is not contingent on appreciating rationality in the same behavior.

Someone can both believe that something is the case and disbelieve that very same thing. This would be the height (or depth) of irrationality and incoherence.

There are at least two difficulties with purported counter-examples like the one mentioned above to RIT, however. One is whether real persons are like those described in alleged counter-examples and really do or can assert, think or believe what a counter-example says that they do. Do I *really* understand what it means to sincerely deny that I have a brother in Cleveland, if I say also that I believe that I have a brother in Cleveland? Am I prepared to be so flatly or even flamboyantly inconsistent? If so, this looks like a real problem for the RIT view that rationality is constitutive of believing and other attitudes with Intentional content. But isn't it better or wiser to question my understanding of the meaning of my denial (or the sincerity of my purported belief report) rather than to assume that I am being flatly inconsistent and logically irrational? Whatever the source of my utterances, it is not (Searle or Davidson may argue) the possession of explicitly inconsistent attitudes or speech act intentions. Perhaps I am intending to be ironic or humorous or not to be taken literally for some reason. Or perhaps I am ambiguously using the word 'Cleveland' to designate two different locales, one the city in Ohio, the other the small town in Alabama. Perhaps I am denying that I have a brother in Alabama, but affirming his existence in Ohio.

Another (and connected) difficulty with criticizing RIT is that RIT, to some extent, is an elliptical target. A fan of RIT needs not to deny the occurrence of 'irrational' behavior on the part of a person. All of us can be foolish or imprudent. RIT does not assume that we are all *perfectly* rational or responsive to reason (whatever perfection means). And perhaps we can harbor contradictions or inconsistencies of some sorts of which we are not explicitly aware.

The following may be a relevant example. We often count as reasons for a person's behavior motives or emotional dispositions that he fails to consciously appreciate. Your colleague's reason for voting against your promotion may be that he envies you, although he may not recognize this as such; and his envy may be incompatible with other traits that he has, such as his generosity or appreciation of merit. In such a case, the best RIT course of interpretation may be to concede that reasons or attitudes may not be ideally coherent one with another or free of potential implicit contradiction, but we can accommodate them in our person (and in the RIT thesis) by allowing that they would not be tolerated by a rational person if brought out in the conscious open and reasoned about. Learn if alleged contradictions are or would be pruned when known and inspected. RIT predicts that they would be.

Another form of accommodation of at least some departures from perfect rationality is to note that sometimes attitudes do not function as genuine attitudes. A purported belief may not behave like a belief (at least prototypically speaking). Just as an artifact may not behave as designed, but function in an atypical or un-designed manner, so a belief or desire may not function as a belief or desire, although it may still help to control behavior in some other and albeit a-rational or mechanical way.

A number of philosophers use references to various mental disorders to argue that Searle/Davidson RIT picture must be wrong. Some mental disorders, it is claimed, demonstrate that the possession of attitudes (with Intentional contents) requires no rationality or reason-responsiveness on the part of a person possessed of a relevant disorder or within the bounds of a particular relevant mental illness (for discussion see Bortolotti 2005; Campbell 2009;

Gerrans 2004). A starkly deluded person, for example, may hold inconsistent or incoherent beliefs or attitudes. Just observe the so-called 'word salad' of a victim of (or person diagnosed with) schizophrenia (Fulford et al. 2006: 164): "I am sure we can get from planet to planet by mesmeric Father Christmas's children, and, if you like, the giant." "I am like 'em." "I'm a trichlorinetic pilot." Rational intelligibility seems utterly absent in such remarks. But I am loath to flat-out agree with any anti-RIT interpretation of a mental disorder. For me, as long as a disorder is a *mental* disorder, then it carries an autograph or stamp of Intentionality (of mentality) on its more or less proximate propensity conditions and symptom displays (still more on this topic later in the chapter and book). Independently coincident with this conviction on my part, plausible efforts have been made to defend RIT or theses like RIT against mental disorder-tethered counter-examples (see Reimer 2011). In a word salad case, for example, we may claim either that such patients are not as unintelligible or irrational in their speech as they may at first appear, although we ourselves just cannot figure out what is going on inside their heads, or that such speech is, on occasion, what Berrios calls "empty speech acts" or random Intentional-content-less fragments of non-rational nonsense (Berrios 1991: 12). If content-empty, they are not expressions of beliefs at all; hence not expressions of flatly irrational beliefs and no counter-example to RIT. They are faux attitudes.

If RIT is correct, broadly speaking, a description of the Intentional states and attitudes as content infused states of a person in no way resembles a list of brute causal connections, correlations or mere 'mechanical' associations between states and behavior. This is because in order for states to be genuine beliefs, honest-to-goodness desires, and so on, and to act as such and not as non-attitudes, they must conform to standards or norms of rationality and reason-responsiveness.

Suppose you learn that your best friend has just died in Boston. You grieve because you love him deeply and know you will never see him again. You feel his death as a profound loss. The world is cold and empty without him. You don't feel his death as if you have just won a lottery. You don't delight in the news. That would be bizarre, senseless. It would mean that your states or attitudes are not connected according to norms of coherent reason-responsiveness. Loss of a loved one ought to spell grief, not frivolity. If you do feel delight, this may mean that your mind somehow is being pushed or pulled into senseless or unreasonable reactions. How can you possibly be pleased as punch that he is dead? That's not how the loss of a loved one *ought* to be received if they are loved but believed lost forever.

If, however, reason can sometimes fall short of the ideal and still behave like reason, what is an ideal rational or reasonable person like? The *ideal* rational or reasonable person, in the RIT sense, is not merely devoid of inexplicit illogical, incoherent, or inconsistent attitudes, but possesses a definite positive description of their person and goals in life (see Feinberg 1989: 107). An ideal rational agent chooses after deliberation, avoids acting on unreflective impulses, and maintains a level of prudence, self-regard and self-responsibility that balances present or current preferences against next week's and next year's, those of mid-life and possible old age. He or she is a person who takes pains to manage preferences or goals and to connect themselves with the world as well as with other people in important and satisfying ways, so as to try to achieve a measure of satisfaction or fulfillment over the course of a life (of which more in the next chapter). After all, we live in relation with others and so to a significant extent, a person's rationality or reason-responsiveness should be evaluated, in part, in terms of our relationships with other persons and the world. Recognizing this is important for the theory of mental disorder, for at the level at which judgments of the presence of a mental disorder are made, a person is not positioned just in relationship to himself, his or her powers of reason are not characterized just in terms of internal or logic textbook type features, but in terms also of what is required in order for them (as William Bechtel aptly puts it) "to operate as a situated organism" (Bechtel 2008: 258). That is, to deal with the world in reason-responsive ways and to lead a purposive and purposeful life in social contexts and a variety of environmental circumstances.

I assume that RIT is true. As noted, I cannot examine all that needs to be examined to systematically defend this assumption. But I am pledging allegiance to the general spirit of the view and anxious to show how the view helps to evaluate the significance or clinical severity of impairments and harmful incapacities that are distinctive of a mental disorder. I must mention again, though, that Intentional states do not always function as states with Intentionality, just as hammers, keys or other artifacts do not always function as hammers or keys.

Consider the following three explanations of a behavior:

1. I phoned my friend's wife because I wished to offer her my sympathies.
2. I got a bad backache because I wanted to see my deceased friend again.
3. I got a bad backache because I slept on a mattress with hard lumps and broken coils.

The first two explanations look quite similar in that they each make reference to an Intentional state, namely a wishing or wanting, in explanation of behavior. Number 3 makes no such reference. Its form is simply *C caused E* (i.e. sleeping on hard lumps and broken coils caused a backache). But 2 actually is as much like 3 as it is like 1, although in a different sort of way, for 2 also is of the form of C caused E (i.e. wanting to see my deceased friend caused a bad backache). In that sense (namely, the C-caused-E sense, the mechanical cause/effect sense), my state of wanting to see my deceased friend acted like broken mattress coils. Even though the state in question was a wanting (an Intentional state and not a sleeping on coils), it did not function as an Intentional state. It was not a reason for action. It functioned somehow just like the coils. Purely mechanically or brute causally. My desire to see my friend did not make sense of, rationalize or warrant my getting a backache, although it somehow was responsible for the ache. (How it may operate fully mechanically I do not surmise. Perhaps the answer is through its neurochemical or physical-level realization base, associatively and a-rationally.) By contrast, the Intentional state referred to in 1, namely of wanting to express sympathy, did perform like an Intentional state. It made sense of or provided a rationale or reason for my phoning my friend's wife. Phoning her stemmed from wanting to express sympathy. Phoning her was sensible or warranted – reasonable. Being rational, I made the call. It was part of my trying to connect with various other people in a purposive and satisfying way.

The general lesson here? Intentional states, once an agent is capable of them and once they possess their identity or distinctiveness through rational and conceptual connectivity with other attitudes and behavior, may not always function like Intentional states. (They do not always express their identity or functionality as endowed with Intentional conceptual content.) So, reference to them does not always help us to make sense of a person's behavior. Making sense of behavior requires that we discern some rationale or measure of reason in behaviour, namely a premise or premises from which the behavior follows. But there can be brute causal connections between Intentional states and behavior without any rational connection being in place. When Intentional states or attitudes actually do function or function properly as Intentional states, as states connected in rational patterns, when, that is, they perform as beliefs and desires and not like coils or elements in brute causal relations, they therein measure up to norms or standards of rationality. That's RIT's point. To be Intentional, to possess aboutness, directionality, or Intentionality, and for an Intentional state to guide, direct, or control purposive behavior in terms of its conceptual content, it must measure up to norms of reason.

Philosophers who are sympathetic to physicalism about mentality often worry about the physical makeup or constitution of Intentional states and attitudes and of the nature of the rational and inferential connections among them. How can neurochemical/neurobiological states or conditions help to existentially base Intentional states and attitudes and also respect or comport with the reasoning powers of persons? We are not as rational agents like clay statues, which come into being when a lump of clay is molded in a certain way, and then perish, outlived by the lump, when the statue is squashed. Intentionality is no mere matter of the shape of neural cells or particles. It's a matter of Intentional content, of aboutness or directionality, a radically different feature from the statue-likeness of a lump of clay. Much of the energy and intellectual efforts of such fields as cognitive neuroscience, sub-personal information processing psychology, so-called teleosemantic theories of conceptual content and other brain and behavior research programs are devoted to figuring out how the material mechanisms of the brain (together with activities outside the skull and skin and in the environment) enable or generate Intentionality, and permit persons to be rational and reasoning creatures. I alluded to such a worry in our earlier discussion in Chapter 4, of Intentional content efficacy and of Fred Drestke's example of a soprano and her aria.

But my interest here in this book is not in deciding how Intentionality or rationality comes into being through neural processing or activity (and whatever else is involved, such as the interactive role of a surrounding environment and culture). It is not even in demanding that there be a physically kosher account someplace in Metaphysical Heaven (that avoids anti-realism about mental disorder and dualism about mind/body) of the neural base of Intentional attitudes. My interest here is in deciding whether we can and should deploy a thesis like RIT in classifying some conditions or disturbances as mental disorders and in understanding when an incapacitation or impairment counts as clinically serious enough to qualify as a mental disorder. So, my question now is: Does a disorder's manner or mode of reason-unresponsiveness or unreasonableness help to serve as a standard for a mental disorder? My answer is yes. It does help.

Depending upon how an incapacity is understood, if it is an incapacity in reason-responsiveness and harmful to a person, then such a fact helps to constitute a mental disorder. The subject of a mental disorder is disposed to think, feel, or act in unreasonable and deleterious ways, not because they are fatigued, foolish, or under severe time constraints, or out of ignorance or ill-humor, but because of impairments or deficits in rational or reason-responsive functioning of those capacities that are associated with a mental disorder. Those of us who are more reasonable may govern our own affairs, feel as we should when a beloved friend dies, and refrain from impulses to act in self-injurious ways. But a subject of agoraphobia, like Arthur, may be unable to enter a mall to buy a blouse or to be present, as he should, at a parent/teacher association meeting. He may tell you that he would rather die than have a recurrence of his intense anxiety. From a reason-responsive point of view the disorder keeps him from leading a satisfying life and endangers him.

Or: A drug addict may consume a drug, and decide to take the drug at self recognized grievous danger to bodily health, and we may ask "how could anyone do that?" or were they "out of their mind" or do they possess "some sort of irrational death wish". We may be mystified by their pattern of self-destructive consumption. If the person knows that the behavior harms them, why engage in it? It just does not seem to make sense. The behavior appears to be utterly uncalled for.

Now a complexity or qualification arises. A distinction needs to be made when we look closer at the unreasonableness associated with a mental disorder. Interestingly, the above general sentiment about mental disorder, namely that the domain of disorder is the domain of sense-lessness or unreason, is a notion that Karl Jaspers endorsed (see Fulford, Thornton, and Graham 2006: 170; Bentall 2004: 28). Jaspers offered the standard specifically to apply to the presence of a *severe* mental disorder or psychosis (as in stark forms of schizophrenia), which he described as un-understandable or as intelligible only in non-mentalistic and neuromechanical coil-like terms and not in terms of an individual's beliefs and desires.

I don't agree with Jaspers about the *utter* lack of reason or the complete and engulfing pre-sence of a-rationality in mental disorders (even truly severe ones). In mental disorder, there is causation both without (rational) Intentionality (mere coils) and with (rational) Intentionality (responsive reasons). Interactive co-signatories. Unreason and reason. Even in a severe mental disorder, as long as a disorder is something *mental*, it is not utterly senseless. In it reason is truncated, compromised or impaired, but not obliterated. Incapacitated but not totally incapacitated. Senselessness is present, to some hefty measure, but not exhaustively or unabashedly promiscuously so.

So I like to distinguish between two possible ways (only one of which is the right way) in which to understand the unreason of a mental disorder, which I call the *total* and the *partial* presence of unreason. In neurological disorders reason is totally or utterly absent or un-present (more precisely, along relevant dimensions of behavior). Consider, for example, the class of such disorders known as neurologically degenerative diseases or diseases that are associated with degenerative atrophy of the brain (perhaps as a result of pathology of the nerve cells, Andreasen's literal "cells gone bad"). Numerous such disorders produce a diffuse loss of brain function across the cortex and within multiple subcortical structures. Multiple sclerosis. Pick's disease. Progressive epilepsy. In a mental disorder, by contrast, rational and a-rational forces operate and unfold in characteristically interactive and dynamic ways. If we understand a disorder by reference to such forces, we can and must admit to an ongoing role for reason-responsiveness or rationality in both the proximate onset of a disorder and the expression of its symptoms.

To illustrate: Let's return to Arthur. This time we will deploy the notion of the rational Inten-tional mind that we have been outlining as RIT. On the normative conception of the mental that I am sketching and endorsing, Arthur's impairment in public behavior, his disability, counts as clinically important (as the sort involved in a mental disorder) not just because it robs him of various social freedoms and is a source of conscious distress or harm, but because it makes his behavior, in effect, something quite impossible for him to control in a reason-responsive way, absent abnormal incentives or a dramatic change of circumstances. Why should he be panicking? For him to avoid parent/teacher association meetings as well as other public occasions is inconsistent with his duties as a teacher and discordant with his desire to be a successful professional educator. Yet he cannot help it. No matter how hard he tries. No matter the efforts of others to persuade him.

It may be wondered why our explanatory understanding of a mental disorder requires reference to a-rational neural activity at all if the brain is undamaged. Why not just deploy the language of Intentionality in a case like Arthur's, together perhaps with discussion of his temperament, judgmental biases, biography or learning history – but nary a word about brain activity? Refer only to powers of reason, situated or contextualized to the biographic details of the person. Call such a rejection of the need to deploy brain science in the explanation or understanding of a mental disorder an *anti-neural* concept of disorder.

If anti-neuralism is to tell us that the subject's mental capacities are unimpaired (in part) by a-rational mechanical forces, this seems to imply that mental disorders, so to speak, are not uncontrollable or involuntary. They truly are not gummed up. The 'mental' of such a condition (the mental pictured as essentially rational) would seem to rule out the disorder of it, although it may permit numerous other liabilities, such as wishful thinking, prejudices, and so on. This would make something highly puzzling about a case like Arthur's. We would lack a full under-standing of just why he not merely fails to favorably respond but cannot favorably respond to his reasons for mixing among crowds. His responses are not under appositely rational control. Any reference to the overall behavioral gumming up or impairment that his autonomic nervous system helps to contribute to his personal condition (e.g. to his fight/flight response) in interaction with his psychology would be unwisely neglected by the explanatory story.

By this I don't mean to imply that mechanical forces are solely responsible for the onset or presence of a mental disorder. Down that road lie the fault lines of a brain disorder. I also don't mean to imply that there is a malfunction or incapacitation of the brain (like Arthur's) in a mental disorder (again, that spells brain disorder). Although a mental disorder must always reflect the inherent limitations of the brain in some sense, the standards for normatively appropriate mental or psychological behavior are not (and should not) be those for the natural design specifications or adaptational fitness functions of the brain. Among other things, too much sheer evolutionary speculation is required to identify such specifications.

However, a concept of mental disorder that insisted upon *neglecting* the brain may not just be metaphysically unwise, but explanatorily unhelpful. So, according to the view of RIT that I am promoting or in the process of promoting here, there are irruptions of brute a-rationality/neural processes into the rational operation of this or that faculty or competence and that negatively affect otherwise less harmful behavior of a person. But these irruptions still leave operative and complementary elbow room for reason in the onset and character of a disorder as well.

An analogy may help with this idea.

Suppose you are picnicking with some family and friends on a beach. You take a nap. While you are napping the tide comes in and irrupts into the space of the picnic. You feel the wetness of the water, awake startled, gather your blankets and food and then retreat to higher ground. The picnic has been disrupted. It's not the same event anymore. It's not what you wanted in a picnic. Certain of its purposes have been blunted. Everyone is disappointed. But the picnic has not totally been wiped out or destroyed. Some corn on the cob and salad remains to be eaten, though the blanket is wet in spots and some family members, especially the cousins from Newark, now want to go home. Call this an analogue of the *disruptive irruptive way of the neural in a mental disorder*. It helps to produce disorder. It contributes gum. It impairs or helps to incapacitate, but does not obliterate. A picnic of sorts (some measure of reason) remains.

Suppose the very next week you and the others picnic on the same beach again. Again you take a nap. While you are napping the ocean floor is damaged by a huge meteorite. The reverberations cause a tsunami. At the moment it is miles out to sea. You awake. You hear something both sonorous and sinister. A thunderous ocean mass is approaching in the middle distance. You spot nothing yet. But sense it. Leaving all manner and matter of the picnic behind, you and your family hurriedly leave the beach. You run to your motel. Once in the lobby you are directed to the top floor. This does not merely compromise or truncate your picnic, but it enters into the space of the picnic in a destructive way. The beach is cleared. Call this analogue the *destructive irruptive way of the neural in a neurological disorder* (or a case of brain damage). A person sees; but then his striate cortex is severely damaged; he is rendered blind. A person speaks; but then cysts form on her third ventricle; and she speaks no more. She is rendered mute.

This may sound like a neat distinction. Simply drop the thought that all irruptions of neural mechanisms into the exercise of a person's reason, broadly understood, are the same in impact and purport. Simply say that some irruptions of the neural compose neural disorders (the rational destruction ones), some not (the rational function truncating or partially incapacitating ones, the mental disorder ones). But if this helps to distinguish between the role of the neural in a neurological disorder and the role of the neural in a mental disorder, it creates its own problems, of course. Alas, though, no account of either sort of disorder is problem-free. You pick your theory; you accept your problems.

LOGIC OF ITS OWN

Let's re-inspect the normative failure of Arthur's panic attacks. Is his behavior *utterly* mindless, senseless? If that particular conclusion is hard to swallow, namely of Arthur's complete sense-lessness, the following may be the explanation. Isn't the mind *sometimes* infused with at least a sliver or shadow of reason-responsiveness or rationality even when the person appears to be behaving in a rather reason-unresponsive fashion or to be suffering from a mental dis-order? Certainly not every behavioral performance in which a mind is at work has to display robust or perfect rational competence or coherence. Sometimes a good reason for someone's behavior is buried in noise, distraction, or gummed up by the unhelpful interactive influence of some a-rational if not impaired brute causal neurological mechanism.

Jonathan Lear refers to the proclivity or vulnerability of the human mind to lapse into partial but not complete unreason as a tendency to exhibit a "strange logic of its own", a "weird intelligibility" or "cunning of unreason" (Lear 1998: 84). The vulnerability in question, he says, does not turn mental disorder into order, "but it does bequeath to [a mental disorder] its own intelligibility" (84). When *robust* reason is absent, some measure of rationality may still, albeit perhaps in a hidden and complex guise, exhibit its presence, and therein reason is not totally missing in behavior. So, how may it be present?

Panic attacks, paranoia, addiction, grandiose delusional disorder, each of these and other mental disorders, possess their own partial rationales. Each contains its own mix of reason-responsiveness and unreason. Just how robust the 'logic' or 'reason' is in each case depends upon how close a disorder is to being exemplary of mental disorder and less like a neurological disorder. The more exemplary, then the more prominent is its presence. In non-mental neurological disorders like (I assume) Alzheimer's, by contrast, reason-responsiveness and associated rational self-control do not figure at all in the immediate propensity conditions or proximate sources of a disorder. There is no doubt that states of Intentionality or aboutness play a role in the progression of some of Alzheimer's symptoms (once the disorder itself is present). Victims may suffer from thoughts of theft and paranoia, which, in the context of the amnesia and confusion associated with the condition, may be misinterpretations of mislaying or misplacing objects (forgetting where they have been placed). Additionally, sadness and depression often are present in individuals with Alzheimer's, perhaps reflecting changes in a victim's perception of disturbed social relationships and diminished personal autonomy. A kind of learned helplessness or hopelessness may set in or take over. Sad but true.

But I do not count (and neither does Kleinman or Bentall) Alzheimer's as a mental disorder. This is because, much like, say, Down's, reference to Intentional states or attitudes just does not (seem to) figure in the best explanation of its origin, source or proximate developmental propensity. The disease (and, yes, it may also be classified as a disease and not just neural impairment) appears due to plagues and neurofibrillary tangles that form in the hippocampus and spread throughout the cerebral cortex, in specific areas or systems of the brain that are associated with both dementia and amnesia (Andreasen 2001: 263–65; Lovestone 2000: 392). It's a neurological disorder. The mental plays various subsequent or post-onset roles in Alzheimer's (once the pleats of its symptoms start to spread apart and influence each other) and is responsible, quite directly, as just noted, for some of its symptoms, emotional disorientation or content. But no form of genuine Intentionality plays a role in the proximate onset of the condition itself. Brute neurological or mechanical forces are the source of its degenerative progression and memory impairment. Or so I (and current neuroscience does) assume.

In exemplary mental disorders Intentionality or attitudes with Intentional content constitute proper aspects of the conditions of onset or origin of a disorder. Not Intentionality in the full flower of unfettered rationality and apposite connectedness with the world, but with, to use Lear's apt expression, a strange logic or rationality of its own. Rationality truncated by interaction or dynamic interplay with brute a-rational mechanisms, but evident on careful inspection.

Arthur's behavior? Autonomic nervous system activity in Arthur's case, for illustrative purposes I assume, helps to contribute a misplaced rationale but a rationale no less to his anxiety. The case is hypothetical and illustrative, but here is a representative kind of explanatory story that I have in mind for mental disorders in general.

Suppose that the regulation of the autonomic nervous system occurs (in part) in the hypothalamus, a small region of the brain just below the thalamus. Suppose also that there are reverberating electrical circuits in the hypothalamus that help to modulate emotional responses associated with fear and anxiety. Suppose that in Arthur's case fear and anxiety have become conditioned to locations, smells, discordant noises or other cues associated with crowds of unfamiliar people (in malls, churches, and so on) and these are not dampened down by the regulative mechanisms of his hypothalamic circuitry. For some reason, perhaps going back to the various reinforcement schedules of his past, he experiences the arousal of his autonomic nervous system as an impending heart-attack, and cannot otherwise explain to himself just why he wishes to avoid crowds. It appears so foolish and misshapen of him to avoid them. He knows he cannot properly function in this way. Blips of autonomic nervousness, which another person may feel in crowds, but dismiss as completely harmless, Arthur reads as signaling the need to consult a cardiologist. It is not utterly unreasonable of him to believe this, however, given his reaction to crowds and the significance of that reaction to him. A kind of logic is there; a rationale or reason-responsiveness of sorts is present. A premise for avoiding malls. But so, too, is a disorder. Assuming that his hypothalamus is not damaged, dysfunctional or impaired (and there is no particular reason to think that; the circuits presumably were not tuned to permit shopping with strangers), his condition then is a mental disorder and not a neurological disorder. Having his particular form of anxiety (while not utterly devoid of a rationale) is unreasonable for him – in the sense that it is not responsive to his best interests or appraisal of his duties. It also is harmful and freedom depriving. He can't function socially and may lose his job. But he cannot help it. It reflects an incapacity or impairment.

Or more exactly: Arthur cannot control his unwelcome behavior at least without assistance. Hannah Pickard, a philosopher and professional clinician, who works with people who are diagnosed with Personality Disorders, points out that effective clinical treatment for mental disorders often presupposes that patients can "exercise ... at least a degree of control over [their] behavior" if given proper assistance (Pickard 2011: 215). All sorts of therapies and therapeutic treatment communities are based on the premise that service users ultimately are capable of rational self-control (213).

Barbara Grizutti Harrison, a recipient of the O. Henry Prize for short fiction, was a victim of panic disorder. "A panic attack has the force of an oncoming train," she writes. It contains a sense of panic "grotesquely heightened" (Harrison 1998: 3–7). That's Arthur's train, too. But it is a train that can get back on its tracks.

Often whatever activities take place within the human nervous system, autonomic or otherwise (peripheral, central), both enable and preserve the rationality of behavior. Our nervous system both sponsors and respects reason's sense and sensibility. Rationality sustenance existentially based in brain activity helps to make it possible for us to refer to Intentional states, their contents, and to the rationality inherent in them in the explanation of goal directed and deliberate behavior. It enables us to refer to sources of behavior as *reason-responsive*. Such references and explanations, as Dennett notes, do not require that we know "of the ... mechanisms that accomplish" the behavior (Dennett 2009: 349). Sometimes, however, neural mechanisms are no respecter or robust sustainer of reason and reasoning. Sometimes the sheer, raw shifting power of their seismic neurochemical tides or reverberating circuits is inconsistent with maintaining a robust normative character to our beliefs, desires and to links between them and our emotional responses and behavior. When this failure of rationality maintenance occurs (and it occurs along different dimensions and to different degrees) I like (as noted) to refer to such occurrences as 'irruptions' of brute a-rational mechanisms into the domain of the mental or

Intentional or the space of reasons. Arthur prepares for flight with an incapacitated power of reason that otherwise is geared to be more prudent or rationally responsive to real threats. Given, however, that Arthur's bodily activity has gone into a consciously detectable mode (his heart palpitates, he sweats, and so on) and is undaunted by hypothalamic circuitry, and that he misreads his body's preparedness for fight or flight as an impending heart attack, he panics.

Premised on his fear, it's reasonable for Arthur to be anxious in public circumstances that are associated for him with impending danger. There is a logic or rationale there, although, from a more properly informed or robustly rational perspective, given his woeful ignorance of the nature of his autonomic nervous system and of the absence of real threat, Arthur's behavior possesses only a truncated logic. He is gummed up by a mechanical process and by his mis-reading of the significance of that process. Crowded elevators and busy malls are not truly risky. No need to avoid them. It's unwise or unreasonable to do so.

In Arthur's case, as I have sketched it, the dynamic intersection of two sorts of forces lies behind his behavior, one requiring reference to his hippocampus and autonomic nervous system activity and the other to his rationalizing reasons, together lending a sort of strange intelligibility or logic to his retreat from malls. Jonathan Lear notes: "A mind is part of a living organism over which the mind has incomplete [rational] control" (Lear 1998: 85). Indeed. In Arthur references to thalamic and autonomic nervous system activity and his own self-inter-pretation combine to explain his uncontrolled proclivity to panic attacks. The intersection of these two sorts of forces or sources disables or incapacitates him.

Do only *consciously* interpreted (by the agent) mechanisms figure in mental disorders? That is one aspect of Arthur's story from which we should not generalize. Surely some disorders are like that, but many are not. Conscious interpretation is not an invariant requirement of the intersection of the two forces. Non-conscious mechanisms may get a grip on the proximity conditions of a disorder without a person knowing anything whatsoever about them. Consider a substance abusing addict. Each substance that contributes to substance-dependent addictive behavior, for instance, may work differently in the brain without ever showing up at a conscious level or its user knowing anything about brain chemistry. Sorted out in different ways for differ-ent molecules, we may be able to appreciate the distinct reinforcing effects and withdrawal consequences of Substance A (e.g. alcohol) as opposed to Substance B (e.g. cocaine) and help to appreciate why patterns of temporary abstinence may differ in each case. An addict may have utterly no idea of what is going on at that neurochemical or somatic level.

Psychologist Andy Young says that in understanding certain disorders "we need a way of bringing together neurological and psychological factors" (Young 2000: 58). We should not agree more. That's a central premise behind the conception of mental disorder that I am promoting in this book. I want to bring unreason (mechanism) and reason (rationality, Intentionality) together in a conception of mental disorder.

Someone is bound to reply to this picture of mental disorder, perhaps having forgotten things that I have said earlier in the book (about involuntariness, harmfulness and other aspects of a disorder), that the picture risks treating any failure or decrement of rationality that is not a brain disorder as a mental disorder. Consider wishful thinking. Cases of wishful thinking stand out as violations of various rationality norms, such as the principle that we should avoid motivationally biased belief (when relevant evidence runs grossly contrary to it), although exactly how motivation may derail rational belief formation and persistence in such cases requires analysis. Why isn't wishful thinking a disorder? Consider a case.

> Betty has good evidence that her son has been killed in the Iraq War. His death was reported by a fellow-soldier who accompanied him on a combat mission and by a journalist who said that he saw her son's lifeless body. She has not heard from him in over a month. Yet she remains convinced that her son still is alive. She loves him and refuses to admit that he is dead.

Cases of wishful thinking as such are not disorders, mental or otherwise. This is not because they are always harmless. Many are harmful. Betty may be harmed by her attitudes. Much depends upon how intractably contrary a person's attitudes are to disconfirming evidence. If Betty displays involuntary indifference to disconfirming evidence, or is irresistibly hostile to different attempts to situate her in front of the facts, perhaps her state or condition has descended into a disorder (a delusional disorder perhaps?). But as long as her wishful thinking remains 'mere', that is, if it simply is hyper-responsive to motivational incentives that influence belief formation, then, in such a case, nothing is needed to explain such a phenomenon except the language of consciousness and Intentionality. Nothing except psychology. No partial mechanical gum up of psychology's works. Reason-responsiveness is in charge (albeit in a motivationally biased manner). In such cases of wishful thinking it's nothing but the Intentional mind.

Indeed, something like a proclivity to wishful thinking may be built into the processes of human belief formation in order to optimize having positive expectations and hopes in the face of manageable hardship or adversity. Such wishful thoughts need not require false beliefs or so-called 'positive illusions' (Taylor and Brown 1988; see also the third section of Chapter 8). Provision may also be made in human psychological economy for evidence gathering and reality checking, telling the wishful thinker that their thoughts are over-influenced by preferences or desires, and that a wishful thought in certain situations should be abandoned.

The empirical question of when wishful thinking shifts from being 'merely mere' into being a disorder lies, in part, in determining when a thought or belief or set of beliefs is something a person could abandon if contrary evidence and reality checking wears down her indifference or refusal to change, or instead is something that she involuntarily refuses to examine no matter what – perhaps even when confronted with the extraordinary presence of the dead body of her son. One may start to live in a fantasy world of corpses as imposters for those invisibly living. The empirical difficulty lies in distinguishing between a belief that a wishful thinker cannot give up and one that she chooses not to give up – and in how the inability to give up is best explained.

In general, the tale of rationality mixed with brute mechanism, the Arthurian Legend about a mental disorder, as it were, if I may call it that, is central to the notion of mental disorder that I am promoting or trying to regiment in this book. Intentionalistic (rational) and neurological forces work together in human psychological capacities (or incapacities). When they do so in a harmful way, and depending on the incapacity, mental disorder may be present. How the twin forces work or intersect depends upon the type of condition, the particular case or circum-stance and the specific psychological capacities in question. But, and here certainly is where much more work needs to be done in this book, exactly which specific sorts of psychological disabilities or incapacities help to constitute disorders is a topic that has yet to be tackled. Not the capacity to ace exams. Not GOD. But then what?

An important but still remaining chapter in this tale should be obvious. I have not described the particular kinds or sorts of capacities or faculties that, when disordered, constitute mental disorders. Reason impaired, yes, but that notion is much too vague. It fails to distinguish the disability evident perhaps in GOD from that evident in Arthur. So which faculties or capacities in particular? I plan to answer this question in the next chapter. My answer consists in arguing that exemplary mental disorders are constituted by impairments or incapacities in the rational operation or reason-responsiveness of *basic* or *fundamental* psychological faculties or capacities. Not in non-basic ones (like acing exams). But in fundamental ones, like not knowing one's way around the world.

SUMMARY

This chapter was organized around the following single question. What sort of normative criterion of clinical seriousness or importance is appropriate for a mental disorder or for any form of psychological impairment that constitutes a mental disorder? The chapter explored three possible criteria. Two were found wanting: (i) cultural conventionalism and (ii) an ancestral and once biologically adaptive response pattern's being evolutionarily mismatched to a current environment. A third criterion is more promising. It says: A mental disability or impairment counts as clinically serious, in part, when it constitutes an impairment or truncation in a person's reason-responsiveness or rationality. Much of the energy in this fifth chapter was devoted to describing just why rationality is so central to being minded or to Intentionality. Intentional states and attitudes refer to objects and states of affairs in the world beyond themselves and they do so subject to various norms of rationality or reasonableness.

The content of disorders is often highly sensitive to cultural or social context, but this does not undermine the status of disorders as in some culturally invariant way wrong or bad for a person or very typically (in a wide variety of social contexts) harmful for a person. The occurrence of disorders may also sometimes reflect ancestral response patterns. But without some reason to suppose that we know what those patterns were or likely were, then the question remains as to how to assess the harmfulness or seriousness of a disorder in current environmental terms.

Most of the troubles that plague accounts of the norms or standards for a mental disorder or illness can, I would suggest, be blamed on the failure to appreciate the full nature of the reason-responsiveness or lack and impairment of it in a disorder. What reasons for thought and action we recognize and act upon may be felt in our bones (in our emotional and affective dispositions) as well are grasped by logical analysis and deliberation, and so all the sensitivity and responsiveness of a person participates in the rationality and reasoning capacities of a person. The more we discuss these matters and the more we appreciate the background of rationality that accompanies a mental disorder (as opposed to a brain disorder), the more we should come to realize that both psychological and neurological forces are at work in such a disorder.

SUGGESTED READING

Bolton, D. (2001). "Problems in the definition of mental disorder," *Philosophical Quarterly* 51: 182–99.

Lee, S. (1996). "Cultures in psychiatric nosology," *Culture, Medicine, and Psychiatry* 20: 421–72.

Nesse, R. M. (2000). "Is depression an adaptation?," *Archives of General Psychiatry* 57: 14–20.

Richardson, R. (2007). *Evolutionary Psychology as Maladapted Psychology* (Cambridge, MA: MIT Press).

Searle, J. (2001). *Rationality in Action* (Cambridge, MA: MIT Press).

6 An original position

Reasons – arguments, pro and con considerations, goals, incentives, purposes, aspirations – move people to act. Some do so with a bang. Others do so with a whisper. Some run against the tide of other considerations. Others ride within a tribe of complementary reasons. But reasons move.

Describing reasons as movers of behavior is thinking of them as motives or causes and as the objects of reference for psychological explanations for why people do (or fail to do) things. Not brute mechanical causes but causes or perhaps better 'becauses' that can and often may reflect deliberative reasoning. Reason itself is sometimes described as the capacity for reasoning or for being responsive to argument, deliberation, calculation or self-reflective analysis. To understand why Ian, the victim of paranoia mentioned in the first chapter, refuses to leave his apartment, we need to appreciate his reasons, or the peculiar logic that governs his deductions from his conviction that the government is spying on him. To recognize why Alice complains about her husband, we need to grasp her reason. Howard cheated on her.

Reasons don't move when a person is unable to act on them, of course, or when a person's ability to reason or react to reasoning is impaired, incapacitated or relevantly disabled. Take the disorder of clinical depression. It may leave a person, say, like Alice, unable to get out of bed in the morning. So, if you ask, "But doesn't she have sufficient reasons to get out of bed?," you are inquiring as to why those reasons (for example, the need to get dressed and go to work) fail to motivate her. Alas, the character of her depression, and the answer to your question, depends on the fact that the condition impairs her ability to respond positively to or even perhaps to appreciate reasons for getting out of bed. The reasons, although otherwise normally sufficient to move her, don't move her. Being incapacitated or 'disordered', she can't react in a desirable or reasonable way. The gravitational inertia of her condition weighs down upon her.

There are various psychological capacities whose incapacitation or impairment helps to explain why subjects of a mental disorder behave harmfully or risk serious harms. It is a matter of controversy, however, as to just which impairments in which capacities constitute a mental disorder. To speak of an impairment being 'clinically significant' points in the direction of an answer, insofar as it points to something that is bad or pathological about the incapacitations of a disorder, but it does not describe it. For what does 'clinically significant' mean? Inside the causal explanatory foundations of a clinical depression, for example, just which mental faculties or capacities are impaired? Which failed powers of reason and responsiveness are implicated clinically and perhaps call for medical attention or assistance?

The more psychologically 'well ordered' a person is, the more effectively will they behave in a reasonable or reason-responsive manner. When psychologically unwell, however, a person's behavior will not be in harmony or coordinated with their welfare or well-being. A person may be unable, as the philosopher Owen Flanagan, who himself suffered from a disorder, has written, "to get a grip [and to] find a way to regain order and harmony and integration" (Flanagan 2011: 291).

Consider depression again. Depression is said to be a disorder or incapacitation of mood. It's thought that the despondent mood or hopeless affect of a depressed person keeps them from getting out of bed, even if or when they recognize the desirability of rising. But that can't be the whole story, can it? It is worse than elliptical. People do all sorts of things when in the same or similar moods. My depressed mood may lead me to listen to Mahler and drink scotch on the couch in the morning. Yours may lead you to tighten the laces on your track shoes for a self-punishing pre-dawn run. Alice's may stitch her to her sheets.

Depression, when it is a disorder, a mental disorder, is not just a mood, emotion, or affect. It is also not a condition whose identity or nature is constituted by just one characteristic effect or symptom and a single proximate path into its onset or origin. It is an unfolding process, a condition that endures and persists, inner in thought and feeling, outer in expression and behavior. It emerges over time, appears in phases and periods, and is best classified in quite heterogeneous terms, exhibited by different individuals in different circumstances in different ways. It involves a family of crisscrossing and overlapping moods and feelings, judgments, imaginings, and forms of interactivity with the environment as well as interpretations of self and situation. It stems from a harmful mix of reason and mechanism (or, as I like to say, unreason).

Specific mental faculties or psychological capacities are incapacitated in a mental disorder. But which faculties? Not all classes of capacities. Not the power to have cool nerves when taking a calculus test. Not the ability to decide whether Rembrandt is a better artist than Vermeer. But powers that are more, as it may be put, basic or fundamental for a good life or essential to the satisfying and worthwhile lives that persons wish to lead.

By 'basic', I don't mean powers or capacities of a standard pedagogical or psychology textbook sort. We normally possess capacities for memory, emotion, perception, motor movement, and learning. Any entry level psychology text examines faculties that go by those names. The word 'basic' may be applied to them. But the utility of that particular sort of list or scheme when offered as a menu of basic mental faculties or capacities depends upon the pedagogic purposes to which it is put. Pedagogy is one thing; understanding a mental disorder and its place in a life is another.

William James once noted that if a person is wondering which breed of horse is best, the answer depends on the purposes to which the horse is put. Racing with alacrity on a track is one thing. Moving a heavy plough through a muddy field is another.

What holds for rating horses holds for identifying or comprehending the capacities implicated in a mental illness. It is one purpose to organize a review of experimental and research results in psychology or cognitive science (see Bechtel and Graham 1998). For such a classroom goal, memory period, emotion period, and so on may be treated as basic capacities. But it is another to develop a taxonomy of basic capacities that is intended to assist in understanding a mental disorder. For this second and distinct purpose, the identification of basic psychological capa- cities should be coupled or informed, I believe, with an appreciation of the preferences, projects or aspirations that help to give structure, meaning and purpose to a human life. What do we want a faculty of memory for? Merely to remember period? Hardly. What do we wish our emo- tional response patterns to do? Merely to feel – no matter what? Again, hardly. Why bother to perceive – merely to notice paint chips on a wall, gnats in a sleeping dog's hair? 'Hardly' hardly needs to be said.

The questions are rhetorical. Capacities *as we value* them are contextually situated, environ- mentally operative, and tethered to existential and not impersonal textbook needs.

Psychological faculties of a standard textbook sort, such as memory *full-stop*, emotion or mood *simpliciter*, and so on, when so listed are not perspicuously pictured as enmeshed in the contexts, goal directed structures, and purposes of our lives. Stripped of descriptions of our goals and aspirations, and of the discriminatory and reason-responsive operations of our mental faculties, such faculties appear like personally desiccated or unlined structures, highly generic and much too abstract to be fit for a theory of the mental faculties or abilities impaired in a mental disorder.

Think, by analogy, of bodily limbs and organs. People deploy their limbs and organs, notes George Henrik Von Wright, "to satisfy various wants and needs" (Von Wright 1963: 58). Our wants or needs normally can be satisfied only if relevant parts of our bodies perform or function in *this* or *that* way. To move we need operative legs; to breathe we need functioning lungs. The same general point, I assume, is true of mental faculties or capacities. If certain uses of memory "were not vital to the satisfaction of [certain] needs", it would be a puzzle, Von Wright notes, why we should never refer to a faculty of memory as incapacitated or impaired (Von Wright 1963: 59). "Perhaps we can imagine circumstances [in] which remembering would be a [rather] useless activity" (Von Wright 1963: 59). If that were to happen, in some distantly possible world, no doubt, if, that is, a functioning memory somehow became useless, what would this odd fact tell us? It would tell us, I believe, that any 'deficit' in memory would be considered too trivial or inconsequential to count as a mental disorder. Nothing basic to a worthwhile life would be lost in some such distantly possible circumstance.

But what about the capacities needed for our world, the actual world, and our lives in this world? The capacities for types of memory that we desire and need are situated in the context of the lives that we aim to lead. Some forms of memory are much more useful to and for us than others. Some, I shall claim, when impaired help to constitute exemplary mental disorders. The same general point holds true for other mental 'limbs' and 'organs', other psychological capacities. Some are much more useful than others and, when impaired, help to constitute disorders.

SOCIAL ORDER, MENTAL ORDER AND VEILS OF IGNORANCE

How, on earth, can we identify basic mental capacities, life-enmeshed or situated mental 'limbs' and 'organs'? Capacities that, when impaired in their rational or reason-responsive operation, help to constitute mental disorders?

We need a principled way of identifying the relevant psychological capacities or of making them determinate and explicit. Which capacities do we need to give structure and meaning to our lives? Which ones should a 'this world' basic tool kit of mental faculties contain?

I assume that there are psychological capacities or faculties that are valuable or required for any or virtually any satisfying and worthwhile life. When they function well, or in a suitably rational or reason-responsive manner, reference to them helps us to describe or assess just how mentally well or healthy a particular person is. Reference to them also lets us determine, when they are impaired or incapacitated, just how psychologically unhealthy a person is. They are, whatever they are (to be identified later in the chapter) "what we need to survive, to be healthy, to avoid harm, to function properly" (Griffin 1988: 42). And they also are, as the philosopher Harry Frankfurt puts it, what is required by "the universal exigencies of life, together with … other needs and interests that derive more particularly from the features of individual character and experience" (Frankfurt 2004: 47).

There is, of course, much that has been written on capacities or abilities that we human beings need or require in order for us to lead worthwhile lives. Some theories, like Aristotle's (384–322 BC), focus on one purported main capacity. In Aristotle's case this is the capacity for reason and rationality (or the ability to reason and to respond or react to reasons). His *Nichomachean Ethics* describes how reason is situated in everyday life, considers various demands of everyday affairs, weighs conflicting values and preferences, and tries to show how we can strike a balance between them. The book's main lesson? This is that each and every mental faculty or decisional power that a person possesses must be deployed or exercised in a rational or reason-responsive manner if it is to be properly functional or wisely operative and active. Reason at its situational best and most useful supports and underlies leading satisfying and worthwhile lives.

I shall take Aristotle on his word. Reason has a pivotal role to play in mental health and well-being and in the necessities of a worthwhile life. But is that all? Reason? What else is in the toolkit of basic psychological capacities other than a faculty of reason or for reasoning? What capacities need to be exercised rationally?

To assist in answering this question, I plan to appropriate a thought experiment of John Rawls (1921–2002), the late Harvard social thinker and moral philosopher. In Rawls's thought experiment, which I will describe momentarily, he is concerned with how to distinguish between morally acceptable and unacceptable forms of social order or social justice. He wishes to learn what basic structures of a society are principled, just, and fair. I, by contrast, am concerned with distinguishing between mental order/health and disorder/illness. I wish to identify which basic capacities or faculties of mind are desirable, valuable, and when sufficiently 'well-ordered' or functioning in a reason-responsive or rational manner, enable satisfying and worthwhile lives to be led. Rawls's thought experiment has social or moral ends. My use of Rawls's experiment has psychological or mental health ends.

First a brief background to Rawls's concern.

Social coordination and cooperation make possible all sorts of goods in life. Schools, hospitals, highways, science, and religion. Phones, libraries, and movies. Families and friendships. You name it. Without social cooperation little that truly is good or valuable in life can be accomplished or achieved.

Social cooperation of the sorts that help to produce hospitals, sciences, religions, and so on requires conventions, rules or norms for acceptable social behavior. If social participants are truly to be enthusiastic or engaged and cooperative, the rules or norms of social cooperation must be perceived by cooperating parties to be fair and respectful of their interests and needs. Ideally, the rules or conventions of social fair play are rules that give each person recognizable status as a respected member of the society or social order, no matter one's individual station or particular lot in life. These are rules that a person may commit themselves to without fearing that they will be short changed, devalued, or disrespected as compared to other persons with whom they socially cooperate.

Here is a simple domestic example. You and I are apartment mates. We throw a big dinner party with many guests. I buy potato chips but neither purchase nor prepare the meal. You buy the main dishes (which are expensive) and prepare a multi-course dinner (which is labor intensive). I arrange the cutlery and answer the doorbell. You slave in the kitchen. "Unfair", you think. You feel short-changed. Your enthusiasm for the party wanes. I fail to carry my proper or fair weight. What we need if we are to help each other cooperatively and enthusiastically is a fair distribution of responsibilities. A measure of impartiality or of 'domestic distributive justice' is wanted, lest either of us carry too much or too little weight. Rawls has a hypothesis for how a fair distribution is best understood.

In his magisterial book on socio-political theory, *A Theory of Justice* (1971), Rawls aims to identify which moral rules or norms for fairness should govern the basic or foundational structure of a social order and therein serve as a framework for enthused and committed social cooperation. Rawls does this by asking which principles of social organization would be chosen by persons from an impartial or unbiased perspective or point of view. To help our imagination to picture this neutral and globally invariant standpoint, he asks his readers to assume that we are "situated behind a veil of ignorance" in a position, an "original position" so-called, prior to commencing our particular individual lives and before the adoption of explicit rules of social order. What makes the veil one of ignorance, so-called, no doubt with an air of irony, is that behind it "no one knows his natural assets or abilities." Each person is assumed to know "the laws of human psychology", but not their personal lot or "own plan of life" (Rawls 1971: 136–37).

Rawls asks us to decide, as if from behind the veil, which basic rules or principles we would desire a society, in which we may live, to embrace and institutionally or conventionally enforce. He assumes that each and every person wants a satisfying and worthwhile life at least in some broad and general sense. He assumes that whatever each of us puts in and takes out of society can vary greatly. He also assumes that if we agree on basic rules of fairness or principles of social cooperation, then each of us would be better off than we would be without such agreement. He says that we (again, from behind the veil) would want rules that give each and every person an abundance of freedom or liberty, but that would also insure that no one is made intractably worse off by other people's exercise of freedom or liberty. When, then, the imagined veil is lifted and our individual lives or biographies have begun, a society with such rules is one in which, Rawls claims, we would prefer to live, no matter whom we are or whatever our personal assets and liabilities or goals and stations in life. Whether we end up being rich or poor, female or male, young or old, sick or healthy, such is the social order in which people would prefer to live.

Another of Rawls's key assumptions is that the rules or norms that would be chosen in the original position possess an eminent claim to actually being fair or just. How so? This is because the rules would impartially balance each person's potentially competing preferences and interests over and against those of other persons. The intuition pump of the imagined veil therein is designed to impose an unbiased or impartial standpoint in terms of which to adjudicate between interpersonal preferences. In Rawls's terms, it accomplishes this task because it expresses people's "respect for one another" (Rawls 1971: 179). It asks us to imaginatively project ourselves into possibly being any one of a number of other persons of different types, talents, and stations and "unencumbered by the singularities of the circumstances in which we find ourselves" (Rawls 1971: 516). We are to assume "a point of view that everyone can adopt on an equal footing" (Rawls 1971: 516). So, no single person is mistreated or disrespected by the chosen rules of social order. Each person and each person's interests or preferences are respected by whatever are the chosen principles. Or such is Rawls's aspiration or aim.

Consider our dinner party from behind a veil. It's not enough for me just to buy the chips. It's too much for you to do all the work. If I was in your shoes, I would see right away that the situation disrespects your interests. In whatever rules we adopt, apartment mates must be prepared to be in each other's shoes. My freedom not to cook, incompetent chef that I am, must not put you in the unfair position of being a 'slave' in the kitchen. Some compensatory benefit or gain must be available to you if I escape the heat of the stove. Such, roughly, is a Rawls-like assumption.

I mention Rawls here in a book on mental disorder not because of his theory of fair social order or person-respecting institutional arrangements or because I endorse the theory. I mention Rawls because of his thought experiment of a Veil of Ignorance in the Original Position and his use of this imaginative idea to uncover desirable rules of social order. A good thought experiment may be used independent of its original clips and chips. A truly good one is, as Daniel Dennett notes, "more robust than any one version of it" (Dennett 1984: 17–18). Rawls's experiment truly is good, I believe, even if it does not produce everything that he intended. So, I wish to explore how we may use something very much like it to help to identify basic psychological capacities. Humanly invariant ones, ideally, required for any life or virtually any life that is satisfying and worthwhile.

Suppose, again, we want to talk not about social order/disorder, as Rawls does, but mental order/disorder. Suppose we wish to engage in such talk not as a gratuitous exercise, but because we believe that mental disorders are 'out there'. They are real and undesirable conditions of people. They are *objective* conditions of the, as it were, *subjectivity* (psychology and behavior) of persons. Suppose we wish to identify these objective conditions. We want to explain and predict types of human behavior in terms of them. We want to help people who harbor disorders.

So, I ask now, which mental faculties or capacities are those that when disordered (incapacitated, impaired) help to constitute (depending upon their propensity conditions and harmfulness) a (prototypical, exemplary) mental disorder – conditions blessed (or cursed) with clinical significance? Here is where Rawls's experiment, I believe, becomes relevant to our task.

Or *nearly* here. Not quite yet. Not quite 'right now' or immediately.

Not every part of the answer to the question of 'which capacities' needs Rawls's thought experiment. Rawls's veil is not needed to warrant this next claim or thesis. It's a thesis about the personal or existential importance of our psychological capacity for consciousness or for conscious awareness or phenomenal experience.

Rocks and worms are not conscious, but we are. We not only are conscious period, we are conscious of things – of objects, the properties of objects, events, and facts. Being conscious of things (events, facts, etc.) is being aware of them and being aware of them means it is something it is like to experience them.

If some things are conscious and some things are not conscious, why be conscious? Why value consciousness or a capacity for it? Why put a capacity for consciousness in our toolkit? I am not asking about the biological or human species general advantage of being conscious, although reference to a capacity's contribution to genetic fitness, or to our desire to be fit genetically, could be part of the answer to my question. I am asking what contribution consciousness makes or may make to our individual or personal lives and to leading a worthwhile life. What personal use does consciousness possess? Is this a foolish question, whose answer is obvious? Not really.

THE IMPORTANCE OF CONSCIOUS EXPERIENCE

I taste an orange, smell a sweet rose, see the purple color on the BMW owned by my neighbor, feel pride on winning an award, and struggle to pronounce a foreign language term that is phonetically alien to my native speech patterns. In each of these cases, I am the subject of a very different form of awareness or conscious experience. In the case of conscious experiences, there is always something it is like to undergo them, some phenomenology that they possess. As the what-it-is-likenesses or phenomenal qualities of experience change, the contents of conscious experiences themselves change. If phenomenal features disappear entirely, no consciousness remains. The light goes out. The room is dark.

Here is a thought experiment about the value of consciousness. It is owed to Robert Nozick's *Anarchy, State, and Utopia* (1974). "Suppose there [was] an experience machine that would give you any experience you desired" (Nozick 1974: 42). While floating in a special tank, you could be hooked up to the machine. Super-duper neuroscientists would stimulate your brain so that you would think and feel as if you are climbing a mountain, making love to your soul mate, or preparing to visit Paris. All the while, however, "you would be floating in a tank, with electrodes attached to your head" (Ibid.). Should you plug into this machine for life, perhaps having in some manner preprogrammed all your future experiences? "While in the tank [assume] you won't know that you're there; you'll think it's all actually happening" (Nozick 1974: 43). The program blocks out that you experience yourself as being in a tank and hooked up to the machine. As far as you know or are concerned, you are out and about in the real and objective or external world.

You could be musically tone deaf, but believe you are composing a wonderfully melodic symphony. Scaling a mountain? Sure, though your feet are floating. Would you take a virtual hike?

I have asked this question of students. Most respondents answer no, but a few say yes. The outliers, the yes-sayers, claim that they would readily plug into an experience machine and do so for the rest of their lives, if they could trust in the continued operation of the machine. Why should it matter otherwise to a person, they ask rhetorically, whether he or she is in the dark (the tank) about the non-veridical origins or objective falsehood of their conscious experience? Positive or pleasurable experience is the *only* true measure of personal well-being or life satisfaction, they say. As long as you *feel* good, why worry about the authenticity of your experience? Consciousness has value to us as human beings because and only because it makes pleasure possible, they say, not because it makes for actual contact or interaction with the real or external world.

I wish I was able to argue these students out of this position of stated utter indifference to authentic connection with the world. My suspicion is that if they were actually faced with the Nozickean choice, they would not choose the machine (even if they trusted in its operation). They would think twice about never seeing their actual friends again or about being completely cut off from family and normal activities in school, work, and so on.

Loss of actual contact with the real world would certainly be rejected by John Stuart Mill (1806–73). Authenticity or external world engagement doesn't matter? It's inconsequential whether a person is locked into their own phenomenological space? Mill would never claim such things. It is better he would (and did) say to be a Socrates dissatisfied, than a pig satisfied. Better, he would say, to be out in the world and unfulfilled, than to plug into a machine and be deceived about the sources or causes of your feelings of fulfillment. A pig afloat.

At 22 years of age Mill underwent what likely was a protracted major depressive episode. He describes it in his *Autobiography* as a "dull state of nerves" in which he "seemed to have nothing left to live for" and experienced "the dry heavy dejection of … melancholy winter" (Mill 1969: 80, 81, 84.). On eventual liberation from his condition Mill claimed the following: "Those only are happy … who have their minds fixed on some object other than their own happiness." "The only chance is to treat, not happiness, but some end external to it, as the purpose of life" (Mill 1969: 85, 86).

What did Mill mean by such remarks? He meant this, I believe.

People certainly prefer to feel good rather than to feel bad. Pleasurable feelings or positive affects play an essential role in personal welfare and well-being and not just in our own hedonic satisfaction. But it is not true that feeling good is ultimately all and only what matters in life or that the exclusive and exhaustive merit of our capacity for conscious experience consists in affording pleasurable experiences. Some periods or episodes of pleasure are essential to a satisfying and worthwhile life, but pleasure alone is not sufficient or enough. Or so thought Mill.

For Mill we persons assess or evaluate our pleasures and their merits and demerits. This is one way in which, for example, we differ from nonhuman animals. A pig or bird does not take stock on its sources of fulfillment. We do.

Pleasures are judged and evaluated on the basis of how they come about, not just on what they feel like on the subjective inside. Feeling good, Mill believes, if it is to count or be judged as a valuable or truly worthwhile feeling, typically has to come about as the by-product of pursuing *other* good things that we believe to be worthwhile and meritorious. These other goods are not pleasurable feelings per se. They are states of the real or objective world, of one's family and its well-being, of one's career and its accomplishments, of one's friends and their health and happiness, and so on. "Aiming thus at something else, [one finds] happiness by the way" (Mill 1969: 86).

Individuals differ, of course, in how much, or even whether, they care about things or people external to themselves. Some of us are more egoistic or selfish than others. But, for Mill, we persons normally possess a psychological preference for authenticity over deceit, for real world connectivity over a mere virtual reality to our lives. We possess this preference provided we are not confused or befuddled about the role that consciousness plays in our lives or pressed by tragic vicissitudes or overwhelming heartaches into preferring some sort of real world personal oblivion. (In some dire circumstances one can easily imagine that a life of experience machine "highs", for example, would be preferable to an authentic life hooked up to the real world.)

Mill, I believe, makes a valid point. It is one thing to value conscious experience because it may be pleasurable (and note that it may be painful, too, of course). It is another to value it because of the roles that consciousness normally plays in helping us to secure, produce and experience other good things – good things or states or affairs in the external world.

What bothers Mill about emphasis on mere subjective feeling as the sole or exclusive criterion of the merit or importance of our capacity for conscious experience is that he doubts whether anyone can really and truly feel good without first caring for things other than good feelings, as paradoxical as this may sound. A mother takes pleasure, for instance, in the welfare and accomplishments of her children, because she wants them to flourish. She does not wish them to flourish in order that she may feel good. True, it makes her feel good to know that her children are flourishing, and she feels poorly when they don't. But she wants them to thrive for their own sakes and not for the sake of something that occurs just within confines of her own head.

Feeling or consciously caring for something or someone other than oneself is risky business, of course. Feelings make us vulnerable if we commit ourselves to things or externalities that fail. I want my former student to be a successful doctor. She does not do well. I am distressed. I want the newly elected president to address perplexing problems of global warming. Suppose, however, that once elected he lapses into indifference about the environment and cares only for the financial interests of big oil companies. I am upset.

A person must learn to feel or consciously care for things or persons that somehow are worth caring about, even though one's feelings and attachments are not protected against disappointment. The sorts of things we human beings care for, and which help us to lead satisfying and worthwhile lives, include pursuing various sorts of personal accomplishments, sustaining intimate personal relationships, addressing our curiosity about the world, helping other people in need, and so on, and not self-absorption in one's own conscious affect. Put again paradoxically, for Mill, it is only by more or less casting aside primary concern for one's own feelings and conscious experiences and becoming concerned for things (persons, etc.) in the real world, other than one's own states of mind, that therein an individual person may truly be happy or enjoy a satisfying and worthwhile life.

So, reason or a capacity for reasoning and reason-responsiveness is in the toolkit. A capacity for consciousness also is in the kit. What other psychological faculties or specific conscious or mental capacities are in the kit?

If we are successfully to engage in the world, we need more than a capacity for conscious experience. We need more than the ability to reason and be reason-responsive. We need capacities for performing activities that, in our being committed to them and aiming for their outcomes, help to make life structurally satisfying and enable us to lead worthwhile lives. Not capacities to plug into a machine. But powers or faculties that enable us to function well in the world. What are those capacities? How can we identify them?

Here and now Rawls.

BASIC PSYCHOLOGICAL CAPACITIES

Reasonable, intelligent persons, such as each of us, I assume, if we imagine different but desirable life projects as well as a likely range of genuinely possible (and not outlandish) circumstances in which we may live, and wish also to give ourselves decent life prospects virtually no matter our individual goals and circumstances, is in the best possible position to identify or appreciate just which capacities are basic (truly and generally valuable) for a human being. These are capacities or faculties that people are generally bound to need or care about, regardless of which particular goals they may have. They are similar to what Rawls speaks of as primary goods (Rawls 1971: 93, 263). Primary goods are conditions required for seeking virtually any other and more particular goals or goods.

To try to bring the required capacities out into the analytical open, I propose that we follow Rawls's example and construct a thought experiment of an original position type. Imagine ourselves situated behind a veil of ignorance about our individual talents, particular goals and situations. Look at things with an eye on the capacities people (including one's own person, of course) need or likely need in life. Assume the following empirically: We know a good deal about human psychology. We know what people tend to want out of life. We know basic facts of history, anthropology, and sociology. We know of personal and circumstantial challenges that individuals face, of tragedies and heartaches that must be endured. We know of various forms of human achievement and of the skills and talents required to secure them. We know existentially relevant bits of natural science. We have a good sense of what the human brain can do as well as what it cannot do. All of this empirical or factual knowledge qualifies as information about 'the universal exigencies of human life' (to use Frankfurt's phrase). What we don't know (and are unconcerned about here) are the individuating or particularizing features of our own personal lives. We don't know whether we ourselves wish to become tailors, tinkers, sailors, or spies. We don't know whether we wish to live in city or country, to father or mother, to counsel or command. We don't know whether we wish to affect the lives of others with small graces or to sweep people up from hardship with grandiose acts of heroism and personal self-sacrifice. We don't know whether we will be cooks or tennis players, spinsters or spoilers. We may well do some such things or be some such persons and we wish to be equipped for those possibilities. But we should also assume that any person may wish to be basically equipped for them.

My presupposition in the thought experiment is that we 'veiled' people (we Everyman, we Everywoman) are to identify a set of psychological capacities, not derived from our individually specific or variable talents or capacities, but from general capacities or competencies that we and other persons are bound to value and need. So, I am asking about an aptly-capacitated, well-'facultied' or mentally well-ordered person, as so conceived, and not, as Rawls did, about a well-ordered society.

I hope that four factors are in imaginative play or operation in this thought experiment.

The first factor is obvious. As noted: I am not asking us to pick out or identify capacities that may suit you or me but no one else or are too circumstantial or circumscribed to be of interest to the majority of humankind.

The second factor is that we individuals in the imagined position are to purge ourselves of unrealistic demands or overly idealized conceptions of what a satisfying and worthwhile human life requires from a generally deployable capacity-toolkit. What is wanted is a *basic* psychological endowment, not a treasure chest.

The third factor is that capacities will be identified that, although they make one vulnerable to illness and disorder when disabled or impaired, if exercised in a rational and reason-responsive manner, are valuable for a life lived temporally large and not a life confined small. We participants in the thought experiment should expect to derive satisfaction from the capacities' responsive operations over the whole course of a life, not just in discrete and isolable phases, or in youth rather than old age.

The fourth and final factor is connected with not focusing on worse case scenarios or being too risk averse. Sometimes in life decisions as to what to do next are literally matters of life and death. Although the abilities needed for threatening and aversive decisions should not be discounted from behind the veil, they should not be over-valued either. Consider the following analogy. We value our eyes because they are the source of enormous amount of information about the world, not just information about tsunamis and house fires. It is satisfying lives we are after, not lives aimed primarily at avoiding heartache and misfortune.

So: What are the primary (basic, fundamental) psychological competencies or capacities that are bound to be required or desired, regardless of particulars – both in bad times and good times? Which ones would we recognize as requirements for a human psychological capacity tool-kit?

Alongside our capacities for conscious experience and rationality or reason-responsiveness, I assume (or predict) that we, if we follow the terms of this thought experiment, would identify needs for non-negligible measures of each of the capacities briefly described in the list that follows just below this paragraph. This is not to assume that we would (or should, prudentially) wish for the same or equivalent measures of each capacity in each and every situation that we confront as human beings. Some capacities or faculties may strike us as more important in their measure or exercise at different times or periods in life than others. It is the capacities themselves that interest me, not their precise 'amounts' or contextually variable weights. Besides which, the list as offered here is described in pretty threadbare terms.

1. *Bodily/spatial self location*. We persons need to be able to identify our somatic or bodily position in the environments in which we live, so that we can utilize our motor capacities in the service of bodily movement and self-maintenance as well as in various forms of goal pursuit. To locate myself physically is to know where I am and what my location is vis-à-vis other objects of importance. Am I behind a door or underneath a willow tree? Am I far from a precipice, near a portal, or too close for comfort to a predator? What is important is not just

seeing a precipice or portal, but recognizing it as germane or helpful in determining the location in space and place of me. Am I headed this way or that way? I need to know.

2. *Historical/temporal self location.* We persons need to be able to identify our present position in time and to apprehend ourselves as (what may be called) enduring or historically extended agents or individuals with a past and future or at least (since people die, of course) a possible impact on the future. Quite apparently, no non-human animals possess conceptual or reflective appreciation of themselves as individuals extended in time. They don't conceive of themselves as possessed of a past and possible future. They remember the past (and learn from it), but arguably not as factually their past. None apparently remember past events in the sense of being able to deliberately relive them in the imagination. But as human beings we wish a sense of where we are, temporally, autobiographically, that "extends through time from the past we have experienced to the future we have planned" (Bechtel 2008: 259). I am more than halfway finished writing this book. You are more than halfway through reading it, assuming we each began at the beginning and plan to labor until the end. We wish to think or know of a past as our past and of a future as our future.

3. *General self/world comprehension.* We persons need to be able to comprehend ourselves and the world to the practical extent or degree necessary to lead a life in an at least a moderately well informed and knowledgeable fashion. Ignorance of self or world is no bliss. Oftentimes we make mistakes in what we think we know, misremember what we have done, or infer to some false proposition, belief or hypothesis about the world or ourselves. But without some modicum of successful comprehension, without knowing whether the food in my refrigerator is poisonous, if my car is safe to drive, whether my neighbors are trustworthy, or if the hot cup of coffee on my kitchen counter is too hot to hold, my ignorance is dangerous and deleterious. (Think of Arthur here, whose generalized and misplaced mistrust of strangers in crowds cripples him socially.) The capacity for self/world comprehension that we need is not angelic; it is situated or contextualized. Knowledge of certain facts or states of affairs is more practically important to us than knowledge of other facts. If I plan to get theater tickets, I need to know where to get them. If you plan to join me, you need to know where to meet me and how to get there. Neither of us needs to know the phone numbers of strangers sitting around us in the theater. And there would be no point in either of us attending the performance if we each know ahead of time that neither of us is likely to enjoy the play.

4. *Communication.* We persons need to be able to communicate about ourselves and the world with other people, and this requires sufficient competence in some system of communication (such as a native language). We need both speaker competence and listener competence if we are to be successful communicators or participants in communicative interaction. I may be a journalist reporting the atrocities of a political regime under which I lived. A skeptical reader will wonder if I distort the truth, but before assessing the soundness of my testimony, the reader must at least comprehend or understand what I mean by what I say or write. You may be a pedestrian answering my question about the location of a theater, adding no distracting detail to directions, but wishing to offer me the information I request. If you are to succeed in communicating the requested information to me, you must not speak of irrelevant effluvia, but of the location of the theater. You must know the right words for doing so. Communicative encounters and interactions are a pervasive activity in

human life – a source of knowledge as well as of social connectivity and coordination, a bond with others and the world. Good vision, a sensitive ear, and an apt sense of context are of little help in communication without the ability to comprehend what is said and heard.

5. *Care, Commitment and Emotional Attachment or Engagement.* We persons need to be able to care about and be committed to persons and things other than ourselves. (Mill's lesson.) To care for and be committed to something is to be invested in it, to identify oneself with it and to regard it as important to oneself, so that we make ourselves "vulnerable to loses and susceptible to benefits depending upon whether what [we care] about is diminished or enhanced" (Frankfurt 1988: 83). We appreciate, too, that normally the capacity for care and commitment requires or is constituted, in part, by emotional or affective attachment to what we care about. A reliance on affectless care or commitment alone, in the words of Harvard psychologist, Jerome Kagan, "without the capacity to feel ... joy, guilt, sadness or anxiety ... would lead most people to do many, many foolish things" (1994: 39). Without emotional commitment "the level of [a person's] mental energy and activity diminishes" (Frankfurt 2004: 54). Our responsiveness to the world and to other people "flattens out and shrinks" (Ibid.). We would possess no felt real or vested interest in what happens. We need to be capable of real or vested interests.

6. *Responsibility for self.* There are some things or people that practically no person can help caring about. This is most true of caring for oneself. A person who cares not for themselves hardly counts as a person at all. Complete indifference to oneself is tantamount to a cessation of caring. So, we need the ability or capacity to care about and be responsible for ourselves – for the kind of person one is and wishes to be. We would want to be able to govern, guide, manage or control our own behavior in a reason-responsive way. To form intentions, evaluate impulses and inhibitions, make practical judgments and self-reflective decisions, and act on those decisions with at least a modicum of freedom from immediately surrounding circumstances (the push/pull of the surrounding environment) as well as from unwelcome or intrusive personal characteristics. A person, for example, who is totally heedless of themselves, promiscuously impulsive in behavior, acting without prudent selectivity or restraint, will not be long for this world.

7. *Recognizing and Acting on Opportunities.* We need to be able to recognize or appreciate opportunities for alternative courses of action or behavior and to act on them. Circumstances and occasions present themselves as choice or decision points for variable and varying courses of action. Being able to recognize choice points or affordances (as they may be called, co-opting a term of J. J. Gibson out of context [see Reed 1996]) and then acting on them is essential for securing a variety of different goods and for the development of our own plans and policies, character and personality. True, an opportunity for a goose may not also be one for a gander. An affordance may be open to one person but not to another. But recognizing opportunities and then acting on them, when possessed of appreciable or sufficient reason, is essential for a satisfying and worthwhile life. To use a metaphor of John Martin Fischer's, when I act on an opportunity or respond to an affordance, "I write a sentence in the story of my own life" (Fischer 2009: 167). We want to author that story – our story.

It is, I believe, instructive to picture the above psychological capacities or needed faculties (and they crisscross, overlap and interpenetrate one other quite obviously), if luck permits and circumstances provide, as enabling us persons to achieve satisfying and worthwhile lives. Not painless lives. (Remember Freud noted the impossibility of that.) Not flourishing or utterly self-fulfilling lives. Flourishing requires (in addition to sheer good fortune) capacity levels in excess of those pre-supposed, albeit vaguely, by my talk of 'non-negligible measure'. Flourishing is above and beyond mere satisfaction. It means flowering into the sort of existence that is immensely well worth living and profoundly worthwhile. A gift of the gods perhaps. No such elevated or inflated standard suits the identification of faculties or capacities for a baseline level of mental order or well-being – for a tool kit.

The purpose behind my list is not to propose that each and every one of the above capacities, or impairments or incapacitations in them, is operative in any and all exemplary mental disorders. When, for instance, the poet Sylvia Plath (1932–63), who suffered from depression and com-mitted suicide, wrote in her diary in 1952 of "corrosive emotions of insecurity biting away at my sensitive guts", she was speaking of an undermining emotional tone to her life that left her "nerves paralyzed" and her "action nullified" (quoted in Kagan 1994: 2880). Such is the disorder of depression that it leaves a person, as T. S. Eliot phrased it in *The Waste Land*, with "a handful of dust". Emotional dust. Without resonance: without the emotional commitments, engage-ments or forms of caring that enable a person to lead a decent life. Plath, as a victim of clinical depression, was impaired in her capacity for care (of self) and perhaps also in related capa-cities for self responsibility and opportunity recognition. She, however, had no trouble, say, in locating herself spatially or temporally or in communicating (she was a gifted poet). So, to impair one or more capacities certainly is not necessarily to disable others, let alone all.

I am also not proposing that the relevant psychological capacities mentioned above, however incapacitated, disabled or impaired, utterly preclude living a worthwhile life. Disability per se does not preclude living at all well or satisfyingly. Perish the thought. Some disabilities may be effectively managed (especially with assistance from others); others may admit of compensation; still others, in context, may be moderate and relatively inconsequential – a chronic low grade depression like a low grade fever. As two well informed clinical observers put matters, "even people experiencing repeated episodes of mildly psychotic symptoms" may do so "without ever becoming floridly unwell" (Frith and Johnstone 2003: 43–44). Disorder, after all, is not an all or nothing affair, anymore than the boundary between disorder and non-disorder is clear cut. Rather, my assumption here is that the disabling of one or more basic psychological capacities raises the risk or likelihood of harms or losses and therein of the loss of a healthy quality to life. Moderate instances of a disorder are moderate, not by themselves life shattering. Exemplary instances, however, are serious and severe and may be shattering.

I am also not assuming or claiming that capacities in being disabled must be disabled by the two kinds of proximate forces proper to a mental disorder. While such a twin or two-level pair of final pathway sources holds, I believe, of a mental disorder or of conditions or disturbances that deserve to be classified as mental disorders, both kinds do not operate in all forms of disorder (say, in neurological disorders where only lower level mechanical forces are at work). Just because a psychological capacity is impaired does not mean that mental forces must be part of its disabling conditions. Capacities may be disabled by pure brute a-rational mechanisms.

I am also not proposing that basic capacities admit of only one sort of impairment or dis-abled state or condition. Goodness (sadness) no. There are multiple (and for some capacities a bewildering variety of) ways of disabling a basic capacity (especially those composed of complex and multi-level sub-capacities). Multiple ways, for instance, of disabling a person's ability to locate themselves spatially (blindness is but one) or of impairing the capacity to effectively comprehend oneself or the world (Down's syndrome and paranoia are but two). In addition, too, disabilities come in different degrees (as noted), may be restricted to expression in specific situations or environments and, under certain circumstances, may be muted or muffled. Disabilities of different sorts also may affect, influence or interpenetrate each other. Someone with a dramatically diminished power of self comprehension or temporal self-awareness may become so depressed that they are unable to properly care for themselves. (I am thinking here of various cases of advanced Alzheimer's dementia, for example, in which autobiographical memory loss so disturbs a person that they become frightened, withdrawn, and hopeless.) Or a person may cease being emotionally committed to their own personal well-being and suffer a disability in self-care and concern. (Think of a clinical depression. A depressed person may be unable to recognize important opportunities for self change and transformation, which is a failure to grasp decisional affordances.) So, one type of incapacity may break into another faculty, helping to produce a second or even a third dimension to a disorder. Remember: "A totally specific [incapacity may] be extremely unlikely" (Karmiloff-Smith 1998: 390).

I am vividly aware, of course, that the above list of basic capacities contains numerous vague, loose and imprecise terms or expressions. Ability to locate self. Comprehend world. Be self responsible. These are all capacities that come in different sizes, shapes, colors and varieties and operate along a variety of different personality fronts, cultural landscapes and biographical dimensions. Each also has exemplars; each foils. Failures of rationality and reason-responsiveness can be quite specific to each capacity or set of capacities. A reckless and ambivalent imprudence in the consumption of drugs may be a sign of addiction and impairment both in acting on affordances and being responsible for self. Irrationally distrusting others may reveal paranoia and a truncation in comprehension of self and others. Imprudently staying in bed rather than reporting to work may signal an instance of clinical depression. It may reflect an incapacity for enduring emotional attachment to other people to whom one is responsible (the children who need breakfast, the elderly parent who needs help with their finances, and so on). Just how one should understand and apply notions of impairments in the rational exercise or operation of the capacities (listed above) and for specific types of mental disorder depends on the needs and contexts of particular cases of disturbance and distress (of which more in the rest of the book).

Although it may be theoretically nerve wracking to base a theory of basic psychological capacities on phenomena that are loosely defined and subject to contextual parameters, there is no way around it. As pointed out earlier in the book, there are some physical diseases (not exemplars of somatic illness perhaps) that also possess loose or vague borders. One illustration is hypertension, an abnormal elevation of blood pressure, which increases the risks of strokes and heart attacks. The boundary between low and high blood pressure is vague, and determined contextually by physicians, who assess a person's risk of vascular disease (in terms of family history, analysis of work stress, and so on). But no one wishes to deny that hypertension is a genuine somatic malady. What is missing from vaguely defined conditions is precision, not necessarily objective reality.

What attitude should we take towards vagueness or looseness in capacity designation? Wanting to eliminate vagueness or looseness from the idea of a basic capacity has a scientifically idealistic ring, but eliminating it is an unwise theoretical aspiration for a theory of mental disorder. Remember: In referring to mental disorders we are not talking of conditions with the often relatively more precise descriptive specifications and origins of diseases like malaria or scurvy. Disorders are states that lie on a continuum alongside normal variations in human mental health and well-being, have multiple (not small sets of) symptoms and origins, and lack empirically tractable necessary and sufficient conditions. In speaking of mental disorders we are also referring to conditions that transgress norms of rationality and reason-responsiveness, broadly understood, and therein must be flexibly described given the contextual and rather loose nature of such norms. Reason's rules are not rigid, smothering or algorithmic (as we noted in discussing RIT). The very idea of rationality can and should be adjusted to fit particulars of purpose, person, capacity, and circumstance.

What of the manner in which my list of the capacities/incapacities proper to a disorder presupposes contestable norms or values? What about my Rawlsian predilection for identifying relevant basic faculties in terms of the sorts of lives to which people aspire, albeit under 'veiled' conditions devoid of favoring the preferences or circumstances of certain individuals over others? Desirable lives seem like ripe subjects for evaluative contestation. Thomas Szasz may take ironic delight in the 'original' position strategy that I deploy, recognizing in it the recurrence of the sorts of presuppositions that render the very idea of a mental disorder medically otiose to him. I can hear his voice if not see his face behind the veil. "I told you so." "The notion of a mental disorder is a conceptual sham."

Recall that Szasz and certain other anti-psychiatry critics pick out the presupposition of values (especially morally contestable values, of which at the end of the chapter) as an insurmountable obstacle to counting mental disorders as genuine illnesses. Values presupposition strips the idea of a mental disorder, so they charge, of medical-scientific legitimacy or objective factual authority. Of course, legitimacy or objectivity may have a foundation other than absolute freedom from values presupposition. In the fourth chapter, we were encouraged to think of certain mental conditions or disturbances as mental disorders by virtue, in part, of the following fact. Presupposing values (albeit perhaps often hidden) hasn't stopped bodily diseases from being described as genuine or objective illnesses. So, it should not prohibit a mental disorder from counting as a bone fide disorder either. What's dignifying for the somatic goose is respectful of the mental gander. When someone is physically ill, there necessarily is something *wrong* with them. No surprise, then, if or when something is mentally or psychologically *wrong* with a person, the person may be the subject a mental disorder, depending on how the condition is best explained or understood.

But still the Szaszian objection annoyingly persists. As one sympathetic reader of his position puts it, "Szasz got mired in questions of the meaning of terms." "But his conclusions [are] in many ways correct" (Pickard 2009: 98). The relevant norms for the diagnosis of a mental disorder may seem so much more contestable than those that warrant the attribution of a somatic illness. They are, if I am right, norms that depend upon assessments of the rational or reason-responsive exercise of basic psychological capacities. Norms associated with desired patterns of behavior and the purposive structures of a life. To make this explicit, think of the example of our capacity for care, commitment and emotional attachment. It is natural to believe that some things are worth caring for and others not. It is worth caring for one's children, not the wrinkles in one's sheets or the freckles on the back of an overweight sun bather in the seaside cabana summering next to you. Whatever the precise nature of such norms may be, and whatever sort of irrationality or imprudence caring for wrinkles or freckles rather than children exemplifies, such norms may appear highly controversial, eminently contestable. The relevant norms in somatic illness may seem not so contestable. They consist of standards for proper or satisfying bodily function. They may be thought less controversial and markedly less debatable than mental disorder norms. It may appear that it is one thing to say that a heart or kidney is not functioning as it should, another to say something similar about a person's capacity for emotional care or commitment, viz. that it is not functioning as it should.

One response to this reintroduction of the Szaszian worry is to claim that the normative or evaluative differences between standards for somatic and mental disorder are differences of degree only and not of kind. Each notion of disorder relies on norms for the sorts of persons we wish to be or want to become and which faculties or capacities are needed to realize those aspirations.

Complementary to that response is the following response. It is customary in discussions of the existence of a mental disorder to worry over whether there is such a thing as the objective truth about a diagnosis. This worry has two parts. First, are our beliefs and assertions about a diagnosis of mental disorder true? If a psychiatrist says that someone is, say, clinically depressed or delusional, is such a statement true? Does the patient harbor the condition or not? It is, as a physician may put it, up to our diagnostic judgments to get a diagnosis right. And second, is a mental disorder something that exists independent of our diagnostic classifications or judgments? If someone has a mental disorder only because or when we say that they have it, it's not the disorder (the real and independent existence of the disorder) that is the truth bearer of our diagnosis, but the act of diagnosis itself makes it true that the person 'has' the disorder. It's a matter of diagnostic fiat. A performance, not an inference from evidence. Saying so makes it so, as it were.

Nothing could be less objectively real for a condition or disorder than to be possessed by diagnostic fiat. In a baseball game, the home plate umpire 'makes' a pitch a strike by calling it a strike even if it is out of the formal strike zone. A clinician is no maker or should not be – if mental disorder realism is true.

One might be tempted to straddle the fence here and say that the jury still is out on whether mental disorders are real objective conditions of persons or whether mental disorder realism is true. But I don't believe that the jury is out. At least at a coarse-grained level of analysis, which allows for ragged borders between disorders and non-disorders, mental disorders are real. There is no deep or ultimate difference as a harmful condition between that of a clinically depressed person who cannot get out of bed in the morning and tragically ends the day by committing suicide and that of an individual who dies of a heart attack in their sleep or office. What is present in both cases are the effects of something wrong with a person, something which they cannot manage, something that is undesirable and harmful – an emotional incapacity, a hobbled heart.

We are exploring the character of the question of what makes something the sort of impairment that is characteristic of mental disorders. We are noting that it is an impairment in a basic psychological capacity, one whose effective operation is required (or usually required, absent compensations or lucky environments) for a truly satisfying and worthwhile life.

It may be noted that the identification of capacities conducted from behind the veil of imagined ignorance excludes as well as includes capacities as germane to a class of mental disorders. GOD (Grade Obsessive Disorder) is not a mental disorder. There is no reason to confer medical respectability on GOD as a diagnosis. Failure to achieve high academic performance in a stress-free manner reflects no basic impairment or incapacity (assuming, of course, that GOD is not a specific symptom of a more general impairment). Particular desires of particular individuals may be hampered by GOD. No doubt, they are. But life is like that. Not everyone can succeed at everything all of the time.

GOD is what may be called a problem or difficulty in living, a circumstantial or academic liability, and not the disabling of a fundamental capacity. It stymies in quite specific circumstances certain wished for accomplishments or forms of success only.

Panic attacks with agoraphobia, by dramatic contrast, infect and disable a person much more broadly, generally or profoundly. Suppose I am victim of the condition. So, if someone asks me to walk with them through a mall, I decline. I cannot get to work in a bus or subway. My office is on the 25th floor, but I cannot ride an elevator. Unmarried, I am eager to find a spouse but cannot attend church services, join a club, or vacation at a singles resort. Such circumstances are crowded with strangers. All to the good are such places if a person is looking for a spouse. But I get hyper-anxious. All to the bad if I am hoping myself to find one. So, it has become practically impossible for me to meet new people. Practically, no one could live well under such circumstances. The propensity to stranger-induced panic locks me in a closet socially. It reflects a reason-responsive impairment in a capacity to comprehend others (if I am right) as well as perhaps in both self responsibility and acting on affordances. People matter to me. I've read Mill and labored through Augustine. I want someone to love in order to give meaning to my life, but I can't control myself well enough to meet them. I need to maintain my job but struggle to do so. Such and more would be the case if I was a victim of agoraphobia.

Let me now sum things up and bring the bulk of this chapter to a close by describing the concept of mental disorder that has been regimented or constructed, so as to best fit, I believe, and to guide, I hope, mental health clinical practice and research. It is designed to apply to prototypes or exemplars of disorder. The concept was mentioned in the second chapter. It has since, I hope, been plausibly derived or defended and sensibly extended with additional details. So, the statement below is not just like the one in the second chapter. (This coming statement mentions rationality/reason-responsiveness, for instance, rather than just, as in the second chapter, mentality.)

A CONCEPT OF MENTAL DISORDER

Here is the concept or idea. Since it is the concept that is being offered in this book, given the title of the book, I refer to it here in this section of the chapter as the *TDM Concept*. Using the language of theses to articulate it, the TDM Concept contains four main theses or sub-parts.

The concept goes like this: The very idea of a mental disorder, prototypically understood and regimentally clarified, is the concept of a (i) [*rationality disability thesis*] disability, incapacity or impairment in the rational and reason-responsive operation or exercise of one or more fundamental or basic psychological capacities of persons, that (ii) [*harm thesis*] causes harmful or potentially harmful symptoms/consequences for the person (and perhaps also for others). Also: The disability of a disorder possesses a special general and immediate source, proximate genesis or set of final propensity conditions. It is (iii) [*mixed or dual-level source thesis*] brought about by an admixture of Intentionalistic, psychological or mentalistic activity, on the one hand, and brute a-rational neural causes or mechanisms, on the other; (iv) [*some preservation of rationality thesis*] and the combination or intersection of these two forces infuses a mental disorder with a truncated 'logic' or compromised rationale of its own. This sub-thesis of 'iv' means, in part, that in a mental disorder, wherein a basic capacity is impaired, the capacity itself is not rendered senseless. In its reason-responsive operation, the faculty is not destroyed or obliterated. The incapacitation is not *total and complete*, as may occur in cases of severe brain damage or neurophysical disorder. A victim of depression, for example, may be able to get out of bed given extraordinary incentives or reasons for doing so – like a fire burning her house down around her. However, a person with quadriplegia, with paralysis of all bodily regions below the neck (a severe neurological disorder, resulting from "high" spinal lesions, in the cervical portion of the spine), cannot move. They are incapable of moving appropriately even away from a fire.

The concept of a mental disorder offered in this book, viz. the TDM concept, compares and contrasts with at least five distinct and opposing types of concepts.

One is any concept of a mental disorder that attempts to describe a disorder in value-free terms – as, say, a case of statistical deviance or mere abnormality. A second type of concept, which is represented by cultural conventionalism, is any concept that tries to define a mental disorder in terms of culturally conventional judgments of disorder or mental illness. A third type attempts to define a mental disorder in terms of damage to or dysfunction in brain mechanisms or processes (describable in neuroscientific terms) and which issue in psychiatrically salient symptoms (such as a depression or delusion). A fourth type of concept of a mental disorder is conceptually self-restricted from investigative concern with the causal role of brute mechanisms in a disorder. It is a concept of disorder that discourages the effort to "look down" (to use a helpful visual metaphor of William Bechtel [Bechtel 2008: 156]) into lower level neurobiological/neurochemical processes that may help to explain one or more features of a disorder (even when such processes are undamaged). It insists upon only "looking up" at propensity conditions described in psychological terms, and "looking out" at environmental factors with which person interacts. Finally: a fifth concept of a mental disorder is wedded to the idea that mental disorders are diseases or natural kinds. The TDM conception swings free of such marital entanglements (although it may perhaps accommodate them, depending upon how loosely the ideas of disease or natural kind are developed). The TDM concept takes disorders to be real and objective conditions of persons independent of whether they also count as diseases or natural kinds.

The challenges for the particular four sub-theses TDM concept offered in this book consist, in part, in the empirical challenge of figuring out just which sorts of evidence may adjudicate whether a particular case or disturbance is a mental disorder as opposed to a brain disorder. The TDM concept of a mental disorder conceives of the proximate causes of or forces behind a mental illness as part of its identity, nature or constitution as a mental disorder. And so, if an illness (any illness) has *nothing* whatsoever in its immediate genesis that needs to be described in psychological terms, it does not count as a mental illness. If, for example, syphilis is caused by the spirochete *Treponema palladium* in the central nervous system, then a case of this condition, according to the TDM concept, is not a mental disorder/illness, although, of course, it is a disease (of the central nervous system). This is objectively true of syphilis (or neurosyphilis), even though the condition was once believed, at one time historically and before its sources were discovered, to be a mental illness. Spirochetes a disorder does make, to be sure, but not a mental disorder (for the TDM concept).

Another challenge to the TDM concept is a conceptual challenge. Theorists (including philosophers) need to figure out just which types of concepts or descriptions of activity at the two main levels of causal or propensity conditions for a disorder (one marked by reason and Intentionality, and the other marked by unreason and mechanism) are most appropriate or best suited for understanding processes associated with a disorder. This no small chore, since within causal explanatory levels there may be sub-levels or methodological options for which concepts to use. In neuroscience, for example, there are different sorts of vocabularies and levels of analysis of brain mechanisms (from neurons to computational neural networks) – each descriptive level with its own history, important questions to answer, research techniques, criteria for explanatory success, and so on.

Finally, still another challenge is a normative or values challenge. Theorists, especially perhaps philosophers, need to figure out which norms or standards are the best or most appropriate for understanding the 'disorderliness' or clinical significance of a condition that qualifies as a mental disorder.

So far in this book I have tried to work on each of these challenges. But there are a lot of blanks or details yet to be filled in. In the next and final section of the current chapter, I try to partially fill in at least two of those blanks. These are blanks occasioned by some of the taxonomic efforts and commitments of DSM and by debates about the borders between mental disorder and non-disorder. The rest of the book is also devoted to filling in details. Not all of them. Some of them. More work remains when a book is done.

COMING TO GRIEF OVER PSYCHOPATHY

Augustine once more. In AD 371 Augustine went to Carthage for an advanced education. There he found a mistress, who bore him a son. Augustine named him 'Adeodatus' ("given by God"). The young man died at 18. We do not know how helpful Augustine as a father was to the son, but we do know that death became no stranger to the father. Augustine confronted a deep personal loss during his period of philosophical and religious soul searching. This was the death of a beloved friend from Tageste. Augustine devotes a whole section of Book 4 of the *Confessions* to it. He does not give his friend's name to the book's readers, but he does describe, in a passage with which we already are familiar (from Chapter 5), the intense grief that it produced in him. "My eyes looked for him everywhere," he writes, "and he was not there." "I hated everything because they did not have him, nor could they tell me 'look, he is on the way', as used to be the case when he was alive and absent from me." "I had become to myself a vast problem." (Augustine 1992: 57).

One commentator remarks on Augustine's description of the overwhelming personal significance of the death as follows:

> [The reader] is attracted both by the intensity of his love and grief, and by his willingness to expose that grief to his friends and the readers of his *Confessions*. To any who may have experienced torments similar to those Augustine here describes, the passage also has the mysteriously balming quality of expressing with delicate precision the grief they themselves have felt. All the places and all the objects that once whispered "Here he comes" or "Here she comes" have lost their voice and fallen achingly mute.
>
> (Wolterstorff 1988: 196)

Well over a dozen centuries after the death of a friend affected Augustine, Ted Bundy (1946–89) was put to death in a Florida electric chair. Bundy confessed to 30 homicides (though he likely committed more) of young women, some of whom he decapitated and whose naked and decaying bodies he continued to abuse sexually. He was diagnosed as a psychopath by Hervey Cleckley (1903–84), a famous psychopathy researcher and the author of a seminal work on the condition in 1941, called *The Mask of Sanity* (1982, St. Louis, MO: Mosby).

Confessing to the murder of Georgann Hawkins, Bundy, described what he did to the young woman in the following way (Keppel 1995: 418):

> "And, gee, this is probably the hardest part." [...] Ted shut off the recorder. He regained his composure for a moment and turned it back on. [...] "I hope you understand that this is not something I find easy to talk about after all this time." [...] Ted took a big sigh and said, "One of the things that make it a little bit difficult is that at this point she was quite lucid, talking about things. It's not funny, but it's odd the kinds of things people will say under those circumstances. And she said that she had a Spanish test the next day, and she thought that I had taken her to help tutor her for her Spanish test. It's kind of an odd thing to say. Anyway." [...] Another sigh, and then he approaches the subject by saying, "The long and short of it, I mean, I'm only trying to get there by degrees. The long and short of it is that I again knocked her unconscious, strangled her, and drug her about ten yards into the small grove of trees that were there."

Bundy and Augustine. Centuries apart in life. Light years apart in personality and moral character.

But despite dramatic disparities of time and person, the relationships of Augustine and Bundy to the topic death indirectly are connected. Grief and psychopathy are and have been the source of much taxonomic controversy and contestability within the history of DSM. Consider first the place or non-place grief or bereavement in DSM.

The publication of DSM-III in 1980 marked a turning point in the psychiatric profession's attitude towards grief. Rather than admitting the process of grieving as a possible form of pathology as Freud did, DSM-III bars a bereaved person as such from being diagnosed with a disorder until or unless their grieving changes into and is independently describable as a full-blown major or clinical depression. Only major depression in a 'complicated' case of bereavement is classified as a disorder. In the language of DSM-III-R, which was published in 1987, grief cannot be considered a mental disorder "even when associated with the full depressive syndrome," although it can be "complicated by a Major Depressive Episode" (APA 1987: 222). Complicated by but not itself a disorder? Is that all to be said psychiatrically for grief?

Not every special committee and workgroup of the American Psychiatric Association agrees. Some want the grief exclusion excised from DSM-5 (see Hughes 2011; Carey 2012). (While I am writing this chapter before DSM-5 appears in print, it appears that it will be excised.) Why so? Some clinicians claim that just as losing a treasured job, being betrayed by a trusted spouse or discovering that you have an inoperable cancer may figure in the propensity conditions or onset of clinically significant and diagnosable episodes of hopelessness, bitterness, a sense that life is meaningless, so, too, the inability to effectively adjust to the death of a beloved person may lead to the very same results. It may contribute to a condition of clinical and diagnosable significance. As Mardi Horowitz, a professor of psychiatry at the University of California, San Francisco, puts matters, "grief [can predict] a lot of bad outcomes – over and above depression [and it is] worthy of clinical attention in its own right" (quoted in Hughes 2011).

Symptoms of grief and depression overlap, of course, but Horowitz appears not to be making the claim that a bereaved person may suffer from a clinical depression. Horowitz seems to be making a distinct claim, namely the claim suggested by use of the words 'over and above'. This is that, in certain cases, grief can disable and merit classification as a type of mental disorder on its own and should be included in DSM-5. Numerous other clinicians agree with this claim. They want the bereavement exclusion excised from DSM-5 in order to leave sufficient conceptual and clinical elbow room to categorize a certain form of grieving as a disorder, whether it is a major depression or not. (This form is likely to be called, judging from a proposal from one of the DSM-5 work groups, Bereavement Related Disorder.) Other clinicians urge simply that the grief exclusion be eliminated from DSM *full stop*. The reason for doing so? This would rest on the conviction that some forms of grief change or descend into a major depression. So, even if grief fails to count as a disorder on its own, grieving may be part of a disorder (major depression) or a source of a disorder (again, a major depression).

Critics of excising the grief exclusion worry about the medical and social consequences of removing it. A pathology focus on grief, critics say, would be encouraged by the exclusion's removal. Such a species of medicalization is to be feared, charge critics, for it will lead the mental health profession to misidentify grief's problems, the contexts and durations of their occurrence, and the cultural and social routes (such as family and religious practices) available to address and dissipate them. A pathology focus will tend to assess grieving and bereavement in terms of medical and clinical treatment norms to the neglect of non-medical social and personal interrelationship norms, such as those associated with loss of personal intimacy, emotional attachment, and loving relationships. So, for example, Allen Francis, M.D., a prominent critic of eliminating the exclusion (Francis chaired the task force that produced DSM-IV), complains that removing the exclusion is "a disastrous and foolish idea" (Hughes 2011).

Disastrous? Foolish? But can't some forms or constituents of grieving be genuinely negative mental health states or processes, and pathological or harmful for a person? Much depends, no doubt, on just how or if a line can be drawn between grieving healthily and unhealthily.

There is no doubt something it is like for a person to grieve. Grieving has a phenomenology. But 'the experience of grief' is not the name of a single or isolated sensation or feeling. It is part of a process, called 'grieving' or 'bereavement', and it occurs, to use apt and concise words of Wittgenstein, "with different variations, in the weave of our life" (Wittgenstein 1958: 174; see also Goldie 2011). Grieving has a characteristic or generic shape or contour for a person, from first, as it were, hearing the terrible news of a death onwards. But it is quite particularistic or individualized, focusing on a particular fact (such as the death of a specific person), events (such as the circumstances surrounding the death) and a bereaved person's history of shared experiences with the deceased.

The notion of grief is sometimes used to describe reactions to things or events other than the death of a loved one, to be sure. Grieving may accompany loss of a limb, a reputation, a treasured opportunity, and much else besides. It may also be a feature of human reaction to the results or contents of calamities and disasters. One may grieve a town destroyed in a tornado. A valley demolished in a tsunami.

I shall focus here on the case of a lover or dear friend who grieves for a beloved person. This is Augustine's type of grief and is the form of bereavement often presented to psychiatrists and other mental health professionals.

Consider the attitude of a lover towards his or her beloved. Suppose loving this particular person is categorically or intrinsically important to the lover. It is not important to them as an instrument or means for advancing other goals or aspirations that the lover may have. The value of loving the beloved to the lover, as Harry Frankfurt puts it, "derives from his dedication to [the] beloved" (Frankfurt 2004: 59). "The interests of [the] beloved are not actually other than [the lover's] at all. They are [the lover's] interests too" (Frankfurt 2004: 61). So, it is not surprising or unexpected, of course, that grieving over the death of a beloved occurs. The lover may experience the death as a terrible loss. Solidarity with the beloved does not evaporate just because or when the beloved dies and the love can no longer be shared. To love someone and to suffer over their annihilation is an expression of continued attachment to the person. The griever may say "No" to the death or try to deny its occurrence, as Augustine did, but there is no mere volitionally contingent dissociation between death and the aversive experience of bereavement. The two processes, loving and grieving, are emotionally and psychologically entangled.

Facts like those just mentioned, I assume, we would know, in some shape or form, in our 'original position'. We would recognize that one way in which our general capacity for care, commitment and emotional attachment will be exercised or expressed is in grieving over the deaths of people whom we love and to whom we are emotionally attached. We would accept this fact, this painful truth, I assume, as a tolerable cost or part of the burden of love. Wanting a life with the prospect of love, rather than one coldly or dispassionately stripped of the possibility, requires grieving, painfully grieving. It's a steep price but payable.

Pathologizing or medicalizing any and all cases of grief is indefensible. It would be a mistake to "bite the bullet and admit that normal grief is a disorder" (Wilkinson 2000: 290). It would be a mistake because doing so, not that any clinician wishes it, possesses the downsides feared by critics of the elimination of the grief exclusion (see also Kopelman 1994). Recognizing, however, that some acute and protracted forms of grief, just like comparable forms of sadness or hopelessness, should qualify as a mental disorder makes sound sense, I believe. Importantly, this means that the grief exclusion should be eliminated. Anti-eliminativists are in error if they suppose that grief can never assume the character of pathological or mental disorder, independent of being associated with a major depressive episode.

Which cases of grieving should qualify as a disorder?

Some cases of grief are associated with persistent pain, heightened vulnerability to disease and morbidity and loss of social responsibility (expressed in difficulties with completing job obligations, following through on social promises, and maintaining attachments to other loved persons). In such cases of persistence and loss of responsibility, a bereaved person may be permanently fixated on a death – torturing themselves with recollections of the dead person. They may search for the individual, be on the look out for them, or call out to them, reluctant to discard even minor artifacts associated with the beloved. The bereaved may be unable to form or even to conceptualize opportunities for loving other people or to deepen pre-existing emotional attachments. The bereaved may think "I have suffered an irreparable loss, and must do whatever I can to avoid situations and relationships in which I may incur such a loss again." A grieving person may even desire to join the dead person in death. Suicidal ideation may accompany a desire for reunion.

Any grieving that possesses a disabling contour or course like that just sketched above, and which persists for many months, showing no signs of dissolving or diminishing, may be wisely regarded as a plausible candidate for clinical classification and attention. Not because the line between grief-as-order and grief-as-disorder is fine or sharp. It's not. It's vague. But because grief's anguish, when protracted or undiminished with the passage of time, may serve no good purpose and exhibit no satisfying or able exercise of a person's capacity for care, commitment, and emotional attachment. Grieving is involuntary, of course, at least in its initial and many of its successive stages, but if the bereaved is unable to resist the process's negative impact, or somehow to "develop out" of it and to realistically hope for non-torment in the future, such a case may qualify as a mental disorder.

Many individuals, of course, like Augustine, grow out of or work through their grief. John Bowlby (1907–90), a British psychologist known for his work on child development and emotional attachment, suggests that when grief is healthy it typically passes through a number of distinct phases (Bowlby 1980/1998). An initial numbing or state of shock, followed by a phase of searching for signs of the beloved, then a phase of desolation or despair, and then a period of reorganization, recovery, or reclamation. Good or healthy if still more than occasionally painful grief does 'end', not necessarily with never again suffering over the loss, but with stopping to torture oneself for no good purpose and in identifying and coming to re-appreciate the importance of other personal commitments and attachments. "Through grief," writes Carolyn Price, "as much as through joy, we perceive what matters in our lives" (Price 2010: 20). Recovery and renewed commitments to others should become part of what matters in diminishment of grief.

I now turn to Bundy. Hacking says that the term 'disorder' denotes something undesirable (Hacking 1995: 17). No doubt it does. But can a category of profound moral 'disorder' like that of psychopathy also count as a label for a mental disorder or illness (and I shall suppose here that the issue with Bundy is one of a mental and not brain disorder, although speaking in the light of a fully empirical day the possibility of a brain disorder cannot automatically be excluded). One may think that people who possess traits that count as incapacities of moral character and ethically and grossly mistreat others should not be diagnosable as subjects of a mental disorder (see Charland 2004, 2006). Moral failings (rights violations, criminal behavior and the like) are just the sort of conditions that some critics of the idea of a mental disorder like to argue should not be part of medicine, given the contestability of judgments about such failings (Szasz 1960, 1974).

Of course, numerous sorts of disorders have a profound negative impact on people other than the individual with an illness, and greatly affect other persons' reactions or reactive attitudes towards the individual with a disorder (see P. F. Strawson 1962). These attitudes or reactions may consist in various negative responses of indignation, resentment, blame and the like, that persons (such as caregivers, family members, colleagues and so on) may have towards a person with a disorder – to their impulsivity, obsessiveness, paranoia, depressive withdrawal, desire for interpersonal control, and so on (depending upon the illness).

So, why not admit that a profound moral failing may sometimes also count as a mental disorder? Why can't a moral 'disorder', a disability with a dramatically negative moral impact, also be a mental illness?

Bundy was a horrific moral failure as a person. He habitually tortured and killed innocent people. The rules against torture and killing are fundamental moral rules. Without following them, human beings just could not live in cooperative, peaceable societies. So, what then of psychopathy? Is it, may it qualify as, a mental disorder?

Psychopathy generally has been regarded as a mental illness or disorder and has had a place in DSM as a sub-type of a so-called personality disorder, consisting, in part, of a "pervasive pattern of disregard for, and violation of, the rights of others" (DSM IV-TR, APA 2000: 645–50). Psychopathy is sometimes spoken of as an anti-social or dissocial personality disorder or as sociopathy, although different theorists sometimes press for different or distinct meanings (meanings that don't always capture the very idea of psychopathy) for each of these various expressions. In DSM IV-TR psychopathy is located as a personality disorder in Axis II Cluster B, which also includes so-called borderline, histrionic, and narcissistic personality disorders, colloquially called the 'bad' disorders, as opposed to the 'mad' or 'sad' disorders, of clusters A and C, respectively. Disorders in A and C are not so clearly connected with failures of moral behavior; those in B are so connected. Someone with a diagnosis of Narcissistic PD (Personality Disorder), for example, may possess a lack of empathy, an overwhelming need for attention, and a pronounced willingness to exploit other people.

What is the condition of psychopathy or its behavior like? How is it described?

The description most germane to someone like Bundy goes something like this (see Cleckley 1982). A psychopath is someone who appears to have no moral compunctions to speak of. Other persons matter to him only to the extent that he can satisfy some need or desire of his own. A psychopath may manipulate, cajole or coerce others to satisfy his wishes. He is incapable of love; is devoid of compassion; does not respect the emotional welfare or well-being of others. Human pain and suffering are of little or no concern to him. As for moral and social rules, they have little relevance to his actions, except insofar as their social enforcement does, for he himself does not wish to be captured or caught and punished. He violates moral norms with no sense of guilt. He expects other people to respect his rights and needs and uses their reliance as a basic platform for manipulation. If caught he blames others. He insists on being treated himself as morality requires, but refuses to reciprocate the treatment. Psychopaths also are pathological liars, self-impressed and grandiose. They tend to be relatively impervious to punishment, devoid of long-term personal plans, and stripped of empathetic reactions to the negative plight of other people. As best one can tell, in brief, such people are immoral to the core. Or perhaps they are better described as amoral to the core. Living or trying to live outside the world of moral and social rules, not merely violating them.

Philosophers recently have devoted a hefty amount of attention to the topic of psychopathy. Much of this attention is focused on the potential lessons of psychopathy for understanding moral judgment and moral motivation. I have no intention of discussing such morally complex and complicated issues in this book. My interest here is in whether psychopathy deserves to be classified as a mental disorder, given the TDM concept of disorder, even though or given that it is a moral failing or 'disorder'.

First off, as the philosopher Jeanette Kennett reminds us, a person like Bundy is "the psychopath of popular imagination: the embodiment of evil, who ... derive[s] particular satis-faction from murder and the like" (Kennett 2002: 341–42). The more common occurrence of the condition is of a much less odious and petty criminal variety, and "as they exist around us, [psychopaths] are not usually active and purposeful pursuers of the bad" (341). This fact is important because it helps to locate wherein the non-moral psychological difficulties of psychopathy may lie for psychopaths themselves. They lie, as the philosopher Heidi Maibom notes, in their "proneness to boredom/need for stimulation, shallow affect, and lack of long-term realistic goals" (Maibom 2008: 178). My description above (where Cleckley is cited) of the psychopath fits Bundy, and it is the Bundy-type that interests me here – someone amoral to the core.

Second, the exercise of our basic capacity for comprehension of self and world (a capacity that we identified in the 'original position') often takes the form of discriminatory and reactive sensitivity "to a ... range of environmental features" (Churchland 1989: 299). We observe that an apple is ripe, that a refrigerator is broken, that a local church is under repair, that a school yard is full, and that a neighbor's dog barks at dawn, and so forth. "These [sensitivities] are," as the philosopher Paul Churchland points out, "the sorts of immediate and automatic discriminations that one learns to make, and on which one's practical life depends" (299).

Now that Jack for the first time has eaten Vidalia onions, he gets a craving for them now and then. In the supermarket he looks for them, never having noticed them before. Now that Jill has seen a Van Gogh in a museum in Amsterdam, she hovers in front of a reprint of one of his paintings hanging on a wall of the bank in Fargo, North Dakota, where she has a savings account. Since Jerry has seen the neighbor's dog attack his cat, the dog has changed from being a pet in his eyes to being a predator. The story that emerges in such cases of observation and comprehension is of a dynamic process of perceptual discrimination, and of an increasing sensitivity and conceptual sophistication that our powers of comprehension may acquire in virtue of their application to a vast and changing variety of environmental features.

Churchland expands his list of examples. He notes as follows. "The discrimination of ... *moral* features is surely an instance of the same process, and it is made possible by training [or experiences] of a similar kind" (299). Churchland illustrates what he means by the discrimina-tion of moral features of the environment by offering examples of conceptual and cognitive development in children.

Children learn to recognize certain prototypical kinds of social situations, and they learn to produce or avoid the behaviors prototypically required or prohibited in each. Young children learn to recognize a distribution of scarce resources such as cookies or candies as a *fair* or *unfair distribution*. They learn to voice complaint in the latter case, and to withhold complaint in the former. They learn to recognize that a found object may be *someone's property*, and that access is limited as a result. They learn to discriminate *unprovoked cruelty*, and to demand or expect punishment for the transgressor and comfort for the victim. They learn to recognize a *breach of promise*, and to howl in protest. ... What the child is learning in this process is the *structure of social* [and moral] *space* and *how best to navigate one's way through it* ... This is as genuine a case of learning about objective reality as one finds anywhere. It is also of fundamental importance for the character and quality of any individual's life.

(Churchland 1989: 299–300)

Note the expression: 'quality of any individual's life'. Maibom remarks that the "psychopath is more bad than mad" (2008: 179). I am not sure exactly what Maibom means by this remark. Does she mean that psychopathy is not or never is (even in dramatic cases) a mental disorder? Does she mean that we should restrict our notion of a mental disorder to disorders that could occur in a world, as she puts it, "bereft of moral value" (180). I think not (for see below). I don't believe Maibom means to insist upon such a diagnostically exclusionary imperative. Insofar as morals matter to powers of mind, some moral failings may also qualify as disorders.

How to properly characterize the moral content or features of situations often is no easy issue, of course. Churchland's point, however, is that provided we do not set the bar too high or restrictively (by, say, insisting that moral sensitivity requires a storehouse of reflective moral concepts), the social and cultural environment contains moral content or morally relevant features that even a quite conceptually unreflective person can apprehend and to which persons may and do learn to sensibly and sensitively respond.

How a child learns to observe or respond to moral/social situations like those described above by Churchland, and not just to apples and refrigerators, is a matter (to use the language of the original position thought experiment) of the operation of at least two basic psychological capacities. One is the capacity for environmental *comprehension* (including comprehension of the interpersonal world). The other is the capacity for *engagement* in and emotional care and concern for other people. An individual does not need to be socially caring to recognize that an apple is ripe. But the observation of cruelty and a morally apt response to it typically express features of care and concern for others. Cruelty is no ripe apple.

We could, hypothetically, if we wish from behind the Veil of Ignorance, insist that basic psychological capacities such as comprehension and emotional engagement must be understood as restricted, in their relevance to the lives we desire and to mental health/illness, only to non-moral environmental features. This would mean that the description of the reason-responsive operation or proper working order of each such capacity (relevant to the attribution of mental disorder) not include learning how to exercise the moral sensitivities to which Churchland refers. Recognizing cruelty? Not in the range of relevant discriminations. Responding to injustice in the distribution of goods? Again, what has this to do with *mental* health or illness? Being sensitive to moral content has nothing to do with mental health or illness. Or so, in effect, we may decide or claim. Unwisely, I counter-claim.

Contrarily, there is, I believe, good reason to include (in deliberations behind the veil) features or events with moral content or relevance as among those that we should wish to comprehend and with which we should engage, as Churchland's remarks help to illustrate. The natural world is also a moral world. It possesses moral content. We would be worse off if we failed to think of our ability to recognize that content and engage with it as part of our reason-responsive capacities and mental or psychological well-being. To stop a Bundy from behaving badly, we must first recognize that he is behaving badly. He is brutal and sadistic. Then, we must care enough about his brutal and sadistic behavior, recognized as brutal and sadistic, to somehow accost or prevent him or to notify others who may prevent him.

An impaired capacity to grasp and understand moral features of social situations and to react reason-responsively to them may then count, depending upon its propensity conditions and harmfulness, as a form of mental illness or disorder or aspect of some disorders. We should hardly wish to prune our capacities for comprehension or engagement of moral sensitivity and sensibility without wanting ourselves to live a perceptually stunted and stultifying form of social life, myopically focused on situations that are devoid of moral significance or resonance. Apples and refrigerators. Not the inherent complexities of people and the puzzles and dilemmas of personal relationships and social behavior.

Medicine alone is neither equipped, nor suited, nor needed to handle all moral failings, to be sure. Nor certainly should we wish it to be. Our human dignity and respect for each other as responsible persons and rational agents morally constrains the reach of medicalization and medical practice. But should a *profound* moral failing like psychopathy (especially in a brutally sadistic case like that of Bundy) be precluded from being classified as a mental disorder? It may be challenging empirically and normatively to add reference to certain incapacities that are deep moral failings to a list of mental disorders. Addition adds controversy to a list, no doubt. But this does not mean that we *never* possess sufficient reason for doing so. The horrible facts of Bundy's behavior are not dulled or muted by embracing a psychiatric diagnosis, although the outrage we feel towards the behavior must somehow yield to an apt clinical response (see Pickard 2011 for insightful discussion of the complex topic of the clinical treatment of personality disorders).

The world in which we live is not stripped of moral content. Neither should our concept of a mental disorder be precluded from relying on *some* moral assessments of *some* persons and *some* behaviors. So, we may aptly hold that certain cases of psychopathy fall within the domain of mental disorder, even though we acknowledge that a psychopath is, as Maibom succinctly puts it, "mentally disordered in a very special way" (Maibom 2008: 179). A way constituted by a profound moral disability.

What of the implications of admitting moral assessments into the domain of attributions of mental disorder for moral skepticism or anti-realism about mental disorder? Different and overlapping themes contribute to the morally skeptical position (as noted in Chapter 4). One consists of reflecting on the differences between the moral judgments or conventions of different societies or cultures and the negative impact of cultural conventionalism about mental disorder on the objectivity or truth of a psychiatric diagnosis. Another consists of the fact that a diagnosis of a somatic or bodily disorder may seem so different from that of a mental disorder or illness. In psychiatry, disagreement about a diagnosis of schizophrenia or delusional disorder may seem endless, whereas in cases of somatic diseases like malaria, breast cancer and scurvy, not so. All this is challenging enough for a concept of mental disorder. In order to avoid making things harder for psychiatric medicine, then isn't it dangerously unwise to include a moral failing like psychopathy within a psychiatric diagnostic framework?

Culturally relative moral judgments may be worrisome for some issues about mental health, such as the challenge of achieving cross-cultural consensus about a social policy for the care and treatment of those who are mentally ill. Social disagreement breeds policy contestation. However, cultural differences are not necessarily problematic for the objectivity or truth of a diagnosis. The theory of mental disorder offered in this book proposes a culture-neutral or socially unbiased standard or norm for a mental disorder. The theory's standard or norm does not play cultural favorites. The norm is whether a basic or fundamental psychological capacity is impaired or disabled and therein whether a person is harmed or otherwise markedly worse off in any or virtually any cultural or social setting. Psychiatric diagnosis requires taking all the facts about desirable general abilities or capacities for a human being and weighing them against evidence in particular individuals of incapacitation in reason and behavior – in those capacities.

The source of the norm or standard for a mental disorder does not lie within one particular culture or historical period. It lies in an original or 'pre-cultural' position. It lies in capacities of mind and behavior required for living a satisfying and worthwhile life. The situation specific content of a satisfying and worthwhile life may differ from culture to culture, of course, and disagreements may occur over the dynamics and relevance of a capacity from one circumstance to the next. But there is baseline agreement over such issues as the undesirability and harm of being unable to remember one's past, act on affordances, take responsibility for self, and so on – no matter the different contents or specifics of a life.

As for the difference between somatic and mental illness diagnoses, somatic illness diagnosis may be distinct, in some ways, from diagnoses in psychiatric medicine. If I say that Smith has carcinoma of the esophagus this may be easier to demonstrate than that Jones is delusional or that Brown is agoraphobic. A diagnosis in somatic medicine may be easier to demonstrate because there are reliable methods in a laboratory or clinic for reasoning about the truth or falsity of a diagnosis. Biopsy of a lesion may be sufficient to demonstrate the presence of esophageal carcinoma. The diagnosis of a mental disorder or illness, by contrast and comparison, often is complicated by inaccessible information about a patient's social or environmental situation, ignorance of a patient's biographical history, various sorts of looping effects within the clinical setting, and the fact that some kinds of data useful in somatic medicine may normally be irrelevant for psychiatric inspection (such as the results of a biopsy or roentgenologic findings). But that does not mean that somatic medicine is not values based, whereas mental health medicine is values based. It also does not mean that disagreements are not possible about the proper norms for a somatic illness (see Chapter 4 for discussion). Contrary perhaps to superficial impression, there does not appear to be any essential or ultimate difference between the norms for somatic and mental illness. All of medicine agrees about a large body of capacities or faculties that we human beings need if we are to live satisfying and worthwhile lives.

SUMMARY

This chapter has focused on some of the concepts to be used to identify when a disability is 'clinically significant' – a mental disorder. It argued that a disability is clinically significant and otherwise qualifies (given requisite foundations) as a mental disorder when it takes place in a basic or fundamental psychological capacity. It claimed that capacities required for a worthwhile life are basic capacities and of the kind that when truncated or impaired may figure in a mental disorder. It explored how basic capacities may be identified from a perspective that possesses global or general human applicability.

The chapter summed up the concept of mental disorder that has been developed over the course of the book, distinguished it from other concepts of mental disorder and then applied it to two controversial questions in the psychiatric literature. One concerns whether grief may ever qualify as a mental disorder. The other concerns whether a dramatic moral failing or 'disorder' like psychopathy may qualify as a mental disorder. The chapter argued that to recognize that psychopathy can count as a mental disorder is to appreciate the morally significant content of our lives and the capacities needed to discriminate that content. It urged that we dismiss moral anti-realism's exclusion of mental disorder; and that we approach the domain of mental disorder realizing that the presence of immoral elements in a condition is no litmus test for the impropriety of a mental illness diagnosis. Psychiatric assessment is not moral judgment. But moral failing in a condition of mind and behavior need not dispel it from the domain of mental illness.

SUGGESTED READING

Frankfurt, H. (2004). *The Reasons of Love* (Princeton, NJ: Princeton University Press).

Griffin, J. (1988). *Well-Being: Its Meaning, Measurement and Moral Importance* (Oxford: Oxford University Press).

Kopelman, L. (1994). "Normal grief: good or bad? Health or disease?," *Philosophy, Psychiatry, and Psychology* 1: 209–20.

Kukathas, C. and Pettit, P. (1990). *Rawls: A 'Theory of Justice' and its Critics* (Stanford, CA: Stanford University Press).

Maibom, H. (2008). "The mad, the bad, and the psychopath," *Neuroethics* 1: 167–81.

7 Addiction and responsibility for self

Often we persons do things because we expect them to be rewarding or to confer benefits, although we may simultaneously know of and be willing to accept various negative aspects or consequences of what we do. I shop for a car. I need one. My old car is on its last cylinders. I discover one that I decide to purchase. It has a good consumer rating, reliably infrequent repairs, excellent gas mileage, and I can afford it. It's not made in colors I like. Nothing but Precambrian Pink or Geothermal Green. But I believe I can put up with incredulous stares from neighbors and the occasional snide remarks of pedestrians. Situation is: Among the options for a good car that I think are open to me, this one strikes me as the best at the time.

Are addictive patterns of behavior like that? When we spot a gambler living in financial debt up to his neck, having wasted away his life savings, divorced from his spouse, separated from his children, living in a run down efficiency apartment in a dangerous part of town, waiting on tables in an all night diner, is this the life-style he has chosen? Among the options or afford-ances that he actually believed were open to him, did habitual gambling strike him as the best at the time? Is it wrong to suppose that there is something wrong with him? That he is the subject of a disorder?

Gary Becker and Kevin Murphy (1988) propose just such a 'no disorder' model of addiction. An addict, they say, may act self-destructively or objectionably by social or moral standards. And they may be ignorant of certain harmful consequences of their behavior. But, Becker and Murphy add, addictive behavior is the upshot of rational efforts to satisfy desires or preferences for various goods, given circumstantial and temporal constraints. So, while addictive behavior is something mental, for it's a choice and deliberate, it is not a disorder or illness. An addict's behavioral preference for drugs or wagers at a horse track just is a decision, and like any other decision maker addicts try to get as much preference satisfaction overall as believed possible. Out of bad luck, ignorance or an ill-considered or fearless devaluation of the future, they may not succeed, of course, just as we may fail to be satisfied by our behavior. When, however, an addict consumes a drug or places a series of wagers at a track, at the time, this is a good choice from their subjective or personal point of view. Or at least it impresses them as what they should do. Yes, an addict may harm themselves, and, yes, we may try to help them to avoid situations in which they do so. But we should not help under the faulty assumption that addiction is a disorder or that something is wrong or psychologically unhealthy with them.

So say some theorists. Of course, denying that addiction is a disorder depends upon just how addiction is more fully understood. If we assume that addiction, properly so-called, puts a person's health or welfare at serious risk, that an addict's preferences or desires often are unsettled or in serious conflict, and that addicts are not indifferent to or ignorant of the harmful consequences of their behavior but often have difficulty (an impairment in rational or self-responsible impulse control perhaps) avoiding such behavior, even though they wish to and sometimes do succeed (albeit temporarily), then the case for classifying addictive behavior as a type of disorder starts to become strong. Certainly, it is stronger than depicting it as mere preference satisfaction. The assumption is that the addict would not act so disastrously on their own preferences, unless an illness or disorder of sorts is responsible.

So: Is addiction a disorder? Is it a mental disorder? The terms of these questions – 'disorder' and 'mental' – are subject to interpretative disagreements. In previous chapters in this book, I have tried to regiment or explicate their proper meaning. I have spoken, for example, in connection with the second term ('mental'), of Intentionality, and in connection with the first ('disorder'), of a-rationally gumming up the rational or reason-responsive works of mentality. If all or much of what I have said is accepted, we are in a position to decide whether a particular case of addiction is not just a disorder but (also in certain cases) a mental disorder. No mere preference satisfaction, but something wrong with a person in a manner that merits being classified as a mental disorder.

I shall begin by coming to fuller terms with the main term for this chapter. Addiction.

'Addiction' is used by ordinary folks as well as most behavioral scientists to identify excessive and deleterious behavior, behavior that is repeatedly engaged in despite its negative consequences, and often prefaced by impulses or motives that the addict wishes to control but finds difficult to consistently master, self-control or govern. The term 'addiction' hasn't always had such an unfortunate reference. At one time (in Britain in the early seventeenth century) the word referred to a devotional or obligatory attachment to a particular pattern of activity (Ross et al. 2008: 4). In that sense of the word, I am addicted to philosophy, for I am devotedly attached to it. That's not, needless to say, the reference of the term on which I plan to focus here in this chapter.

Lest in this chapter we be unsure of how 'addiction' is being used, I offer the following outline of the stages of addiction or addictive patterns of behavior. I take there to be eight main stages or steps in a typical clinical coal-face case of addiction. In referring to addiction's clinical coal-face, I mean the behavior pattern of an addict who appears in an addiction clinic or professional mental health care setting and seeks and receives treatment for addiction. Clinics for alcohol addicts, cocaine addicts, and so on, are "largely populated by people who are in the process of making a serious attempt to stop their behavior" (West 2006: 128). We may speak of such addicts as *unwilling* addicts as opposed to those who may, in some sense or other of 'addiction' and 'willing', be addicted but willingly or preferably so (if perhaps unaware of the deleterious consequences of their behavior or indifferent to them). Here are the eight stages or steps:

i   A person commences a behavior that is potentially harmful or deleterious. They consume a deleterious drug or other chemical substance or gamble.

ii   The behavior eventually becomes an object of focal attention and periodically repeated or habitual activity. The focus is such that at times or in some cases it may be "the only tune or story in the addict's head, and nothing else drives it out" (Morse 2011: 189).

iii   The behavior produces consequences that are not just harmful or that seriously risk harm to self (and/or to others) but are perceived as harmful or destructive by the agent.

iv   The perception or self-conscious experience of harmful consequences leads the person on certain lucid, critical or self-reflective occasions to negatively self-evaluate the behavior and attempt to refrain or quit. This does not mean the addict knows how to quit or how difficult it may be to quit or whether they can quit for any consistent period of time. But an attempt to refrain is made.

v   The addict refrains, quits or inhibits the behavior during certain periods (perhaps without assistance, perhaps only with assistance – individual cases and occasions vary). (I shall be interested in those cases in which an addict seeks or is receptive to help.)

vi   Quitting or cessation ultimately (timing and intervals vary) proves unsuccessful, however. The addict relapses. They 'fall back' into the detrimental behavior after a period of temporary stoppage. The behavior returns together with its negative consequences or risks.

vii   Relapse is interpreted by the agent as a form of personal disappointment or failure, not just as something destructive or risky, but as a source of shame, regret, self-blame, and embarrassment or as grounds for diminished self-confidence or self-esteem.

viii   The steps or phases of harmful behavior, temporary abstention, and relapse cycle repeatedly. The recycling, in some cases, may cease permanently, perhaps without harmful long-term residue. And the person just plain quits. (Thousands of addicts just plain quit for good at some point. They "age out" of their addiction.) Or the addictive pattern may lead to an addict's enduring exposure to harm or personal demise.

Each of the eight steps, which steps, I assume, help to constitute a prototypical addictive pattern, are not present in any and all cases of behavior that may be classified as addictive. They are not all present, as has just been noted, in what are sometimes referred to as 'willing' addictions, for instance, namely, in cases of addicts who make no attempt to free themselves of an addiction or of self-destructive behavioral habits. And I do mean 'free' – permanently liberated from the pattern. Some addicts do sometimes deliberately try to abstain from an addictive behavior for a temporary and prolonged period, and succeed, but only in order to decrease the extent or cost of the behavior in which they otherwise wish to indulge. Abstinence is not sought; merely a less costly manner of indulgence. However, in order to make progress on the topic of addiction, a theorist has to make certain background classificatory assumptions. So, I assume that addiction, at least in prototypical or exemplary cases where treatment is sought or received, possesses or cycles through the full eight steps.

There has been much discussion in the clinical and therapeutic literature of the actual and possible objects (substances, forms of activity) of addictive behavior – drugs, gambling, smoking, food, sex, shopping, internet, shoplifting. In this chapter I have nothing directly to say about the possible range of substances or activities to which people may be addicted or why in each case. I plan to focus on activities such as the consumption of drugs (like alcohol and cocaine) and gambling. These are the prototypical objects of addictive behavior. They are the exemplars.

Some steps in addictive behavior are more or less well understood. We certainly know that people behave imprudently and engage in risky behaviors (Step [i]). We know that such behaviors have variable motives. Sometimes risky behavior is engaged in simply as a form of entertainment; other times it possesses more serious, sinister, or dramatic motives. In some impoverished social or personal circumstances, for instance, one can easily imagine that a person may begin to take drugs in order to "alleviate the misery of existence" (Morse 2011: 178). We also know that non-human animal models of addiction help to explain some forms of habitual but deleterious or risky behavior, as does as reference to certain well known features of human psychology, such as the fact that imprudent risk taking may be pleasurable or perceived as adventurous, reinforced by peers or promoted in one's sub-culture. But other steps in addictive patterns are not well understood.

Relapse (Step [vi]) and some of the negative attitudes experienced after or during relapse (Step [vii]) are poorly understood. So, in this chapter I plan to concentrate not just on addiction but on relapse, namely, the episode of relapse itself and the agent's interpretation of relapse (the sixth and seventh stages of addictive patterns). I also plan to examine just what makes a case of addiction (of the sort outlined above; hereafter I shall refer to this simply as 'addiction', unless otherwise indicated) qualify as a *mental* disorder, when it does qualify, rather than as a disorder of the brain or neurological disorder. This is not to deny that some cases of addiction are or may be brain disorders. But it is to commit to conceptual elbow room for speaking of some cases of addiction as mental disorders.

To clarify: There is a great deal of behavioral heterogeneity among addicts, and the abuse of some drugs certainly may cause brain damage, so the possibility of a brain disorder classification of addiction must be considered in some cases. But from this it does not follow that any and all cases of addiction constitute "a disorder of the brain's reward system" (Gastfriend 2005: 1514). Currently, whatever is known of the biological substrates of addiction is consistent with the view that in many cases of addiction, the brain is in proper working order by strictly neurological standards, and so given that addiction is a disorder, the condition is, in such cases, a mental disorder.

So, in this chapter, I will use 'addiction' for a pattern with the eight steps and without the connotation that addictions must be brain disorders. I will assume that the phenomenon of relapse is central to the pattern. It is partially definitive of what makes addiction a disorder. The gambler or substance abuser, at one time, may truthfully report and make sincere efforts to gamble or consume less or not at all, so as to improve their lives and resist ruin, but at a later time their behavior reverses and they indulge. Relapse occurs. Then, regret or shame may set in, and they are confronted with their inconsistent behaviors and the harmful excesses of gambling or consumption. In cases in which such phenomena occur and cycle through reoccurrences, relapse may occur not because addiction has 'hijacked' the brain and its "reward system below decks, [and] then commits mutiny on the bridge by sabotaging the cognitive systems that would otherwise check its influence", that is, not because the brain is damaged (Ross et al. 2008: 156). It may occur because what leads some people to relapse and to become addicts is something that is best explained or understood in both psychological/reason-responsive and brute a-rational or mechanical terms, that is, in terms suitable for a mental disorder (as that phenomenon is understood in this book).

IMPULSE, INHIBITION AND RESPONSIBILITY FOR SELF

Addictive patterns are constituted, in part, although only in part, by "impaired control over behavior" or by an incapacity to inhibit behavioral impulses that lead "to significant harm" (West 2006: 10). (DSM talks not of addictions but of "disorders of impulse control".) I say 'only in part' because the full-bodied tale of the cognitive-motivational dynamics behind addiction is, I claim, a story of an incapacity or impairment in taking evaluative stock of oneself and of exerting reason-responsive self control. Following a terminological practice introduced into contemporary philosophy by Charles Taylor (1976) and others, I call taking stock and exerting reasonable self control taking 'responsibility for self'. No small chore that: taking responsibility for self. Telling a tale of the failure of self responsibility in addiction requires going well beyond trying to understand addiction just in terms of impulse control, inhibition failure or deleterious habit formation.

Consider impulse and inhibition first, though. William James tells us: "Impulses [push] us one way and obstructions and inhibitions [hold] us back" (James 1901–2/2002: 287).

References to impulses and inhibitions help to explain why people do what they do. Adam smokes cigarettes because he enjoys lighting up. He has an impulse to light up. Eve doesn't indulge because she is worried about her health. She is inhibited.

To correctly attribute an impulse or inhibition to a person means that they are inclined or disinclined, respectively, to behave in a certain manner on certain occasions. A person may push forward (impulse) or pull back (inhibition). Offer me a delicious piece of chocolate cake in a four star restaurant. I will take it. Offer me the same piece off the back of a garbage truck. I will refuse. The first situation reflects impulse. The second reflects inhibition.

We human beings, of course, are not mere creatures of impulse and inhibition. Normally, we have and exercise a power or capacity to reflect upon our impulses or inhibitions and to decide whether we should, or should not, act upon or even continue to possess a certain impulse or inhibition. Our capacity for evaluative self appraisal and assessment (taking stock of one's own person) the philosopher Harry Frankfurt aptly calls a "capacity for reflective self-evaluation" (Frankfurt 1988: 12).

As reflective self-evaluators we persons try to put in place self-appraised reflexive motivational relations to our impulses and inhibitions, our acts and abstentions. If I positively evaluate or appraise a disposition, say, judge it to be good or approve of it, I may attempt to stand by this judgment or assessment and act in terms of it. If I negatively evaluate a disposition, disapprove of it, I may try to inhibit the impulse. Tempted to steal or cheat, but judging the behavior to be base, degrading or incompatible with cherished character traits or with the life I wish to lead, I may decide that I don't wish to be tempted. I may yearn to be free of the disturbing impulse. Inclined to sample a recreational but potentially unhealthy drug and appreciating that consuming it jeopardizes plans or projects that I hold dear, I may try to restrain myself. Perhaps I will turn away from the site or sight of temptation.

The twin or related powers or capacities, the one of evaluative self-reflection, the other of behavioral self-control, are constituents or elements in the capacity for responsibility for self (as I will explain momentarily). It's a clear cut linguistic distinction between them, to be sure, but any hard and fast separation in practice or situation between the two powers can be tricky. Behavioral self-control or mastery often is itself a feature of reflective self-evaluation. The intensity or seriousness of mental effort behind or required by evaluative attention, for example, through which a person appraises their impulses or inhibitions, is not always a purely cognitive matter, not a mere matter of a spectator-like intellect. It is not always easy to control one's deliberations and mental activities. A person often has to take an active or authorial role in them.

A persistent theme in the literature on the manic episodes distinctive of bipolar disorder is the enormous surge of energy that a person in manic states acquires. Nancy Andreasen speaks of mania as like "riding a horse that is out of control" (Andreasen 2001: 233). "If the increased energy and richness of thought could be harnessed and focused, a time of mania could be a time of great creativity and productivity" (Andreasen 2001: 232–33). But, sadly, people in manic states typically lack prudent inhibition and respond to all sorts of indiscriminate thoughts. When mania is acute or severe, a person may experience a 'flight of ideas', thoughts or feelings whose wealth and abundance skips so rapidly from topic to topic that they cannot self-reflectively step back and effectively evaluate their impulses. The person may be incapable of asking themselves whether their behaviors are deeds in which they should be engaged. They may not even experience their agitated or excessive impulses as disruptive or upsetting. All of which seems best described as difficulties of self-control within the very effort of self evaluation. Focusing prudently on consequences of anticipated behavior, directing one's thoughts to desired traits of character, not allowing one's own ideas of possible behaviors to be swayed by attractive temptations to dangerous activity, and so on, all may require exerting a sizeable measure of self-rule or self-governance over one's mental processes and not just over one's physical movements or overt behavior.

The possible and more than occasional need for self-control within self-evaluation aside, the two dimensions of self responsibility are distinguishable. Philosophers have been intrigued by the roles of the capacities for self-evaluation and self-control in human agency and personhood. "Is there a sense in which the human agent," Charles Taylor asks in a classic paper on responsibility for self, "is responsible for himself which is part of our very conception of the self?" (C. Taylor 1976: 281). Taylor answers, yes, a human person is "not just a de facto kind of being, with certain given desires, but it is somehow 'up to him' what kind of being he is going to be" (Ibid.). He writes:

> Human subjects are capable of evaluating what they are, and to extent that they can shape themselves on this evaluation, are responsible for what they are in a way that other subjects of action and desire (the higher animals for instance) cannot be said to be. ... My dog 'evaluates' [a piece of] beefsteak positively. But the kind of evaluation implicit in the above [remarks] is a reflective kind where we evaluate our desires themselves.
>
> (C. Taylor 1976: 282)

The evaluative power of which Taylor speaks is the capacity for reflective self-evaluation. The corresponding power to shape, sculpt or mold oneself along the lines of one's evaluation is the capacity for reflective self-control. Both powers are proper parts of self responsibility. To possess a power of self responsibility, a person must not only be capable of evaluating which desires, impulses, or inhibitions she acts upon or possesses, but "of controlling ... behavior in the light of such reflections" (Kane 2005: 165).

Robert West, a professor of health psychology at University College London and the Editor-in-Chief of the flagship journal on addiction aptly called *Addiction*, has noted that when addicts (remember, I am using 'addiction' for the eight stages outlined above) evaluate themselves, appraise who they are and how they should behave or act, they may want to stop their deleterious behavior or quit for good (West 2006: 128). (Indeed, thousands of addicts, as noted above, ultimately do give up their addictions voluntarily and often without assistance from others.) Of course, an addicted person's desire to quit may not be sustained in effective purport and may undergo alteration or reversal. Motivational alteration should not surprise us, however. People quite ordinarily change tastes or preferences. Sometimes we adopt completely new and contrary preferences or aspirations. West remarks: "[I]t is unrealistic to assume that the situation would be any different for addiction" (West 2006: 128).

Many forms of motivational alteration are normal and not deleterious. They raise no judgmental eyebrows. Their effects are not harmful or destructive. But one can hardly take a casual attitude to reversal or alteration when harm to self as well as perhaps to others is a consequence and a subject's self-evaluation urges inhibition or restraint. One of the core elements of addiction, in cases of persons undergoing voluntary clinical treatment, and unlike more pedestrian forms of behavioral inconsistency, is that the agent knows that a behavior is deleterious and may make genuine and successful, albeit not enduringly successful (as long as they remain addicts), attempts to refrain. When things are going well and self responsibly, I (suppose I am an alcoholic) don't enter a bar and order a drink. When something goes wrong, abstention fails, and there is a self responsibility problem. "A shot of Scotch, please." Taking a drink, if desired and close at temporal hand, may be an impulse to which I succumb, when the deleterious consequences are far ahead or "the recollection of having suffered them in the past is ... already fading" (Von Wright 1963: 113).

The phenomenon of failed abstention and return to harmful behavior in a case of addiction is known, as noted, as relapse. Relapse is a psychologically puzzling state of imprudent affairs. It is difficult to explain how something that is negatively evaluated or believed by the agent in lucid or reflective moments to be harmful retains a grip on behavior. Unwanted behavior, rather than being a docile and easily mastered servant, may possess a motivationally salient grip on action.

Why does relapse occur despite the fact than an addict knows or feels that it represents a subversion of their prudent efforts to refrain? If there is a single answer to this question (and I am not sure whether there is) it is not simple.

Some say that relapse is, in each and every case, evidence of addiction being a brain disorder. "A disorder of the brain's reward system", as Gastfriend puts it (2005: 1514). But that cannot be right. In some cases of relapse an addict may remain to a considerable degree incentive sensitive or reason-responsive and also show an ability to refrain, especially when given extraordinary incentives or when reasons for refraining are presented in the right manner or context prior to relapse. If relapse occurs, though, because a brain disorder prevents the addict from refraining, powers of abstinence effectively are defeated no matter the incentives.

Perhaps relapse has something to do with the fact that addiction is a form of compulsion or compulsive behavior. That's what numerous theorists and clinicians claim. So: Is relapse due to the fact that addictive patterns are compulsive? And, if so, what exactly is meant by calling it 'compulsive'?

Some of the most striking statements in the literature about addiction and relapse are about drug addiction and the perils of certain drugs. Several scientists speak of drug seeking and consumption as compulsive. Alan Leshner, in a special issue of *Science* devoted to addiction, writes that the essence of drug addiction is "compulsive drug seeking and use, even in the face of negative health and social consequences" (Leshner 1997: 46). A publication of the Institute of Medicine claims that drug addiction consists of "drug seeking behavior involving compulsion [and] resulting in substantial impairments of health and social functioning" (Institute of Medicine 1996: 19).

Is addiction a species of compulsion? Not just drug addiction but addiction period? Reading the memoirs or autobiographies of addicts may suggest that it is.

Jack London (1876–1916) was a prolific American novelist and short story writer. He wrote *The Call of the Wild* and other books. London apparently struggled with alcohol dependence or addiction. "It is the penalty", London wrote, that a person's "friendship with John Barleycorn [beer and whiskey] sends [them into] the pitiless spectral syllogisms of ... white logic." A person "sleeps a drugged sleep" and "looks upon life ... with the jaundiced eye" of a pessimist to be "flung into the scrap-heap at the end" (London: 1982: 940).

Caroline Knapp (1959–2002), columnist and editor, also battled with alcohol dependence. (She died in 2002 of lung cancer.) She drank cognac, double shots of Johnny Walker Black, expensive red wine, and silky Merlots – among other types of alcohol. In a post-recovery memoir entitled *Drinking: A Love Story* (1995) Knapp reports that drinking occurred "when I was happy and ... when I was anxious and ... when I was bored and ... when I was depressed" (Knapp 1998: 167). This meant Knapp drank, as she puts it in one simple ironic word, "often". Knapp says she experienced "pangs of horror" when she thought back to what she did to herself (169). Alcohol had become "a kind of liquid glue that gums up all the internal gears" (168).

Cocaine, too, of course, may be immensely addictive. Consider the case of a woman named Helen. Paramedics found her "sitting alone on the floor in a corner of the kitchen." "Her legs ... pulled up underneath her chin and her arms ... wrapped tightly around her knees." "She was too agitated and disorientated to comply" with their request to lie down. (Flynn 1998: 181–82). Helen now reports that during the cocaine addicted period of her life "the only thing ... important ... was cocaine" (184).

Not just substances but activities, too, may be addictive. Consider sports wagering or casino gambling. "What did gambling do to me?", asks one victim (Heineman 1998: 163). He answers: "It removed all the positive characteristics my parents worked so hard to foster within me." "I cursed them, blamed them, stole from them, and, in the end, I attacked them physically" (163–64).

Compulsives, although certainly there is more to compulsion than this, fail to refrain from the 'compelled' behavior, even though possessing good reasons to refrain. They somehow get derailed from responding to incentives to refrain. The addicts described above seem to fall under this description. To save her physical health, Helen had good reason to abstain. To avoid attacking his parents, the gambler had good reason to quit gambling. So as not to be mired in the 'glue' of alcohol, Knapp had good reason to stop drinking. London, speaking from personal experience (as I assume he was), knew better than to end-up in a scrap-heap. But neither person consistently or unfalteringly did what they possessed self acknowledged good reason for doing. Quitting. Refraining.

COMPULSION AND ADDICTION

Frankly, I am not sure if it makes good sense to classify addiction as a form of compulsion. Much depends on what counts as compulsion.

Compulsive motivations are sometimes referred to as irresistible impulses. So, addictions are sometimes pictured as compulsive because they are said to stem from irresistible impulses. Relapse, in particular, it is said, amounts to yielding to irresistible impulses. Addiction, remarks Carl Elliott, "holds the leash" (Elliott 2002: 48). The attribution of irresistibility or leash holding, however, is in general not an illuminating way in which to depict addiction. If addictive behavior generally was irresistible, no addict could quit for good. Yet many addicts do eventually age or phase out of their addictions. Many addicts also exhibit a sizeable measure of circumstantial self-control, periodic self regulation or modulated abstention over the character or tempo of their impulse to behave (e.g. to consume a drug, to gamble). If the price, say, of a drug is too high, or a preferred dealer is inaccessible, a drug addict may temporarily curtail consumption and then re-seek their drug of choice only when its price falls or the special supplier returns. An alcoholic office worker may abstain from drinking when her boss or colleagues visibly are present. Some alcoholics are sensitive to the cost of a drink even after an initial drink. Some cases of abstinence often take place when a contrary incentive is strong, like the need to take care of an infant child (Levy 2011: 109). It is not as if the impulse itself is irresistible. At the very least it is circumstantially variable and felt in some circumstances to be resistible.

Compulsions are sometimes said to be insatiable. So, some clinicians, who are fond of classifying addiction as a form of compulsion, claim that certain substances or activities induce insatiable appetites or desires and this, so also they claim, means that addictive behavior is a species of compulsion. Relapse, it is said, stems from a failure to be satiated or to effectively eliminate a craving or insatiably intense desire for a drug or form of behavior.

The portrait of addiction as insatiable craving also is not illuminating, however. Attribution of insatiability is not in general a veridical way in which to picture the impulse or motivation behind either a general addictive pattern or the stage of relapse, although it may depict certain individual episodes or cases. Presumably, if certain drugs (say, alcohol) or behaviors (say, gambling) induced insatiable cravings, then seemingly everyone, circumstances being equal, who drank alcohol or gambled would become an addict. But they don't. Relatively few people who consume drugs or gamble end up as addicts. Even with a drug like cocaine less than 20 percent of users become addicted (Robinson and Berridge 2003: 26). The desire to consume or engage is not so stable, intense, and all-encompassing that, as West notes, it necessarily "sweeps all other considerations before it in a myopic and single-minded search for the object of desire" (West 2006: 77). People become addicted at different rates and under diverse circumstances, some perhaps in states of single-minded craving or insatiability, but most not. Some addicts do not even experience unpleasant withdrawal discomfort or negative or aversive affect prior to relapse. Besides, as Stephen Morse points out, "no sufficiently valid metric and instrumentation can accurately resolve questions about the strength of craving and the ability to resist" (Morse 2011: 185). So, appeal to the phenomena of craving or insatiability hardly warrants saying that any and all addictive behavior patterns are compulsive. The very idea of craving seems just as elusive as the very idea of being compelled. One notion hardly helps to illuminate the other.

So then, what explains why addicts do not lastingly abstain, but relapse and then persist in addictive patterns? If not insatiability or irresistibility, what? Is it time to give up on the very idea of addiction as a form of compulsion? Some commentators urge that we should abandon the idea (see Levy 2006). But perhaps that's too hasty. Perhaps we should think of addictive behavior as compulsive, *provided* that the concept of compulsion is free of essential reference to irresistibility or insatiability. Is there an empirically sound and clinically sensible alternative notion of compulsion that lacks such explanatory commitments?

Aristotle was emphatic in insisting that compulsions are not voluntary, but his notion of being non-voluntary is not a form of compulsion that addictions share. Aristotle's influential characterization of compulsion occurs in the *Nichomachean Ethics*. (The quotes that follow are taken from *The Nicomachean Ethics of Aristotle*, translated by Sir David Ross, and published by Oxford University Press in 1971. See Book III, Section 1, pp. 48–52. See also Stephens and Graham 2009b from which the next several paragraphs are adapted). Aristotle claims:

> Those things, then, are thought involuntary which take place under compulsion or owing to ignorance: and that is compulsory of which the moving principle is outside, being a principle in which nothing is contributed by the person who is acting ... [for example] if he were carried somewhere by a wind or by men who had him in their power.
>
> (48)

> What sorts of acts, then, should be called compulsory? We answer that without qualification actions are so when the cause is in the external circumstances and the agent contributes nothing.
>
> (48–49)

According to Aristotle, behavior is compelled only when its causes or sources are physically "external" to the agent and dominate their internal state or suffice to produce the behavior irrespective of the agent's internal state of reason-responsiveness or cognitive-motivational economy. An example is that of a sailor whose boat is caught by a powerful wind and driven onto the shore of an island. From the moment the wind takes hold of the boat, the sailor contributes nothing to determining the boat's course. What he wants, believes, decides or intends or reasons he should do is irrelevant to explaining what happens to him. The outcome of ending up on the shore is entirely determined by external forces.

Aristotle stresses the externality of causes of compulsive behavior, but internal forces, internal to an agent's body, may also dominate the agent's desires and expectations. Suppose, for instance, that a cerebrovascular accident (CVA) in my left hemisphere renders me mute. My failure to respond to a question about the city of my birth is entirely due to the brain damage I suffered. I know of my native city and wish to pronounce it as requested, but it matters not what I desire. My stroke has rendered my desire irrelevant. I am, we might say, compelled to remain mute. Suppose, then, that what counts for compulsion, in the spirit if not letter of Aristotle, is not that it puts my behavior under the control of forces outside my body, but that it removes it from the control of my cognitive-motivational states or reason-responsive capacities. It puts it outside of my Intentionality dynamics, not by virtue of being motivationally irresistible or insatiable, but by some other means.

What then? If 'compulsion' implies by-passing the control of one's cognitive-motivational states, this, too, is not a useful way in which to understand addiction. Here's why.

Terry Robinson and Kent Berridge, two biopsychologists at the University of Michigan, who have written extensively on drug addiction, offer an answer.

> An addict who steals, another who scams, another who has money and simply must negotiate a drug purchase – all face new and unique challenges with each new ... negotiation. Instrumental ingenuity and variation are central to addictive drug pursuit in real life. ... We believe that the flexible and compulsive nature of drug-seeking behavior in the addict requires ... motivational explanation.
>
> (Robinson and Berridge 2003: 34)

Addicts are motivated to obtain certain objectives and they exercise cognitive capacities and reason-responsiveness to devise flexible strategies for achieving them, appropriate to the challenges presented by changing circumstances. If addiction is compulsive, then it must be a form of compulsion that works *through* or somehow taps into the addict's cognitive-motivational dynamics or Intentional attitudes, not operates outside of them. Behaving addictively is something a person does, not something that happens to or befalls them. The cognitive-motivational processes involved in addiction no doubt differ in their operation from those of the non-addicted, but they are not by-passed or rendered impotent in a manner analogous to the wind that strikes Aristotle's sailor.

OK? So, what now? Should we *still* use 'compulsive' to refer to addictive behavior patterns? Perhaps. But we have not yet hit upon an appealing and applicable analysis of the meaning of the term.

Robinson and Berridge describe addiction (or drug addiction, their interest) as compulsive. They write:

> Addiction is more than mere drug use. It is ... a compulsive pattern of drug-seeking and drug-taking. ... The key questions in addiction, therefore, are why do some susceptible individuals undergo a transition from causal drug use to compulsive patterns of drug use, and why do addicts find it so difficult to stop using drugs.
>
> (Robinson and Berridge 2003: 26)

Addictive behavior is compulsive behavior. So they say. But what do *they* mean by this label? In a remark made more offhand than addressed explicitly to the character of compulsion, they mention a promising possibility for understanding compulsion. They say that even if an addict "has a stable rational resolution to refrain from taking drugs", the motivation to take a drug may compete with and "momentarily surpass rational intentions, precipitating a binge of relapse" (Robinson and Berridge 2003: 45). Elsewhere they refer to such rational resolve as a "dominant cognitive intention or desire" and of the contrarian impulse that produces a relapse (and that violates that dominance) as "transient" (Berridge and Robinson 2011: 39).

The picture that they have of compulsion and of the compulsiveness of addiction seems to go something like this: Addictive behavior is risky, destructive or harmful. Addictive behavior is habitual or repetitive. But the typical addict (remember, of the type who passes through the eight stages), also periodically reflectively or in lucid periods negatively self-evaluates the behavior and they may, on various occasions, resolve, decide or intend to break the addictive pattern and to inhibit the impulse. A decision ('rational resolve') to break is evident in their efforts to refrain and in the experiences of shame, regret, remorse and similar self-critical reflexive attitudes on relapse. Owen Flanagan, for instance, describes the content of his own remorse, when an addict who relapses, as follows: "Self-loathing was my constant morning companion." "I was a wretched, worsening train wreck of a person – a whirling dervish, contaminating, possibly ruining, the lives of my loved ones" (Flanagan 2011: 277–78).

Call these experiential elements of regret, shame, and so on, parts of the subjective or conscious phenomenology of relapse. When some rational choice theorists (like those mentioned at the beginning of this chapter) deny, in effect, that addiction is a disorder, they seem blind to the conscious phenomenology of relapse and to intra-personal conflicts or forms of ambivalence that addicts often feel or experience towards their own behavior. Deciding to quit, then quitting, which may be or feel immensely difficult, but then also lapsing and being disappointed in oneself. Such are the consciously unstable wages of addiction.

I propose that we refer to the desire to break an addictive pattern and avoid relapse as an instance of wanting or resolving to take responsibility for self. It is, to use Robinson and Berridge's term, a case of rational resolve. What the addict lacks, as evident in relapse, is the power or ability to *consistently* act in a reflectively self responsible manner. Addicts may try to correct themselves and to strive for more consistent across-time self control, but, while addicted, they cycle through periodic failure. They break, as I wish to put it, promises to self to refrain, promises that stem from what otherwise is a matter of more or less stable rational resolve or enjoys some sort of evaluative and not merely ephemeral dominance.

I will return to this idea of breaking resolve in a moment, but first, before doing so, I wish to examine what is meant by referring to the *self* for which an individual takes or wants to take responsibility and to whom a person may make promises to refrain. The psychiatrist George Ainslie's work on alternation and time inconsistency of impulses and inhibitions provides a useful vehicle for commentary on the reference of the term 'self' in a context like that of addiction and addictive relapse (Ainslie 2001).

On Ainslie's picture preferences or impulses to engage in certain behaviors in pursuit of perceived rewards or goods may *dramatically* oscillate or reverse themselves over time. Reversals may be harmful to a person. An individual may regret the behavior that stems from them.

But the closer in time a particular perceived good (no matter how small) is to a person the more likely they may be to follow the impulse to seek or consume it. As a result of proximity, an individual's evaluation of the merit of future goods may be inconsistent and therein 'irrationally unstable' and not in the person's best or prudent interests over time.

Suppose X and Y are mutually exclusive goods, one large-scale, the other small-scale, respectively. Say, X is protecting health and well-being. Y is snorting cocaine. When each of X and Y is far off in time, I may believe that the value or desirability of X far outweighs the value of Y, but as Y gets closer to me or becomes temporally more immediate, I may convert to thinking of Y (consuming the drug) as more valuable or desirable. If the 'self' of responsibility for self refers just to the time slice of me at the moment of my decision to consume, then there is nothing rationally inconsistent or unstable in deciding to take the drug. Clearly, I want it here and now. The drug, just like the slice of me at a time, is here and now. Health and well-being belong to a distant and possibly never existing slice or segment of my life. (I may die in the interim.) Self resolutions are not surpassed; promises to self are not broken. The self is wholly and only present. Consumption helps to satisfy the stronger preference of the time-slice. What *I* want just is what here-and-now-me wants.

It's not easy to have an articulated grasp of what a mere time slice of a person is. The idea is not just metaphysical (nothing is wrong with that, of course) but esoterically and phenomen-ologically so. So much of who we are as persons as well as our sense of ourselves as persons are connected with past acts and future possibilities. A slice may seem like a dissociated, desiccated or all-too merely molecular fragment. Hopefully, as a reason-responsive person, too, I am not so foolish as to judge that all that matters to me is here and now. Hopefully, impa-tience to consume does not overwhelm whatever judgment I may make about the value to me of my long-term future. Hopefully, whenever or if ever I prefer current rewards, I do so but not at all costs. My reflective or considered intentions call for a temporal distribution or blending of benefits, not of 'always more now is better', as if I am a slice, but of balancing and coordinating short and long run interests or preferences. Not so the individual addict during relapse, whose 'impatience' surpasses or suppresses whatever desire for across-time benefits they harbor or self-reflectively endorse.

Preferring present to future benefit is not utterly and absolutely indefensible or unreasonable, of course, even when the future good markedly is greater, for in the meantime misfortune (in say, death, as just noted) may overtake a person. Better something now than nothing later. We cannot be certain we will live to experience a future benefit. But self responsible people both acknowledge the possibility of unkind future fates and commit to across-time projects, aspira-tions and goals. After all, we are *temporal-historical* beings pursuing enduring and sometimes far-off achievements. Self responsible people care about the future.

The self evaluation that is constitutive of being a self responsible person is tied to being an individual who has a "sense of ... historical continuity", to use a helpful phrase of Erik Erikson (1968: 16). One of the most important ways in which we as persons think of ourselves is as persistent things or as creatures with biographies or stories of our own lives. Without an his-torical or autobiographical sense of one's own person and temporal endurance as a person, there is no self for which to be self reflectively responsible. There are no long-term plans, projects or commitments to hold dear. Without a sense of persistent selfhood there are no aspirations to care about in the sense that a person makes themselves (in Harry Frankfurt's words) "vulnerable to losses and susceptible to benefits depending upon whether what [they care] about is diminished or enhanced" in an outlook that is "inherently prospective" and that "both entails and is entailed by [their] own continuing concern with … what goes on in [their] life" (Frankfurt 1988: 83–84).

For persons as self-reflective, historically or temporally self-aware creatures, the fact that some rewards induce preference reversals does not mean that other preferences (desires for distant or less proximate goods) are obliterated or set at motivational or phenomenological naught. Our self reflective evaluations and aspirations may remain psychologically active within us even when they are behaviorally ineffective. Failure to act in conformity with them in relapse often is painful and regretful precisely because such forces remain subjectively and affectively alive.

The lapse of a relapse is a barometer of the power of addictive impulse. But relapse should not be seen as a mark of the *total* impotence or evisceration of an inhibition or reflective desire to refrain. The desire may still be in place, true, and not exercised in the act of consumption, but experienced in the shame and personal disappointment of drinking in a bar or snorting cocaine.

The philosopher Neil Levy has a crisp and effective way of making the point that I am making here, which is that we are not time slices but creatures persistent in time and that addiction reflects a failure to take responsibility for ourselves as historical beings with across-time commitments and concerns. Levy speaks in terms of personal autonomy and of a faculty of will or volition rather than of responsibility for self, but the spirit of his message is similar to mine despite its difference in conceptual letter. Levy writes:

> Addiction impairs autonomy … because it fragments the agent, preventing her from extending her will across time. … Her preference is temporary, and does not reflect her will.

> (Levy 2006: 12)

One striking feature of addiction, which is sometimes observed in clinics, is that while a preference to consume a drug or gamble may win a battle with self-evaluation in guiding an agent's behavior, this is not so much because the agent's evaluation is impotent or has evaporated, but because (despite its being negatively evaluated) the impulse to consume or to engage is life-defining for an addict. It's a part of a person's subjective persona: their sense of self and of what they are like as a person. And this phenomenon of self definition or partial self definition through addiction can in turn imbue non-addiction with an element of personal risk or unwanted indeterminacy about one's future. The impulse may not be effectively counter-balanced or inhibited by an affectively articulated or emotionally rich conception of life without addiction. Addictive consumption or engagement may be felt to express, for an addict, who they are fundamentally. It may be their way of locating themselves in their social and cultural environment.

An addict may have trouble imagining how they could reinvent, redesign or reconstruct themselves, no matter how much they may regret the failure to do so, as someone who does not gamble or consume. They may also try to appease themselves with quasi-intentions to take the steps of self-redefinition later (after one more drink, etc.). So, the failure of successful abstention may have less to do with its being temporally discounted, than with an inability to imaginatively feel for or affectively or empathetically engage with what it would be like to be someone who does *not* to enter a bar and consume a drink. To be someone who is not an addict. To be someone who does not wake up each day "thinking about where, when, and how [I] will next use [if a drug], or continue using, even while seeming on task" (Flanagan 2011: 280). The motivation to refrain may be stunted by a failure to grasp new life defining affordances. 'This is who I am, the person in the bar, not someone who returns to his air conditioned room to watch CNN and sip a Diet Coke.' An addiction-free future may seem as barren and unarticulated to a person as that of the desiccated time-slice, albeit immensely more extended. "I found the idea of complete abstention from alcohol inconceivable [and] terrifying", is how Flanagan once conceptualized his own addiction-free future (2011: 290).

The problem for some addicts (and I stress 'some' and not all) may be, in short, with the whole possible life-style of non-addiction and the project of reconstruction required to live it. Andrew Garner and Valerie Hardcastle describe this situation succinctly. An addict may "remain addicted because they don't know, in a profound and fundamental way, how else to be" (Garner and Hardcastle 2004: 377). "Becoming someone else is hard to do, and most of us simply cannot do it." An addict may "feel no [emotional] kinship with the world of recovery", the world of non-addiction (377). If so, promise to or responsibility for self is compromised or surpassed not or not just because of oscillating or changing impulses, but because a person is unable to imaginatively compensate for the perceived emotional emptiness or detailed affective vacuity of an addiction-free selfhood.

So then, what about the term 'compulsion'? What may this word aptly mean if it applies to addictive behavior? In light of the notions of reflective self-evaluation and responsibility for self, another way of understanding the category of compulsive behavior suggests itself. This is not the notion of behavior under physically external or motivationally by-passed control. Not the notion of repetitively dangerous behavior. Not that of behavior driven by essentially insatiable cravings or irresistible desires. But of behavior that contravenes an agent's efforts to take responsibility for self – a self understood as an historical person, when lucid, who prudently takes account of their future. Such a notion of compulsion may be put this way: A person behaves compulsively when they act against the motivational grain of their aspirations for responsible selfhood. In so doing, they exhibit a failure to take control of themselves namely, a failure of stable rational resolve. This failure takes place when acting on desires or impulses that are incompatible with their appraisals of how segments of their life should hang together. I enter a bar and order a drink, even though I know full well that I have reason for not doing so and likely will regret it afterwards. The impulse to drink wins out over my more or less persistent and reflectively desired inhibition.

ANIMAL MODELS

It is widely believed that work on non-human animal models of addiction provides helpful insight into the behavioral grip of addiction. And it does, no doubt. But if addiction is understood as behavior that contravenes efforts to take responsibility for self, which, in turn requires thinking of oneself as an individual with a history, animal models can't tell the whole story of addiction even if they tell important parts or address non-conceptual or non-self-conscious aspects of addiction.

Suppose that a subject is addicted (and perhaps compelled, in relevant clinical cases) only if their behavior runs against the grain of efforts to take responsibility for self. This self-evaluation or reflexive higher-order attitudinal component of addiction cannot be addressed by animal models. Animal models may help us to describe phenomena that are parts of addiction such as behavioral persistence in spite of harmful consequences or continued seeking for a substance even when it is visibly missing from the environment (Robinson 2004). (Seeking visibly missing substances is called "chasing ghosts".) Without, however, a component of negative self-assessment or evaluative disapproval, it is difficult to draw a line between 'mere' dangerous and dramatic preference reversals, on the one hand, and patterns of behavior that deserve also to be described as addictive (in the relevant clinical sense), on the other hand. Can a rat try to abstain from taking a drug, relapse, regret relapse and then pass negative judgment on itself? It can't, of course. Rodents lack the cognitive or conceptual resources required to make self-reflexive judgments. Rats may dramatically and dangerously reverse preferences over time, from the naturally prudent to the grossly imprudent. But reference to a mere change of preference fails to capture the full content or character of human addiction.

Berridge and Robinson (I switch the order of names depending upon the first named author of the relevant cited work) offer a theory of addiction or of drug addiction (of which more below) that owes a great deal to efforts at animal modeling. The conceptual nerve of their theory is that there is a special type of motivation for behavior, which they call 'incentive motivation', which may persist and control behavior, and even when human beings and non-human animals no longer take pleasure in it or dislike the behavior in which they are engaged. Persistent consumption of certain drugs may "change brain cells and circuits in susceptible individuals" making them "hypersensitive ('sensitized') in a way that results in pathological levels of incentive salience" to certain stimuli, such as drugs and drug cues that predict opportunities for drug consumption (Berridge and Robinson 2011: 31). "Mere sensory shapes, smells or sounds [may be transformed] into ... attention-riveting incentives" or (as they also put it) "motivational magnets" (37).

There is much in Berridge and Robinson's theory that I personally find attractive (see discussion below), but not its effort to capture the distinctive pathology or disorder of human addiction. Setting off addicts by describing them as riveted to pleasure-less incentives, in spite of harms to themselves, does not distinguish them from non-addicts whose failures of self-control may also be harmful or from laboratory animals who are riveted to harmful incentives. Finding certain stimuli to be, in some sense, magnetic although not liked and pursuing them in harms way may be part of addiction but it cannot be the whole story.

The brain reward system of non-human animals is a device for getting them to approach certain things or engage in certain behaviors rather than others, but it encodes no distinction (available to animals themselves) between what is of ultimate prudential benefit or reflects reason-responsive self responsibility and what simply reinforces behavior. People, however, are self-evaluators, self-interpreters, and we are built for active deliberation, conscious decision making and personal self-assessment. As the philosopher William Bechtel notes, "a major factor in developing such [talents] to the level that they can best serve our functioning as [self responsible] agents is our representation [or comprehension] of the self" (Bechtel 2008: 266–67). Unlike non-human animals, we persons can and do form representations of ourselves as "future possibilities" and "what we might become" (West 2006: 164). These future possibilities can be the targets or Intentional objects of our motives or reasons for action. They may function as incentives for doing one thing rather than another. *This* is who I want to be. Or: *That* is who I hope to become. Such self-conceptions together with the failure to consistently respond to them help to explain both why addicts feel regretful or remorseful and try to make continued efforts to refrain or abstain. Not so with rats or rodents, whose preferences may reverse or 'relapse' or become harmfully inconsistent with one with another, but whose behavior is never inconsistent with the sense or judgment, on their part, that they are failing to become the individuals (rats? rodents?) that they responsibly wish to be. They harbor no such conceptually enriched sense of self.

Addicts, in their self-evaluation, as witness the cases of Caroline Knapp and others, don't report after relapse that they regret mere reversals in wants, desires, or preferences. No, they report shame or regret over acting on preferences (for drugs, for gambling) that they themselves wish not to possess or to be moved by namely, preferences that represent failures of responsible selfhood. Theirs is not a complaint about preference oscillation. It's a complaint about letting themselves down, breaking promises to themselves, selves understood as historical entities. It's a complaint about sacrificing health and well-being to drug consumption or wagers at a track.

Robert West writes of such an addict:

> When ... restraint fails, there is ... no sense of having changed (one's) mind and deciding to engage in behavior as a positive step; rather the sense is of a failure to exert control followed by regret and a feeling of having let oneself down.
>
> (West 2006: 133)

West's observation rings true. Addicts fail to control impulses. True. Addicts engage in harmful or risky behavior. True. Addicts may engage in such behavior knowing that it is deleterious. True also. But what really marks a pattern of behavior as addictive (in the clinical coal-face of human addiction) is the inability to muster consistent motivational energy or strength around the effort to take responsibility for one's own self coupled with the feeling of, as it were, letting oneself down (and perhaps other people as well, as Flanagan poignantly notes). Even if some addicts are ambivalent about the reasons that they possess for avoiding a harmful behavior pattern, they are capable of recognizing the reasons as reasons and of evaluating them. Nonhuman animals are not.

NEURAL MODELS

The neurological existential bases of addiction and of drug addiction, in particular, lie, in part, in the brain's internal reward system, primarily in the mesolimbic dopamine system. This is a system of neurons projecting from the ventral tegmental area to the nucleus accumbens (NAcc) that use dopamine as their neurotransmitter (Malenka 2004). So, one hypothesis for addiction that a broken brain or neurological disorder theorist may offer is that addiction always is a breakdown or incapacitation of the reward system of the brain. Addiction is a disorder *of* the system and not just existentially with*in* it. If such a hypothesis is correct, this means that no case of addiction is, contrary to my explication of the concept of mental disorder, strictly speaking, a mental disorder. It is essentially and inescapably a neurological disorder. Addictive behavior stems strictly and purely from damaged neural hardware/wetware.

A lot of theorists endorse a brain disorder conception of addiction. Tempting and neurologically stalwart as the assumption may be, however, it is not a truly warranted hypothesis for any and all cases. To justify interpreting a disorder like addiction as a neurological disorder and not just as physically based, one must demonstrate that the base itself is damaged or impaired. It's one thing to possess a physical base. It's another for the base to be damaged or impaired and for us to be able account for addiction just in terms of the base.

No one would assert that a thermometer is anything but a physical artifact. If, however, an oral thermometer mistakenly is placed in an oven hot loaf of bread and breaks, then this does not mean that the thermometer broke because it was physically 'disordered' or 'dysfunctional'. The thermometer's failure is physically based certainly, but it is a situational failure. The break is due to the fact that the artifact was situated in an environment in which it was not designed to function and therein was unwisely placed. Or, to take another example, no one would assert that just because I am shivering and my shivering is controlled by neural mechanisms, there must be something wrong with my brain. The weather may be cold and I need a coat or sweater. So, likewise, a person may engage in behavior in a 'wrong situation', at a horse track, growing up in a family with alcoholic parents, and so on, where the processes of learning, memory and preference development and satisfaction produce objectively harmful or imprudent results that conform to addictive behavior patterns. This is not to say that the brain of such a person is broken, disordered or impaired. The brain may be doing just what it should be doing, neurologically speaking.

How are neural impairments or neurological disorders demonstrated in clinical neurology? There is no simple or short answer to this question. Various experimental procedures are used, studies of anatomical sites, searches for toxins (e.g. carbon monoxide poisoning), and so on. I do not hope to shed systematic light on the methods or demonstrations of clinical neurology in this book. But I would like to briefly focus on two sorts of neural impairments for the lessons that they contain about brain disorder identification. My intent is to help to explain why many addictions of the sort that follow the eight steps are not neurological disorders.

It has been known since the nineteenth century that damage to the striate cortex and to the region known as V1 produces a blind field or scotoma, such that patients normally report not seeing anything when stimuli are presented to that portion of their visual field (Weiskrantz 1986). Quite fascinatingly, some patients with the scotoma possess a form of competence of their visual system in which consciously *invisible* stimuli influence (reliably above chance) judgments about the location, brightness, orientation and even shape of those stimuli. For instance, if asked to 'just guess' whether a presented stimulus is of vertical or horizontal grating, subjects may respond rather accurately, in spite of sincerely denying that they see anything relevant.

The subjects themselves are completely unaware consciously of what they are looking at or that they are able to give rather accurate reports of a limited range of features of a surrounding environment. This phenomenon of limited and personally unrecognized success is known as "blindsight". The brains of blindsighted subjects are damaged cortically. Just how or where they are damaged is a matter of empirical contention, but there is no doubt that blindsight is a disorder of (and not just in) the brain. Reference to damage in the striate cortex explains the performance and decrements or limits in visual judgment. Note, again, blindsight is not a mental disorder, although it has mental consequences (namely, scotomas), for nothing Intentionalistic (cognitive or motivational or reason-responsive) figures in a scotoma's proximate propensity conditions. No reference is made to a person's beliefs, desires or to other reason-responsive attitudes in the description of its origins. Explanation is conducted in terms of a failure or decrement in the brute a-rational machinery of conscious vision and that's it. Emphasis is placed on finding an explanation in terms of the various cortical regions and brain systems that are involved in processing retinal inputs to discriminate specific aspects of a visual stimulus, such as its color, motion, and so on.

There are numerous examples of behavioral dysfunctions or disorders that possess exclusively a-rational brute causal (non-cognitive, non-motivational, non-Intentionalistic) neural sources. The field of clinical neurology is filled with references to them. Consider, for another example, ideomotor apraxia. This is a disability in carrying out simple voluntary gestures such as saluting or waving goodbye. When, for example, given a request to salute, a patient with the condition may be unawares that his hand needs to be raised in an appropriate fashion. They may appear confused, "being unable to either complete the movement or place the hand correctly" (Rogers 1999: 101).

When testing for ideomotor apraxia (or analogously, testing for blindsight) it is critical that the patient's non-performance is not under voluntary or reason-responsive control and that the misplacement of, say, the saluting hand is not a purposive action. Neurologists debate just where damage or injury to the nervous system must occur to produce the condition, but presumably "lesions in the posterior regions of the dominant hemisphere, specifically the parietal or temporoparietal region, are essential" (Rogers 1999: 101). Again, once voluntary or cognitive-motivational control has been ruled out and a lesion is said to be responsible, nothing Intentionalistic or reason-responsive is thought to figure in ideomotor apraxia's immediate sources or causes.

To be sure, each and every behavioral upshot or consequence of a neurological disorder is not necessarily completely and utterly non-Intentionalistic. When brain damage or a neurological disorder is present, as Derek Bolton notes, "there is a fundamental ... dysfunction caused by damage to neural structures" but the person with the disorder may still "seek to act despite this". In such a case, what may be observed in behavior "will be strategies for coping, as well as ... direct signs" of the brain damage itself (Bolton 2001: 196). Perhaps, for one illustrative example, the repetitive, isolated play of an autistic child reflects avoidance of situations that require understanding other persons. Neural damage presumably is responsible for the incapacity to understand, but the child's repetitive and isolated play may be a reason-responsive compensatory strategy. Perhaps playing is aimed at or reinforced by reduction of the disorientation associated with social incomprehension. Signs of a brain disorder may therein not be immediately open, as the example of autism illustrates, to an unencumbered clinical or empirical view. Such signs may be "disguised in some way by coping strategies, and will need special tasks, circumventing the coping strategies, to elicit them" (Bolton 2001: 196). Special investigatory clinical tasks may be needed to learn if Intentionality (beliefs, desires, and so on) is not a proper part of a disorder's immediate propensity conditions and if brute neural processes are the sole sources of a condition.

Clinicians may vary in their approach to neurological examination and diagnosis. But the search is for non-Intentionalistic mechanical damage – infections, tumors, traumas, toxins, metabolic disorders, strokes, lesions, developmental abnormalities and the like – and a subject's inability to control for the manifestation or expression of direct symptoms of a condition (and not the sometimes attendant compensatory behaviors that Bolton mentions).

Is addiction always and everywhere like that? Is it the result of brute neural or mechanical damage? No doubt, as just noted above, the neurological base of addiction (and of drug addiction in particular) lies (in part) in the brain's mesolimbic system and concentrations of dopamine in the extracellular space in the nucleus accumbens and NAcc related circuitry. No doubt, too, addiction is a disorder: an unhealthy or harmful disability. But is it always and everywhere a disorder not just based in the brain but also, like blindsight or ideomotor apraxia, of the brain? Does it result from neural impairment? I am claiming 'no'.

In thinking of the brain as damaged and of such damage as responsible for a behavior or set of harmful or undesirable behaviors, it isn't enough that neural activity, in some broad sense, is responsible for the behavior. No, the behavior must depend upon the brain in a particularly specific way. Something must be wrong not just in the behavior but with the brain itself. Think, by analogy, of the ringing of a door bell. Suppose my door bell rings at odd times of the day or night, and when I answer it, no one ever is there. Is it broken? This depends not just on the fact that it rings at odd times or that no one is at the door, but on whether the bell is failing to operate as it should because of something wrong with the bell itself. If squirrels are pushing the doorbell button, there is nothing wrong with the bell. If the bell was installed surreptitiously by my unfriendly next door neighbor, purchased to give me a hard time, and designed with a random ringing mechanism for just that sort of annoying purpose, then the bell is in perfectly good working order. Unfortunately for me, it works.

What about the brain and addiction? Note that the very same reward system that is responsible for addiction serves a whole variety of psychological as well as biologically adaptational or fitness enhancing functions, such as endowing safety, food, water, and sexual partners with reinforcing properties. Facilitating prudent consumption of a recreational drug or temperate betting at a horse track presumably is not what Mother Nature designed the neural reward system to do, however, anymore than she constructed the brain to help individuals to study ballet at the Julliard School of Music – itself risky behavior. If the brain reward system regulated drug consumption or gambling (or ballet dancing) well, it might do a lot of more significant and prudentially important tasks poorly. So, imprudent drug consumption or deleterious horse wagering is no reliable sign or trustworthy criterion of a damaged brain. The brain, in general, is not hardwired for personal prudence. Neural activity may systematically underwrite unwise behaviors for an individual without exemplifying a breakdown or something wrong or damaged in its biochemical wetware or hardware machinery.

Of course, addictive behavior patterns over time may *produce* a brain disorder given, say, the prolonged consumption of an alcoholic substance or other drug. Toxins may destroy relevant neural circuitry making it impossible for a person to control a wide range of responses. Parkinson's, for example, is a degenerative disorder in the dopamine system. Dopamine signals entrain motor habits and one of the symptoms of Parkinson's is loss of motor control. Chemical antagonists found in certain drugs (such as cocaine) may do something comparable in certain cases of addiction, causing difficulties of concentration, learning, planning and motivation. But it is one thing for a pattern of behavior to cause brain damage and another for it to be a neural disorder. So, my claim is that addiction (gambling, cocaine consumption, and so on) is not necessarily a neural disorder, as such, although it may harm the brain and become an effect or mark of brain disorder over time.

The claim that addiction, although (as I am assuming) brain based, is not per se or necessarily a disorder of the brain, combined with the proposition that addiction qualifies as a disorder because of its harmfulness or undesirability, has implications for the proper role of neuroscience in the study of addiction. Investigators should not ideologically presume that the brain reward system is broken in a case of addiction, although neuroscientific investigation still should play a prominent role in our explanatory understanding of addiction. Various important questions about addiction's origins and behavior patterns (in the eight step case) cannot be answered just by reference to states possessed of Intentional content or to an addict's reason-responsive or cognitive-motivational dynamics (beliefs, desires, and so on). I plan to outline one specific possible contribution of neuroscience to the study of addiction in a moment. It's a contribution that has been offered by Berridge and Robinson (see Berridge and Robinson 1995 and 2011).

HOW BRAIN MECHANISMS MAY GUM UP THE WORKS

Why, in particular, do addicts relapse? A number of different hypotheses about the irruptive role of a-rational neurobiological/neurochemical mechanisms into the space of reasons in relapse are available in the literature. These range from attributions of fluctuations of glucose levels in fronto-cortical blood flow to chemically impeded learning from punishment (West 2006; Levy 2006; Robinson and Berridge 2003). I am not going to sort through them. Rather, I plan briefly to describe one hypothesis that strikes me as a potentially fecund suggestion for how neurological mechanisms may contribute, in part, to relapse and contrary to an agent's considered disapproval of addictive behavior and deliberate attempts at self control. (Remember we are talking of addicts of the eight steps sort, and, in particular, of persons who seek or at least consent to treatment.) The explanatory hypothesis in question focuses on the onset of relapse i.e. on its first or incipient steps, not on the full blown behavior pattern of relapse, which may be immensely complicated and, of course, infused with Intentionalistic activity. The hypothesis, which is owed to Robinson and Berridge, comes in three main parts or progressive steps (see Stephens and Graham 2009b for related discussion). It goes like this.

Step one

The impulses or dispositions behind addiction and relapse are not forces that necessarily are irresistible. They may be (often, as noted above) resistible. Addicts are not all and always like (to borrow a metaphor of Stephen Morse) hapless cliffhangers, hanging over a deep chasm, strong enough to hold on for awhile, but too weak to pull themselves up (Morse 2011: 180). Indeed, some addicts successfully abstain for long periods. Addictive impulse may also be independent of pleasure seeking motivation. Gambling or drug consumption are not necessarily associated with either (i) expectations regarding pleasurable effects of behavior, for there may be no pleasurable effects in some instances, or (ii) a desire to make withdrawal less painful, for addictive patterns may recur long after withdrawal discomfort has disappeared. (See Stephens and Graham 2009b; West 2006.) As Berridge and Robinson note:

> The truth is that addicts continue to seek drugs even when no pleasure can be obtained, and even when no withdrawal exists. For instance, addicts seek drugs when they know those available will be insufficient for pleasure. Further, addicts crave drugs again even before withdrawal begins: ... And addicts continue to crave drugs long after withdrawal is finished.
> (Berridge and Robinson 1995: 71)

(Parenthetically, I am not sure why Berridge and Robinson speak of addicts 'craving' drugs when no pleasure or withdrawal discomfort is involved, but I shall let their use of this phenomenological term pass unexamined here.)

Rather, according to Berridge and Robinson, addicts find it difficult to avoid relapse because they do not remove themselves, or fail to appreciate the necessity of removing themselves, from environmental cues or circumstances that evoke impulses to seek drugs (or to gamble) – to pursue harmful or risky rewards. Environmental cues help to determine the emergence of the impulse to indulge. They signal the prospect of impending reward.

So, wherein resides the behavior gripping strength of environmental cues? Why is it important to remove oneself from the premises (their presence)?

Step two

The strength of cue-response-reward connections is based in a distinct neural substrate from the substrate that underlies liked or pleasurable goals as well as conscious representations of environmental situations that are occasions for pleasurable reward (Robinson and Berridge 2003; Berridge and Robinson 1995). NAcc-related circuitry underlies cue-response-reward connection strengths, whereas prefrontal and other cortical areas help to serve as substrates for conscious intentions as well as for anticipations of pleasure associated with behavior. These two substrates can dissociate or control behavior independently of each other. When that happens 'wanting' (that is, whether a person has an impulse, bias or disposition to behave) splits off from 'liking' (that is, whether a person expects to gain pleasure from the behavior). Berridge and Robinson cite a combination of, in their words, "neurobiological and behavioral evidence that ... suggest that ... dopamine-related systems [incentivize] rewards by a ... process that is separable from ... pleasure" (Berridge and Robinson 1995: 73).

Berridge and Robinson do not insist that pleasure seeking and reduction of withdrawal discomfort never play a causal role in addiction. Such phenomena sometimes do play important roles, especially perhaps in the early stages of development of addiction (as in e.g. recreational drug taking). Berridge and Robinson insist, however, that "after one has accounted for all instances of drug use by addicts motivated by pleasure or withdrawal, a vast amount of compulsive drug use remains to be explained" (1995: 73). They conclude, then, that there must be some other form or system of motivation at work in addiction that is distinct from pleasure seeking ("liking"). This other system is (what they call) "wanting".

> The sensitized neural systems responsible for ... incentive salience can be dissociated from the neural systems that mediate the hedonic effects of drugs, how much they are 'liked'. In other words, 'wanting' is not 'liking'. ['Liking'] is a different psychological process that has its own neural substrates.
>
> (Robinson and Berridge 2003: 36)

Step three

Dissociation between wanted or incentivized and liked or pleasurable behavior or reward means that the environmental cues that signal reward may help to trigger an onset of relapse via a process that, partly because it is not consciously associated with expectation of pleasure, is difficult or impossible for an agent to introspectively recognize and therein deliberately or voluntarily to inhibit. Wanting per se does not make addictive highs more pleasurable or withdrawals more painful. If it did conscious affective signals would presumably reveal to an agent the presence of an initial impulse to seek a drug or to re-begin a pattern of deleterious behavior. Rather, it's as if there are two ways of being motivated to engage or re-engage in addictive behavior, two motivational systems. One uses pleasurable or affectively salient signals or incentives to re-motivate. The other deploys wanted incentives. The two systems (as noted) can operate independently. A person may want what they don't like (or indeed like what they don't want). So, even if a person's self-declared goal and self-reflective judgment is to refrain from a behavior, wanting to indulge or consume may momentarily slip past personal aspirations to inhibit, constituting the first movements or time slices of an imprudent behavioral relapse pattern. Such a tilt is not itself a full relapse, but a relapse cannot occur with some initial tilting whose full or ultimate import may ultimately be hard to inhibit.

As they write:

> Once it exists, sensitized "wanting" may compel drug pursuit whether or not the addict has any withdrawal symptoms at all. And because incentive salience is distinct from pleasure or "liking" processes, sensitization gives impulsive "wanting" an enduring life of its own.
>
> (Robinson and Berridge 2003: 44)

Robinson and Berridge's three-step approach to the onset of relapse offers a neurological explanation for the impulse to re-engage in a form of negatively self-evaluated behavior. It helps to explain what may be called the tilt to lapse (or to relapse). Once the impulse or want is activated, then what happens?

To re-secure a drug or to place a wager consciously flexible and deliberate behaviors are required. Not just an initial 'tilt' in behavior but the activity of purchasing a substance, avoiding the law, and so on. I offer no surmise here (and neither do Robinson and Berridge) about the neural processes that may underlie these more complicated behaviors (all of which may take place during relapse) and whose explanation requires reference to an agent's cognitive-motivational dynamics/reason-responsiveness. Planning, decision making, emotional variables, and long term memory processes all play a role in full-scale relapse. So, for me (and apparently also for Robinson and Berridge), at post-tilt points, Intentionalistic explanation (reference to an addict's cognitive and motivational dynamics) is required for our explanatory understanding of relapse. Of course, again, reference to ongoing Intentionality or reason-responsiveness does not kick-in to the *exclusion* of continued reference to neural activity or to its irruptive role. It has been claimed that references to mechanisms of protein folding, monoamine production, as well as to various other neural processes must also be part of the full neural story of addictive motivation and reward. No doubt, too, in the case of drug addiction, we may expect that different substances or drugs may work differently in the brain (Kuhn and Koob 2010). References to such differences in brain system operation may be needed to explain various features of, for instance, drug withdrawal (like irritability and anxiety) (see also Flanagan 2011: 285). But explanatory reference to Intentionality (to reason-responsiveness, to cognitive-motivational dynamics) does, I believe, often operate to the exclusion of a fully or otherwise purely neurobiological/neurochemical explanation of relapse, depending on the form of addiction and whether it is a mental or brain disorder. What the brain often has to do to help to get a person addicted and to relapse is permit continued responsiveness to reasons but impair fully responsible self-control.

Here is a complementary hypothesis to that of Berridge and Robinson's for an explanatory role for neuroscience in understanding relapse. It is known that concerted or strenuous efforts at inhibition may cause falls in glucose levels and a general loss of what is sometimes referred to as mental energy (Levy 2006; 2011; Bayne and Levy 2006). So, one additional possibility, to that of 'like-less wants' noted by Robinson and Berridge, is that the resources in the brain that are required to resist or inhibit emerging impulses or wants are depleted or may be exhausted by prior efforts to sustain abstinence, and that such 'mental exhaustion' (which may be quite normal or normatively normal) may make resistance to the full complement of relapsing behaviors difficult. Some addicts may engage in full-scale complex drug seeking or gambling behavior in part because the 'will-power' or motivational energy needed to inhibit the behavior has become weak or depleted by past efforts to refrain. This depletion may occur in spite of the fact that a person sincerely negatively evaluates their addictive behavior and anticipates regretting relapse. They may then take a drug or gamble in a "compulsive degree" (Robinson and Berridge 2003: 44). This would be contrary to their otherwise self responsible resolve.

I am not here, as noted above, prepared to offer anything like fulsome speculation about the place of reference to brute neural mechanisms alongside reference to Intentionalistic and reason-responsive forces in the total story of relapse or addiction generally. I assume that the complete story will give interactive places to both strictly neural and mentalistic/Intentionalistic or motivational elements and that reference to neural elements will be useful in understanding how addiction helps to impair the effort to abstain. (I also assume that all cases of addiction or of relapse may not be alike. What is craved on Monday may be merely wanted on Friday, after Tuesday's imprudent indulgence.) Above I have only sketched some neural speculation that may be relevant to understanding the initial onset of relapse behavior.

If I might use a metaphor, the productive elements of any mental disorder, in general, and not just of addiction when a mental disorder, in particular, may be conceived as like a pale gray fabric woven tightly of thin black threads representing a-rational (non-Intentionalisitic) processes described in strictly brain science terms and white ones representing a subject's cognitive and motivational dynamics and described in Intentionalistic or psychological idiom. Were a disorder all black in descriptive onset and persistence, it would be a brain disorder or neurological illness. It is at just this point (deciding what type of disorder a disorder is) that some neuroscientific theorists of mental disorder end up painting themselves into a tight explanatory corner. They urge that we drop reference to the role of mind or mentality from a disorder's architectural specifications. They assume that a disorder with a physical basis is therein a non-mental physical disorder. Down that monothematically mechanical explanatory path lies not only anti-realism about mental disorder, I believe, but the inability to properly understand and appreciate the complex and dual proximate sources of a mental disorder. The contrary theoretical disposition, which is to view a disorder in all white or Intentionalistic terms, puts reason too much in charge. It neglects the subtle and complex ways in which neural activity and brute mechanical processes (even when they are themselves in proper working order) may help to impair or incapacitate reason's works. Down such a rationalistic or all-white explanatory path lies the inability to grasp the physical forces underlying a disorder as well as to appreciate the various 'mechanical' treatments or forms of clinical address or therapeutic intervention that may help to dissolve or control a disorder.

SUMMARY

The focus of this chapter has been on the nature of addiction. In examining the nature of addiction, the chapter explored what makes addiction a disorder, and a mental disorder when not a brain disorder. One question is whether the pathology or disorder character of the condition is a function of whether addiction is a species of compulsion. The chapter argued that the prospects for thinking of addiction as compulsive depends on whether addiction is understood as a form of impairment in a person's basic or fundamental capacity for self-responsibility. A necessary condition for effective self responsibility is the ability to extend one's aspirations and intentions effectively across time. A person who is unable to exert control over their future behavior by reflectively controlling their current impulses, wants and desires lacks the capacity for effective responsibility for self.

A challenge to understanding addiction as a mental disorder is how to distinguish between the causal explanatory roles of reasons and of mechanisms in the onset, course, and character of an addiction. How can choice and voluntary control be impaired in addiction, while yet remaining somewhat intact? To help to answer this question, the chapter concentrated on the phenomenon of relapse. Addicts are often able to recognize reasons to abstain and to control their behavior in light of those reasons, but when confronted with certain situations or environmental cues, they may revert back to harmful and self destructive behavior. Relapse may occur when addicts no longer like or find pleasure in a drug or activity (like gambling) or when the desire to avoid the unpleasantness of withdrawal has long subsided.

A suggestion of Berridge and Robinson was used to help to understand relapse. A stimulus cue can evoke a want or motive that is not associated with anticipated pleasurable motivation or conscious awareness and may therein be difficult initially to control in spite of otherwise contrary aspirations or intentions. Hedonic 'liking' or pleasure has its own distinct neural substrates from those of 'wanting'. Reference to the dissociation between those substrates or between wanting and liking is a potential explanation for a bias or tilt towards relapse.

SUGGESTED READING

Berridge, K. and Robinson, T. (1995). "The mind of the addicted brain: neural sensitization of wanting versus liking," *Current Directions in Psychological Science* 4: 71–76.

Fingarette, H. (1988). *Heavy Drinking: The Myth of Alcoholism as a Disease* (Berkeley, CA: University of California Press).

Poland, J. and Graham, G. (eds) (2011). *Addiction and Responsibility* (Cambridge, MA: MIT Press).

Ross, D., Sharp, C., Vuchinich, R., and Spurrett, D. (2008). *Midbrain Mutiny: The Picoeconomics and Neuroeconomics of Disordered Gambling* (Cambridge, MA: MIT Press).

West, R. (2006). *Theory of Addiction* (Oxford: Blackwell).

8 Reality lost and found

Where are we now? In the last chapter we examined a general instance of one of the exemplars of a mental disorder. This is a disorder of reactivity or impulse (to use the language of Chapter 2) known as addiction. To be sure, some cases of addictive behavior patterns may be expressions of a brain disorder, but the focus of the chapter was on cases in which addictive patterns express a mental disorder or illness and wherein psychological forces are an important part of the condition's causal explanatory foundations.

The present chapter examines a disorder of incoherence (again, to use the language of Chapter 2) known as delusion or delusional disorders, and it gives special attention to paranoia and grandiose delusions. The chapter also looks at schizophrenia, autism, depression and the subject of therapy for a mental disorder.

The topic or focus that holds the chapter together as a single chapter is our basic or fundamental capacity for comprehension of self and world and various impairments within that basic capacity. There are several disorders that mean that a person is 'out of touch with reality' and in which the possession and expression of patently false or bizarre attitudes or dramatic and harmful failures to comprehend engenders suspicion of mental illness.

SYMPTOM AND SCHIZOPHRENIA

The novelist James Joyce's (1882–1941) daughter Lucia was diagnosed with schizophrenia at the age of 25. Joyce took Lucia to a clinic of Carl Jung (1875–1961) in Zurich for observation, even though Jung had written a negative appraisal of Joyce's great masterpiece *Ulysses* (Frith and Johnstone 2003: 70). The strain of the young woman's illness (whatever its exact nature) became so acute that "the slightest setback could plunge Joyce into a depression" (Bowker 2011: 446).

Was Lucia really and truly schizophrenic? If one believes that such a diagnosis is quite possibly true, one will be impressed with claims like the following about this particular illness or disorder. "Schizophrenia is a term applied to a severe form of mental disorder that exists in all countries and cultures [and] about 1 person in 100 may experience this disorder at some time in their lives" (Frith and Johnstone 2003: 1). "This lifetime risk of 1% is about the same as that for developing rheumatoid arthritis" (Ibid).

Not every scientifically informed mental illness theorist believes that any diagnosis of schizophrenia can be true. As creatures of our own efforts to make sense of mental illness or disorder, the category of schizophrenia is hardly an uncontested fixture of diagnostic taxonomy. Some theorists are skeptics or anti-realists about the disorder.

"Schizophrenia," says Hanna Pickard, may not be "a category that carves the world at its joints" (Pickard 2009: 91). What Pickard, who is both a therapist and a philosopher, means by this remark is that to her the category of schizophrenia does not appear to be a genuine or distinguishable type of mental illness or disorder. 'Schizophrenia' may not to refer to a real mental illness. An alleged or nominal one, yes. A real one, no. However, if schizophrenia, she notes, is not a true mental disorder, this fact does not mean that the various symptoms or behaviors associated with a *diagnosis* of schizophrenia are not real or fail to be matters of impairment, disturbance and undesirability. The symptoms or behaviors connected with the diagnosis can and should be studied ("scientifically explained" is the expression she uses) even if skepticism about schizophrenia is warranted.

Pickard is not alone either in being skeptical about the reality of schizophrenia or in trying to push a-categorical doors open when it comes to the category (see also Boyle 1990; Bentall 2004; Poland 2007). Skeptics charge that the assumption that the term 'schizophrenia' identifies a single illness or disorder (whether a mental disorder or, indeed, for that matter, a brain disorder or disease) has failed to be not only vindicated by scientific evidence, but also constitutes a harmful assumption in terms of which to manage the varieties of patients and associated clinical strategies and therapeutic uncertainties associated with the diagnosis.

The category or concept of schizophrenia certainly has played a major role in describing certain forms of mental illness for over one hundred years (witness the case of Joyce's daughter). It commands, in the words of Jeffrey Poland, who is himself a skeptic about the reality of the condition, "entrenchment ... in clinical and research practices and in the public imagination (Poland 2007: 168). So, as Poland notes, skeptics about schizophrenia suffer from an initial disadvantage over and against those who believe that there is a real, honest-to-goodness disorder that deserves to be described as schizophrenia. What is the disadvantage? Poland puts it as follows: "critics ... have a burden to carry that involves the development of viable alternatives to current [schizophrenia] research, clinical and other practices" (Poland 2007: 183). Poland calls this the "put up or shut up" rejoinder to schizophrenia skepticism. If we don't talk about schizophrenia per se, then how should we classify and deal with patients who have the symptoms otherwise thought constitutive the condition? If relevant patients are not possessed of symptoms of schizophrenia, of what condition or conditions do they possess symptoms?

One response is to take the symptom-orientated rather than an illness-orientated approach to understanding patients with a schizophrenia diagnosis, which Pickard recommends. Symptom-orientated approaches are favored by a number of prominent skeptics about schizophrenia as well as by some mental health professionals who, while perhaps not absolute skeptics, nonetheless appreciate that, in the words of the psychiatrist Garry Honey, it is "unreasonable to expect any model [of schizophrenia] to reproduce all of [its] symptoms" especially given that "two patients ... with the same diagnosis of schizophrenia could have no overlapping symptoms" (Honey 2009: 253).

The symptoms whose identifications most frequently are cited for a diagnosis of schizophrenia tend to segregate or cluster into three groups: (i) Psychomotor poverty (including blunted or flat affect, poverty of speech, decreased spontaneous movement, and a-sociality). (ii) Disorganization (including incoherent speech and behavior, inappropriate affect, and problems of attention). (iii) Reality distortion (including delusions and hallucinations). These last (those of reality distortion) are the classic signs of psychosis, and indicate that a person is "out of touch with reality" (Frith and Johnstone 2003: 62).

I am intimately familiar with them. Just to describe one of several symptomatically similar patients, in the psychiatric facility in which I worked, one of the patients for whom I cared was a Roman Catholic priest. One day I entered the priest's room early in the morning shift. I found him underneath his bed on the chilly linoleum floor in his pajamas. He grinned as he grasped his hands around the underside of the metal bed frame. I had at most a few minutes to see that he was in his robe and escorted to the unit's dining room for breakfast. Most of the other patients in the unit had eaten. Many already were back in their rooms or in one of the recreational areas. A lingering three or four were finishing their meals or having a final cup of coffee.

The priest appeared to have been awake all night. He spoke to me. "Graham," he said, "you are the worst kind of a devil." "You seem like a good angel."

"But you're bad." "*Really* bad."

I had had encounters with him previously that were similar, marked by his disorientation and distrust. In them I had little or no control over his behavior. So, I thought I would be unable to fulfill my dining hall escort assignment.

The priest spoke to me of feeling the "tidal pull" of evil, of communion wafers being an "ordeal" to swallow, and of his wish for no "contrivance" with the devil.

"You contrive me, Graham", he said.

Contrive him?

What, if anything, was he meaning or intending to say? I could only guess. Perhaps he wished to dissuade me from seeing to it that he had breakfast. Or perhaps he was offering a gibe or joke, possibly a humorous neologism with a touch of theological irony. But he did not seem to be in a humorous mood. His grin was more anxious than friendly. Or perhaps he was hearing voices, the verbal auditory hallucinations common in someone with his diagnosis. Perhaps he was sharing their content or his interpretation with me.

The priest's diagnosis? Schizophrenia. Christopher Frith, a neuropsychologist at the University of London, describes it as "the most devastating" disorder "seen by psychiatrists" (Frith 1998: 388). Or if one wishes to put Frith's description in schizophrenia-skepticism terms, the symptoms or problematic behaviors associated with the alleged condition, by any other name, would still disrupt or disturb as much.

Regardless of whether schizophrenia is a genuine disorder, clearly the priest was at the very least delusional. (Note: I do not take a stand in this book on whether schizophrenia is a real illness or condition. This is partly because I am undecided about the issue, though I incline towards skepticism. I shall write as if it is a real illness. I plan to focus, instead, on the specific topic of the disturbance or symptom of delusions. Much of what I say can be translated into schizophrenia-skepticism terms, however.) The priest had a penchant for losing contact with reality. I may have been no angel, but I was no devil.

People who are delusional may utter strange and contextually bizarre things such as

- My food is being poisoned by the police.
- I have the power to forgive sins.
- I am infected by insects crawling under my skin.
- My uncle's thoughts are being carried on snowflakes that fall on my head.
- My wife has been replaced by an imposter.
- I exist in two separate places at the same time.
- Barack Obama's thoughts are being inserted into my mind.
- I am dead. I do not exist.
- I have been metamorphosed into a beast.

The possible intentions behind such strange utterances are hard to fathom. They do not express claims that one can easily imagine oneself sincerely making. They are alien. How alien? Karl Jaspers surmised:

> The profoundest difference … seems to exist between that type of psychic life which we can intuit and understand, and that type which, in its own way, is not understandable and which is truly distorted and schizophrenic. … [W]e cannot empathize, we cannot make them immediately understandable, although we try to grasp them somehow from the outside.
> (As quoted in Frith and Johnstone 2003: 124. See also Jaspers 1913/1963)

If Jaspers is right, then the utterances of classified schizophrenics or of individuals diagnosed with stark or severe delusions often are so alien and bizarre that they ultimately defy empathetic understanding. Empathy, when successful, consists of taking the mental perspective of another person, i.e. imaginatively assuming another's frame of mind or conscious mental attitudes. If Jaspers is right, then certain stark and symptomatic utterances of a schizophrenic just cannot be rendered imaginatively or intuitively understandable. If he is right: We cannot imagine our speech being congruent with their speech. We cannot imagine what sort of meaning or intentions their speech acts may have. We may say of such people "It's not as if she really believes that Obama's thoughts are being inserted into her mind" or "It's not as if he actually thinks that his wife has been replaced by an imposter". "It's only a malfunction of their nervous system speaking" or "They are exhibiting neurochemical impairments and not genuine speech acts infused with Intentionality". So, it would be no wonder, again, if Jaspers is right, that we can comprehend such episodes only from the outside. Only impersonally. Only mechanically. There is nothing Intentionalistic or reasonable going on inside such subjects when delusions are expressed. No general frame of a rational mind into which to project ourselves. If so, their disorder is a neural disorder or set of neural disorders flat out.

G. E. Berrios seems to make a similar point when he claims of the delusional utterances that they are "empty speech acts … not the symbolic expression of anything" (Berrios 1991: 12). There is no clear evidence of any identifiable Intentional content, he suggests. No logical or rational connections of the kinds which are required of the conceptual media of Intentionality. The utterances are mere (albeit quasi-articulate) noise but in the guise of mentality.

Is Jaspers right? In thinking of Jaspers and wondering if he is right, I think of my priest patient. I liked him a lot. At times he was quick, candid, ironic – traits in his speech and of his person that I enjoyed. So, did he really mean *nothing* in calling me a devil? In saying that I contrived him?

One must be cautious in making a Jaspers-like judgment of un-understandability, 'unproject-ability', or non-meaning. Bentall warns that if we fail to empathize "hard enough, we may fail to recognize the intelligible aspects of [another] person's experiences" (Bentall 2004: 29). The affected person may have, on the whole, a very different conscious or mental life from our own, yours and mine, to be sure. But to their disorder or behaviors, we should not add, if Bentall is correct in his caution, the loneliness and isolation that may come from our not making a con-certed effort to understand them – from the 'subjective inside' if possible. If we make that effort, if we attempt to empathize, how should we do that? Here is an idea that may help to orientate our effort.

In a paper that appeared in *Mind and Language* in 1997, Tony Stone and Andrew Young outline an account of the intelligibility or reason-responsive sensibility of delusions of the sorts exhibited in the kinds of speech acts above. The account proposes that deluded individuals have bizarre, unusual or anomalous perceptual experiences that help to give rise to delusional beliefs and to genuine speech act intentions (Stone and Young 1997). The perceptions precede the utterances and help, as it were, to 'rationalize' them. Stone and Young propose that linkages between unusual perceptual experiences and delusions are, in effect, from-the-inside imaginable or empathetically understandable. A deluded person treats their bizarre experiences like a datum or 'reason' for making their bizarre claims. Here is part of what Stone and Young say:

> [Some] delusions can be best explained in terms of the person suffering from the delusion trying to make sense of or explain a disturbing perceptual experience that is brought about by … brain injury. On this view, the brain injury does not alter beliefs directly, but only indirectly by affecting the person's perceptual experiences.
>
> (Stone and Young 1997: 330)

On Stone and Young's view, some delusions may be subjectively reasonable responses to unusual perceptual experiences. The unusual experiences themselves and a subject's need to interpret them are responsible for the delusion. If this hypothesis is true, empathetic under-standing of delusions and their associated speech acts may be achieved if we can somehow mimic or imagine undergoing relevantly similar unusual perceptual experiences. Claims about Obama's thoughts being inserted or of one's spouse being an imposter are not like psychic coughs or sneezes. They are spontaneous efforts at trying to make sense of one's own phenomenology.

That's an intriguing conception of delusion. It's one that may open up an empathetic window inside at least some symptoms of (a diagnosis of) schizophrenia (delusions in particular). And it may do so independent of whether schizophrenia is itself a distinct or determinate kind of illness. As we will see momentarily, it's not an idea that is original to Stone and Young, as they readily admit.

On the question of empathetic understanding of unusual symptoms compare schizophrenia and its symptoms with autism. Autism is a neurodevelopmental or brain disorder, although the precise neurological details are not known. Its central symptom is, in two words, social aloneness – an obsession with objects (not persons), a paucity of imaginative play, a lack of normally expressive social engagement (such as eye contact with others or with the eyes of others), and engagement in monotonous, repetitive activities with, say, numbers or the material innards of physical objects. Presumably, there is something it is like to a person to undergo at least some its symptoms. But what is it like to be autistic?

Understanding autism from the inside or empathetically presents a serious intellectual challenge to the imagination of family members, clinicians and other persons engaged with autistic people, although by drawing upon the memoirs of high-functioning autistics, a variety of clinical and experimental studies, and other sources, seemingly it has proven possible to describe various aspects of the inner life of autism. Indeed, attempts to describe the experience of autism offers a method for describing what it may be like to suffer from at least certain elements in schizophrenia. This is to focus not on the total composite condition, assuming that there is one, but on particular symptoms or types of behaviors or complaints and to ask just what those particulars may be like to a person. Symptom-focus in the case of understanding autism does not necessarily presuppose that some symptoms (say, paucity of imaginative play) are neatly walled off from others (say, repetitive activities). Various symptoms or their causes may affect or be affected by other symptoms. But focusing on symptoms does require not automatically lumping or 'gluing' all sorts of symptomatic behaviors together. Whether a symptom can be understood empathetically and apart from other symptoms is, in the broadest sense, an empirical question. Not to be decided in advance or on a priori taxonomic grounds.

Symptom focus is a common orientation among clinicians who treat disorders. Sally Satel, a psychiatrist and lecturer at Yale, remarks that often "it is symptoms, [and] not formal diagnoses, that direct the clinician" (Satel 2008: 42). Satel is right, of course. Symptoms constitute the evidence base for a diagnosis and are the primary behaviors marked for initial clinical attention.

A symptom orientated approach may help us to inside-understand the conscious states that underlie the lack of expressive social engagement in persons with autism. It may make 'rational' or 'logical' sense of their lack of engagement. Normally, when we see a happy face, our smile muscles react, and when we see the face of someone who is suffering or in pain, our face may react in the way in which we ourselves would if we were in pain. One quite common result of our power for spontaneous facial mimicry is that we come to feel the same emotion that we are observing. A person does not need to be an astute clinician or tenured social psychologist to notice this phenomenon. We all are familiar with it. Attempts at deliberate affective mimicry were imaginatively made by the nineteenth century poet Edgar Allan Poe (1809–49):

> When I wish to find out how wise, or how stupid, or how good, or how wicked is any one, or
> what are his thoughts at the moment, I fashion the expression of my face, as accurately as

possible, in accordance with the expression of his, and then wait to see what thoughts or sentiments arise in my mind or heart, as if to match or correspond with the expression.

(Quoted in Goldman 2006: 17–18)

Capacities or abilities for facial or affective mimicry are often impaired or absent altogether in autistics and this suggests that autistic persons may miss much of what the philosopher Jonathan Glover aptly dubs "the small change of everyday life" (Glover 2003: 513). The possibility that autistics miss the communicative meaning of face-to-face encounters, namely Glover's small change of daily life, may help to explain why autistic individuals become socially confused and withdraw or are preoccupied with impersonal objects. One high-functioning autistic friend of Glover (a woman with Asperger's Syndrome) asked him to imagine what his social interactions would be like if other persons actually had no faces whatsoever. This thought experiment offered Glover a metaphorical prime for an empathetic glimpse of her inner world (Glover 2003: 514). Absent non-facial cues, social contact with other people would appear mysterious in the extreme. What person would not withdraw or become confused under such 'face-less' circumstances?

Consider a diagnosis of schizophrenia with delusions again. A person with the diagnosis may think, for example, that "her thoughts, emotions, bodily sensations, or movements are under the control of some alien being or force" (Sass and Parnas 2007: 71). Or an individual may be withdrawn and lacking in expressive levels of affect. They may also be depressed. Bentall notes: "Depression is … commonly experienced by [people diagnosed as schizophrenics], both during acute episodes and also during the prodormal phase that precedes the appearance of positive symptoms" (Bentall 2004: 234).

All sorts of delusions may occur in deluded people and not just in those who are subjects of schizophrenia. Just to name a few: grandiose delusions (e.g. that one is divine or divinely inspired), delusions about the state of one's body (e.g. that it is diseased or infected with parasites), sexual delusions, and delusions that one's ideas, impulses and intentions are under the control of or being broadcast to other persons or agents.

Laura, a young woman diagnosed as schizophrenic and the subject of a case study by McKay et al. (1996), helps to illustrate a range of delusions that may occur in people. Laura reported that the hospital staff was plotting against her (persecutory delusions). She complained of being forced to urinate on herself and to pace the ward (delusions of control). She said that other people sometimes invaded her mind, banishing her other thoughts (delusions of thought withdrawal) or projecting their thoughts into her stream of consciousness (delusions of thought insertion). She lamented that other persons were directly aware of her thoughts as soon as they occurred to her (delusions of thought broadcasting).

How can we understand what it is like consciously to undergo a delusion? Delusory ideas, feelings, or beliefs may seem, as noted, utterly weird and unintelligible. Normally, when we describe another's thoughts, we can imagine (or at least think we can imagine) them harbored within ourselves. But how can we imagine what it is like to think Laura's thoughts or those of the priest for whom I cared in Boston? I am forced to urinate on myself? The nurse's aide literally is a devil? What is the subjective or conscious Intentional content of such attitudes like? What do the attitudes mean or what are they about to their victim? Do subjects of delusions possess any warrant, reason or factual evidence, no matter how subjective, behind them? Where did *this* or *that* delusion come from? Did it come from an anomalous perceptual experience as Stone and Young suggest? Regardless of where it came from, why does the person persist in and not reject it? Don't they know that it may ruin them?

To get a handle on all this, I begin with a pair of unusual attitudes taken from the Bible. I am going to examine whether they are delusions and how best to understand them if they are delusions.

Yes, that's right: Scripture. Two cases. One case is Abraham; the other is Christ. Yes, that's right: Christ. I plan to examine these two candidate cases, in part, because the psychiatric literature occupies itself with pre-established clinical cases (like that of Laura) and typically under a sponsorship of a diagnosis like that of schizophrenia. I want no such pre-sponsorship or no prior impulse to diagnose our cases (in order to allow for skepticism about schizophrenia). I call this exercise an exercise in examining some possible grandiose, that is to say, *grand delusions*.

GRAND DELUSIONS

The Bible reports a case promoted by the Church as a triumph of religious faith, although it may be a better fit for classification as delusional. It's the story of Abraham and Isaac. The tale goes as follows: God orders Abraham to sacrifice his only son Isaac. To add poignancy to Abraham's situation, Isaac had been born after Abraham's wife was past her years of childrearing. Abraham is told by God to "Take now thy son ... and offer him ... for a burnt offering upon one of the mountains that I will tell thee of" (Genesis 22).

Here is a quick and imaginary analogical version of the tale that the Christian philosopher Robert Adams says he presents to his students:

> What would you think if you asked your neighbor why he was building a large stone table in his backyard, and he said, "I'm building an altar because God has commanded me to sacrifice my son as a whole burnt offering. Won't you come to the ceremony tomorrow morning?" All [Adams's students] agree that the neighbor should be committed to a mental hospital.
>
> (Adams 1999: 284)

Should we say the same thing about Abraham? Yes, he was deluded. He had lost contact with reality. He should be committed to a mental hospital. But, if so, why classify him as deluded? Why answer 'yes'?

Suppose the following assumption is true of subjects of delusion. Delusional thinkers or deluded people are unrestrained by common sense or relevant background factual knowledge that they should possess. Laura should know better. People don't force other people to urinate. As for Abraham? Abraham fails to filter the command of an apparent divine voice through "his knowledge of right and wrong" (Adler 2007: 282). The philosopher Immanuel Kant writes of Abraham's reaction to the experience of an apparent divine voice as follows: "Abraham should have replied to this supposedly divine voice: 'That I ought not to kill my son is quite certain.' "But that you, this apparition, are God – of that I am not certain, and never can be, not even if this voice rings down to me from [visible] heaven" (quoted in Adler 2007: 271). Allowing an apparent divine voice to overrule one's background ethical knowledge is not triumphal faith. It's delusional.

But we must be careful. Is a delusional state or attitude *necessarily* unwarranted or evidentially unrestrained? (Remember the Stone and Young hypothesis here.) Even if, objectively speaking, Abraham should not have taken the voice experience seriously, if we were in his phenomenological or experiential shoes, isn't it understandable that he thought of God as communicating with him? Such a belief may have helped him to make sense of the bizarre voice experience.

Harvard psychologist Brendan Maher (1974, 1988 and 1999) has argued, in a manner that has influenced Stone and Young as well as several others who write about delusions, that delusions sometimes are spontaneous attempts to make personal sense of bizarre or unusual perceptual experiences. Maher writes: "the processes by which deluded persons reason from experience to belief are not significantly different from the processes by which non-deluded persons do" (Maher 1999: 550). Not significantly different? Maher's hypothesis is that delusional attitude generation may be just as rational or reasonable, from an agent's personal point of view, as certain forms of attitude formation in non-delusional people. Reasonable in the following sense: Just as we normal folks try to make sense of our perceptual experiences, so, too, do victims of delusions. The pathology or wrongness of a delusion, for Maher, therein lies not in the bizarreness of a delusional attitude or conviction as such, but in the experiential aberration that helps to generate it. From a deluded subject's point of view, such an experience cries out for an explanation, and in a manner that suggests to them not that something minor has happened to them, but that "everything [has] changed in a fundamental way" (Maher 1999: 560).

If anomalous experiences figure in the generation of delusions, perhaps we should not be surprised if the Intentional or conceptual content of the corresponding delusion is close to the phenomenal or conscious content of experience. In such a case, the content of an anomalous experience may be taken at face value and the deluded subject more or less just endorses it (Bayne and Pacherie 2004). For example, if it seems to me in some auditory experience that I have as if God is speaking to me, then although the content of the experience is utterly bizarre and not normally to be expected, the experience itself (perhaps given its vividness or forcefulness) is taken by me as reliable and trustworthy. So, I believe that God is speaking.

If the Bible is to be believed, just such an anomalous (bizarre, unusual, and endorsed as veridical) perceptual experience occurred to Abraham. Kant, however, still would insist that Maher would be mistaken if he was to claim, in, say, Abraham's case, that "I should kill Isaac" is an instance of a reasonable response to a supposedly divine voice. A divine call to kill one's son? That sort of interpretation of any experience dramatically outstrips the norms or limits of common sense or warranted assertion, subjective constraints and the failure to ignore background base rates or likelihoods and all. Abraham should have believed that something was wrong with him, that he was hallucinating, not that he was struggling with a genuinely divine imperative. He over-accommodated his experience of a divine voice. Vivid or significant as the experience of the voice may have been, it betrays (Kant argues) a tell-tale theological and moral flaw. No optimal divinity, or at least none worth worshipping and loving, would command killing one's own son. So: Maher may be right about the subjective warrant of *some* delusions, but he would be wrong (if he applied his perspective to it) about *that* particular one. No parent should believe that God wants him to kill his child. The experience as of hearing a nurse's voice commanding you to urinate is one thing. Perhaps on a hospital ward, it may make sense to believe that a medical authority is barking orders to you. But kill your son? Hell no. God would never ask for *that*. Such is Kant's position.

So, was Abraham deluded? There is much to be said for the proposition that, yes, he was. But I do not wish to pursue a detailed interpretation of his case here. My target is the phenomenon of delusion, not Abraham.

So what, then, is a delusion? Is it merely something bizarre and objectively unacceptable or without proper evidential support and out of truthful or veridical touch with objective reality, as the case of Abraham may teach us? DSM (1994) offers the following gloss on the notion of a delusion.

> A false personal belief based on incorrect inference about external reality that is firmly sustained despite what almost everyone else believes and despite what constitutes incontrovertible and obvious proof or evidence to the contrary. The belief is not one ordinarily accepted by other members of the person's culture or subculture (e.g., it is not an article of religious faith). When a false belief involves a value judgment, it is regarded as a delusion only when the judgment is so extreme as to defy credibility. Delusional conviction occurs on a continuum and can sometimes be inferred from an individual's behavior. It is often difficult to distinguish between a delusion and an overvalued idea (in which case the individual has an unreasonable belief or idea but does not hold it as firmly as is the case with delusion).
>
> (APA 1994: 765)

The DSM gloss is unhelpful. It describes delusional thinking, in part, in terms of the possession and falsity of a belief. Let's examine this description for a moment.

Beliefs can be notoriously difficult to identify or individuate. Giving grounds for believing that we ourselves or another person possesses this or that belief is not a gratuitous exercise. This is especially true in certain cases of mental disorder. When a victim of schizophrenia says "I'm a trichlorinectic pilot" or "I don't know a Turkish drug addict when he sleeps in a box" does he believe all that? (Fulford et al. 2006: 164). And that is *what*? A trichlorinectic pilot? How can delusions be beliefs, when we may have pronounced trouble, in many cases, attributing any conceptual content whatsoever to some of a patient's delusional attitudes? We may be tempted to say that such people have delusional beliefs, but we just cannot figure out what they are. Or we may be tempted to say that in certain cases Berrios is right. Delusions are content-empty speech acts. Whatever certain deluded patients are expressing, it is not beliefs. Either way, a rigid absolutism requiring of delusional attitudes the status of beliefs creates difficulties and is arguably an unwise clinical constraint on the very idea of a delusion.

There are related objections to the presumption that delusions are beliefs. Some subjects of delusions act on their 'beliefs' or attitudes – sometimes violently – while others utterly fail to act in accordance with them or even to be inclined to do so. Victims of the Capgras delusion, claiming that they live with an imposter who is substituting for their wife or husband, may fail to submit missing person reports on behalf of their displaced spouse. Those who claim to be Jesus Christ are rarely observed trying to walk across lakes.

Perhaps some delusions are beliefs, while others are not. Or perhaps some deluded attitudes may be similar to beliefs, but fall short of belief prototypes. They may be quasi-beliefs, half-beliefs, or some such. Stuart Hampshire notes: "There may be many shades and degrees of ... half-belief and half-imagination." "The phenomenology of belief is very various, and beliefs may exist at many different levels of explicitness and rationality" (Hampshire 1965: 101). Hampshire is right. There are many mixed, in-between cases of beliefs and half-beliefs, and the requirement to segregate a deluded person's thoughts or opinions into two bundles, those that are delusional beliefs and those that are not delusional at all because they are not beliefs, seems to run against the clinically coarse grained manner in which delusions often present themselves. When I, for one, worked in a psychiatric clinic, doctors rarely discussed whether a deluded subject really or genuinely believed what they claimed or said that they believed. They did not understand their project to be getting clear about the concept of belief. The usual worry was whether or how a patient might act on their claims or interpret them to themselves – not whether the individual genuinely believed them.

Another response to the question of whether delusions are best understood as beliefs is to hold that a deluded person is someone for whom there is an Intentional or conceptual content to the delusion (pace Berrios), such as that, for example, one's wife has been replaced by an imposter, but that the content may not necessarily be believed. The deluded person does not necessarily believe the content to be true. The person may decide against the prospect, present to his mind, that he should refrain from being with his imposter wife or call the police. But in spite of not acting upon the content of the delusion, he finds that the thought or content lingers on and he also thinks he should not rid himself of it. When he comes to appraise the content, he may disclaim responsibility for its occurrence and persistence in him, but he will not try to dissociate himself, publicly or privately, from the thought. Even if unpleasant and harmful consequences follow upon the thought or even if other people claim it is groundless, he may cling to it. He may therein take what may be called a 'delusional stance' towards it, whether it decisively qualifies as being believed or a belief state or not (see Stephens and Graham 2004 and 2007; Currie 2000).

To an extent, the issue of whether delusions are best understood as always and everywhere beliefs is pragmatic or contextual, turning on which definitions of 'delusion' as well as 'belief' one adopts and on the clinical and therapeutic utility of one's definition. There are, for example, some well-worked out conceptions of paranoid delusions as beliefs, interpretations that are said to have clinical utility in treating victims of paranoia (see Kinderman and Bentall 2007). Given the clinical contexts in which diagnoses of delusions are made, trade-offs may arise between the overall strategy of treating delusions as types of beliefs or treating them as complex concatenations of attitudes or as enveloped in a delusional stance that a person may take towards their own thoughts. The upshot is that it may be difficult, if not impossible in some cases, to adjudicate which conception of a delusion is best, and the territories between one and another conception are imprecise and perhaps quite irrelevant in some circumstances of clinical practice.

In any case, resolving disputes about the identity of beliefs and about the role of beliefs in delusions is not something I want to make crucial to the rest of the discussion of delusion in this chapter. So, let's assume, for the sake of discussion, with DSM that delusions are beliefs at least in certain cases. Are they also, as says DSM, false and firm?

Delusional attitudes may sometimes be true. Some paranoid people are persecuted. When she was charged by Henry Kissinger with being distrustful about her Arab neighbors, Golda Meir, then prime minister of Israel, is supposed to have quipped: "Even paranoids have enemies."

DSM leaves epistemic elbow room for such a possibility. Here is its description of the jealous type of delusional disorder. It says: "This subtype applies when the central theme of the person's delusion is that his or her spouse or lover is unfaithful." "This belief is arrived at without due cause and is based on incorrect inference supported by small bits of 'evidence' (e.g. disarrayed clothing or spots on the sheets), which are collected and used to justify the delusion" (APA 1994: 297). Note that this leaves open the possibility that a delusional conviction of jealousy may be true, albeit insufficiently supported by a subject's own evidence or warrant base.

Are delusions (as DSM says) firmly sustained? Some are. But delusional convictions, so called, may fluctuate. Clinicians report that some of their delusional patients occasionally entertain the possibility that they are mistaken in their beliefs or may not have decisively made up their mind about their truth (Bentall 2004: 324).

How about the notion that delusions are inferable from a deluded person's behavior? Such inferences are possible, of course, oftentimes, but not always. There may be "'double or multiple bookkeeping', whereby the delusional [belief] is kept separate from the rest of experience" (Sass 1992: 275). A man may say, "My wife has been replaced by an imposter" and then let her fix his meal or sleep next to him in bed. Or a "patient who insists that her coffee is poisoned with sperm still drinks it without concern" (Sass 1992: 274). A delusional 'belief' or content may be so shorn off from apt behavior as barely to appear (and as already suggested above) belief-like.

Then, too, why should articles of religious faith secure exemption from the category of delusion? Perhaps license for exemption depends upon social or cultural contexts in which religious attitudes typically are embraced. Articles of religious faith are parts of peoples' normal cultural equipment and among the belief stocks acquired from a surrounding community. "It is undeniable," Dominic Murphy writes, "that normal maturing brains do pick up on religion, along with many other ... theories of the world" (Murphy 2006: 181). So "religion is not delusional even if religious beliefs are false" (181). But Murphy adds: "Numbers matter with delusions." "If only a tiny minority of humans were religious we might be more tempted to call them delusional" (Murphy 2006: 182). If Murphy is right, if religious attitudes may count as delusional when numbers of religious believers are small, then where does such a possibility leave, say, a religious leader like Jesus Christ, who presumably believed that he is God Incarnate? Was Christ deluded? The initial number of Christians was small.

One common type of delusion is of a grandiose variety in which an individual is convinced that they possess special powers or are on a special mission – as Abraham seemed to think he was with respect to the divine voice. Was Christ possessed of grandiose delusions? If he and only a tiny minority of others (immediate followers, Doubting Thomas aside) believed that he was God Incarnate, then perhaps the more delusional his attitudes towards himself should appear to be.

The temptation to picture Christ as deluded, of course, demands clarification. Reflecting on the temptation is helpful, as I hope to show, in understanding delusion more generally.

Grandiose delusions occur in several different types of disorder, including mania, so-called delusional disorder, and schizophrenia (Munro 2006: 140–42). Grandiosity consists of inflated and evidentially unwarranted estimations of one's power, worth, knowledge or importance. Did Christ suffer from it?

Perhaps ironically, given the imprimatur, a number of Christian apologists have worried about this question. Here is C. S. Lewis in *Mere Christianity*:

> A man who was merely a man and said the sort of things that Jesus said would not be a great moral teacher. He [might be] a lunatic – on a level with a man who says he is a poached egg.
>
> (1952: 55)

But Lewis raises the possibility of Christ being deluded only to dismiss it. "It seems obvious to me," writes Lewis, "that he was [not] a lunatic" (56). (See also Davis 2002.)

The physician, musician, theologian, and Nobel Prize winner, Albert Schweitzer in a book with the fascinating title of *The Psychiatric Study of Jesus*, considered whether Christ was a victim of delusion. But Schweitzer denied it. He summed up his appraisal as follows: "The high esti-mate that Jesus [had] of himself ... fall[s] far short of proving the existence of mental illness" (1948/1913: 72).

If we take certain aspects of the Gospels at face value, however, a plausible case can perhaps be made that Jesus was truly or genuinely delusional. Let's see how such a case may be constructed. It will, I believe, teach us something about delusion itself. Or at least that is my aim.

Numerous eyewitnesses who were familiar with his activities and teachings claimed that he was "raving mad" (John 10:19) and "out of his mind" (Mark 3:21). He said bizarre and grandiose things such as:

- I am the Way, the Truth, and the Life; no man cometh unto the Father, but by me. (John 14:6).
- I and my Father are One. (John 10:30).
- Before Abraham was, I am. (John 8:58).
- I am the light of the world. (John 8:12).
- Whoever acknowledges me before others, I will acknowledge before my Father in heaven. (Matthew 10:32).

According to historical orthodoxy, shared by both Christians and non-Christians alike, Jesus claimed to be an equal to God or to be God in incarnate form. (Not every scholar, agrees with this orthodox interpretation of Jesus. Bart D. Ehrman, a distinguished historian of the Gospel period, claims that "the historical Jesus did not believe in his own divinity." "His concerns were those of a first-century Jewish apocalypticist" [1999: 243]. Here, however, I merely report or assume interpretative orthodoxy, not defend it.) Christ believed himself to be carrying out various divine prerogatives like forgiving sins, not just wrongs or sins against his own person, but wrongs to others, as if he himself had been wronged in the harms done to other people. He also thought himself to exemplify the best or most secure or reliable way in which to have a proper relationship with God.

Imagine, borrowing a brief thought experiment from the philosopher Daniel Howard-Snyder, that you have a pious neighbor by the name of 'Florence' (Howard-Snyder 2004). She claims to be divine and offers to forgive your sins. Florence is a nice person. Kind and generous, in fact. Wouldn't you be tempted to believe that she is delusional? Howard-Snyder says he certainly would.

Our question, again, though, is as follows: Is it plausible to claim that Jesus was deluded in believing, assuming he did so, that he was equal to God or God in incarnate human form?

Remember Jesus could have been deluded in believing such things, but not utterly irrational or without subjective warrant for doing so, if Maher is right. Perhaps "I and my Father are one" was a reasonable proposition for him to embrace, even if he was deluded about it. Remember Maher's (and Stone and Young's) claim that some delusions are subjectively reasonable responses to anomalous perceptual experiences. Consider the following hypothetical Maher-like story.

> *The Maher Story of Jesus*: Jesus had all sorts of bizarre and anomalous experiences. He perceived himself to be able to cure various ailments (fever, leprosy, lameness, blindness, and so on) and to raise people from the dead (see Mark 5:35–43 and John 11:38–44). He appeared to himself to be able to walk on water, still storms, multiply loaves (see Mark 6:30–44). While many contemporaries rejected him, and although he himself lamented that though foxes and birds have places to stay he has nowhere (Matthew 8:20; Luke 9:58), his 'miracle-performances' had numerous purported eyewitnesses. So it came to pass: Jesus explained these bizarre perceptual experiences to himself by believing that he was the kingly Messiah, the fusion of God and Man – divine, the Son of God.

The psychiatrist Alistair Munro writes of delusional grandiosity as follows: "An interesting element in grandiosity is that of centrality." "Highly unusual and improbable things happen to him, yet he does not question these." "Centrality is often associated with ideas of ... persecution" (Munro 2006: 142).

Suppose we add the following ingredients to the Maher Story. Jesus's self-attribution of divinity was reinforced by his interpretation of the Messianic Story in the Scriptures and by the messianic culture of first-century Palestine. Christ viewed his suffering and persecution not as a miscarriage of justice, but as having been foreshadowed by and endowed with apocalyptic significance in the writings of the prophet Isaiah. The persecution is God's plan, he thought. True, during Jesus's time, a lot of other persons claimed to be messiahs. Scores of followers believed in them without empirical confirmation. But Jesus's own I-am-God belief continued to grip his personal imagination. It helped him to account for the otherwise unusual and improbable things that appeared to happen to him at the end of his life. These were perceptual experiences that possessed for him a deep "feeling of significance [so that] everything must have changed in some fundamental way" (Maher 1999: 560). "There is something profoundly different about me," he may have thought. "I must be the Son of God." Such would be a rather full-bodied Maher-like tale. It may not be good Christology, of course, but it is useful, I think, in understanding whether Jesus was a victim of a psychopathology or disorder.

So, again, *was* Christ deluded?

Some examinations of Jesus's delusional or mental health status confuse the question of whether his belief in his divinity was true with whether he was deluded. Here, for example, is the psychiatrist O. Quentin Hyder on whether Jesus was deluded. It begins with a quote from a diagnostic manual.

> "A delusion is a persistent false belief not in keeping with a person's cultural and educational background or level of knowledge." Jesus' belief that he was the Messiah was by contrast totally in keeping with his background. The whole of the Old Testament Scriptures look forward to and actually spell out the coming of a Messiah together with his characteristics and qualifications. Jesus was thoroughly familiar with the Old Testament and knew that his birth and early life had already fulfilled many prophesies. "Search the Scriptures – for – they are they which testify to Me" (John 5:39). His own prophesies about his own death and resurrection, later literally fulfilled, indicate further that he *knew* [italics added] that he was the Messiah that Israel was waiting for (Hyder 1977: 8).

I certainly do not wish to examine here whether, in fact, Christ actually was the Messiah. If he was divine, or omnisciently divine, he could not have been deluded, of course. An omniscient deity does not make that sort of mistake. But, again, it's delusion I am after, not Christology. For my target, which is understanding delusion, I am going to assume (without argument) that Christ was not God incarnate. I am going to presuppose he was not divine. A human being only. What then?

Munro notes that "some individuals with grandiose beliefs can adopt a lifestyle which accommodates and sanctions their delusions and their behavior" (Munro 2006: 141). One obvious way in which this may happen is by propagating a kind of extreme apocalyptic religious ideology "which allows the person to share and even propagate his strange beliefs" with a group of "equally deluded individuals" (Munro 2006: 141). Such group sharing may help to explain the testimony of alleged eyewitnesses to Christ's miraculous performances and other 'evidences' of his divinity. None of the observers truly may have been reliable or trustworthy. Perhaps they were as deluded as he may have been. Or perhaps they were self-deceived or wishful thinkers.

Let us, however, take another approach to delusion, not in terms of the actual truth or falsity of its content, as with Hyder, or in terms of the subjective anomalous experiential warrant, hallucinatory or otherwise, for its acquisition, as with Maher, or even in terms of reference to a shared group delusion, but in terms of its persistent and self-represented or self-interpreted role in and consequences for a person's (like Christ's) overall psychological economy and well-being. Consider, for example, claims by psychologist Mike Jackson about what he calls "benign psychosis" (Jackson 2007).

Benign psychosis? I am not pleased with this locution. It seems oxymoronic, like referring to a harmless disorder. But there is an important point about delusion behind it that I wish to extract. This is its emphasis on downstream or forward looking considerations in classifying delusions. Not or not merely their upstream origins or sources, but their downstream persistence and effects.

Some people's religious convictions and experiences, Jackson notes, are neither disruptive nor intrusive, but inspirational, "involving a sense of authority and meaning" and exemplifying "creative thinking" (Jackson 2007: 245). By contrast a delusion as such (or a 'malignant' psychosis, adopting Jackson's awkward terminology) harbors or risks a "devastating impact on [a person's] well-being and ability to function" (2007: 247). "Rather than resolving ... existential concerns, a situation of radical and threatening social dislocation is likely to exacerbate them" (2007: 248). Jackson notes: "People ... tend to be isolated by their delusional beliefs" (248).

Jesus was neither socially isolated nor emotionally devastated by conviction in his own divinity (assuming that that's exactly what he, in fact, did believe). Hyder, in a passage devoid of the question begging assumption that Jesus *knew* that he was the Messiah, writes of how Christ's belief in his own divinity helped to inspire his moral insights and to develop his moral character:

> The Sermon on the Mount is still the best ever summary of principles of living in this life (Matthew 5–7). Psychotherapy today uses many of the principles he first enunciated. The principle of self-love means having a good sense of self-worth, esteem, or respect for oneself which is the vital prerequisite to obeying the commandment, "Thou shalt love thy neighbor as thyself" (Matthew 22:39). The principle of forgiveness is essential to all healthy interpersonal relationships (Matthew 18: 21–22), as is also the so-called Golden Rule of doing to others what you desire that they would do to you (Luke 6:31).
>
> (Hyder 1977: 11)

The historian Philip Schaff offers praise of Christ's moral and social acuity, when he asks the following rhetorical question about him (meaning to answer it affirmatively):

> Is such an intellect – clear as the sky, bracing as the mountain air, sharp and penetrating as a sword, thoroughly healthy and vigorous, always ready and always self-possessed – liable to a radical and most serious delusion concerning his own character and mission?
>
> (Schaff 1918: 97)

Suppose Jesus was grossly mistaken in thinking himself to be divine. Suppose that this attitude was not just bizarre and grandiose but overall or objectively unwarranted by the evidence. Christ may have had unusual perceptual experiences, perhaps even hallucinations, which felt immensely significant to him and in need of explanation, but suppose that these did not truly or objectively warrant his believing that he was God. Suppose that they were evidentially deficient. Suppose Christ, much like Kant's Abraham, should have filtered them out and not used them to ground belief in his own divinity, if that is in fact what he actually did. Jackson assumes that such a belief (despite its lack of evidential pedigree) qualifies as delusional (or 'malignantly' psychotic) *only if* it results in pragmatic distress or has a destructive personal impact. But *if* Hyder and Schaff are correct, Jesus's conviction in his divinity had no such impact. The belief or conviction contributed to Christ's sense of meaning, purpose, moral insight, and capacity for benevolent and productive social engagement. If they are right, it had a negative impact on his biological longevity, of course, but not on him as a person and morally compassionate agent.

Jackson urges that we adopt just such a forward-looking criterion for a (for him 'malignant') delusion. If so, a belief or attitude fails to qualify as delusional if it contributes positively to leading a worthwhile life and is integrated helpfully into a person's overall psychological makeup or economy. Such an attitude may still qualify as some other sort of normative error – a superstition, an instance of wishful thinking or self-deception, whatever. But if Jackson is right, and if our standard for delusion should include reference to harmful personal consequences, Jesus was not deluded. He was not deluded because his belief played a positive role in his life.

I am not being detailed in my examination of Jesus here, quite obviously. The elusive historicity of Jesus is being bypassed. So: Think of what I am saying as a conditional: If there were overall positive consequences (for Jesus and others) and if these consisted of his flourishing as a person and moral agent and were due, in important measure, to his belief that he was the Son of God, then even if or although he was mistaken in this belief, and even if or although this conviction may have arisen in the wake of bizarre and untrustworthy perceptual experiences, then Jesus was not deluded. He was not the victim of a grand or grandiose delusion. The conviction did not drive him into despair or wreck havoc on his powers of reasoning and communicative expression. Quite the contrary, if Schall and Hyder are correct, it contributed to his intellect and moral vision.

The single and simple moral I want to draw from examining the case of Christ is this. Consequences matter for delusions. Helpful beliefs are not delusional.

I am reminded of a remark about the relevance of consequences to mental abnormalities of a religious nature that William James makes in his masterpiece on religious psychology *The Varieties of Religious Experience*: "What then," to quote James, whom Jackson acknowledges as an influence on this own thinking, "is more natural than that this temperament should introduce one to regions of ... truth, to corners of the universe, which your robust Philistine type of nervous system, forever offering its biceps to be felt, thumping its breast, and thanking Heaven that is hasn't a single morbid fiber in its composition, would be sure to hide forever from its self-satisfied possessors?" (James 2002: 29).

James's and Jackson's point is well-taken. Harmful consequences matter for delusions. Helpful or beneficial consequences matter for non-delusions. Even if a belief or attitude is false, bizarre, or otherwise immensely suspect, as long as it enhances a person's adjustment to or positive contribution in the world, this leaves room for classifying it as non-delusional. Not otherwise faultless to be sure. But not delusional.

So what, then, does make a belief or attitude qualify as delusional?

Karl Jaspers claimed, perhaps in a manner not totally consistent with his skepticism about the inability to empathetically understand schizophrenia, that being deluded involves being in a special mood or frame of mind, which possesses both affective and cognitive components, namely, a "delusional mood", and that even true beliefs may count as delusional, if they are enveloped in such a mood (Jaspers 1963). What this mood amounts to, Jaspers claimed, is difficult to describe with precision other than that it (among other things) invests a belief or attitude with great personal consequence or importance, dominated by its atmospherics (its 'centrality', to use Munro's term, or 'significance', to use Maher's), so that to deny it (and here is one of a delusion's negative effects on behavior) would be perceived or interpreted by the person as shattering their sense of self or world. Jaspers writes: "Delusion proper ... implies a transformation in ... total awareness of reality" (Jaspers 1963: 94). It is something that, as the philosopher Shaun Gallagher notes, a "deluded subject experiences and lives through" (Gallagher 2009: 257). A deluded individual lives 'in and through' their delusion.

The psychiatrist and philosopher K. W. M. Fulford (like Jackson, James and Jaspers) also offers a consequence oriented approach to understanding what makes a delusion a delusion. He writes that "the irrationality of delusions should be understood in terms not of defective cognitive functioning but rather of impaired reasons for action" (1993: 14). That is, what makes a delusion a delusion is not or not so much how the patient or person acquires the attitude, but the manner in which they self-represent, appeal to, or rely upon it in reason giving and action guidance. How it affects their life. The pathology or disorder of delusion is practical (related to choice and action). And it is prospective namely, what a person does with or because of a belief, thought or attitude. Not retrospective namely, how a person acquired the belief or attitude in the first place.

Consider the priest for whom I cared in Boston. Thinking of me as the devil was bizarre. Who knows how this particular idea may have arisen or of the basis of its personal appeal? Perhaps, if the Maher–Stone–Young-line is correct, it helped the priest to explain something experientially anomalous and felt by him to be immensely important. However, by walling this belief off from contrary evidence, being wedded to it in spite of being under his bed in bedclothes, and not properly evaluating or appreciating its imprudent impact on his behavior, this helps, for Jackson, Jaspers and Fulford, to make the priest's conviction delusional. Not how he acquired it or came to believe it. Not whether it is false. Rather how he lives harmfully within it.

Consider Laura. She believes that unseen speakers are urging her to pace up and down the ward and to urinate on herself. Whether she is deluded does not hinge on whether this belief is bizarre (surely, it is) or radically unsupported by available evidence on the hallway (certainly, it is). It depends on her deployment of the attitude and its effect on her. Does it lead her to deeper insights or to effective social intercourse with other people? Or does she over-identify with it, failing to appreciate the negative impact it has on her behavior? When prior to treatment Laura is asked if she was sick, she replied that she was suffering from things that bothered her. When asked why she was in the hospital, she replied "I do not know". She failed to appreciate that something was genuinely wrong with her. After a year of treatment, however, in a prescient sign of recovery, when asked about her delusions, she offered the following telling response: "I think I was getting sick at this point" (Young and Leafhead 1996: 107). Negative consequences were self-recognized and halted the persistence of her delusions in a moment of diagnostic insight. Her delusional world began to dissolve.

Crack the acquisition or source code, the generation conditions of a delusional attitude, some say, and one should be able to determine whether an attitude is delusional. Dominic Murphy writes for the majority of theorists that "we need to appeal to some general ideas about belief acquisition to explain why certain beliefs count as delusions in the first place" (Murphy 2006: 180). In the first place? Delusions? Acquisition? I am unconvinced (and Murphy himself seems unconvinced; see below). Certainly that is not the way in which clinicians commonly identify delusions.

Clinicians normally are not privy to acquisition or generation conditions. They are a party only to the persistence and effects or consequences of a person's attitude. When confronted with a patient who seems to hold unusually distorted or evidentially bizarre or unfounded beliefs, it is not the origin that directly confronts the observer, but the manner in which the attitudes are dealt with, assessed or evaluated by the subject and the person's failure to properly respond to challenges that their beliefs or attitudes present to them as persons or rational agents. Do these attitudes actually lead people to become more sensitive to evidence and to attain successes that contribute to their welfare? Or is a harmful cost or overall liability evident in a person's lack of insight into or the unmanageability of an attitude? G. Lynn Stephens and I put matters as follows: "As bizarre as it may be to think that, for example, worms are devouring one's bones, delusion consists not in [the contents of] such thoughts but in the pathological manner in which we respond to them as persons" (Stephens and Graham 2004: 241). It is one thing to learn how a belief or attitude that becomes delusional is initially acquired. It is another to understand "why it is maintained and not rejected in the light of everything else that the patient knows" or believes or experiences – including exposure to its harmful or imprudent consequences (see Bell et al. 2006: 221). This last feature of delusions, namely persistence in spite of bad and perhaps even self-appreciated harmful consequences, is typically the focus of clinical concern and treatment. As well it should be. Living through a delusion hurts a person.

REALISM AMONG THE RUINS

It is obvious that sometimes we succeed in comprehending the world correctly and sometimes we do not. Take the case of beliefs, for example. They are true if the world is as the believer believes and false otherwise. Our beliefs are accurate or in proper cognitive contact or touch with the world in some circumstances and inaccurate or false in others.

There are, of course, so many possible factors that may affect a person's ability to be in proper cognitive contact with the world. Suppose depressed people, not persons who are so profoundly despondent that they never get out of bed, but 'moderately depressed' individuals who experience persistently sad or melancholic moods and emotional outlooks, while trying to lead normal lives, are in more accurate cognitive contact with the world than non-depressed persons. Suppose that depressed people (of the moderate sort) make more realistic appraisals of events and describe themselves and their abilities or inabilities to control events with greater accuracy and less self-serving bias or error than do non-depressed people. Suppose also that whatever it is that depressed people, insofar as they are depressed, believe about the world more closely or evenhandedly corresponds to the actual facts than whatever ordinary non-depressed persons do recognize. This set of suppositions, together with various observations about human psychology and the evidence that allegedly back them up, is known as the thesis of *depressive realism* or the *sadder-but-wiser* thesis (see Alloy and Abramson 1979 and 1988).

Here is some more supposing. Is close cognitive contact with reality a benchmark of mental health? Some say yes (see Maslow 1950; Valliant 1977). Others say no, arguing that mental health is often secured or maintained only by harboring positively unrealistic attitudes and beliefs (Taylor 1989; Taylor and Brown 1988). Such 'positive illusions', as sometimes they are called, include exaggerated positive self-evaluations and unrealistic optimism about one's powers of personal control and the future.

Suppose, for example, that in order to maintain one's physical and mental energy and to be capable of moral and socially useful action as well as perhaps to avoid being depressed and unhappy, people need to make overly optimistic assessments both about the probability of good things taking place in the future and about their own power or ability to bring about good events. A person may need, for example, to make self-serving or personally biased assessments that they are much less likely to suffer calamities than other people. Or a person may need, again, for another example, to over-estimate the degree to which they will do well in life, especially concerning matters that require personal effort and judgment. Suppose, in one way or another, persons need 'positive illusions' (again, as such falsehoods are called in the literature) if they are to cope effectively with life and to engage in productive and creative work (see also Taylor 1989).

How should we to react to each of these two sets of suppositions or hypotheses. They pose an awkward dilemma, do they not? Depressive realism versus positive illusions. Sadder but wiser versus happier but less veridical. Here's the dilemma.

In facing the world be either (a) (as depressive realism says) realistic or cognitively in touch with reality but, alas, moderately depressed or (b) (as the thesis of positive illusions urges) optimistic but, alas, cognitively unrealistic and inaccurate or out of proper overall cognitive contact with reality.

To avoid a protracted discussion, although at the risk of oversimplification, I want to quickly bundle a variety of considerations together into something that may be called a 'passing assessment' of the warrant base for each of the two hypotheses. I wish to reach judgments about each hypothesis that come filtered through concern with whatever each hypothesis tells us about being in touch, or in proper or comprehending cognitive contact, with reality, the world and ourselves. This brief dynamic will reveal or show, I hope, just what it means to value (as mentioned in Chapter 6) our capacity for comprehension of self and world. Let's look at the (b) hypothesis first.

The (b)-hypothesis that we need positive illusions to live by is in conflict with the ideal of truth-seeking and reality-monitoring. Illusions I cannot positively maintain if I self-classify or recognize them as illusions. "I must," as Hampshire notes, "regard my own beliefs as formed in response to free inquiry; I could not otherwise count them as beliefs" (Hampshire 1965: 87). A person who thinks of his beliefs as illusions and therein as devoid of genuine warrant should know that maintaining them is misplaced.

Illusions also often have disastrous consequences, especially in contexts (like investing in the stock market [see Odean 1998]) in which overconfidence tends to undermine one's ability to achieve important goals. Although, with luck on one's side, you may be happier believing that your spouse is faithful, loves you, and is not having an affair, when they unexpectedly depart with their adulterous intimate for Paris, Texas, and empty your mutual bank account, you may regret that you were never told the truth.

David Dunning, a psychologist at Cornell, notes that the "literature is filled with numerous [examples], strewn across business, education, and policy worlds, in which positive illusions prove costly and even disastrous" (Dunning 2009: 518).

Of course, it must be asked, just what constitutes an illusion? The mere fact that our beliefs (our cognitive contacts with the world) often are tied up with hopes, wishes, and aspirations doesn't mean that we turn off your reality or evidential inquiry detectors when belief forming mechanisms are in gear. And it certainly does not mean that hopeful beliefs, just because they are hopeful, are false. Belief formation may be framed by motivational or affective influences which, on the negative side, may lead people astray from the truth. But, on the positive side, such influences may result in a pragmatically effective realism that is formed by facing the ambiguities of this world (when or where it is ambiguous) with a hopeful or positive interpretation of the evidence.

Social reinforcement, too, may offer evidence in support of convictions that are 'biased' and positive, but not illusions as such. Suppose you receive mostly positive feedback about yourself from others or were consistently told you are special and above average by loving parents, family members and friends. Objectively speaking, you may have an exaggerated positive estimation of yourself, but this is not so much an illusion as an errant or objectively unwarranted belief formed in response to a skewed evidential set. As Dunning puts it, "even a perfectly rational [person] could come to hold types of beliefs" that advocates of positive illusions may classify as positive illusions "because the environment more frequently provides people with incomplete or misleading data" (Dunning 2009: 518).

One general situation in which it seems perfectly wise, sensible and rational to adopt beliefs that turn pivotally on hopes or aspirations is when doing so is permitted by the evidential indeterminacy of a situation and when the energetic pursuit of a goal or valued purpose demands a goodly measure of optimism. If the power of pessimistic evidence massively exceeds any room for optimism, of course, it's time to face the sullen facts. But the world often is an ambiguous place. Sometimes terribly ambiguous. Not just in the ambiguity or equivocation it presents to our perceptual systems, but more profoundly in the indeterminacy it offers to our attitudes and moods.

Consider a doctor who is trying to save a patient's life in a desperate situation in which she does not really *know* whether his life can be saved, but her ability to help is indissolubly bound up with her believing that she can. The question of the 'realism' or accuracy of her conviction or belief depends crucially on how things look from the standpoint not just of the evidential situation (medical track record, patient's age, and so on) but in term's of such a conviction's practical consequences. If the gods could speak, they might whisper in her ear: "Proceed in the belief that you will save this person and you will therein improve your chances of saving his life." "The evidence that he will die is far from decisive." To win the battle against the patient's illness, given the epistemic latitude or evidential ambiguity of a clinical situation, the norm or rule that whatever the doctor believes should correspond to reality ought to presuppose a loose and contextualized sense of correspondence. What is truthful correspondence often is neither known nor knowable. Setting one's beliefs against what utterly is obvious is, of course, unrealistic and foolish. An illusion perhaps. But when a person adopts a belief that is hopeful or purpose serving, we should not disparage this as an illusion. It may be a helpful and proper response to ambiguous circumstance. A person's optimism may in the end prove unrealistic, perhaps – but being illusory is a separable matter.

Nicholas Rescher expresses the point well:

> We face a fundamental contrast. [T]he future [is] factual. ... But our warranted attitudes can be practical. ... [T]hey can reflect our appropriate hopes as we assess them pragmatically with reference to their potential consequences.
>
> (Rescher 1987: 106)

Finally, and related to what has just been said, suppose we consider positive illusions as (as advertised by their advocates) false beliefs – as misrepresentations by a person of a particular state of affairs (e.g. "I am above average in intelligence and power") as actual. If so, illusions depart from reality. But we must be careful not to conflate whether a person's optimism or exaggerated assessment qualifies as belief or instead is a hope or positive mood or attitude. Positivity or optimism may be associated with a range of attitudes and feelings. A measure of 'unrealism' may be just what some human hopes, for example, need. Believing that you will survive a normally fatal illness may not be recommended, but hoping that you will survive may be just what your poor soul needs.

The quick take-home point is that the (b)-hypothesis that we need positive illusions/beliefs to live by is at best misleading and at worst requires much more careful defense and fine-grained analysis and distinction making than thus far it has received in the literature (at least on my reading).

So, what then, in turn, about the (a)-assumption that moderately depressed people are more realistic or in more accurate or veridical in cognitive contact with the world than those who are non-depressed? This assumption, too, rests on controversial premises about just what it means to be realistic or in contact with reality. Consider paranoia. A co-worker, who is moderately paranoid, may be able to give a more detailed and accurate description of her boss's comings and goings than a more trusting office mate. It scarcely follows, however, that she is a better worker, more rational or "for that matter more in touch with reality" (Garrett 1994: 88). Richard Garrett notes:

> People who trust the world, trust in themselves, trust their spouses, and in general trust others may get duped in many small ways. But people who trust little or not at all get duped in very big ways. [They may] happen to see the individual trees better, [but] lose sight of the forest. And this leads them to do and say things that frustrate their deepest longings and hopes.
>
> (Garrett 1994: 88)

Garrett's general point about distrust applies to depression as well. Even if it should turn out that moderately depressed people are more accurate in certain observations than normal non-depressives, it does not follow that they are in superior cognitive contact with reality. What a depressed individual may miss is "the larger picture, the larger truth that in general it is better" to possess a "positive and constructive" picture of the world and of the future (Garrett 1994: 88, 89). This is not just because trustful or hopeful attitudes may be self-fulfilling or self-confirming. But it also is because people often objectively are worthy of being trusted, and the world, too, is, in some measure, oftentimes good. So, arguably, often the deepest and most useful or helpful cognitive contact with the world is achieved only if we harbor or maintain for ourselves a moderately positive conception of things, not illusory, and certainly not desultory, but as pragmatically sensible and evidentially sound as purpose and circumstance permits.

Bertrand Russell once announced that "the life of Man is a long march through the night" as one-by-one we are "seized by the silent orders of omnipotent Death" (1989: 172). Some philosophers have argued that the fact that we will all be dead in two hundred years and that millions of years from now the solar system will cool or wind down and collapse, and all remnant of human effort will vanish or be ruined, means that a positive or optimistic image of anything (no matter how moderate) is unwarranted. But such a deep, dark cosmic pessimism is very hard to take seriously as a rational response to life, to things. Even if there is no ultimate point to *everything,* there are points to the many immediate, smaller or local dimensions of life. When we care about particular things and persons and are committed to them, "the feeling with which we do so is not ... one of dispirited impotence" (Frankfurt 1988: 89). We find ourselves most fully realized and fulfilled when we focus not on global solar death, but on the smaller-scale aspects of human life and appreciate that our capacity for care and commitment is one of our most cherished faculties as persons. In rejecting a measured or moderate optimism, and embracing a global pessimism, a person is contending not so much with trying to live in a ruined world (if unbeknownst to us it ultimately is or will be ruined) as living, in sense, against themselves and their own best interests, hopes, and aspirations.

PARANOIA, BENEVOLENCE AND IMAGINATION

Above I mentioned paranoia. I want to say more about it. Such discussion will help to remind us that the understanding of a mental disorder is morally contentious territory. I begin with a remark about morality.

Morality often requires us to be kind and benevolent towards other people and sometimes, too, to make compassionate efforts to intervene in another's behavior for their own sake or on another's own behalf. Morality also requires us, in helping others, to be respectful of their dignity as persons, assisting only in the most unobtrusive or essential ways or only when our assistance is urgently or drastically needed or asked for explicitly.

Caring for victims of delusional disorders poses special difficulties for the discharge of our duty of benevolence. To begin with, deluded persons may actively resist our help. The effects of assistance or intervention may be the opposite of those that we compassionately intend. To a victim of persecutory delusions or paranoia, for instance, attempting to help them may reinforce their distrust of other people's motives. A paranoid may misinterpret another's efforts at assistance as a cover for manipulative designs or intentions. As Munro notes: "Delusional disorder sufferers are notoriously difficult to engage in treatment and persecutory ones especially so" (Munro 2006, p. 131). In addition, assuming that we ought to help a victim of delusion, it may not be possible to feel the compassion or sympathy that motivates and modulates help. Perhaps our moral imagination or ability to empathetically project ourselves into the shoes or situation of a deluded person may be blunted. When caring for a victim of a flood, one can imagine "all one's possessions being washed away" (Torrey 1995, p. 29). But, by contrast, what about caring for someone with full-blown schizophrenia or florid delusions? What then?

E. Fuller Torrey, a psychiatrist specializing in schizophrenia writes:

> Sympathy for those afflicted with schizophrenia is sparse because it is difficult to put one-self in the place of the sufferer. ... Those who are afflicted act bizarrely, say strange things, withdraw from us, and may even try to hurt us. ... We don't understand why they say what the say and do what they do. ... [And] the paucity of sympathy for those with schizophrenia makes it that much more of a disaster.
>
> (Torrey 1995: 29)

Sympathy is empathy extended or filtered though compassion. The philosopher Arthur Schopenhauer (1788–1860) requires of compassionate motivation that we successfully put ourselves in the place or shoes of the sufferer and that we must be sympathetic. "How is it possible," he asks, "for another's weal and woe to move my will immediately?" His answer: "Only through [my feeling] his woe just as I ordinarily feel my own" (Schopenhauer 1841/1965: 143–44). Schopenhauer regards the ability to emotionally identify with another's subjective situation as the source of our benevolent impulses and the main "incentive to morality" (Schopenhauer 1841/1965: 170). But is empathetic mixed with compassionate identification truly required if we properly are to help? In order to treat another benevolently, must we empathize with their weal? Sympathize with their woe? Compassionately project ourselves into their shoes or straits?

One has to be careful in morally insisting upon the psychological-moral standard of effective projection. Suppose, as it is often assumed in ethical theory, that 'ought' implies 'can'. Suppose, that is, that the presence of a moral obligation presupposes a capacity for relevant action (for fulfilling the content or directive of the obligation). You ought to repay a debt, for example, but only if you possess the capacity to repay. You ought to keep a promise, but only when you are able to keep it. If 'ought' truly does imply 'can', and if, in addition, Schopenhauer is correct about the proper motivational source of morally benevolent impulses and duties, then there is no good reason to say that you ought to help another person, unless, in fact, you really are able to imagine yourself in their place or to project yourself into their shoes.

The simulated experience of another's state of mind requires assuming one or more of the other's sorts of mental states. It requires 'mimicking' aspects of the subjective world of the other. Is this always possible? Nomy Arpaly cautions that there is a lot to be said for the empirical possibility that another person's inner world or what it is like to be in their subjective situation, may be "very, very different from our own" (Arpaly 2005: 298). Another's mind may be too different from our own in which to project ourselves. Attempts to project ourselves into another's situation may come up empty.

Of course, a claim of 'cannot' as in "cannot successfully project" or "unable to imagine" may reflect a misreading of the evidence for one's own simulationist powers. It may be hard to tell apart the presence of a deep incapacity, about which the agent can do nothing, from that of a mere performance failure or transient inability, which, after proper learning or additional experience, may convert to competent performance. A developing ability to project oneself into another's situation may outrun the reach of current evidence for one's imaginative powers or potential.

Imagine, then, a case of imaginative projection into a paranoid person's delusion. Everything in a paranoid's psychology crystallizes around distrust of others and "an intense preoccupation with an individual's [own] position in the social universe" (Kinderman and Bentall 2007: 280; see also Bentall 2004: 330–46). Let's briefly consider the challenge of trying to be benevolent towards a paranoid via, in part, projection into their subjective circumstances.

> Individuals [with the disorder] are known for their hypersensitivity, mistrust, and suspi-
> ciousness of other people's motivations. They are always on guard, easily slighted, and
> quick to take offense. They believe that others are trying to trick or harm them, and will go

to great lengths to prove it. They question the loyalty of others and often see plots where nobody else can see them. They are often rigid, argumentative, and litigious. ... They appear to have few tender feelings, disdain weak people, and lack any sense of humor.

(Torrey 1995: 92)

Is that the sort of person whose weal and woe, whose distrust of others, I can feel or imagine harboring in myself? With what exactly must I empathize in the distrust harbored by an individual who is a victim of paranoid delusions?

Kinderman and Bentall remark that "patients who are diagnosed as suffering from that kind of delusion [typically] say that they are the target of some kind of organized conspiracy to cause them harm, although patients vary in the agencies to [which] they attribute this intention (which may be specific persons, religious or ethnic groups, or organizations such as the CIA or MI5)" (2007: 281). Kinderman and Bentall's comment is a helpful hint about the inner world of paranoia. Let's pursue it by talking briefly about the epistemology or evidence base of conspiracy theories.

In a discussion of the epistemology of conspiracy theories, the philosopher Brian Keeley claims that one of the more striking features of conspiracy theories is that evidence against a conspiratorial explanation is construed by its advocate as evidence in the explanation's favor (Keeley 1999). Contrary evidence is presumed to intentionally misdirect or mislead the effort at its proper interpretation or explanation. Consider the following vignettes:

Charles says that his Protestant co-workers discriminate against him because he is a Roman Catholic. Charles refers to the fact that he has not gotten a pay raise in two years as proof that he is the object of a discriminatory conspiracy. When it is pointed out that his boss is active in a local Catholic parish, he says that "he", the boss, just wants Charles to believe that he (Charles) is not being mistreated by the firm. "My boss really is not a Catholic."

Darlene is an 18-year-old college student, who sought treatment at the student health center at the request of her dormitory supervisor. A shy and rather "rigid" looking young woman, who had never been involved in any counseling before, she complains of being uncomfortable and unhappy because of the noise and lack of privacy in the dorm. She told the dormitory supervisor that other students are watching her using hidden cameras plugged into her bedroom light fixtures. "They are attempting to catch me in cheating or sleeping with my underage boyfriend, so that they can have me expelled from the school." When asked why other students care about expelling her, when she has just been admitted to a popular sorority, Darlene retorts that her admission to the sorority is part of a plot to keep the expulsion plan a secret. The more popular she thinks she is the more likely she is to let her guard down.

David, a successful Toronto engineer, is agitated and upset. He says that a paramilitary Canadian national agency is out to get him, and that some powerful data that he has gathered, about which he speaks only in vague terms, will prove that fact. David says that a number of his friends in the firm where he works have been killed in recent weeks in mysterious accidents. When it is noted that no colleagues of his have died within the last two years, he replies that the recent deaths have been disguised as leaves of absence or terminations of employment and that he himself has just recently been offered a vacation leave.

Partly because conspiratorial hypotheses require an increasing and increasingly complex amount of skepticism about contrary data and falsifying evidence, a paranoid's delusions embody a deep pessimism or skepticism about the behavior and motivations of other people (the boss, sorority sisters, the firm). As Jennifer Radden points out, "while it is neither prudent, nor virtuous, nor mentally healthy to trust too much, or injudiciously," it is, of course, also unhealthy to "trust too little as the paranoid does" (Radden 2007: 267). So what, then, is it to trust others too little as the paranoid does? Whatever a victim of paranoia does as a paranoid, in their relations with other people, even if they try to minimize their reliance upon others, a paranoid person trusts and does so injudiciously their own distrust of others. They over-trust their ability to recognize the untrustworthiness of other people. In trusting others too little, they trust themselves too much and are insufficiently epistemically humble or appositely critical about themselves.

A simple example from ordinary life, owed to Annette Baier, offers an insightful observation about the inseparable connection between trust of others and self-trust (see Baier 1989: 278). I trust my mailman not to discard my mail on days in which he may feel too fatigued to deliver it. I trust myself in this judgment to trust him. I realize I may be disappointed, however. So, suppose that one rainy day, while in a melancholic frame of mind, I try I guard myself emotionally against the disappointment that the mailman may not deliver my mail by distrusting him. Suppose I become suspicious of him. Such an attitude if widely extended to other ordinary forms of reliance on others would make social life utterly unbearable. Trusting neither mailman, nor bank clerk, nor waiter, I am precluded from all sorts of necessary or desirable patterns of social engagement. True, in trusting others I am vulnerable to being neglected, manipulated and used. The mailman may hurt me in various ways. He may read my private correspondence or encourage the neighbor's dog to defecate under my mailbox. If, however, I wish my mail to be delivered, and to engage in other normal social behavior and mutual reliance, I must develop a taste in people, and then trust it (Baier 1989: 279). I must trust in my trust of others. If my trustful judgment fails, others (among them a mailman, waitress or whomever) will let me down. But that's a small risk to be undertaken for entering into beneficial relations of social cooperation and coordination.

Trusting usually is not the product of a deliberate predictive cost/benefit calculation about other people's behavior. It is something more akin "to a kind of faith in the other" (Radden 2007: 267). It's a form of faith that may require imagining the other as being in certain relevant respects like me. Guided by the thought that I myself would deliver the mail if I was both a mailman and fatigued, I imaginatively simulate his delivering the mail. Tired or not, I would deliver it. So, I assume he will do so as well.

A deficiency in the capacity for projection, empathy or simulation may be part of what impairs the paranoid's capacity for trusting others and comprehending the actual motives of other people. A paranoid may over-trust their own self and distrust others, perhaps because the subject cannot extend or project their self or implicit trust in themselves to the other. This failure to extend, project or mimic produces a blindness or evidential tunnel vision towards the paranoid's own self-trust. It deprives them of evidential feedback from others about their own attitudes or feedback from a "second self, to give [them] sight" (Baier 1989: 279). If I am paranoid, others are not allowed to teach me or model for me whom to trust, how to trust or whether or when distrust of others is well- or ill-founded.

However note: The difficult challenge, stated earlier, of imagining the inner world of a paranoid person appears to be dissolving the more we think about it. We are developing a sense of what it is like to be a subject of paranoid delusions. Paranoia represents a deformity in self-comprehension (of when to trust one's very own person) as much as categorical skepticism about the motives of others. Additional analysis may continue to help in this task of inside-understanding paranoia, too, of course. But our suggestions for describing the 'inside' of paranoia are also raising a difficult therapeutic or treatment issue.

At first blush, it may appear obvious that in order to therapeutically intervene in a benevolent and genuinely respectful manner in the outlook and behavior of a deluded person, we must be able to imagine their inner world. Perhaps compassion requires it. In a case of paranoia, this means having empathy for a paranoid's distrust of others. The better the subjective inside of a deluded person is understood the better is the patient cared for. Such is the recommended clinical-moral maxim. However, we are also revisiting a misgiving about helping certain sorts of deluded persons that was mentioned earlier. When it comes to treating paranoia, Munro says, "pessimism pervades the literature" (Munro 2006: 135). Not only may paranoids resist treatment, but they may be reinforced in their paranoid attitudes by treatments that require caregivers to enter their world imaginatively. Such entry may be received as manipulation and deception. David may read a therapist's expression of misgiving over David's misreading of the offer of a vacation leave as an effort to soften his suspicions about the firm. Darlene or Charles may make comparable distrustful interpretations of relevantly analogous therapeutic responses. So, entry must be cautious and unobtrusive. As Munro counsels, "a patient, low-key, nonjudgmental approach by the psychiatrist is necessary" (ibid.). Hanna Pickard notes that a somewhat "submissive, non-challenging stance" may need to be initially adopted by a therapist (Pickard 2011: 213). But just what does a cautious and low-key entry involve? No doubt, there is more art than science here. If one can't blurt out "I feel your pain", what can one do?

If a person, although a subject of paranoid delusions, has some (however weak) warrant or rationale for some of their distrustful attitudes (remember, the mere fact that a person is delusional does not automatically mean that each and every aspect of their delusion is utterly unreasonable or even false), there may be room to reason with them. There is increasing clinical evidence that a delusion per se, although perhaps not the total illness (like schizophrenia) in which a delusion is embedded, may be modified by Cognitive-Behavioral Therapy (CBT) if conducted with sensitivity, skill and diplomacy. CBT recognizes that a deluded person has difficulty interpreting evidence against their delusional convictions. (CBT is a form of therapy derived from the so-called cognitive theory of depression, developed by Aaron T. Beck. CBT has received influential application to depression and recent extension to other disorders including delusions [see Bentall 2004: 507–9; Morrison 1998; Beck and Wieshar 2008]). But if a supportive non-confrontational relationship is established with a therapist, the therapist may then gently and inquisitively apply practical logic, rules of evidence, and Socratic questioning in a manner that encourages the deluded person to expose, question, and moderate or modify their delusional outlook, mood or stance (see Munro 2006: 227). Knowing when or whom to trust is knowing when or whom to distrust. And both trust and distrust are attitudes that possess a composite nature, neither solely cognitive or judgmental, nor exclusively affective or volitional. Judicious therapeutic focusing within a CBT or comparable framework on the affective or volitional components of paranoia should also be part of the psychotherapeutic mix. Why is the person refusing to abandon their persecutory convictions? What is required for therapy is that the patient or client should assess the merits of competing hypotheses (trustful ones), while questioning the veridicality of distrusting and suspicious moods, thoughts, or convictions.

CBT is one of a type or form of therapy that I call *pass through reason* treatment. Numerous varieties of this form of treatment are practiced in the mental health profession including Freudian psychotherapy, rational emotive therapy, interpersonal therapy, and reality therapy, among others. Pass-through-reason treatments share one common goal: to redirect and improve a person's self-knowledge and understanding or comprehension of their current situation (see Graham and Stephens 2007: 359–63; see also Levy 2007). Different forms of the general type of therapy differ in how this goal is best achieved as well as the manner in which proper comprehension and cognitive contact with the world or with others is understood. A cognitive behavioral therapist, for instance, puts emphasis on a person's knowledge of how to cope with current circumstances and unwelcome or distressful behavior. It is hoped that a patient can learn to monitor or reflect on their own thoughts and feelings, find means of examining their validity, and of substituting more helpful attitudes. A Freudian explores a patient's understanding of a disorder's supposed etiology, perhaps as far back as childhood trauma. It would make sense, for example, for a person, who as a child was surrounded by threats and attendant and genuine harms, "to become gradually more hyper-vigilant for threat-related information" when an adult, although "this kind of bias in processing information [may] tend to the maintenance of paranoid beliefs once established" (Kinderman and Bentall 2007: 285–86).

A spectrum of states of mind and attitudes, extending from mere passive feeling or thought to outright belief, may be the objects of focal attention in pass through reason therapies. Efforts made to find the causes of, and the means of changing, displacing or replacing those states of mind with others are not always to use methods of rational inference and deliberation. A pass through reason therapist may identify entirely non-rational sources of a state of mind (such as the mechanisms of classical conditioning) and use techniques like "thought stopping" or "systematic desensitization" to expunge the belief or thought. Take someone like Arthur, for example, whose fear of crowds of strangers blocks his free social intercourse. He may be asked to concentrate on his anxiety-inducing thoughts, and, after a brief period of time, the therapist may suddenly and emphatically say "stop" or produce a loud and aversive noise or unpleasant shock. Having been repeated several times, and after Arthur reports that his thoughts have stopped or been blocked, he may be asked by a therapist to emit his own subvocal "stop" whenever he begins to embark on self-defeating anxiety. Reason pass through is operative here not in the form of Socratic inquiry, but in establishing that the object of focal attention and a patient's ultimate self-control is the Intentional or conceptual content of a thought or attitude.

In cases of disorder in which a person is explicitly resistant to reason-pass-through intervention (as may happen in paranoia) or in which delusions are too florid or bound up with other symptoms to be questioned, conversationally examined, or displaced by contrarian thoughts, what then? How should we treat them? The most popular alternative forms of intervention or treatment are a-rational somatic, namely psychopharmacological (neuroleptics, antidepressant drugs, mood-stabilizers, anticonvulsants) and non-pharmacological (electroconvulsive therapy). I call such types *bypass reason* treatments.

Bypass reason treatments share a common goal: they try to reduce or suppress the symptoms of a disorder or delusion. Except in cases in which reduction or suppression is deemed an end in itself (as sometimes happens), the assumption behind them is that a patient may be better able to manage or understand their own behavior and ultimately to respond to pass-through-reason therapy only if or when they are no longer in the overbearing grip of the delusional stance or emotional distress.

Big issues of both a moral and therapeutic nature loom large over the comparative pros and cons of reason pass-through and bypass treatments for mental disorder (see Elliott 2003; Levy 2007). This is especially so given that how we interpret and think about ourselves, and the kinds of treatments we design or accept for ourselves, deeply affect how we are.

Some mental health professionals are reluctant to countenance psychopharmacological or bypass reason treatments for delusions even in cases of paranoid schizophrenia. There may be good reasons for reluctance. These include worries about a patient's immediate personal safety, concern about long-term health effects, apprehension over drug dependencies that may somehow undermine self-comprehension and personal autonomy, recognition that delusions may remit on their own without any sort of intervention, the charge that bypass interventions tend to treat or suppress symptoms only and not the illness itself, and so on. Of course, pass-through treatments also harbor problems. Some pass-through treatments or cases of such treatments enhance rational capacities, to be sure, but others are manipulative, aimed at creating long-term profit-motivated dependence on therapy, delivered by incompetent therapists, or based on erroneous and misinformed assumptions about the nature of a mental disorder. Neil Levy wisely cautions: "Psychotherapy is not a synonym for truth-seeking" (Levy 2007: 111). Pass-through treatments may also be more labor-intensive, time-consuming, and expensive than by-pass interventions. On each side of the treatment ledger, therefore, bypass or pass-through, the risks or potential liabilities are real, even if the desired and possible or normal benefits also are real.

How may bypass treatment be morally or benevolently justified in a case of paranoia? There are different ways of answering this complex ethical question, depending upon the actual circumstances or reasons for resistance. One possibility is to assume a moral principle of *future-orientated consent* to assist in the justification (Battin 1982: 155). Here briefly is the principle: Although a person may *now* object to whatever bypassing interference is made on their behalf, *later* (when they discover the harm that their paranoid attitudes were doing to themselves and which now can be avoided) they "will be grateful that the interference was made" (Ibid.). This later gratefulness warrants present bypass intervention. So, for example, in a case of paranoid delusions, although a subject of paranoid delusions may now reject bypass intervention made on their behalf, later (when the person has come to their better senses or discovers that they had, when paranoid, broken off from social reality) they will be glad that a bypass was conducted. Their future self or state of mind will embrace or retrospectively endorse what was done to and for them. Or so we may hope. If so, we may justify, say, some forms of involuntary drug treatment. A person may realize and appreciate that what was done was best for them.

Justification via future-orientated consent, of course, presupposes that there will be future consent, rather than that the post-paranoid person will express anger or regret over the fact that they were subjected to mechanical intervention or involuntary medication in an effort to eliminate or dampen their distrustful world view. Post-paranoid Peter may miss the self-definition and world-view that his paranoia afforded him, although post-paranoid Polly may be delighted to be free of the vigilant burden of distrust. Frith and Johnstone note: "After recovery, many patients, although not all, will accept that treatment has helped them" (Firth and Johnstone 2003: 168). Note the 'not all'. Some persons may wish not to have been 'helped'. What then?

Of course, it should be noted, not all interventions in cases of mental disorder in general or of paranoid delusion in particular are aimed just at the interests of the individual paranoid. Bypass treatments may also serve the interests of other persons (e.g. family members who must care for the deluded person) or the public at large (e.g. those who are victims of violent psychopaths or alcohol addicted automobile drivers). So, although it may not always be recognized, there are moral complexities to intervention that are not focused just on the dignity or self-respect of the patient or paranoid person. Other people may need to be assisted or protected, too. However, as remarked, even focusing just on one individual subject or person is no small moral chore. What happens if someone desires to remain distrustful, resents taking a drug that turns them into a less socially vigilant person, and claims that a non-paranoid worldview is inaccurate and precludes the sorts of hard-boiled success that they want in life – despite the harms of paranoia? (Kinderman and Bentall quote a tongue-n-cheek quip of the CEO of a major computer technology firm that "only the paranoid survive" [Kinderman and Bentall 2007: 275].)

The moral autonomy ideal that a person's life is their own is widely endorsed in the thinking of many anti-psychiatry critics like Thomas Szasz. One key component of one's life being one's own is deciding for oneself how to live. Even if I worsen my life, and even if you would do better for me if you took charge of my life, I may not wish you to do so. Take, for example, Darlene. She may protest if she is sent home and forced to take medication. A person's right to cut themselves off from treatment (even if this makes a mess for them) is recognized in cases of somatic illness. Just because I have breast cancer does not mean I must take treatment. Why not in cases of a mental disorder, especially when the ragged edges between mental health and illness produce heated forms of contestability as to just where the relevant borders lie?

The attitude that each and every person should decide for themselves how to live their own life is among the deepest moral convictions that we have. But, I believe, there is a potentially powerful reason for doubting whether this conviction is morally legitimate in cases in which a paranoid patient resists treatment and is in danger of harming themselves or being cut off from any and all significant social relations. The reason again has to do with our capacity for responsibility for self.

Day-to-day responsibility for oneself involves a commitment to one's welfare and the comprehension of one's best interests that a paranoid person just cannot self provide. Frankfurt notes that there are a number of respects in which the care and concern that a person ought to have for their personal well-being is closely analogous to the care and concern parents ought to have for their children. Parents should care about the good of their children and be "concerned to protect and to pursue [a child's] true interests" (Frankfurt 2004: 83). They should wish the child's life to be satisfying and worthwhile.

Suppose that a parent is attempting sincerely to add to the training of their child the formation of character traits and social interpersonal habits and attitudes. Suppose that one of the desired traits is a sound and sensible trust of others. Children need to be told when and whom to trust. They need competence in trusting as a character trait or habit. Something that is quite persistent and spontaneous. It would seem that whatever the detailed guidance would or should be, a child must feel pleasure in trusting others – otherwise it will not become a character trait or be perceived as a habit worth preserving (by the child when grown up). It would also appear that a child needs to be the recipient of trust and that "he or she needs to experience how nice it is to be [trusted themselves]" (Pickard 2009: 95). But when we consider the unhappy complexities and anxieties of generalized distrust of others or paranoia, this seems not at all the sort of habit or character trait that a parent would wish possessed by their child. A persecutory worldview is often accompanied by feelings of victimization and powerlessness, pleasure-less engagement with other people, and a depressed and fearful mood, as everywhere there seems to be for a paranoid, in the words of Kraepelin, "hounding and backbiting, jeering and chicanery" (quoted in Radden 2007: 266).

Therapists and clinicians should hope that a post-paranoid individual will be appreciative of and grateful for the treatment that they receive. But if, by chance, they aren't, then that fact, by itself, arguably counts as a failure of proper self-responsibility and concern. "Barricading ourselves against all possible attackers," to quote Baier, so that the social world and our need for other people cannot break in, certainly is not what a responsible parent would wish for their child if the parent loves them and the family lives in a normal environment (Baier 1989: 279). Intervention, then, may be morally justified independent of the prospect of a post-paranoid's positive appraisal of the effort to help. Suffering persecutory paranoia is not what I should wish for my child. It is not what I should wish for myself. Not to underestimate the moral complexities or details of treatment, or possible side effects of bad treatment, but others (clinicians and so on) may do me (if paranoid) no moral wrong if they try to direct me down a trusting path, even though I resist and end up resenting them for doing so.

One final point needs to be made about paranoia and the issue of contact with reality. As John Martin Fischer notes in another context, "surely there are many deeply unhappy persons – persons who grew up under conditions of horrible poverty or terrible physical or emotional abuse" (Fischer 2009: 60). "Why wouldn't these people be willing to take the risk involved in having a different personality?" (Ibid.) Fischer's rhetorical query or point (which he himself applies to another topic entirely) applies to paranoia. It seems obvious that if a paranoid person was able to experience life as a non-paranoid (and outside the horrible reality in which they may have had to live) any person would want to discard their paranoid personality and be unwilling to revert to paranoia. The point though made with humor is insightful: "I so rarely left my house," the comedian Richard Lewis remarks, "I think it would be nice to see people for a change" (Lewis 2002: 244–45).

SUMMARY

This chapter explored various disorders or symptoms in which a person disconnects from or somehow loses cognitive or comprehending contact with reality. It paid attention to the presence of delusions in schizophrenia and to the hypothesis that delusions consist of false and bizarre beliefs. It argued that there may be *some* subjective warrant for a delusional attitude and that a delusional attitude may not be false. So, it sought for another mark or aspect of delusion. The mark is found not in whether a subject of delusion falsely represents the world or in other upstream aspects of an attitude, but in the failure downstream of the deluded person to grasp the deleterious nature or manage the harmful consequences of their own mental activities. Understanding the nature of delusion requires understanding a deluded subject's failure to control or direct their own cognitive activities in a satisfactory and prudent or reason-responsive manner.

The chapter also examined just what it means to accurately or truthfully represent reality as well as to empathetically understand conceptions of the world and other people that some delusional subjects harbor, paranoids in particular. Why do some people over-identify with imprudent attitudes? Why are some individuals unduly pessimistic or distrusting of others? The chapter noted that often what we should believe of the world or others is quite indeterminate evidentially. This leaves elbow room for shaping our cognitive attitudes in a manner that enables us to properly care for ourselves and to protect our capacities for leading satisfying and worthwhile lives. None of this means that people should freely embrace or welcome so-called 'positive illusions'. And it certainly does not mean that moderate depressives possess more realistic or truthful outlooks than non-depressives. But it means that given the evidential ambiguities of the world, moderately positive attitudes towards real world situations and other people may constitute proper or reasonable cognitive contact with the world.

The present chapter introduced a distinction between two types of therapy for a mental disorder. One works through a person's reasoning capacities, while the other by-passes it. Working through reason is not always effective or even possible (depending on the disorder). Perhaps a person is paranoid and essentially bent on distrusting others. A disorder may also pose a stiff challenge to a caregiver to imaginatively simulate the mind set of such a patient. Proper therapeutic care may turn out to be a mix of pass-through and by-pass treatment.

SUGGESTED READING

Bell, V., Halligan, P., and Ellis, H. (2006). "Explaining delusions: a cognitive perspective," *TRENDS in Cognitive Science*," 10: 219–26

Biegler, P. (2011). *The Ethical Treatment of Depression: Autonomy through Psychotherapy*. (Cambridge, MA: MIT Press).

Chung, M., Fulford, K., and Graham, G. (eds). (2007). *Reconceiving Schizophrenia* (Oxford: Oxford University Press).

Flanagan, O. (2007). *The Really Hard Problem: Meaning in a Material World* (Cambridge, MA: MIT Press).

Frith, C. D., and Johnstone, E. (2003). *Schizophrenia: A Very Short Introduction* (Oxford: Oxford University Press).

9 Minding the missing me

ME, MYSELF AND MY SELVES

Children all too easily scratch, cut or scrape their skin. Abrasions and surface wounds over-populate the accidental territory of childhood.

As a young boy, I had more than my share of cuts and bruises. Climbing trees or exploring thick thorny bushes caused minor wounds. Playing stick ball or touch tag on the Brooklyn city street where my family lived produced numerous temporary scars.

Minor and surface wounds disappeared quickly, of course. But they left an indelible impression on me of the body's ability to reconstitute its borders. So, I was delighted, when, in the summer of my eighth year, while vacationing in the mountains of Pennsylvania with my parents and siblings, I discovered something marvelous about the tiny, lowly salamander. (In the evening I collected salamanders, some injured, in shoeboxes and jars.) This is that the adult salamander is blessed with a miraculous power. It can regenerate an entire lost limb over and over again, no matter how often the limb is shorn or amputated from its body. Just how this is done was utterly mysterious to me at the time. One key, I since have learned, is that when a sala-mander's limb is amputated blood vessels in the remaining stump contract quickly so that bleeding is limited. A loose arrangement of stem-like cells in the area of the stump then begins to serve as progenitor of the replacement limb (Muneoka, Han, and Gardiner 2008: 56–63).

Wouldn't it be wonderful if our mental health or emotional well-being, when scarred or damaged, similarly healed autonomously, immediately and fully? Suppose a wounded mind would 'know' of the right repair for its damaged capacity or faculty, access the extent of injury, initiate a regenerative response, clean the emotional scar, restore the contour of cognitive or psychological function, and heal itself. Just as we may watch a lowly salamander grow back a missing leg, we may observe the subject of a severe depression or crippling paranoia quickly and efficiently reconstitute their person.

It would be wonderful, indeed. And, on occasion, something very roughly like that actually does happen after certain episodes or experiences of mental ill-health. At least in this sense: People remit, self regenerate, self reconstruct. Not quickly perhaps, but efficiently. Psychiatric self regeneration, however, is not something on which surely to count. We aren't salamanders. We often need the help of other persons and mental health professionals and cannot properly constitute or reconstitute ourselves without assistance.

'We aren't salamanders.' So, what are we, then?

I intend this 'What are we, then?' to be a deep question. A very deep question. A metaphysical question. A question about our fundamental or essential nature or identity as persons. A straightforward answer like 'author or reader of this book' will not do. A salamander fundamentally or essentially is a type of non-human animal. But what fundamentally or essentially are we?

As bizarre or counter-intuitive as the following claim may seem, numerous philosophers have claimed that, as a matter of strict metaphysical fact, we are nothing at all. We don't exist. Fundamentally or strictly speaking, we are unreal. Thomas Metzinger in a note to his aptly titled book called *Being No One* announces that "strictly speaking, no one ever was born and no one ever dies" (Metzinger 2003: 633, n. 7). "No such things as selves exist in the world," he says (626). Daniel Dennett announces similarly that we ourselves are a "theorist's fiction" (Dennett 1991: 429). If Dennett is right, what I am rather is like, say, Santa Claus, Holden Caufield or Moby Dick: a figure of myth, tale or story. A pretend thing, not a real thing.

There surely is something, as noted, bizarre about such claims. Two bizarre things, in fact, although they are connected. Metzinger and Dennett (and various others) say we don't exist. But you cannot say you do not exist without existing, can you? The thesis seems hopelessly self-contradictory or pragmatically self-stultifying, like saying you cannot open a door while you successfully open it. Furthermore, you'd think that no person should *want* to say such a thing. What can such a thesis contribute? What philosophical problem does it solve? The proposition seems not just self-contradictory but theoretically pointless.

The incredibly counterintuitive idea that we are fictional and unreal has a long and checkered history in the philosophical literature on the metaphysics of selfhood or personhood. Occasionally, fictionalism or anti-realism about we ourselves (as the idea sometimes is called) is mistakenly generated by violating a sensible caution admonished by the philosopher Anthony Kenny. Kenny's warning goes like this: Do not allow the syntactic space that distinguishes the expression 'my self' from the single word 'myself' to produce the appearance of reference to a special metaphysical entity namely, the self and then ask if selves exist, arguing that selves per se do not exist. And then conclude: Therefore we our*selves* do not exist (see Kenny 1988; see also Kennedy and Graham 2007). Or that we are creatures of fiction, not in fact. Such reasoning serves as a foundation for a form of fictionalism or anti-realism about our selves (read 'ourselves'). But it rests on a false distinction between me and my self (or, analogously, between you and your self). I am not a self, though I am, of course, nothing other than myself.

Fictionalism about selves (again read, 'about ourselves') has been promoted on more philosophically subtle and dialectically nuanced grounds, however, than mere syntactic confusion or a misreading of grammar. Such philosophical grounds give it a point or rationale, if not obvious liberation from self-contradiction. The grounds vary in structure, content and contour. Relevant to this book are promotions of fictionalism or 'self denial' that rest upon examination of mental disorders. Multiple Personality Disorder (MPD) has been an especially prominent extrapolation base for the fictionalist case (Dennett and Humphrey 1989; Dennett 1991; Wilkes 1988 and 1991).

Though short on history as a taxonomic category MPD, now known as Dissociative Identity Disorder (DID), is long on metaphysical controversy. Some clinical observers deny the sheer existence or reality of the disorder. Nicholas Spanos in a book length analysis of MPD charges that MPD is an artifact or construct of clinic and therapy. A pseudo-disorder. Spanos writes:

> Patients learn to construe themselves as possessing multiple selves, learn to present themselves in terms of this construal, and learn to recognize and elaborate on the personal biography so as to make it congruent with their understanding of what it means to be multiple ... Psychotherapists play a particularly important part in the generation and maintenance of MPD. Some therapists routinely encourage patients to construe themselves as having multiple selves ... and provide official legitimation for the different identities that their patients enact.
>
> (Spanos 1996: 3)

The philosopher Ian Hacking (1995) appears (and note that I say 'appears') to offer a similar charge against MPD to Spanos's. He argues as follows.

Popular conceptions of MPD exert looping effects on potential subjects of the diagnosis, causing them to behave in manners that conform to the category or concept and therein to think of themselves as multiples. Certain clinicians and therapists notice possible candidates of the condition among their patients and respond by explicitly or implicitly encouraging them to represent themselves to themselves and others as possessed of different personalities, alters or identities. The MPD/DID concept is constituted in part by predictions and proscriptions for what counts as appropriate behavior for people who are diagnosed with MPD (hereafter I drop the 'DID'). Attribution of the MPD classification to certain individuals, who are aware of being so classified, leads them to conform to norms for the disorder. For such persons the disorder may serve any number of conscious or perhaps more likely unconscious palliative or defensive purposes. Perhaps foremost, Hacking suspects, it frees a person from the unbearable suffering or anxiety of real or imagined memories of childhood sexual or physical abuse.

Hacking's position is not that of Spanos, however. For Hacking the role of looping in MPD does not necessarily mean that MPD is not an honest-to-goodness disorder. It means just that the reality of MPD is confined to an unstable or transient cultural, therapeutic or clinical niche. It is socially constructed, as it were, in that niche. But it is real nevertheless. If so, it is a disorder of a sub-culturally embedded or particularized sort and not of the general form captured by the cross-cultural prototype of a mental disorder.

As fascinating as Hacking's depiction of the origins of MPD is, however, I must skip past his discussion MPD here (see Graham 1996 for additional examination of Hacking). Also I am not going to commit myself here in this book one way or another to whether MPD is a genuine mental disorder. (Perhaps, when there is a real disorder present in a person diagnosed with MPD, it is not MPD but some other sort of disorder entirely – a delusional or anxiety order perhaps. Alters are among its symptoms. Perhaps.) I shall merely write as if it is a real disorder. Instead,

I plan to focus on claims about its alleged metaphysical implications (if it is taken to be real). Not the reality, existence or presence of the condition, but the unreality or non-existence of its participants or subjects, namely the 'selves' of MPD. So, here is this different worry about MPD. It is a personal existence concern. One that has to do not with Spanos-like skepticism or with whether MPD itself is real, but with what, if anything, MPD may tell us about our own existence, assuming that MPD or something very much like it actually is real.

On the clinical coal face of it, a good part of what is supposed to be wrong with victims of MPD is that their personal memory or autobiographical self-consciousness is deeply and multiply disturbed. Keeping conscious track of ourselves is crucial to who we are as persons (as noted in our discussion of addiction in Chapter 7). "Self", wrote John Locke (1632–1704), "is that conscious thinking thing … as far as the consciousness extends" (1690/1975: Essay II, XXVII. 17). Possession of an autobiographical memory that extends each of us into the past is a key aspect of *at least* one (actually more) of the basic psychological capacities that I suggested (in Chapter 6) we would pick or identify from behind the veil of ignorance as required for a worthwhile life. This is the capacity for historical/temporal self-location. From the perspective of the 'original position', we would appreciate that we need the ability to remember past personal experiences. We would want to be able to harbor conscious memories of earlier episodes in our life. We cannot lead a truly satisfying life without historical self-awareness or the capacity to extend our consciousness into our past and, indeed, project ourselves into an imagined future.

Locating ourselves historically or in time requires a particular form of self-awareness or self-recognition. It requires in addition to temporally locating some person, recognizing that the person so located is none other than oneself. It requires, in backward-looking cases, personal or autobiographical memories, whereas in forward-looking cases, something sometimes called 'prospection', in which a person mentally rehearses or imagines a situation in which they may or will be involved, and what the situation may be like to themselves then.

Temporal self-location frequently is infused with or accompanied by resonant emotional or affective experiences. In reading a book, planning a vacation, remembering the death of a childhood friend, regretting a past misdeed, being excited over last week's discovery such mental time-travel often is filled with emotional attitudes and feelings. Anticipated pleasure or satisfaction (perhaps when looking forward). Pride, shame, or guilt (perhaps when looking backward). Indeed, arguably the more we examine these matters, the more we come to appreciate that the emotions or feelings often associated with locating oneself in time are not so clearly distinct or so sharply dissociable from other basic capacities such as the human capacity for care, concern, and emotional commitment. The peak of emotional regret or shame taken in a past misdeed, for example, may tend to occur in concert with the realization of how much we care about honoring our commitments and concerns and our disappointment in our own behavior.

> "I remember, much to my shame, that I amputated the limb of a helpless salamander."
> "I held my PhD thesis in my hands, too anxious to deliver it to the department chair's office for my defense."
> "The emotional turmoil of the past weeks overtook her." "The death of her spouse reminded her of her own ambivalence towards him."

Personal/historical or autobiographical memory often is cast as a type of narrative construction, not as "a causally imprinted trace on a passive receiving system forming a 'spool like' cumulative record of self-standing [past] events" (Gillett 2008: 95). But as a product whose content and contour is constantly developed and updated, reinterpreted or rewoven together, often in the light of current concerns and emotional associations and edited and adjusted to fit current circumstances and aspirations.

> When you recall an episode in your life, you [often] reconstruct it in much the same way as you would reconstruct an episode in a story. However, your own life story is much richer and contains many more details important to you than any story you might read. So you need a much finer system of cues and rules to reconstruct your life than to construct a story.
>
> (Glass and Holyoak 1986: 244)

Thomas DeBaggio, once a professional herb grower and newspaper journalist, in *Losing My Mind* (2003), has written a remarkable memoir of living with the effects of early onset Alzheimer's. DeBaggio ends the main part of the memoir with the following testament to the importance of personal historical self-awareness:

> I must now wait for the silence to engulf me and take me to the place where there is no memory left and there remains no reflexive will to live. It is lonely here waiting for memory to stop and I am afraid and tired. Hug me, Joyce [his wife], and then let me sleep.
>
> (DeBaggio 2003: 207)

DeBaggio wrote his memoir, in part, because he said that he wanted to be understood by other people as someone possessing a past, present, and future, or an ongoing biography, rather than as a mere product of his deficits and in need of custodial care.

Autobiographical memory seems to suffer a double disturbance in MPD. One concerns a person's ability to recall or retrieve events from their past history. At given moments, various stretches of a multiple's history appear hidden from them in blank spots or behind so-called 'amnesia barriers'. These juxtaposed patterns of accessibility and inaccessibility may be quite complex. Confer and Ables's (1983) patient, Rene, for instance, originally recalled nothing in her life from age 11 to age 13, despite detailed memories of events both before and after the period. Under hypnosis her powers of retrieval seemed to improve. She was able to offer vivid recollections of formerly blank periods. How this was described or evidenced by her (see below) exhibits the second disturbance of personal memory in MPD.

The second disturbance is an often bizarre and unexpected proclivity, given the frequent drama or purport of recollected events, to recall various events in an otherwise blank period, not as something that happened to or involved oneself, but as having happened to another person (self, alter), namely someone who shared the body of the remembering individual. Rene, for example, recalled in vivid detail her rape by her father, but spoke of the rape while clinically presenting under the therapeutic persona of Stella. She/Stella referred to the victim of the rape as someone else – Rene.

It was Easter. And she was 11. ... I was watching ... but she didn't know it. ... I've been with men, but I wouldn't do nothing like that with my own father. ... She was a wreck. A complete wreck. ... Well, I can see that it was ... hard for her to take.

(Confer and Ables 1983: 127)

It is as if Stella was 'looking on' or 'viewing from the outside' experiences that befell one of her personality states, but without the sense of identity or personal connectedness with that time slice. Stella's/Rene's case helps to remind us that real memory, as opposed to merely apparent memory or a case of misremembering, is what philosophers call an 'achievement'. I do not (successfully) remember some event in which I participated unless I participated in the event. If we persons lose our sense of the person who participated in the event (as apparently happens in MPD), if, that is, I cannot remember what happened to me as something that happened to me, then something truly essential to my capacity for temporal self-location is lost.

What are we to make of recollections like that (assuming their veridicality)? As I remark elsewhere in a discussion of MPD and fictionalism:

These self-conscious recollections described by the patient are typical of MPD. They are cases in which a multiple recalls events from her personal history: things she has done, said, thought, felt, and things that have happened to her. However, she recalls these as things that were done by or happened to another person or agent. Her autobiographical perspective on exactly what parts of her history belong to her and which to someone else varies with her current state. As Stella, Rene has access to some of this forgotten history, but is alienated from it in the sense that she fails to experience it as her own.

(Graham 1999: 161–161)

What do such MPD-like disturbances of personal memory reveal about our existence? Do they help to demonstrate that we are fictions, unreal, myths? If so, just how might they warrant such extraordinary claims? These questions demand more attention than I can provide here. I cannot compose a detailed response. However, here is a reconstruction with simplifications of (and with additions to) what Daniel Dennett believes about the metaphysical lesson of MPD.

According to Dennett, the distorted complexities of autobiographical retrieval in MPD dim any realistic hope of getting a decisive empirical measure or bead on 'who remembers', and hence any standard for what counts as the subjects of MPD. Indeed, the general metaphysical moral, for Dennett, to be drawn from MPD is that we ourselves are a figment, an illusion, of our cognitive system's or brain's mode of operation. We are virtual or fictional rather than real entities. How so?

Suppose we assume, as we do in commonsense, that for a person to be real he or she must be numerically distinct from other persons. If, for example, I remember amputating the limbs of salamanders as a young boy, there is a single, fixed, historically located person that I therein remember performing the procedure. Namely Me. In MPD, however, there is no precise or determinate boundary between one person or individual (say, Rene) and another (say, Stella). The lines or psychological boundaries or distinctions between persons (selves, personalities, or alters) are intractably fuzzy, blurry and vague. So, to announce that Rene is one person and that Stella is another ultimately is a matter of arbitrary decision or practical fiat. There is no independent or objective fact of the matter about just who is who in the condition. *This* person rather than *that* person is a distinction we make up if or when we interact with someone as a multiple.

There are two grounds for this claim of no independent fact as to just which person (or persons) is (are) in the condition. One ground is the lack of successful memory connections to past events. A person or subject like Rene or Stella either (i) has no memory of certain past events performed by the subject existentially based in her biological body or (ii) her memories of past events occur as dissociated from the autobiographical sense of herself as participant in the events. Either way, a proper memory of oneself and one's past is not in place. The other ground is the absence of any sense of personal responsibility for self. Responsibility for self requires (as we learned in Chapter 7) the self-assessment of one's actions and behavior and the possibility of self control in the light of such assessment. Victims of MPD are either "incapable of remembering their prior rational decisions and commitments [as their own], or they are incapable of buying into or being appropriately affected by, the reason-giving force of them" (Kennett and Matthews 2009: 344). Suppose, for example, that Rene/Stella is a drug addict. Without a robust sense of her past as her own past or of her future as her own future, she is incapable of adequately reflecting on the past destructive effects of taking the drug or of feeling constrained in the future by her current effort or desire to refrain.

Some MPD-observers talk, contrarily, as if one and only one individual (rather than an indeterminate or indistinct set) is present in MPD. Not multiples, fuzzy or otherwise. Thus Hugh Silverman remarks:

> MPD is an attempt of a beleaguered individual, unable to … defend against external adversity, to flee inwardly and create alternative selves and alternative constructs of reality that allow the possibility of psychological survival.
>
> (Silverman 1995: 179)

Scott Braude exclaims that MPD is the "dominant coping mechanism of … one subject" (Braude 1991: 179). Grant Gillett writes that "the subject uses different names to collect different clusters of attitudes … ways of thinking, and styles of learning" (Gillett 1991: 107).

According to such 'one person/one body' conceptions, single subjects or selves are the agents, structural and motivational supports of the disorder. Indeed, just above, I, too, spoke in terms of the singularity of a person by referring to Confer's and Ables's 'patient'. It's hard to avoid speaking in that way. But, says Dennett, strictly speaking, we should avoid it, namely the assumption of a single self underlying MPD. For Dennett, however, this is not because there actually are a definite or distinct number of multiple selves in the disorder. Rather, it is because no one is in or behind the disorder. Single selves underlying MPD are no more real than the personas identified as Stella or Rene.

Indeed for Dennett: No one person is us or in us normal folk either. Dennett himself is no more real than either Stella or Rene. "By calling *me* Dan," writes Dennett, we are referring to "the theorist's fiction created by … well, not by me but by my brain" (Dennett 1991: 429). None of us is a real historical singularity or entity.

> Some people [make] a simple arithmetical mistake: they have failed to notice that two or three or seventeen selves per body is really no more metaphysically extravagant than one self per body. One is bad enough!
>
> (Dennett 1991: 419)

You and I are no more real than Stella or Rene? For Dennett the cumulative metaphysical impact of MPD is to put intense weight on how to distinguish or differentiate between selves or persons and to numerically individuate or identify them, to despair of being able to do so, and then to infer that the reason it is so difficult to differentiate between selves is that there really is nothing there to individuate or differentiate between in the first place. Nothing there in them or, for that matter, in us either.

Consider the following analogy. Imagine that you are asked to picture a tiger before your mind's eye. Then imagine being asked, without doing anything whatsoever to your initial image, to count the number of its stripes. (Filling in a number is cheating. You cannot enhance the image. Suppose also that you did not initially imagine a particular number of stripes.) The stripes, for Dennett, are like we ourselves or the selves that allegedly are present in a multiple. We may pretend that the imagined tiger has a certain definite number of stripes, but it does not. We may pretend that there is one of us or (in MPD) two, three, or seventeen selves or alters, but there is not. To suppose that we are real is like supposing that the imagined tiger has a certain definite number of stripes. In a fit of fictive fiat we may claim it's got its determinate stripes. It is a tiger image after all. However, no specific number of stripes truly is present in the image. Likewise: No specific number of us is us. There are no stripes there. There is no self or we ourselves here.

Clever argument? Perhaps. Dennett's work on selfhood and personhood, and his overall defense of fictionalism, rests on considerations in addition to those of MPD. It must do so, for MPD may be an isolated or rare case of the failed numerical identity or distinctness of a person. Perhaps in normal or other cases like our own (with autobiographical memories and responsibility for self more or less intact), we, indeed, are real – distinct from other persons. Perhaps it's just that in MPD or closely related conditions no one is home. Dennett, however, would object that we ourselves are ultimately no more coherent single wholes or singletons than are the victims of MPD. The differences between us and Rene/Stella are differences of degree only. What capacities of a person really are essential to their being a distinct person? Dennett would then ask: If we think we have these capacities, how do they hang together to form one and only one of us? This question, from him, is rhetorical. For him, the capacities of personhood are too multiplex and amorphous to produce a personal singleton.

But (Dennett's own particular brand skepticism or fictionalism aside) I take it that the conclusion that we don't exist should be resisted. Although if so, how so? How resist fictionalism about ourselves?

Well, one possibility is to claim that fictionalism is a kind of realism but in linguistic disguise. Better to exist as a fiction or called a fiction than not to exist at all. But fictional objects do not exist period. A fictional person is not a type of person. It is a non-person. Or: we may claim that denying that we exist is so grossly counter-intuitive, that it defies belief. Dennett, however, may consider that fact, namely, the proposition's counter-intuitiveness, as an iconoclastic plus rather than an unwelcome minus. Much that is true is counter-intuitive, as he would point out. (Just stare at the earth's horizon at dawn. It appears that the earth is flat, but, of course, it's not.) Or: we may claim that

> We ourselves are nothing but –.

Then fill in the blank with mention of something that does exist (say, a brain or a biologically alive human animal). If we ourselves are nothing but, say, biologically living human animals or organisms, then, assuming that animals exist, we exist (see Olson 1997). The animal that is called 'Rene' may also carry different names (say, 'Stella') on different occasions or for different purposes, but she still is one particular human animal.

I have some sympathy for the proposition that we are biologically living human animals fundamentally or essentially. This proposal is known in the philosophical literature on personal identity or self-identity as *animalism* about human persons. If animalism is true, you and I are nothing but particular living human animals. I am a particular living human animal. You are a particular living human animal. But there are difficulties with the position. One difficulty is that a *merely* biologically alive human animal can exist, albeit only with outside assistance, without possessing any conscious or reason-responsive life whatsoever, autobiographical memories or otherwise. But can you and I *really* exist or persist in such a literally 'thought-less' or 'intentionality-less' condition? If animalism is true, I could exist in a permanent vegetative state. To me this consequence of animalism, namely that I could exist permanently non-consciously, just biologically, strips what we essentially are from capacities or powers that, as Lynne Rudder Baker aptly puts it, "matter most deeply to ourselves" (Baker 2000: 227). Powers that we identified in Chapter 6 as required for leading a satisfying and worthwhile life. It matters most deeply to me that I am conscious or possess a capacity for conscious experience and am able to lead a life responsibly and in comprehension of self. Biology may be a precondition for all that (being conscious, leading a life, locating oneself historically and so on), but biology isn't what really and truly matters to me about myself. Biology contains not enough of the 'me-ness' of me. Being stripped down to mere biological features seems like a fate indistinguishable from personal death or annihilation.

Consider the case of Terri Schiavo, who in 1990, at the age of 26, had a heart attack (apparently from a potassium deficiency associated with an eating disorder) and suffered a severe anoxic brain injury. She gradually descended into a permanent vegetative state (PVS) with credible evidence, which eventually included the results of an autopsy, of an irreversible loss of consciousness. If so, while biologically she remained alive, biographically or psychologically she was dead. If such a state befalls me or my body, it would make no difference to me for me to be in the condition. So, I speak of a 'fate indistinguishable' from death. If I don't and never can know that I am alive or exist, why be alive? It hardly matters.

So, then, why do I speak of my 'some sympathy' for animalism? Is there any merit to the position? Yes, there is. The animalist position does pick out something real and numerically single as me namely, an animal. Moreover, in order to account for periods in which I exist but am temporarily unconscious, say, while I am in deep and dreamless sleep, we have to suppose that there is a single entity that is conscious at one time, unconscious at another and later time, persists through unconscious times and then re-engages in various conscious activities at still later times. This entity or individual that is me could well be a particular human animal. Just as there is one animal writing this chapter, so there is one me authoring the book, from start to finish, if I am that animal. Writing the chapter is something that I, a particular organism, do. Our animal identity, too, if we essentially are animals, also helps to make sense of the character of veridical autobiographical memory. If I truly or really do remember something that happened to me yesterday, I am connected objectively (as one and the same object) with that historical personage, namely, me at some past time. Me, then, is one and the same entity as this remembering animal here and now. If a film of my life could rewind, it would traverse a continuous line between the animal now and then. Rene/Stella, too, may be helped metaphysically in her individuation as a single individual if animalism is true. Her memories and interpretations are impaired by amnesia and distortions or dissociations in her sense of personal connectedness over time. But arguably, she is one and the same particular living human animal now and then, either in the persona or guise of Rene or of Stella, memory vicissitudes aside.

Regardless of the merits or demerits of animalism, however, it should also be noted that conventional therapeutic treatment for MPD normally pushes and pulls in favor of picturing 'victims' as single individuals, namely as one distinguishable thing or subject (Putnam 1989 and Kluft 1986). Treatment of persons with MPD often consists of taking a healthy presenting personality and enlisting its services in flushing out and rejecting or unifying with other personalities. A single subject is presupposed as the target therapeutic destination of a multiple and, if achieved, as a healthy gain or improvement from evidence of a beleaguered multiplicity in the initial appearance of a patient in therapy.

However, back now to my original query, whose upcoming 'answer' has just been framed by brief discussion of MPD, fictionalism, animalism and selfhood. What is our fundamental essence? Of what nature am I? What makes me me?

Fundamental essences are powerful, metaphysically speaking. They constitute us. They define us. They, when present, mean we exist. They, when absent, mean we fail to exist. Suppose, for example, that my essence is such that I am a particular non-physical or immaterial mind or substance. Call this substance a 'soul'. If that particular soul exists, I exist. If that particular soul fails to exist, then I also fail to exist, for it is me. Assume the soul is such that it is the subject of all of the person's experiences. Suppose it is singular. Suppose also it is indivisible or devoid of parts. And assume it is present from beginning to end of a person's life. Or suppose, for a contrasting example, that my essence is such that I am a particular living human animal; not a soul. If that particular animal exists, I exist; if it does not, I do not. It, too, is present from beginning to end of a person's life.

As between these two possibilities, an animal essence has a striking advantage over a soulful one. A soul cannot be seen, touched or detected in any conventional way. If, by contrast, animalism is true, we can detect the presence and persistence of a person by normal means of observation. Just look for a living human animal. Of course, which part or parts of the animal are required for its presence and persistence may be debated. Obviously, I could lose a finger and still be me, if I were an animal. But could I survive the loss of one of my brain hemispheres? Different answers may be proposed by friends of animalism.

Despite some personal sympathy for animalism, I don't want to *insist* or presuppose here that the doctrine is true. In good faith I can't. The arguments for animalism don't roll over misgivings about it. For the purposes of this chapter, however, we do not require a definitive or settled answer to the essence question. Indeed, I shall make an assumption. This is that we are not in a position as human beings to *prove* or demonstrate *what* fundamentally or essentially we are, although we know in the experience of self consciousness *that* we are. Built into our experience of being self-conscious is recognition of our own existence (of which more below). However, being aware of our own existence does not require or presuppose that we possess explicit knowledge of our fundamental nature or essence. *That* I am what I am is one thing. That I know precisely *what* I am is another. I like to call this position namely, that we know that we exist but not what essentially we are, *self-serving agnosticism* (metaphysical pun intended). I know that I exist. You know that you exist. But it is left open or knowledge-wise metaphysically topic-neutral precisely in *what* sort of metaphysical class we matriculate. We are not fictions. We exist. We are real, not imaginary. But for essence speculation much beyond that, we are in an ultimately ignorant mode.

Naturally, we may, do and sometimes must make educated guesses about what we are. Some educated guesses may be superior to others. Animalism, despite my misgivings, is my guess. But what makes an individual animal the particular it is? An entire organism, nervous system, brain, cerebrum, or one or another cerebral hemisphere? The lungs are ruled out as essential by realizing that our basic psychological capacities are not associated with lung function. A random collection of particles "taken from toenail and eyelash and tongue does not count as a likely candidate" similarly is discounted (Zimmerman 2003: 492). But numerous possibilities remain.

Knowledge, after all, is "a thick epistemological concept" (Goldman 2006: 223). It's more than just an educated guess. It is a true belief possessed of demonstrable reliability or proveable justification. The epistemological bar or criterion for knowledge is high, too high, I assume, for knowing precisely what sort of creature we are. However, failing to know what we are does not mean, again, that we fail to know that we are. It is evident to me that I exist. When my finger, for example, is accidentally smashed, I feel pain. The pain is experienced as mine, as in my finger. It is pain that belongs to me (even if the pain on some other occasion is of a phantom limb variety). When I feel anxious about climbing a ladder on a cold, windy winter day to get to the roof of my home to remove a fallen tree limb, it's anxiety in me that I know I feel. I do not feel an episode of anxiety and then ask whether it is my own. I experience the anxiety as, as it were, adjectival upon or as a modification of me: as my own apprehensiveness.

Being literally self-evident to ourselves that we exist is a kind of introspective knowledge of our existence. It is direct, non-inferential and not mediated by way of applying identifying descriptions or concepts to one's own person. I don't learn that I exist by first learning how to apply a concept like 'animal' or 'soul' to myself or even by first learning my own proper name. I don't think "This is George Graham's anxiety, so it must be my anxiety, since I am none other than George Graham." "So, also I must exist or else this anxiety would not exist." Even multiples have non-inferential knowledge of their own existence. True, Rene and Stella do not have the sense that they are one and the same person over time, but when Rene feels pain, she knows that the pain is hers (*whoever* she is).

The philosopher Colin McGinn advocates a form of self-serving agnosticism. (I am not sure whether McGinn would appreciate the label or name of 'self-serving agnosticism'. Perhaps not.) McGinn writes:

> We know [of our] existence with a special kind of assurance, but we know next to nothing about [our metaphysical] nature. We know with certainty *that* [we are], but we are grievously ignorant of *what* [we are].
>
> (McGinn 1999: 1630–164)

I wish to rephrase and add to McGinn's claim as follows: Strictly speaking, we do not know exactly what our essential or fundamental thing-hood is. We may embrace a hypothesis about the matter, but we should not think or talk confidently of its truth. The essence of our selves (remember, by 'our selves' I mean "ourselves") is one thing. Our comprehension of that essence (or even perhaps if we have one) is another matter entirely. We just do not know what that essence is. Why is that?

McGinn has an explanation for why we don't, and indeed, on his view, can't know of our essence. It has to do with the absence of scientific, objective or impersonal criteria for the existence of ourselves as well as, for that matter, of our termination or annihilation. We don't know what ultimately constitutes our existence. He asks:

> Does severe Alzheimer's disease put an end to the self or just modify it? What about deep coma? … There is the body, recognizably the same; but is it the same *person* in there?
>
> (McGinn 1999: 162)

Why don't we have an impersonal criterion for the existence of ourselves? Because, he says, we don't have it for the existence of consciousness, and "if we cannot understand states of consciousness [scientifically], then it is hardly likely that we will be able to understand the nature of the *subject* of those states" – namely, ourselves (McGinn 1999: 157).

Terri Schiavo's parents believed that their daughter continued to exist and perhaps was conscious of them during certain periods of the wake phase of her sleep-wake cycle. (Diagnosis of permanent vegetative state is made when a patient exhibits preserved sleep/wake cycles but appears unaware, in the wake phases of such cycles, of self and immediate environment.) We may lament that the truth of her parents' perhaps wishful thought or belief was massively unlikely, but, if McGinn is right, we don't *know* that Terri Schiavo was not conscious or did not as such exist. This point, namely, that the absence of a behavioral or impersonal sign of consciousness may not be reliably indicative of non-consciousness, is acknowledged or conceded by many neuroscientists. Some patients, Martha Farah notes, "continue to experience full awareness of themselves and their surroundings while being unable to indicate their awareness behaviorally" (Farah 2008: 12). Silence may envelop behavior without the thinker themselves being annihilated.

I am not going to commit to an interpretation of the Schiavo case. But I am going to join with McGinn in a refrain of self-serving agnosticism. We don't know what makes for ourselves. What is the particular me? A particular animal? And what is that? Does it require the presence of a capacity for consciousness? But I do not interpret self-serving agnosticism (and neither does McGinn) to imply that we are completely and utterly in the dark about some of our critically important characteristics. Grievous ignorance about our ultimate or categorical essence is one thing. Absolute blindness to important features of our selves is another.

Let me offer a quick mention of some things that I believe we do know about ourselves. Commonsense things. We do know, for example, that we are more or less unified or integrated leaders of a conscious life. Some of us are much more or less unified than others to be sure. (Some forms of mental disorder as well as of brain disorder contribute to degrees or types of disunity.) We do know that our lives cannot be wholly understood without appreciating 'inside' or subjective personal points of view connections between various episodes or stages in a life, namely connections understood from within a person's own perspective. We do know that we are not all 'inside' or private creatures, however. We are publicly observable or at least leave public marks in the world. We possess a public presence and behave in and have an impact as agents upon the physical or material world.

Galen Strawson, the son of P. F., and himself (like his father) a philosopher, writes of

> A friend who recently ... found that the thought 'I don't exist' kept occurring to him. It seemed to him that this exactly expressed his experience of himself, although he ... knew, of course, that there had to be a locus of consciousness where the thought 'I don't exist' occurred.
>
> (Strawson 1997: 418)

No ordinary friend is that friend, of course, for the proposition that there has to be a locus of consciousness where a thought like 'I don't exist' occurs is a quite sophisticated act of conceptual recognition (see Kennedy and Graham 2007). As Strawson-the-father once noted, "it would make no sense to think or say: *This* ... experience is occurring but is it occurring to *me*?" (Strawson 1966: 166). If I am directly aware of a thought and linguistically designating it with a demonstrative like the word 'this' (even a thought like 'I don't exist'), the thought must be occurring to me, and I must be the locus in which, or the subject to whom, it occurs.

> That's why I am in position to refer to it as *this* experience. Its distinctive identity as represented by the demonstrative is inseparable from my own presence or existence as the subject modified by the experience.
>
> (Kennedy and Graham 2007: 237)

Well and good. But what then of persons who seem to have lost their ability to recognize their very own selves as subjects of conscious experience or as responsible agents and who undergo various and dramatic forms of 'inner' point of view disunity or disintegration? Consider a life in which there is no real possibility of integrating one's memories or of revising one's beliefs – a life hobbled by an otherwise discordant or disintegrated point of view. There is a puzzling class of mental disorders or symptoms of conscious disunity and disintegration that vary along numerous and complicated dimensions. MPD is in that class. So, too, are various other disorders. I now plan to look at two other disorders in the class. I plan to begin with a disorder akin to the expressed sentiment of Galen Strawson's friend. It is known as the Cotard delusion.

'I AM DEAD' BUT DO NOT MEAN IT

In the early 1880s Jules Cotard, a French psychiatrist, encountered a 43-year-old female patient who claimed that she had "no brains, chests or entrails and was just skin and bone" (Cotard 1882; see also Bentall 2004: 299 and Young and Leafhead 1996). Cotard introduced the term *delire de negation* to refer to the delusion. After the French doctor's death, it was widely assumed that he had identified a particular type of nihilistic depressive delusion. Its central defining characteristic? A person denies that they are alive or claims that they are dead. Some individuals with the syndrome may claim not just that they are dead, but that they don't exist at all. Subjects may also say things like (see Enoch and Trethowan 1991):

- I have no blood.
- I used to have a heart. I have something which beats in its place.
- I am a corpse that already stinks.
- I have no body.

If there is a distinctive delusion here, which I assume there is, considerable variation characterizes its claims and symptoms (see Berrios and Luque 1995). I plan to focus on two truly striking expressions just mentioned of the syndrome, namely, the claims that

- I do not exist.
- I am dead.

Each may be made by subjects of the delusion.

Early observers of the Cotard condition, it appears, were correct that the delusion tends to be indicative of or associated with depression. Of 100 cases, for instance, in one representative study, severe depression was reported in 89 percent of them (Berrios and Luque 1995).

So, what may lead a depressed person to say (and believe?) that they don't exist or are dead? If I tell you that I am dead, mustn't I appreciate that I am speaking, hence alive? Or if I say that I don't exist, mustn't I recognize this proposition to be utterly false? If I say or think "I don't exist", I must exist. Such 'fictionalisms' should be dismissed by a person, should they not?

A famous assumption of Descartes about the metaphysics of selfhood was driven by his conviction that personal or self-existence denial is incoherent. He wrote:

> I saw that while I could pretend that I had no body and there was no world and no place for me to be in, I could not for all that pretend that I did not exist.
>
> (Descartes 1984: 127)

The Cotard delusion seems like ripe territory for Jaspers's caution that delusions are not rationally intelligible or empathetically sensible or coherent. Perhaps, though, the Cotard delusion is intelligible, at least up to a Maherian point. Perhaps empathetic sense may be made of its outlandish claims and of what they mean to a deluded person, if we can pinpoint aberrant experiences or affective emotional disturbances that underlie it.

The philosopher Philip Gerrans offers a venturesome solution to the 'making sense of' puzzle of the Cotard delusion that is in the Maher mold. Gerrans surmises: "The Cotard delusion, in its extreme form, is a rationalization," by which Gerrans means a Maher-type subjective explanation, "of a feeling of disembodiment based on global suppression of affect resulting from extreme depression" (Gerrans 2000: 112). Gerrans describes the connection between Cotard and depression as follows.

> Nothing that occurs [to the Cotard patient] evokes the normal emotional response. The Cotard patient experiences her perceptions and cognitions, not as changes in herself, but [as] changes in the states of the universe, one component of which is her body, which now feels like an inanimate physical substance, first decomposing and finally disappearing. The lack of affective experience ... produces a feeling of [corporeal] insubstantiality.
>
> (Gerrans 2002: 50) [Expressions in brackets inserted by me]

In an independent and unrelated discussion Nancy Andreasen descriptively fleshes this sort of depressed state out a bit:

> A person who is depressed can have cognitive symptoms so severe that he ... has delusions. ... Sometimes the delusions are turned inward, so that the person [feels as if] his internal organs are rotting away.
>
> (Andreasen 2001: 228)

William James, too, offers an apt description of certain aspects of a relevant depression. He writes that while severely depressed a person may feel as if "they are sheathed in India-rubber", as if there "were a wall between" the individual "and the outer world" (1890: 298). The affective possibility of making emotional contact or engagement with the world and of appreciating its opportunities or affordances is absent from experience.

Gerrans' picture appears to be the following. Patients suffering from the Cotard delusion are shorn or stripped of feelings, on their part, of being in the world and of affective or emotional concern for how they behave in the world as well as of their own corporeality. In bodily action or intentional motor behavior, normally emotions or feelings are associated with specific motivations and dispositions to act. I emotionally care what I do. I care whether my actions turn out successfully and with how my body moves. In people with the Cotard syndrome such care-emotions fail to occur. What do occur are feelings of insubstantiality or of (no pun is intended) not mattering.

The Gerrans-type picture of the Cotard delusion is that dead-feeling (feeling insubstantial and absent affective corporeal connectedness with the world) produces and, in a sense, subjectively warrants believing that one is dead or does not exist. The proposition that one is dead is formed and believed in (perhaps spontaneously and without deliberation) by the subject in order to explain the dead-feeling. I feel dead because, well, I am dead. Or so I believe of myself.

Is this a plausible tale? We should be careful with it. As noted, the story presupposes the Maher premise that delusional attitudes such as those expressed in the Cotard delusion and understood in belief-like terms are generated as explanations by subjects of unusual or aberrant feelings or perceptual experiences. The Cotard delusion that the subject is dead or does not exist (Gerrans primarily is interested in the claim of being dead) is adopted to account for why the person feels (or fails to feel) as they do. The subject feels insubstantial. So, they believe or assume that they are dead or do not exist. They *are* insubstantial.

It is true then, if Gerrans is right, that the assertions of the subject of the Cotard delusion are partially rational. They make a kind of sense. But do they make *that* particular sort of Maher-like sense? The trouble is that although this Maher-like tale of Gerrans looks like it helps to preserve some of the rationality or reason-responsivness of the subject of the Cotard delusion, insofar as it reflects an effort to make intelligible the sense of certain feelings, it still remains, as noted above, notoriously difficult to deny one's own existence or, for that matter, to believe that one is dead without being aware of the gross inconsistency of such speech acts or beliefs with one's living or existing as speaker. No one who denies his existence, for example, can use such words without, it would appear, knowing that the statement is false and knowing that one continues to exist in the very act of speaking.

Suppose I am a victim of the Cotard delusion. Is it that I, while in the grips of the delusion, don't even realize or recognize that I am speaking or saying something that contradicts my very speech act? Gerrans surmises that "the depression is [so] deeply entrenched ... it produces a deficit in reasoning which makes it impossible for the subject to bring countervailing knowledge to bear" (Gerrans 2000: 120). Does Gerrans mean by 'countervailing knowledge' the recognition that I exist or am alive when I speak? But how, then, does the mere entrenchment or power of depression screen me off from recognition of my speech acts as my own or of their implication or presupposition of whether I am alive or exist? It stretches credulity to say that such speech reflects even partially rational beliefs.

Gerrans seems to assume the following about the Cotard delusion. While the subject is quite aware that she feels dead or insubstantial, and also is sufficiently aware of herself to claim "I am dead", she fails to understand that in making this claim she actually is and must be alive. There is awareness of a claiming as well as of feeling insubstantial, but no awareness of one's life or existence as speaker? Gerrans's account of why subjects of the Cotard delusion utter existence denials seems explanatorily inadequate or incomplete, does it not? If I believe that I am dead or do not exist, it must be explained how I may believe this all the while knowing that I am saying these things.

I admire Gerrans for trying both to describe the phenomenal or subjective inside of the Cotard delusion and to make it rationally understandable or sensible. But let's see if we can substitute another and alternative hypothesis for his analysis in a productive way. How can I say something that utterly is incompatible with understanding or experiencing that I myself am saying it?

One possibility is that the speech acts in question are semantically empty and Intentionality-less, like coughs or sneezes. No intention, no rationality, no reason fuels the sound. They are empty or meaningless speech acts (Berrios 1991: 12). But such a construal strips the subject of the Cotard delusion of the speech, as it were, of his speech, namely, of intending to mean something by saying something. It would also be grossly incompatible with Gerrans' effort of reconstruction in the Maher-mold to strip the act of its Intentionality or of any agentive purpose. So, it is worth considering an alternative approach to the Cotard delusion. One with a speech act semantics that is different from that presupposed by Gerrans.

What's missing in the Gerrans' account is an explanation for why a belief such as that I am dead or do not exist is generated rather than some more readily intelligible or non-contradictory expression of a victim's sentiments, such as reports like the following: "I feel insubstantial" or "I don't feel as if I am having a bodily impact in the world".

Here is a brief sketch of an alternative proposal to that of Gerrans, which is aimed at dissolving the appearance of incoherence or irrationality on the part of the Cotard victim's attitudes. It is offered in a speculative spirit and from the interpretational perspective of the delusional stance conception of delusion mentioned in the last chapter (and available in Stephens and Graham 2004 and 2007). The proposal consists of an interpretation of claims like "I do not exist" or "I am dead" as they occur in cases of the Cotard delusion. It goes like this.

Utterances of "I am dead" or "I don't exist" are not reflective of a subject's beliefs that they are dead or do not exist, for these are not (the proposal says) propositions or claims that they actually endorse or really do believe. Rather, such claims are misleading expressions of the subject's feelings of insubstantiality or of the absence of affective connectedness with the world. What a subject of the delusion basically is doing, when he says that he is dead or does not exist, is ventilating or *expressing* the fact that he just does not feel anything like his normally engaged and corporeal self. He feels *as if* he is dead or does not exist and this feeling has become central or hyper-salient to him. His utterance is a tangled, elliptical and misleading way of expressing such feelings or emotional experiences.

Call this proposal an *expressivist* (rather than a creedal or belief) interpretation of Cotard claims. It says: The utterances in question are expressions of feelings (or lack of them), not (also) of literal beliefs. Just why a subject reports feelings as if they are beliefs (e.g. that I am dead) may be explained in a number of ways. One possibility is that the person means to convey the subjective centrality of the feelings. I feel vividly as if I am insubstantial. I feel vividly as if I am disconnected from the world. In order to express that vividness or centrality, I use belief-talk. The victim of the Cotard delusion doesn't have the attitude of belief towards the proposition: *I am dead*. He evinces only that he feels *as though* he is dead. Another possibility is that subjects of the delusion misunderstand the difference between speaking of feelings and beliefs. I've had many a student claim that Descartes *felt* that there is a contradiction between his doubting whether he exists, on the one hand, and his possibly not existing, on the other. This is Descartes as some sort of emotional existentialist, not the ruminative rationalist believer (and no mere feeler) he truly was.

Delusional subjects, in general or normally, do not distance or wall themselves off from the attitudes (beliefs, feelings, thoughts, and so on) that are the elements of their delusion. They are personally entangled in them (even in cases in which a delusion is quite narrow in content or relatively monothematic). This contrasts with the stance or attitude of subjects who suffer from obsessions. Subjects who suffer from obsessions often struggle against their condition and appreciate that their obsessive thoughts draw energy and attention from more prudent and useful activities. Delusions typically, by comparison, are more insidious than obsessions in that delusional subjects may be incorrigibly committed to maintaining them and make no effort be free of them. Persons who typically over-identify with their delusions, are oftentimes blind to their harmful consequences. Deluded subjects fail to realize that the persistence of a certain belief, thought or feeling indicates that something is wrong with them and that their disinclination to abandon the content of a delusion should reveal to them that they are not thinking or feeling properly. (Such is the grip of the Delusional Stance on a thought, feeling, or belief that it keeps a person from distancing themselves from such attitudes.) In the case of the Cotard delusion, such subjective centrality or phenomenological over-identification may mistakenly, at least in some delusional claims, be expressed in the language of belief or report of a belief.

I shall not press for this expressivist interpretation of the existence denial symptom of the Cotard delusion or of the sorts of claims discussed above. Kinderman and Bentall warn that "by denying that delusions are beliefs ... patients [may be] treated with disrespect, and [this may deny] them a voice in determining their treatment" (Kinderman and Bentall 2007: 288). By working with a Cotard's patient's delusion, understood as a 'mere' feeling but reported as if it is a belief, do we risk clinical mistreatment or disrespect? I hope not. Besides which, my proposal is meant to be speculative and to address a problem with or an explanatory gap in Gerrans's account. It is also intended to offer the semantics of certain relevant speech acts of a person with Cotard's. Whether this semantics is shared diagnostically with this or that deluded person is a distinct treatment issue.

A great deal, though not all certainly, of the clinical and neuropsychiatric literature on delusion focuses on a-rational neural or brute somatic immediate causes of delusions (like the Cotard delusion and others). These are sources such as brain tumors, aneurysms, strokes, epilepsy, Alzheimer's disease, and others. One case is of a man who, following a haematoma in his right basal ganglia, somehow believed or thought that he had acquired an extra arm, protruding from the middle of his body (Halligan and Marshall 1996). Prima facie same or similar symptoms, of course, may have different sorts of proximate sources or distinct propensity conditions (and therein are not truly or causally foundationally the same), which fact is worth remembering if we wish (as I urge throughout this book) to preserve applicable conceptual elbow room for a category of mental disorder including certain cases of delusional disorders. Contrastingly: Just because a disorder may seem to be a mental disorder given its syndromal cluster does not mean that it is a mental disorder. If a disorder's presence and symptoms directly or immediately stem from describable or explanatorily identifiable brain damage, it is not a mental disorder. It is a brain disorder.

A tragic case in point: Did Terri Shiavo, whose brain was severely damaged, suffer from a *mental* disorder? No, she did not. Just because her consciousness was 'disordered' (and dramatically so) does not mean that she was the subject of a mental disorder or illness. We should not confuse whether a person has a condition that reflects harm or injury to the mind with whether they are the subject of a disorder or illness that is mental in type or kind. If an injury's or disorder's causal explanatory foundation has nothing whatsoever that requires continued reference to the operative, however truncated or impaired, workings of a person's reason-responsiveness, then the ascription of a mental illness or disorder to them is misplaced and unsound.

SELF SERVING IN A SUPERMARKET

Suppose I am in front of a supermarket. I intend to walk into the market to buy a sack of sugar and a loaf of bread, and, of course, I know this. But how do I know that I possess this intention? It can't be inferred from my current behavior. I am standing outside the market and have not taken a single step inside. Nor can I appeal to my history of walking to this particular store or of buying just bread and sugar. I have never shopped in that market. I have never purchased just bread and sugar. So, my past behavior is no guide for me as to what I now intend. The obvious answer is that the intention is immediately evident to me. My intention is non-inferentially self-evident to me. It wears its presence as well as its 'mineness' or adjectival quality, namely its being mine, on its conscious sleeve.

Now consider the following extension to the story (see John Perry [1979]). I step into the market and grab a shopping cart. I push my cart down an aisle that contains sacks of sugar, pick a sack, and place it in my cart. Then, I set off for a loaf of bread. After exploring two or three aisles, neither of which holds bread, I spot the bread aisle. While pushing the cart, however, I notice that someone is producing a trail of sugar, presumably from a leaky bag in their cart. It's all over the floor. It has formed a distinct line on various aisles. I backtrack to explore a neighboring aisle in search of the culprit whose bag is making a mess. Although the trail gets thicker, I seem unable to catch up to the person. Then, it dawns on me. *I* am the person with the leaky bag. I look down at my cart and sure enough, my bag leaks. My behavior changes accordingly. I stop looking for an unknown person with a bad bag. I cuff my bag to try to keep it from leaking further and return to the aisle that holds the sugar in hopes of finding a better bag. I find one. I put it in my cart. Then, I deposit the leaky bag at the service counter, explaining to the clerk that it has a hole in it, and follow a sign to the bread aisle.

A key feature of this sugar story is that I changed from believing that *someone* has a leaky bag (but not knowing whom) to knowing that I am that someone. It's my bag that leaks. Initially, I failed to make this inference. It certainly was not directly or self-evident to me that I had the defective bag. By contrast, it was self-evident to me that I had the intention to shop in the store. Not just that someone intended shopping. *I* intended. No inference required. Indeed, how could it be otherwise? It seems impossible for me to misidentify the intention as someone else's intention. To appropriate from remarks of P. F. Strawson made in other context: "It would make no sense to say or think: *this* conscious intention is occurring but is it occurring to *me*?"

But hold on. Not so fast. Our short self-serving story continues.

Suppose, sound sack in cart, I visit the bread aisle. I spot the loaves. The following thoughts occur to me: "Good." "Here is a nice loaf of fresh multi-grain bread." "I must purchase this loaf." "It's a brand that my wife and I love." Oddly, though, suppose that instead of experiencing those thoughts as *mine*, I experience them as if they somehow are made for me or done to me by an external agent or individual: as if an intelligent force or person other than me somehow is thinking them inside my own stream of consciousness. I am experiencing 'their' thoughts as if somehow in my stream? Yes, suppose the thoughts 'I' and 'my' occur to me, but I don't interpret them as referring specifically to me. I don't take myself to be thinking that I must purchase this loaf. I don't interpret the reference to 'my wife' as a reference to my wife. It's as if I overhear another person thinking – another's cogitative activity going on inside me.

Two matters appear to be wrong with me or within my conscious experience in the bizarre market circumstance just described. One is that I seem to fail to identify myself as the thinker, although it should be immediately evident or apparent to me that *I* am thinking. How could thoughts occurring to me be other than mine? A bag of leaky sugar, yes, that may be belong to a stranger. But thoughts? In me? How could I experience them as anyone else's but mine? The other matter wrong with my experience is that rather than simply judging that something is amiss with my own thinking processes, I come up with the incredible belief or notion that someone else, some 'alien' or other agent, is doing their thinking inside me. I attribute the thinking to another person. Why, on earth, do that?

In attributing thoughts to another I don't think of the other as exerting a mere causal influence on me. I am not making a claim about another's thought-control over me. (I am not saying, for instance, that by whispering in my ear another person is priming me to pick a multi-grain loaf.) I am also not making a judgment, as I may if I were a victim of MPD, that another person or alter once entertained thoughts in my body. No, I am making a judgment about another's thinking occurring in me right here and now, as I stare at the bread.

Without meaning to be too dramatic, given the above details, imagine that I have become a victim of an occurrence of what is known in the literature on mental disorder and schizophrenia as *thought insertion* (see Graham 2004 and Stephens and Graham 2000). Thought insertion is a type of delusion. It's not the literal insertion of a thought in me (whatever that could mean). Rather, it is the phenomenal experience of one's own thoughts as if they somehow or in some manner belong to another and have been inserted into one's stream of consciousness. Witness the consequences of this attitude. If, for instance, I am questioned in a case of thought insertion as to how a thought in my stream of consciousness could possibly belong to another person, I may offer outlandish explanations such as:

> He treats my mind like a screen and flashes his thoughts onto it like you flash a picture.
>
> (Mellor 1970: 17)

> Thoughts come into my head like ['Get the bread']. It's just like my mind working, but it isn't. They come from this chap, Chris. They're his thoughts.
>
> (adapted from Frith 1992: 660)

Cahill and Frith describe the phenomenon of thought insertion as follows:

> Patients report that ... the thoughts which occur in their heads [are] not actually their own. It is as if another's thoughts have been ... inserted in them. One of our patients reported physically feeling the alien thoughts as they entered his head and claimed that he could pin-point the point of entry!
>
> (Cahill and Frith 1996: 278)

Evident similarities exist in clinical presentation between thought insertion and various other anomalies of self-ascription in self awareness (see Stephens and Graham 2000). Inner or sub-vocal speech may be experienced as the voice of an external agent, for instance, even when there is no acoustic or phenomenal quality to the voice. So-called made feelings or emotions also may be described similarly by patients as inserted thoughts.

> They project upon me laughter, for no reason, and you have no idea how terrible it is to laugh and look happy and know it is not you, but their emotions.
>
> (Mellor 1970: 17)

In cases of schizophrenia (or of its diagnosis), such strange misidentifications or misattributions between the experience of self and of one's own activity occur not just with respect to mental but also bodily motions and activities. Some patients complain that their body is moved by alien or external and irresistible intelligent forces. Others assert that a moving limb that they actually do or may self-control is not a part of their body. It's no wonder, then, that clinical observers of schizophrenia (or of persons classified as schizophrenic) comment as follows: "One of the essential features of schizophrenia is the disturbances of the experiencing 'I'" (Bovet and Parnas 1993: 589). Or: "Schizophrenics tend to lose their sense of integrated selfhood" (Sass 1999: 319). Indeed, they do.

Perhaps the most harmful general consequence of schizophrenia or its symptom clusters (remember the option of schizophrenia-skepticism) is that the condition is incompatible, during disturbances of the experiencing 'I', with properly leading a life and assuming effective responsibility for self. The ability to be self responsible requires that we identify ourselves as ourselves and know that our conscious mental and bodily activity is our own. It requires self-comprehension (another one of the basic capacities mentioned in Chapter 6) or proper self-attribution or self-identification. Lynne Rudder Baker describes the requirement of proper self identification in terms of what is necessary to qualify as a person. She says: "A being that cannot think of itself in a ... first-personal way is not a person" (Baker 1997: 443). Baker's point is that in order for me to be a person (or as I would wish to also put it, someone who leads or is responsible for their own life) I must comprehend my thoughts or deeds as mine, as modifications or activities of me. I must experience my conscious mental and physical activity as mine. I need to do this if I am, for example, to act on my intentions or aspirations. I must be able to compare what I will do or fail to do with what I now intend to do. I must also be able to keep track of myself over time. (This capacity, too, namely keeping track of oneself, it will be recalled, is also one of those classified as basic in Chapter 6.)

Let's look more carefully at the phenomenon of thought insertion. How is this puzzling phenomenon best understood? Does it really and truly consist of a self misattribution of thoughts? The answer is yes and no. Yes and no? How so?

William James once wrote that "whatever I may be thinking of, I am always at the same time more or less aware of myself, of my personal existence" (James 1892/1961: 42). Alvin Goldman makes a similar claim: "The process of thinking ... carries with it a non-reflective self-awareness" (Goldman 1970: 96). James and Goldman aptly note that conscious thoughts present themselves to their subjects as modifications or alterations of themselves. Modifications of the 'experiencing "I"'. This fact does not mean that if I am thinking of something I *judge* or *infer* that I am thinking of it, say, as I may judge or infer on the basis of visible evidence that the leaky bag of sugar is mine. That would be a case of reflective or propositional self-awareness and Goldman, for one, denies that the presentation of self in thought is inferential or judgmental. 'Mineness' is a proper part or constituent of the experience or phenomenology of thinking. It is not a higher-order or self-reflexive comment upon it in the form of a belief or propositional judgment. However, the experience of thinking does mean that I know when a thought occurs to me and I experience it as a modification of or episode in me.

So, thought insertion does not consist of misidentifying my self as *subject* of conscious thoughts. Subjects of thought insertion, like me on the bread aisle, recognize that certain thoughts occur to them. "Thoughts come into my head", I say. What, though, of their attribution to another person or agent? How are we to understand that?

In order to construct an answer to this question, first let us consider an analogy. Suppose a man is looking for a suit in a large clothing store. After trying on four or five suits, the man says to the sales assistant:

I am fat. I am skinny.

Perhaps he says this to vent his frustration at being unable to find the right suit. On the surface, though, it seems that he also is contradicting himself. But suppose that there are some people much thinner as well as other folks much heavier than him in the store. If so, the man is not necessarily contradicting himself. Perhaps he just is being elliptical and therein ambiguous or equivocal. He is saying that relative to the thin people whom he observes, he is fat. Relative to heavy people, he is skinny.

Something similar, I claim, occurs in thought insertion. Reports of inserted thoughts are instances of ellipsis and therein equivocation in one's frame of reference. Relative to one sense or reference point for 'being mine', the thoughts occurring to me on the bread aisle are experienced as mine. This is the sense in which I experience myself as the subject to whom they occur. This is what I wish to call the *subjectivity* sense of being mine. But relative to another sense of being mine, I experience them as another's thoughts. What sense is that? I will come to it in a moment, but first a bit more about the sense of subjectivity.

No special act of judgment (as noted) is required to currently experience one's thoughts as one's own in the subjectivity sense. When you undergo an experience, its manifest character as yours holds true even if you are hallucinating or dreaming, and thus even if the thought otherwise is dissociated from reality (bizarre, false, whatever). Just how vivid is this adjectival or modificational quality of 'mineness' depends on at least two factors. One is the type of thought or conscious mental episode in question. The other is the role played by a person's background intentional activity and surrounding circumstances.

On the topic of type of episode, consider a toothache. Consider your last toothache. Was there ever any question about to whom the ache occurred? No distinctive mechanism for determining that a toothache is one's own should be posited. The ache *self* intimates or directly manifests itself to its subject as one's own. My ache appears to me as mine. Yours appears as yours. Or consider feeling cold, feeling warm, or feeling sad. Such feelings or episodes wear their *being one's own* character on their sensorial and conscious sleeves. So, too, consider cases of thoughts or mental attitudes of a cognitive nature. "This is the bread to buy." Such a thought occurs to me and I know it, even if I report it as an inserted thought and as something I 'observe' or witness rather than 'actively think'. It is 'inserted', as I seem to experience it, but in *me*.

Surrounding circumstance and background is another factor affecting self intimation of thought. A person may have thoughts running through their stream of consciousness, all the while concentrating on some other task. Suppose that I am visiting a close friend in a neighborhood bar and discussing his pending move to another city. The prospect of his move occasions melancholic thoughts in me. I am sad, but my sadness hovers in the moody background. I am not actively attending to it. My focus is on the conversation. However, suppose that two days later I learn of his death in an untimely and tragic automobile accident. I read about it in the paper. I grieve terribly. My grieving is vividly self-evident. Nothing else distracts from my attention to it. It's grief over his death I feel; *I* experience it – and know it.

So, what is the other self-attributive sense to which I refer above? If a thought is experienced as one's own in the subjectivity sense, but, in thought insertion, attributed to another person or agent, what is this second sense? How can a thought be experienced as someone else's if it occurs to a person and he or she knows it?

The hypothesis to which I am attracted I wish to call the *sense of agency hypothesis* (see Campbell 1999; Frith 1992; Gallagher 2000; Graham 2004; Stephens and Graham 2000). A thought, such as my thought about a loaf of bread, may be attributed to oneself in either of two ways or senses. It may be attributed to oneself as the subject to whom it occurs. Or it may be attributed to oneself as the agent who is doing the thinking. Thought insertion represents a misinterpretation of the agency behind a thought (and not of its subjectivity). Before outlining this sense of agency hypothesis, I need to mention three background assumptions behind it.

The first assumption is the reminder that first-person reports of inserted thoughts are elliptical and ambiguous. In one sense (the subjectivity sense), subjects can just tell that a thought occurs to them. But in another sense, they ascribe it to another. I will soon describe just what this second sense is.

The second assumption is that thinking or conscious activity in general often is an active voluntary process. At a semantic level, 'thinking' ('believing', 'desiring', and so on) is an activity verb. "Activity verbs", U. T. Place (1924 – 2000) noted, "refer to an ongoing activity in which an individual can be engaged and on which he or she can spend time" (Place 1999: 381). Forms of being engaged in thought are various and multitudinous: studying, theorizing, scrutinizing, planning, deliberating, wondering, concentrating, pondering, embracing a belief, indulging in a desire, and so on.

The third assumption is that thinking (when an activity) possesses a distinctive what-it's-likeness or conscious or subjective phenomenal character. This what-it's-likeness includes experiences as of controlling one's thinking; as of initiating, directing, redirecting, and terminating one's lines of thought; as of coping with impediments or distractions while trying to think; and so on. To illustrate: Suppose that for years, I have had a number of accounts in a certain bank. But suppose that the bank shows signs of impending financial collapse. Suppose I am trying to decide how to tell my banker that I wish to withdraw my accounts from the institution. I experience myself as not just deciding to withdraw, but as directing germane patterns of thought. I have money concerns. I am looking for a way of disengaging from a bank that has been good to me in the past. I may think to myself: "My relationship with the bank has become too personal." "It's just business." But I also may fault myself for being "an unfeeling capitalist" who entertains the prospect of closing accounts in these immensely difficult financial times.

Perhaps I find myself giving into my guilt feelings over terminating my relationship with the bank. Or I may feel weakened by the effort of deliberation. Just as my legs may feel on the verge of collapse after a long hike or run, I may feel on the edge of mental collapse or depletion after an activity of stressful deliberation and emotional decision making.

A word of caution is needed before proceeding. One should be careful not to conceptually misstep in describing the what-it's-likeness of the activity of thinking. Frith remarks: "Thinking ... is normally accompanied by a sense of effort and deliberate choice as we move from one thought to the next" (Frith 1992: 81). Effort or choice? One thought to the next? Thinking may be effortful in certain respects. But infused with choice? I am not sure what Frith means by such a remark. One interpretation is that he means that, in the activity of thinking, we form intentions or decisions to think *particular* thoughts. But do we harbor or produce such intentions? To think particular thoughts? Hardly. Particular *lines,* patterns or themes of thought, yes. We do form or possess lines-of-thought intentions. But an intention for a *particular* thought content itself, no. We harbor no such intention.

Compare with bodily action, where we may form and act on quite particularistic intentions. Suppose I am at a town hall meeting. I arrive desiring to vote for Eunice Clay for town council. I've known Eunice for years. She's a good person and caring citizen. Suppose the people in attendance are asked to vote by raising their hand, when the name of the person for whom they wish to vote is mentioned. Eunice's name is mentioned. I intend to vote for her here and now. So, I raise my hand to vote. Is thinking like that? First: the intention to do X? Then: the doing of X? First: the intention to think of Y. Then: the thinking of Y. Again no. Nothing like that happens in the world of thought.

We may form intentions to think about problems or themes, to solve puzzles, to make thoughtful decisions, to discontinue unwelcome lines of thought, to resist mental fatigue, and so on. But in so doing there is no intention for *particular* thoughts as one thought progresses to the next. Imagine the following. Suppose I form the intention to think of Paris. *Then* I think of Paris? Note that if I merely form the intention to think of Paris, a Paris thought occurs in the very formation of the intention. So, in cases of thought or thinking there would be no distinction between the intention to do X (say, to think of Paris, as compared with intending in bodily behavior to vote for Eunice) and the doing (thinking of Paris). Nor, likewise, is there a choice or decision as I move from one thought to the next. Suppose, by contrast, I am undecided as to whether to raise my hand for Eunice or for her neighbor Tom. I deliberate and decide to vote for Eunice. Nothing like that happens in the realm of thought. If I am undecided as to whether to think of Paris or of Berlin, I *already* am thinking *both* of Paris and Berlin. If I am undecided as to whether to vote for Eunice or Tom, I am not already in the act of voting.

In the activity of thinking as well as in bodily activity, effort may be needed and energy expended. In certain mental chores, such as trying to solve a mathematical problem or deliberating about a tough career choice, thinking may be effortful and infused with choice, but this is not, as said, choosing *specific* thoughts. The choices may be of themes or desired lines of thought, outcomes or directions of content. "Hard decisions are experienced as requiring effort," Tim Bayne and Neil Levy note, "perhaps as a consequence of the cognitive resources we need to devote to them" (Bayne and Levy 2006: 58). They aptly add:

> Mental effort is also experienced when we actively direct our thoughts. Anyone who has struggled with a difficult conceptual issue has experienced the effort involved in thinking a problem through. It gives rise to characteristic feelings of tiredness and a growing urge to stop. When we do stop for a break, it seems to require real effort to return to the task.
>
> (Bayne and Levy 2006: 58)

So, then, what's going on in thought insertion if this phenomenon is understood as involving not our sense of subjectivity or of ourselves as subjects of experience, but a distinguishable sense? A sense of agency. Here is the hypothesis of sense of agency theory.

In thought insertion, thinking is experienced as an activity. However, although particular thoughts or episodes of thought are experienced as occurring in or to oneself (as subject), the activity itself *qua* or as an activity is experienced as though it is conducted or being engaged in by someone else. Another individual is represented as the agent or author of the activity. An analogous phenomenon occurs in verbal auditory hallucinations, common in a schizophrenia diagnosis, in which I (as subject) seem to myself to hear another person's voice. I experience a voice not as a random or willy-nilly bit of doggerel, but as the intelligent speech act of another person. No other person is, in fact, speaking to me, of course, but I believe that another is speaking. "Donald Trump is urging me to turn a deaf ear and blind eye to my emotional relationship with the bank and to move my accounts to another financial institution," I report as the message of a voice. "It's just business." In thought insertion experiencing oneself as thinker (or as the activity agent) is displaced by experiencing the thoughtful activity as if conducted by another.

Just as there is a distinctive what-it's-likeness to thinking as an activity, there is a distinctive what-it's-likeness to thought insertion. It's as if another is doing the thinking in me. The representation of another as doing the thinking may be voiced in a silent, running introspective narrative on my thinking. "These thoughts belong to Chris, not me." "He loves multi-grain bread." "I don't." "I am strictly a white bread person." "He projects his thoughts into me and treats me like a screen."

Thought insertion, so understood, also reveals that the "sense of subjectivity can survive when the sense of agency is lost" (Proust 2006: 89). Thus, when a person claims that certain thoughts that are occurring in them are not their own, they don't mean this in the sense that the episodes of thought fail to occur to them. They maintain their sense of subjectivity (else they would not know of the thoughts). Rather, they mean that thinking (which is in objective fact theirs) appears to them as if it is being conducted by another agent. Their sense of self as agent is disrupted, which raises a question that is nicely posed by Joëlle Proust:

> Supposing that a patient with schizophrenia is impaired in monitoring her own ... thoughts, why does she not simply recognize that something is wrong with her ability to keep track of what *she* ... thinks? Why does she instead come up with odd judgments, such as that her neighbor, or some unknown person she met in the street, [is thinking in her]?
>
> (Proust 2006: 89)

Victims of schizophrenia (and I am talking here as if schizophrenia is an illness, though I could rephrase matters just in terms of the individuals who receive the diagnosis and possess certain clusters of symptoms) have notorious problems keeping track of themselves. They may, for example, be deluded that other people are watching them (delusions of reference) or plotting against them (delusions of persecution). They may be deluded that their thought processes are being broadcast to others (delusions of thought broadcasting).

Various proposals have been offered in the literature for explaining the generation of the 'odd judgment' of attribution to another and of failing to keep track of one's own activity in schizophrenia.

G. Lynn Stephens and I, for example, suggest that inserted thoughts may be experienced as (what may be called) agentically anomic or alien, that is, as inconsistent with the subject's background beliefs about themselves or of what they are like as a person (Stephens and Graham 2000). If so, then the 'inserted' thoughts that occur in a person's stream of consciousness are felt to be intelligent and seem to be guided or directed, but the person (given background beliefs about themselves) experiences them as personally not theirs and as the presence of another agent's mental activity taking place inside their own stream of consciousness. So, they may automatically assume that another's 'psychology' or cognitive-motivational dynamics is at work in them. ("Someone else is the thinker.")

A second and complementary proposal accounts for the 'alien' ascription of thoughts as due to a failure in short-term working memory. Working memory is a type of short-term declarative or knowing-that memory. It stores and manipulates information needed for "the execution of complex cognitive tasks, such as deliberating, making decisions, and foreseeing consequences of decisions" (Glannon 2007: 62). So, for example, remembering that one is washing one's car or making a phone call would each count as instances of working memory. Perhaps victims of thought insertion suffer from information overload at certain critical moments, with perhaps too many cognitive activities to plan for and execute. This may lead to their temporary forgetfulness about activities or about the intentions behind activities in which they voluntarily are currently engaged. A person may lose track of their plans or patterns of thought, so that when thinking does occur it is not experienced as their own but, given its direction and intelligence, as if it is another's. Short term memory or retention problems are common in people diagnosed with schizophrenia. Without apposite short term memories, "experiences would be deeply disturbing" (Lloyd 2009: 177).

A motor behavior analogy may help. Suppose I find myself taking up a pencil and rapidly inscribing marks on a piece of paper (see Graham and Stephens 1994: 106). The words and sentences express love to a woman named Beatrice. Suppose I recollect no one named Beatrice and that I have no idea of how the letter will end or of the purpose behind it or of my beginning to write it. Given the intelligent momentum of the letter, however, suppose I experience the activity of writing as if another person or agent is writing to Beatrice through me. I am 'possessed', as it were. But now move the Beatrice-phenomenon inside the head, so to speak, from overt writing to covert thinking: from the activity of writing to the activity of thinking.

Suppose that rather than finding myself writing to Beatrice, I find myself thinking of a woman named Beatrice and entertaining loving thoughts about her, although I have no idea who she is. So, I may think of the movements of my mind, my thoughts or inner speech, as belonging to that of another agent. Not that someone merely is influencing me to think of Beatrice (by, for instance, whispering her lovely name in my ear), but that the conscious mental activity inside me literally is that of another person or agent. Another is doing it 'inside' me. I am somehow introspectively observing it. If so, if this may be what happens in thought insertion, perhaps it is not so much that a victim of thought insertion thinks thoughts that are unfamiliar or personally-dystonic (although that may be a factor). It is rather that they have trouble maintaining their goals or intentions in working memory (and perhaps suffer from other attention deficits as well). Whereas normally the sense of being the mental agent or in control of one's thinking activity is automatic, and perhaps self-evident, the self-attribution involved in short-term memory of one's intentions may fail in a case of thought insertion. Thinking, in such a case, carries no sense of authorial 'mineness'. Thoughts occur to me independent of or without my recollection of my own intentions. But I represent them to myself as another's thinking activity, since they still possess, to me, an authorial or purposive quality or 'voice'.

I am sure we don't know yet how best to fully explain attribution to another in thought insertion. I believe that the sense of agency hypothesis is part of the story. But it is not the whole tale. It is merely one hypothesis. There are several questions that need to be answered about the phenomenon. Why do inserted thoughts occur on some occasions but not others? Is this because on certain occasions working memory is overloaded (under conditions of stress, for example) in a manner that compromises keeping track of one's intentions? Are some people prone to be flooded with inserted thoughts in certain circumstances, because, for them, too much mental effort is required to keep track of whatever *they* are thinking? Just how or where does neurobiology/neurochemistry help to impair self-attribution? Does the impairment that is part of thought insertion occur in the prefrontal cortex, which enables a person to hold intentions 'on line' and perform self-monitored intentional activity? Is the impairment perhaps best described as an irruption into the space of reasons but of the destructive sort due to a neural disorder or brain damage?

Despite the presence of still unanswered questions, there is an important lesson about self experience and our capacity for self comprehension to extract from the phenomenon of thought insertion. This is that while we are, as it were, the absolute authorities over the contents of our thoughts (i.e. over what we are thinking) as well as whether these contents occur to us, we are not equally authoritative about our own agentive or causal role or responsibility in thinking. It is quite possible to get one's agency, literally, as it were, lost in thought. Indeed, for a person who is seriously mistaken about their own mental agency, the thought-filled activity in which they engage may come apart to such an extent that it is implausible to say that they themselves are responsible for their own ideas.

Grant Gillett writes:

> A person exercises a quite particular skill [as they] weave together a conscious narrative [of themselves] in a way that locates him or her ... in a world of objects and events presented amidst an abundance of ... information.
>
> (Gillett 2008: 97)

For some persons thoughts occur to themselves that they don't properly self attribute. If there is a narrative of one's own mental agency here, it needs more than a mere tale teller. It needs a good editor. It needs someone, namely, they themselves, to keep track of who is thinking what and when. An editor-less thinker is no real author at all.

EXPLANATION EXPLAINED

In *Content and Consciousness* (1969), one of the classics of twentieth-century empirically orientated philosophy of mind, Daniel Dennett offers a suggestion for when to move from an

Intentionalistic, reason-responsive, rational-person presupposing type of explanation of behavior to a "scientific story about synapses, electrical potentials and so forth that would explain, describe and predict all that goes on in the nervous system" (78). This is when a person's "response to the environment 'makes no sense', and, since it makes no sense" or is not rationally intelligible, then "no Intentional (putatively sense-making) account of the [behavior] will be justified" (78). A behavior or response then "should be susceptible to explanation and prediction without any recourse to ... Intentionality" (78).

One way in which to read the import of Dennett's suggestion goes something like this: Whatever procedure we use to ascribe Intentional states or reason-responsive attitudes to a person in order to explain their behavior or this or that aspect of behavior, if the explanation just does not seem to explain it or seems to reach an explanatory dead-end, then shift to neurobiology/ neurochemisty. Shift to a mechanical explanation. Shift to the language of brain science when features of behavior appear not to be controlled or controllable by reason-responsiveness (content, meaning, or Intentionality). Look for brute causal mechanisms as responsible for the behavior. True, it is not as if Intentionalistic explanation is in principle or *a priori* excluded from such cases. Though straining explanatory credulity and predictive utility, we may continue, for example, to cite an agent's putative reasons or responsiveness to reasons to account for a behavior. But such an explanation may just not aptly or truly plausibly explain the behavior.

Recall, for example, the discussion of addiction in the seventh chapter. It is quite obvious that there are stages or steps in addictive patterns about which our explanatory understanding should or must be complemented by employing the language or perspective of neurobiology/ neurochemistry. There appear to be causal links between a-rational neural activity and the first behavioral stages of relapse, for instance, stages not directly governed or controlled by the rationality of an addict or by the reason-responsive operation of the agent's deliberative capacities. In such cases, we may assume, for example, that there is a neural mechanism that links the impulse or disposition to drug consumption or to gamble with the start of responses that reflect a failure of consistent rational resolve or responsibility to self.

Likewise, there are aspects that are highly perplexing about various cases of delusion or delusional disorder and which the rational-person respecting language of Intentionality has trouble fully comprehending. We may wonder why a person fails to wrest themselves from the grip of a delusion or delusional mood or stance (as in, say, the Capgras or Cotard delusion). Why persist in a delusional attitude (thought or belief)? With respect to such aspects, a distinction needs to be drawn between attitudes or beliefs whose persistence or continued existence is infused with supportive or responsive reasons, and those that endure independently of a subject's reasons or in spite of strong contrary considerations (evidence and so on) or even in spite of the believer no longer accepting the evidence from which the attitude may have been initially inferred. In such cases we may suspend the language of reason and of reason-responsive activities and move or descend literally mechanically to "the sub-personal [explanatory level] of brains and events in the nervous system" (Dennett 1969: 93). At a sub-personal or a-rational level of analysis and explanation, the causal conditions responsible for the persistence of a belief or attitude receive descriptions in brute causal terms.

One recent and widely discussed hypothesis along sub-personal/non-Intentionalistic lines (about the persistence of delusions, in particular) is that dopamine release in the brain, reinforced perhaps by a subject's temperament, situational stressors or moods, invests certain thoughts (through their neurological realization or physical existential base) with a personal importance, salience or centrality that makes a subject feel as if these thoughts are more insightful or veridical than otherwise they should seem to be (Kapur 2003). A person persists in harboring them. The thoughts emotionally rouse a person and awaken feelings of significance. Even the most banal and otherwise neglected thoughts or attitudes may become hyper-salient when excited by sub-personal dopaminergic activity (see also Broome et al. 2005). When this happens the brain reward system a-rationally irrupts into the space of reasons. It irrupts into the linkages between Intentional attitudes and the otherwise more fully reason-responsive conditions of their persistence. This sort of irruptive activity in and of itself may be quite normal. It may not itself reflect brain damage or impairment (even though reference to it may help to explain the impairment of reason in a delusion). Perhaps it occurs in recurrent dreams. It may occur in various forms of creative imagination. It may occur under conditions of emotional stress. It may also be quite thematically specific. Certain sorts of thoughts or beliefs (say, paranoid or grandiose ones), depending upon the individuals involved and their temperaments or learning histories, may more likely be affected than others.

Again, as in a case of addiction, it would be a mistake to automatically assume that any such irruption means that there is something wrong with or damaged within a person's brain or nervous system. Perhaps on occasion there is. But more likely, I think, often not. True, some neuroscientists who talk of the sense of importance or heightened significance attached to delusions being modulated by dopaminergic activity speak also of the relevant neural activity as aberrant. Kapur, for instance, refers to it as a form of "neurochemical dysregulation" (Kapur 2003: 15). Dysregulation? Something wrong at the neurochemical level? But perfectly normal people have bizarre and unusually persistent thoughts, too, especially perhaps when stressed or daydreaming or under conditions of profound disappointment. Sometimes these thoughts or attitudes are taken seriously; sometimes not. Sometimes they change one's orientation to life; sometimes they eventually are dismissed or abandoned as unimportant and inconsequential. Sometimes contrary evidence excises them from a person's belief or attitude stock; sometimes not. Moreover, the bare fact that an attitude or condition may persist in the face of contrary evidence or evidence of possible harm to self does not by itself demonstrate that some sort of neural 'dysregulation' or neurochemical defect is in control or responsible. Perhaps such brain reward system neurochemical activity has the personally helpful mechanical effect in ordinary life of focusing attention, memory and imagination in ways that are wisely resistant to certain sorts of contrary evidence. If a man is convinced that he has found his soul mate, for example, it is perhaps imprudent for him to abandon this conviction just because he spots animosity in her father or stinginess among her siblings. Or: If a woman plans to seek therapy for drug addiction, it may be a good thing to believe that this plan is central to herself or to her preferred form of future life, especially if this means that the prods or encouragements of her clandestine drug dealer to re-consume are consistently resisted. A person's insensitivity to contrary considerations may be suffused with a feeling of immunity to disconfirmation. Not a good feature of one's psychological economy on some occasions, to be sure. But this is not always a bad or imprudent resistance to contrariety either.

Each of psychological and brain science described activities behind behavior are related in complex ways to the mental disorder character or status of a condition of mind and behavior.

The two types of explanatory forces complement and interact. Empirical peace or harmony in applicability between the two types of explanation may not always be readily evident, decisively achieved or permanently secured. But each does not negate the other, when together they make for an explanation of a mental disorder – of its different parts or aspects, of its proximate onset or emergence and progression.

Mental disorder, I have claimed, is a distinct kind of disorder. It is a *mental* disorder and not disorder of the brain. Admittedly, the boundary between mental and brain disorders is vague. They are not precisely discrete domains without borderline cases between them. However, lamenting vagueness between kinds (any kinds) is easier than finding a world without it, for all kinds of things and processes are vague. There is no precise historical or socio-cultural border that marks when or where a war or revolution may begin or end. But this would be woefully insufficient reason to deny that the United States helped to win World War II or that the Russian Revolution led to an untold number of tragic deaths. I am well aware that there is a possible danger here, some critics will say, of constructing an explanatory or categorical distinction between kinds where there is, at present, a lot of empirical ignorance and normative disagreement. A critic may charge that it is much too soon in the medical science of disorder and in our causal explanatory understanding of illnesses for a distinction between mental and brain disorder to command much credence.

My assumption is that it is not too early. I assume that we know or have good reason to believe that we know a lot about disorders already. I also assume that we can and will learn much more if we make the right distinctions between different general types of disorder (see also Graham 2013a; 2013b).

One practical consequence of the theory of mental disorder offered in this book is that when it comes to deciding whether a prima facie mental disorder requires clinical or professional attention, and especially in non-prototypical or non-exemplary cases, personal decisions made by subjects of the condition are an irreplaceable feature of concerns about mental illness. It is no more likely that there is a best way in which to address some mental disturbances or distresses (especially those at mental disorder borderlines) than there is a best horse, best number of children to parent, or best manner of mounting a production of *Hamlet*. From the perspective of the theory of mental disorder offered in this book, it's to be expected that different decisions about classification, care and treatment may prove desirable for different people in the same general condition of disturbance or distress, given different personalities, levels of confidence, learning histories, and personal goals. This is not because mental disorder is a matter of cultural convention or decisional fiat. It is because of the difficulty of describing and understanding the character and role of a mind that is vulnerable to disorder or illness.

Whatever consequences may eventually be forthcoming for the theory of mental disorder offered in this book, my aim has been to take several steps towards describing how to make plausible sense of a category of mental disorder, and thus, too, of a robust role for philosophy of mind in the construction of that theory. I take it as a very special mark of the depth and maturity of an understanding of mental disorder or illness that it does not fear asking difficult philosophical questions. A mature understanding of mental disorder also avoids seeking false harbor in the provincial attitude that there is something wrong with a medical specialization such as psychiatry that needs philosophy at its side. There is much that is right with such cross-disciplinary intellectual companionship or so I hope, for as a philosopher, I believe there is no finer friend.

SUMMARY

I talk and think of myself. I talk and think of other things as well. I break reality down into two types of objects. Me, and all else. The not me. To appropriate an expression of W. V. Quine (1908–2000), I see things that are not me as occupying irregular closed orbits, revisiting me from time to time, "a scattered portion of what goes on" (Quine 1969: 7). In contrast, I see myself with myself all the time.

The same may be said, with descriptive adjustments, about you. You, too, talk and think of yourself. You, too, break reality down into two kinds of objects. You, and all else.

This chapter was about each of us. About me. About you. It was about what various disorders may reveal or imply about us. It asked: What general sort of being am I? Are you? An animal? An immaterial soul or ego? The metaphysical implications of mental disorder for our under-standing of our nature are among its most widely discussed and philosophically puzzling fea-tures. The goal of this chapter was to find out whether the evidence of mental disorder points to this, that, or another metaphysical hypothesis or implication about ourselves.

Does Multiple Personality Disorder (MPD) constitute evidence that we are unreal? No, it does not. Or so the chapter argued. MPD shows that we may not know *what* we are. But it does not show that we fail to know *that* we are. Does the Cotard delusion reveal that a person can coherently believe that they do not exist? No, it does not. It helps to show that feelings may be misread as beliefs as well as that a delusion is a complex multi-layered state which exemplifies a failure of self comprehension and cognitive self management. But nothing in that particular delusion makes the speech act of self-existence denial intelligible as a denial. Does thought insertion show that self-attribution is ambiguous and that a distinction must be drawn between two forms of self experience, namely, of oneself as subject, of oneself as agent? Yes, it does. We have already seen (in Chapter 7) that experiencing oneself as agent and evaluating one's actions are central to our psychological capacity for self responsibility. Experiencing oneself as subject can dissociate from self-experience as agent.

The moral to draw from the chapter is not just about ourselves and the lessons of mental disorder for our understanding of our nature as persons, but about the importance for our wel-fare and well-being – an importance recognized in the Original Position – of our basic capacities for identifying where and when we are and what we are doing as well as for projecting ourselves into a future infused with opportunities.

SUGGESTED READING

Olson, E. (1998). "There is no problem of the self," *Journal of Consciousness Studies* 5: 645–57.

Radden, J. (2011). *On Delusion* (London: Routledge).

Stephens, G. L. and Graham, G. (2000). *When Self-Consciousness Breaks: Alien Voices and Inserted Thoughts* (Cambridge, MA: MIT Press).

Stephens, G. L. and Graham, G. (2004). "Reconceiving delusion," *International Review of Psychiatry* 16: 236–41.

Young, A., and Leafhead, A. W. (eds) (1996). *Method in Madness: Case Studies in Cognitive Neuropsychiatry* (East Sussex, UK: Psychology Press).

Bibliography

Abramson, L. Y., Metalsky, G. I. and Alloy, L. B. (1989) Hopelessness depression: a theory-based subtype of depression, *Psychological Review*, 96, 358–72.

Abramson, L. Y., Seligman, M. E. P. and Teasdale, J. D. (1978) Learned helplessness in humans: critique and reformulation, *Journal of Abnormal Psychology*, 78, 40–74.

Adams, R. M. (1999) *Finite and Infinite Goods: A Framework for Ethics*, Oxford: Oxford University Press.

Adler, J. (2007) Faith and fanaticism, in L. Antony (ed.) *Philosophers without Gods: Meditations on Atheism and the Secular Life*, Oxford: Oxford University Press.

Ainslie, G. (2001) *Breakdown of Will*, Cambridge: Cambridge University Press.

Alloy, L. and Abramson, L. (1979) Judgment of contingency in depressed and nondepressed students: sadder but wiser?, *Journal of Experimental Psychology: General*, 108: 441–85.

——(1988) Depressive realism: four theoretical perspectives, in L. Alloy (ed.) *Cognitive Processes in Depression*, New York: Guilford Press.

American Psychiatric Association (1952) *Diagnostic and Statistical Manual of Mental Disorders*, 1st edn, Washington, D. C.: American Psychiatric Association.

——(1968) *Diagnostic and Statistical Manual of Mental Disorders*, 2nd edn, Washington, D. C.: American Psychiatric Association.

——(1980) *Diagnostic and Statistical Manual of Mental Disorders*, 3rd edn, Washington, D. C.: American Psychiatric Association.

——(1987) *Diagnostic and Statistical Manual of Mental Disorders*, 3rd edn. rev, Washington, D. C.: American Psychiatric Association.

——(1994) *Diagnostic and Statistical Manual of Mental Disorders*, 4th edn, Washington, D. C.: American Psychiatric Association.

——(2000) *Diagnostic and Statistical Manual of Mental Disorders*, 4th edn, text rev, Washington, D. C.: American Psychiatric Association.

Andreasen, N. C. (1984) *The Broken Brain: The Biological Revolution in Psychiatry*, New York: Harper & Row.

Andreasen, N. C. (2001) *Brave New Brain: Conquering Mental Illness in the Era of the Genome*, Oxford: Oxford University Press.

Applebaum, P. (2004) Forward, in J. Radden (ed.) *The Philosophy of Psychiatry: A Companion*, Oxford: Oxford University Press.

Arpaly, N. (2005) How it is not "just like diabetes": mental disorders and the moral psychologist, *Philosophical Issues*, 15, 282–98.

Augustine (1992) *Confessions*, trans. H. Chadwick, Oxford: Oxford University Press.

Baier, A. (1989) Trusting ex-intimates, in G. Graham and H. LaFollette (eds) *Person to Person*, Philadelphia, Temple University Press.

Baker, L. R. (1997) Persons in metaphysical perspective, in L. Hahn (ed.) *The Philosophy of Roderick Chisholm*, Chicago, IL: Open Court.

——(2000) *Persons and Bodies: A Constitution View*, Cambridge: Cambridge University Press.

Barber, C. (2008) *Comfortably Numb: How Psychiatry is Medicating a Nation*, New York: Pantheon.

Barlow, D. H. (1988). *Anxiety and Its Disorders*, New York: Guilford.

Barlow, D. H., Chorpita, B., and Turovsky, J. (1996) Fear, panic, anxiety and disorders of emotion in D. Hope (ed.) *Perspectives on Anxiety, Panic and Fear*, vol. 43. Nebraska Symposium on Motivation, Lincoln, Nebraska: University of Nebraska Press.

Battin, M. (1982) *Ethical Issues in Suicide*, Englewood Cliffs, NJ: Prentice-Hall.

Bayne, T. and Levy, N. (2006) The feeling of doing: deconstructing the phenomenology of aging, in N. Sebanz and W. Prinz (eds) *Disorders of Volition*, Cambridge, MA: MIT Press.

Bayne, R. and Pacherie, E. (2004) Bottom-up or top-down? Campbell's rationalist account of monothematic delusions, *Philosophy, Psychiatry, and Psychology*, 11, 1–11.

Beam, A. (2001) *Gracefully Insane: The Rise and Fall of America's Premier Mental Hospital*, New York: Public Affairs.

Bechtel, W. (2008) *Mental Mechanisms: Philosophical Perspectives on Cognitive Science*, New York: Routledge.

Bechtel, W. and Graham, G. (eds) (1998) *A Companion to Cognitive Science*, Malden, MA: Blackwell.

Beck, A. T. and Weishaar, M. (2008) Cognitive therapy, in R. Corsini and D. Wedding (eds) *Current Psychotherapies*, Belmont, CA: Thomson Brooks Cole.

Becker, G., and Murphy, K. (1988) A theory of rational addiction, *Journal of Political Economy*, 96: 675–700.

Bell, A., Halligan, P. and Ellis, H. (2006) Explaining delusions: a cognitive perspective, *TRENDS in Cognitive Science*, 10: 219–26.

Bentall, R. (2004) *Madness Explained: Psychosis and Human Nature*, London: Penguin.

——(2007) Clinical pathologies and unusual experiences, in M. Velmans and S. Schneider (eds) *The Blackwell Companion to Consciousness*, Malden, MA: Blackwell.

——(2011) The point is to change things, *Philosophy, Psychiatry, and Psychology*, 18, 167–69.

Berridge, K., and Robinson, T. (1995) The mind of the addicted brain: neural sensitization of wanting versus liking, *Current Directions in Psychological Science*, 4, 71–76.

——(2011) Drug addiction as incentive sensitization, in J. Poland and G. Graham (eds) *Addiction and Responsibility*, Cambridge, MA: MIT Press.

Berrios, G. E. (1991) Delusions as "wrong beliefs": a conceptual history, *British Journal of Psychiatry*, 14: 6–13.

Berrios, G. E., and Luque, R. (1995) Cotards syndrome: analysis of 100 cases, *Acta Psychiatrica Scandinavia*, 91: 185–88.

Blasfield, R. (1996) Predicting DSM-V, *Journal of Nervous and Mental Disease*, 184: 4–7.

Bolton, D. (2001) Problems in the definition of "mental disorder", *Philosophical Quarterly*, 51, 182–99.

Boorse, C. (1975) On the distinction between health and illness, *Philosophy and Public Affairs*, 5: 49–68.

——(1976) What a theory of mental health should be, *Journal for the Theory of Social Behavior*, 6: 61–84.

——(1977) Health as a theoretical concept, *Philosophy of Science*, 44: 542–73.

Bortolotti, L. (2004) Can we interpret irrational behavior?, *Behavior and Philosophy*, 32: 359–75.

——(2005) Delusions and the background of rationality, *Mind and Language*, 20: 189–208.

Bovet, P. and Parnas, J. (1993) Schizophrenic delusions: a phenomenological approach, *Schizophrenia Bulletin*, 19: 579–97.

Boyle, M. (1990) *Schizophrenia: A Scientific Delusion?* London: Routledge.

Bowker, G. (2011) *James Joyce: A New Biography*, New York: Farrar, Straus and Giroux.

Bowlby, J. (1980/1998) *Attachment and Loss*, vol. III, London: Pimlico.

Bracken, P. and Thomas, P. (2005) *Postpsychiatry: Mental Health in a Postmodern World*, Oxford: Oxford University Press.

Braude, S. (1991) *First Person Plural: Multiple Personality and the Philosophy of Mind*, London: Routledge.

Brentano, F. (1995 [1874]) *Psychology from an Empirical Standpoint*, trans. A. Rancurello, D. Terrell and L. McAlister, London: Routledge.

Breuer, J. and Freud, S. (2000) *Studies in Hysteria*, trans. and ed. J. Strachey, New York: Basic Books.

Broome, M., Woolley, J., Tabraham, P., Johns, L., Bramon, E., Murray, G., Pariante, C., McGuire, P. and R. Murray. (2005) What causes the onset of psychosis?, *Schizophrenia Research*, 79: 23–34.

Brulde, B. and Radovic, C. (2006) What is mental about mental disorder?, *Philosophy, Psychiatry, and Psychology*, 13: 99–116.

Brumberg, J. J. (1988) *Fasting Girls: The History of Anorexia Nervosa*, Cambridge: Harvard University Press.

Burge, T. (1993) Mind-body causation and explanatory practice in J. Heil and A. Mele (eds) *Mental Causation*, Oxford: Oxford University Press.

Cahill, C. and Frith, C. (1996) False perceptions or false beliefs: hallucinations and delusions in schizophrenia, in P. Halligan and J. Marshall (eds) *Method in Madness: Case Studies in Cognitive Neuropsychiatry*, East Sussex, UK: Psychology Press.

Campbell, J. (1999) Schizophrenia, the space of reasons and thinking as a motor process, *Monist*, 82: 609–25.

——(2009). What does rationality have to do with psychological causation? Propositional attitudes as mechanisms and as control variables, in M. Broome and L. Bartolotti (eds) *Psychiatry as cognitive neuroscience: Philosophical perspectives*, Oxford: Oxford University Press.

Campbell, P. (1996) Challenging loss of power, in J. Read and J. Reynolds (eds) *Speaking Our Minds: An Anthology*, London: Macmillan.

Caplan, P. (1995) *They Say You're Crazy: How the World's Most Powerful Psychiatrists Decide Who's Normal*, New York: Addison-Wesley.

Carey, B. (2012) Grief could join list of disorders, *New York Times*, January 25, A1, A21.

Charland, L. (2004) Moral treatment and personality disorders, in J. Radden (ed.) *The Philosophy of Psychiatry: A Companion*, Oxford: Oxford University Press.

——(2006) Moral nature of the DSM-IV-TR cluster B personality disorders, *Journal of Personality Disorders*, 20: 116–25.

Charney, D. S., Nestler, E. J., and Bunney, B. S. (eds) (1999) *Neurobiology of Mental Illness*, New York: Oxford University Press.

Church, J. (2003) Depression, depth, and the imagination, in J. Phillips and J. Morley (eds) *Imagination and Its Pathologies*, Cambridge, MA: MIT Press.

Churchland, P. (1989) Moral facts and moral knowledge, in *A Neurocomputational Perspective: The Nature of Mind and the Structure of Science*, Cambridge, MA: MIT Press.

Cleckley, H. (1982) *The Mask of Sanity*, St. Louis, MO: Mosby.

Colombo, A. (2008) Models of mental disorder: how philosophy and the social sciences can illuminate psychiatric ethics, in G. Widdershoven, J. McMillan, T. Hope, and L. Van Der Scheer (eds) *Empirical Ethics in Psychiatry*, Oxford: Oxford University Press.

Confer, W. N. and Ables, B. S. (1983) *Multiple Personality: Etiology, Diagnosis, and Treatment*, New York: Human Sciences Press.

Costin, C. (1998) Your dieting daughter, in D. Sattler, V. Shabatay, and G. Kramer (eds) *Abnormal Psychology in Context: Voices and Perspectives*, Boston: Houghton Mifflin.

Cotard, J. (1882) Du délire des negations, *Archives de Neurologie*, 4: 152–70.

Craver, C. (2007) *Explaining the Brain: What a Science of Mind-Brain Could Be*, New York: Oxford University Press.

Crowley, C. and Lodge, H. (2004) *Younger Next Year*, New York: Workman.

Currie, G. (2000) Imagination, delusion, and hallucinations, in M. Coltheart and M. Davies (eds) *Pathologies of Belief*, Oxford: Basil Blackwell.

Davidson, D. (2004) *Problems of Rationality*, Oxford: Oxford University Press.

Davis, S. (2002) Was Jesus mad, bad, or God, in S. Davis, D. Kendall, and G. OCollins (eds) *The Incarnation*, New York: Oxford University Press.

DeBaggio, T. (2003) *Losing My Mind: An Intimate Look at Life with Alzheimer's*, New York: Free Press.

Dennett, D. C. (1969) *Content and Consciousness*, London, Routledge and Kegan Paul.

——(1984) *Elbow Room: The Varieties of Free Will Worth Wanting*, Cambridge, MA: MIT Press.

——(1991) *Consciousness Explained*, Boston: Little, Brown and Co.

——(2009) Intentional systems theory, in B. McLaughlin, A. Beckermann and S. Walter (eds) *The Oxford Handbook of Philosophy of Mind*, Oxford, Oxford University Press.

Dennett, D. C. and Humphrey, N. (1989) Speaking for ourselves: an assessment of multiple personality disorder, *Raritan*, 9: 68–69.

Descartes, R. (1984) *The Philosophical Writings of Descartes* (vol. 1), trans. J. Cottingham, R. Stoothoff, and D. Murdock, Cambridge: Cambridge University Press.

Dretske, F. (1988) *Explaining Behavior: Reasons in a World of Causes*, Cambridge, MA: MIT Press.

——(1997) *Naturalizing the Mind*, Cambridge, MA: MIT Press.

Dunning, D. (2009) Misbelief and the neglect of environmental context, *Behavioral and Brain Sciences*, 32: 517–18.

Edwards, D. and Kravitz, E. (1997) Serotonin, social status and aggression, *Current Opinion in Neurobiology*, 7: 811–19.

Ehrman, B. (1999) *Jesus: Apocalyptic Prophet of the New Millennium*, Oxford: Oxford University Press.

Elliott, C. (2002) Who holds the leash?, *American Journal of Bioethics*, 2: 48.

——(2003) *Better Than Well: American Medicine Meets the American Dream*, New York: Norton.

——(2004) Mental health and its limits, in J. Radden (ed.) *The Philosophy of Psychiatry: A Companion*, New York: Oxford University Press.

Emmons, R. A. (1999) *The Psychology of Ultimate Concerns: Motivation and Spirituality in Personality*, New York: Guilford Press.

Enoch, M. D. and Trethowan, W. H. (1991) *Uncommon Psychiatric Syndromes*, 3rd edn, Oxford: Butterworth-Heinemann.

Erikson, E. (1968) *Identity, Youth, and Crisis*, New York: Norton.

ESEMeD/MHEDEA 2000 Investigators, Prevalence of mental disorders in Europe: results from the European study of the epidemiology of mental disorders, *Acta Psychiatrica Scandinavica* (Supplement), 420, 21–27.

Farah, M. (2008) Neuroethics and the problem of other minds: implications of neuroscience for the moral status of brain-damaged patients and nonhuman animals, *Neuroethics*, 1, 9–18.

Feinberg, J. (1970) What is so special about mental illness?, in *Doing and Deserving: Essays in the Theory of Responsibility*, Princeton, NJ: Princeton University Press, 272–92.

——. (1989) *Harm to Self*, New York: Oxford University Press.

First, M. B. (2005) Desire for amputation of a limb: paraphilia, psychosis, or a new type of identity disorder, *Psychological Medicine*, 35, 919–28.

Fischer, J. M. (2009) *Our Stories: Essays on Life, Death, and Free Will*, Oxford: Oxford University Press.

Fischer, J. M. and Ravizza, M. (1998) *Responsibility and Control: A Theory of Moral Responsibility*, Cambridge: Cambridge University Press.

Flanagan, O. (2007) *The Really Hard Problem: Meaning in a Material World*, Cambridge, MA: MIT Press.

——(2011) What is it like to be an addict?, in J. Poland and G. Graham (eds) *Addiction and Responsibility*, Cambridge, MA: MIT Press.

Flynn, J. (1998) Cocaine: Helen's story, in D. Sattler, V. Shabatay and G. Kramer (eds) *Abnormal Psychology in Context: Voices and Perspectives*, Boston: Houghton Mifflin.

Foucault, M. (1977) *Discipline and Punish*, trans. A. Sheridan, London: Allen Lane.

Frankfurt, H. (1988). *The Importance of What We Care About: Philosophical Essays*, Cambridge, Cambridge University Press.

——. (2004). *The Reasons of Love*, Princeton, NJ: Princeton University Press.

Freud, S. (1989) [1930] *Civilization and Its Discontents*, trans. and ed. J. Strachey, intro. Peter Gay, New York: Basic Books.

——. (1958) [1900] *The Interpretation of Dreams*. In *Standard Edition of the Complete Works of Sigmund Freud*, ed. James Strachey, vols 4 and 5. London: Hogarth Press.

——(1963) [1905] *Dora: An Analysis of a Case of Hysteria*, New York: Collier.

——(2000) [1917] Mourning and melancholy, in J. Radden (ed.) *The Nature of Melancholy: From Aristotle to Kristeva*, Oxford: Oxford University Press.

Frith, C. D. (1992) *The Cognitive Neuropsychology of Schizophrenia*, Hillsdale, N J: Earlbaum.

——. (1998) Deficits and pathologies, in W. Bechtel and G. Graham (eds) *A Companion to Cognitive Science*, Malden, MA: Blackwell.

Frith, C. D. and Johnstone, E. (2003) *Schizophrenia: A Very Short Introduction*, Oxford: Oxford University Press.

Frith, C. D. and Rees, G. (2007) A brief history of the scientific approach to the study of consciousness, in M. Velmans and S. Schneider (eds) *The Blackwell Companion to Consciousness*, Malden, MA: Blackwell.

Fulford, K. W. M. (1989) *Moral theory and medical practice*, Cambridge: Cambridge University Press.

——(1993) Thought insertion and insight: disease and illness paradigms of psychotic disorder, in M. Spitzer, F. Uehlin, M. Schwartz and C. Mundt (eds) *Phenomenology, Language, and Schizophrenia*, New York: Springer-Verlag.

Fulford, K. W. M. (1994) Value, illness, and failure of action: framework for a philosophical psychopathology of delusions, in G. Graham and G. L. Stephens (eds) *Philosophical Psychopathology*, Cambridge, MA: MIT Press.

Fulford, K. W. M., Thornton, T. and Graham, G. (2006) *Oxford Textbook of Philosophy and Psychiatry*, Oxford: Oxford University Press.

Gallagher, S. (2000) Self-reference and schizophrenia: a cognitive model of immunity to error through misidentification, in D. Zahavi (ed.) *Exploring the Self*, Amsterdam: John Benjamins.

——. (2009) Delusional realities, in M. Broome and L. Bortolotti (eds) *Psychiatry as Cognitive Neuroscience: Philosophical Perspectives*, Oxford: Oxford University Press.

Garner, A. and Hardcastle, V. (2004) Neurobiological models: an unnecessary divide – neural models in psychiatry, in J. Radden (ed.) *The Philosophy of Psychiatry: A Companion*, Oxford: Oxford University Press.

Garrett, R. (1994) The problem of despair, in G. Graham and G. L. Stephens (eds) *Philosophical Psychopathology*, Cambridge, MA: MIT Press.

Gastfriend, D. R. (2005) Physician substance abuse and recovery: what does it mean for physicians and everyone else, *Journal of the American Medical Association*, 293: 1513–15.

Gerrans, P. (2000) Refining the explanation of the Cotard delusion, in M. Coltheart and M. Davies (eds) *Pathologies of Belief*, Oxford: Blackwell Publishers.

——(2002) A one-stage explanation of the Cotard delusion, *Philosophy, Psychiatry, and Psychology*, 9: 47–53.

——(2004) Cognitive architecture and the limits of interpretativism, *Philosophy, Psychiatry, and Psychology*, 11: 43–48.

Gert, B. and Culver, C. (2004). Defining mental disorder, in J. Radden (ed.) *The Philosophy of Psychiatry: A Companion*, New York: Oxford University Press.

Gillett, G. (1991) Multiple personality and irrationality, *Philosophical Psychology*, 4: 103–18.

——(2008) *Subjectivity and Being Somebody: Human Identity and Neuroethics*, Exeter: Imprint Academic.

Glannon, W. (2007) *Bioethics and the Brain*, Oxford: Oxford University Press.

Glass, A. and Holyoak, K. (1986) *Cognition*, New York: Random House.

Glover, J. (2003) Towards humanism in psychiatry, *Tanner Lectures on Human Values*, Princeton University, February 12–14.

Goffman, E. (1961) *Asylums: Essays on the Social Situation of Mental Patients and Other Inmates*, New York: Doubleday.

——. (1963) *Stigma: Notes on the Management of Spoiled Identity*, New York: Simon Schuster.

Goldie, P. (2011) Grief: a narrative account, *Ratio*, XXIV: 119–37.

Goldman, A. (1970) *A Theory of Action*, Princeton, NJ: Princeton University Press.

——. (2006) *Simulating Minds: The Philosophy, Psychology, and Neuroscience of Mindreading*, Oxford: Oxford University Press.

Goodman, N. (1968) *The Languages of Art: An Approach to a Theory of Symbols*, Indianapolis: New York.

Goodwin, D. and Guze, S. (1996) *Psychiatric Diagnosis*, 5th edn, New York: Oxford University Press.

Gorenstein, E. (1992) *The Science of Mental Illness*, San Diego: Academic Press.

Graham, G. (1990) Melancholic epistemology, *Synthese*, 82: 309–28.

——(1996) Review of Hacking *Rewriting the Soul*, *Ethics*, 106: 845–48.

——(1998) *Philosophy of Mind: An Introduction*, 2nd edn, Malden, MA: Blackwell Publishers.

——(1999) Fuzzy fault lines: selves in multiple personality disorder, *Philosophical Explorations*, 3: 159–74.

——(2004) 'Self-ascription: thought insertion', in J. Radden (ed.) *The Philosophy of Psychiatry: A Companion*, Oxford: Oxford University Press.

——(2013a) 'Being a mental disorder', in J. Sullivan and H. Kincaid (eds) *Psychiatric Classification and Natural Kinds*, Cambridge, MA: MIT Press.

——(2013b) 'Ordering disorder: mental disorder, brain disorder, and therapeutic intervention', in M. Davies, K. Fulford, R. Gipps, G. Graham, J. Sadler, G. Stanghellini, and T. Thornton (eds) *Oxford Handbook of Philosophy and Psychiatry*, Oxford: Oxford University Press.

Graham, G. and Horgan, T. (2002) 'Sensations and grain processes', in J. Fetzer (ed.) *Evolving Consciousness*, Amsterdam: John Benjamins.

Graham, G. and Stephens, G. L. (1994) Mind and mine, in G. Graham and G. L. Stephens (eds) *Philosophical Psychopathology*, Cambridge, MA: MIT Press.

——(2007) Psychopathology: minding mental illness, in P. Thagard (ed.) *Philosophy of Psychology and Cognitive Science*, Amsterdam: Elsevier.

Graham, G., Horgan, T., and Tienson, J. (2007). Consciousness and intentionality, in M. Velmans and S. Schneider (eds) *The Blackwell Companion to Consiousness*, Malden, MA: Blackwell.

——(2009) Phenomenology, intentionality, and the unity of mind, in B. McLaughlin, A. Beckermann, and S. Walter (eds) *The Oxford Handbook of the Philosophy of Mind*, Oxford, Oxford University Press.

Griffin, J. (1988) *Well-Being: Its Meaning, Measurement and Moral Importance*, Oxford: Oxford University Press.

Gross, G. and Rubin, I. (2002) Clinical theory, in E. Erwin (ed.) *The Freud Encyclopedia: Theory, Therapy and Culture*, New York: Routledge.

Grunbaum, A. (1984) *The Foundations of Psychoanalysis*, Berkeley, CA: University of California Press.

Guze, S. B. (1992) *Why Psychiatry is a Branch of Medicine*, New York: Oxford University Press.

Hacking, I. (1995) *Rewriting the Soul: Multiple Personality and the Science of Memory*, Cambridge, MA: Harvard University Press.

——(1998) *Mad Travelers*, Charlottesville, Virginia: University of Virginia Press.

——(1999) *The Social Construction of What?*, Cambridge, MA: Harvard University Press.

Halligan, P. W. and Marshall, J. C. (eds) (1996) *Method in Madness: Case Studies in Cognitive Neuropsychiatry*, Hove, E. Sussex: Psychology Press.

Hampshire, S. (1965) *Freedom of the Individual*, London: Chatto and Windus.

Harman, G. (1998) Intentionality, in W. Bechtel and G. Graham (eds) *A Companion to Cognitive Science*, Malden, MA: Blackwell.

Harrison, B. (1998) I am not afraid, in D. Sattler, V. Shabatay, and G. Kramer (eds) *Abnormal Psychology in Context: Voices and Perspectives*, Boston: Houghton Mifflin.

Haynes, S. (1992) *Models of Causality in Psychopathology: Toward Dynamic, Synthetic and Nonlinear Models of Behavior Disorders*, New York: Macmillan.

Heineman, M. (1998) Losing your shirt, in D. Sattler, V. Shabatay, and G. Kramer (eds) *Abnormal Psychology in Context: Voices and Perspectives*, Boston: Houghton Mifflin.

Hempel, C. (1965a) Fundamentals of taxonomy in *Aspects of Scientific Explanation and Other Essays in the Philosophy of Science*, New York: Free Press.

——(1965b) Science and human values in *Aspects of Scientific Explanation and Other Essays in the Philosophy of Science*, New York: Free Press.

——(1966) *Philosophy of the Natural Sciences*, Englewood Cliffs, NJ: Prentice-Hall.

Heninger, G. (1999) Special challenges in the investigation of the neurobiology of mental illness, in C. Charney, E. Nestler, and B. Runney (eds) *Neurobiology of Mental Illness*, New York: Oxford University Press.

Herrnstein, R. J. and Loveland, D. H. (1964) Complex visual concept in the pigeon, *Science*, 146: 549–51.

Hobson, J. A. and Leonard, J. (2001) *Out of Its Mind: Psychiatry in Crisis: A Call for Reform*, Cambridge, MA: Perseus.

Hocutt, M. (2000) *Grounded Ethics: The Empirical Basis of Normative Judgments*, New Brunswick, NJ: Transactions Press.

Honey, G. (2009) Psychopharmacological modeling of psychiatric illness, in S. Wood, N. Allen and C. Pantelis (eds) *The Neuropsychology of Mental Illness*, Cambridge: Cambridge University Press.

Horgan, T., Tienson, J., and Graham, G. (2003) The phenomenology of first-person agency, in S. Walter and H.-D. Heckmann (eds) *Physicalism and Mental Causation: The Metaphysics of Mind in Action*, Exeter, UK: Imprint Academic.

Horwitz, A. (2002) *Creating Mental Illness*, Chicago: University of Chicago Press.

Horwitz, A. and Wakefield, J. (2007) *The Loss of Sadness: How Psychiatry Transformed Normal Sorrow into Depressive Disorder*, Oxford: Oxford University Press.

Howard-Snyder, D. (2004) Was Jesus mad, bad, or god? ... or merely mistaken?, *Faith and Philosophy*, 21: 456–79.

Hughes, V. (2011) Shades of grief: when does mourning become a mental illness, http:///.scientific american.com/article.cfm?id=shades-of-grief

Hyder, O. Q. (1977) On the mental health of Jesus Christ, *Journal of Psychology and Theology*, 5: 3–12.

Institute of Medicine (1996) *Pathways to Addiction: Opportunities in Drug Abuse Research*, Washington, DC: National Academy Press.

Jackson, M. (2007) The clinician's illusion and benign psychosis, in M. Chung, K. Fulford and G. Graham (eds) *Reconceiving Schizophrenia*, Oxford: Oxford University Press.

James, W. (1890) *The Principles of Psychology. Volume II*, New York: Holt.

——(1961 [1892]) *Psychology: The Briefer Course*, New York: Harper.

——(2002 [1901–2] *The Varieties of Religious Experience: A Study of Human Nature*, New York: Modern Library.

——(1997 [1910]) *Psychology*, New York: Henry Holt; reprinted in N. Block, O. Flanagan and G. Gulzedere (eds) as The stream of consciousness in *The Nature of Consciousness: Philosophical Debates*, Cambridge, MA: MIT Press.

Jamison, K. (1995) *An Unquiet Mind*, New York: Knopf. Excerpted as An unquiet mind in D. Sattler, V. Shabatay and G. Kramer (eds) *Abnormal Psychology in Context: Voices and Perspectives*, Boston: Houghton Mifflin Company.

Jarvik, L. F. and Chadwick, S. B. (1972) Schizophrenia and survival, in S. B. Hammer, K. Salzinger and S. Sutton (eds) *Psychopathology*, New York: Wiley.

Jaspers, K. (1963) *General Psychopathology*, trans. J. Hoenig and M. Hamilton, Chicago, IL: University of Chicago Press.

Kagan, J. (1994) *Galen's Prophecy: Temperament in Human Nature*, New York: Basic Books.

Kane, R. (2005) *A Contemporary Introduction to Free Will*, New York: Oxford University Press.

Kant, I. ([1793] 2000) On the cognitive faculties, in J. Radden (ed.) *The Nature of Melancholy: From Aristotle to Kriteva*, Oxford: Oxford University Press.

Kapur, S. (2003) Psychosis as a state of aberrant salience: a framework linking biology, phenomenology, and pharmacology in schizophrenia, *American Journal of Psychiatry*, 160: 13–23.

Karmiloff-Smith, A. (1998) Development itself is the key to understanding developmental disorders, *Trends in Cognitive Sciences*, 2: 389–98.

Keeley, B. (1999) Of conspiracy theories, *Journal of Philosophy*, 96: 109–26.

Kendall, R. E. (1975) The concept of disease, *British Journal of Psychiatry*, 127: 305–15.

——(1985) What are mental disorders, in A. Freedman, R. Brotman, I. Silverman and D. Hutson (eds) *Science, Practice, and Social Policy*, New York: Human Sciences Press.

——(2001) The distinction between mental and physical illness, *British Journal of Psychiatry*, 178: 490–93.

Kennedy, R. and Graham, G. (2007) Extreme self-denial, in M. Marraffa, M. De Caro and F. Ferretti (eds) *Cartographies of the Mind: Philosophy and Psychology in Intersection*, Netherlands: Springer.

Kennett, J. (2002) Austism, empathy and moral agency, *The Philosophical Quarterly*, 52: 340–57.

Kennett, J. and Matthews, S. (2009) Mental time travel, agency, and responsibility, in M. Broome and L. Bortolotti (eds) *Psychiatry as Cognitive Neuroscience: Philosophical Perspectives*, Oxford: Oxford University Press.

Kenny, A. (1988) *The Self*, Marquette, Wisconsin: Marquette University Press.

Keppel, R. (1995) *Ted Bundy and I hunt for the green river killer*, New York: Pocket Books.

Kessler, R. C. (2005) Prevalence and treatment of mental disorders, 1990 to 2003, *New England Journal of Medicine*, 352: 2515–23.

Kessler, R. C., Bergland, P., Demler, O., Jin, R., Merikangas, K. R. and Walters, E. E. (2005) Lifetime prevalence and age-of-onset distributions of DSM-IV disorders in national comorbidity survey replication, *Archives of General Psychiatry*, 62: 593–602.

Kessler, R. C., Chiu, W. T., Demler, O., Merikangas, K. R. and Walters, E. E. (2005) Prevalence, severity, and comorbidity of 12-month DSM-IV disorders in the national comorbidity survey replication, *Archives of General Psychiatry*, 62: 617–27.

Kessler, R. C., McGonagle, K. A., Zhao, S., Nelson, C. B., Hughes, M., Eshleman, S., Wittchen, H., and Kendler, K. S. (1994) Lifetime and 12-month prevalence of DSM-III-R psychiatric disorders in the United States from the national comorbidity survey, *Archives of General Psychiatry*, 51: 8–19.

Kim, J. (2003) Lonely souls: causality and substance dualism, in T. O'Conner and D. Robb (eds) *Philosophy of Mind: Contemporary Readings*, London: Routledge.

Kinderman, P. and Bentall, R. (2007) The functions of delusional beliefs, in M. Chung, K. Fulford and G. Graham (eds) *Reconceiving Schizophrenia*, Oxford: Oxford University Press.

King, C. (2007) They diagnosed me a schizophrenic when I was just a Gemini. The other side of madness, in M. Chung, K. Fulford and G. Graham (eds) *Reconceiving Schizophrenia*, Oxford: Oxford University Press.

Kitcher, P. (1992) *Freud's Dream: A Complete Interdisciplinary Science of Mind*, Cambridge, MA: MIT Press.

Kleinman, A. (2000) Social and cultural anthropology: salience for psychiatry in M. Gelder, J. J. Lopez-Ibor and N. Andreasen (eds) *New Oxford Textbook of Psychiatry*, vol. 1, Oxford: Oxford University Press.

Klinger, E. (1977) *Meaning and Void: Inner Experiences and Incentives in People's Lives*, Minneapolis: University of Minnesota Press.

Kluft, R. P. (1986) Personality unification and multiple personality disorder, in B. Braun (ed.) *The Treatment of Multiple Personality Disorder*, Washington, DC: American Psychiatric Press.

Klume, S. (2007) Best selling drugs. On-line at http://psychcentral.com/blog/archives/2006/02/28/best-selling drugs.

Knapp, C. (1998). My descent into alcoholism, in D. Sattler, V. Shabatay and K. Kramer (eds) *Abnormal Psychology in Context: Voices and Perspectives*, Boston: Houghton Mifflin.

Kopelman, L. M. (1994) Normal grief: good or bad? Health or disease?, *Philosophy, Psychiatry and Psychology*, 1: 209–20.

Kosslyn, S. M. and Dror, I. E. (1992) A cognitive neuroscience of alzheimer's disease: what can be learned from studies of visual imagery? in Y. Christian and P. Churchland (eds) *Neurophilosophy and Alzheimer's Disease*, New York: Springer-Verlag.

Kramer, P. (2005) *Against Depression*, New York: Viking.

Kuhn, C. and Koob, G. (2010) *Advances in the Neuroscience of Addiction*, Oxford: Taylor and Francis.

Laureys, S. (2007) Eyes open, brain shut, *Scientific American*, May 2007, 296: 84–89.

Lear, J. (1998) *Open Minded: Working Out the Logic of the Soul*, Cambridge, MA: Harvard University Press.

Leff, J. (2000) Transcultural psychology, in M. Gelder, J. J. Lopez-Ibor and N. Andreasen (eds) *New Oxford Textbook of Psychiatry*, vol. 1, Oxford: Oxford University Press.

Leshner, A. I. (1997) Addiction is a brain disease, and it matters, *Science*, 278: 45–47.

Levine, J. (2009) The explanatory gap, in B. McLaughlin, A. Beckermann and S. Walter (eds) *The Oxford Handbook of Philosophy of Mind*, Oxford: Oxford University Press.

Levy, N. (2006) Autonomy and addiction, *Canadian Journal of Philosophy*, 36: 427–47.

——(2007) *Neuroethics: Challenges for the 21st Century*, Cambridge: Cambridge University Press.

——(2011) Addiction, responsibility, and ego depletion, in J. Poland and G. Graham (eds) *Addiction and Responsibility*, Cambridge, MA: MIT Press.

Lewis, C. S. (1952) *Mere Christianity*, New York: Macmillan.

Lewis, R. S. (2002) *The Other Great Depression*, New York: Penguin.

Litvan, I. (1999) Parkinson's disease, in J. G. Beaumont, P. Kennedy and M. Rogers (eds) *The Blackwell Dictionary of Neuropsychology*, Malden, MA: Blackwell.

Lloyd, D. (2009) When time is out of joint: schizophrenia and functional neuroimaging in M. Broome and L. Bartolotti (eds) *Psychiatry as Cognitive Neuroscience: Philosophical Perspectives*, Oxford: Oxford University Press.

Locke, J. (1975 [1690]) *An Essay Concerning Human Understanding*, ed. with intro. P. H. Nidditch, Oxford: Clarendon Press.

London, J. (1982) John Barleycorn, in D. Pizer (ed.) *Jack London: Novels and Social Writings*, New York: Macmillan.

Lovestone, A. (2000) Dementia: Alzheimer's disease, in M. Gelder, J. J. Lopez-Ibor and N. Andreasen (eds) *New Oxford Textbook of Psychiatry*, vol. 1, Oxford: Oxford University Press.

Luhrmann, T. (2000) *Of 2 Minds: The Growing Disorder in American Psychiatry*, New York: Alfred A. Knopf.

Lycan, W. (2003) The Mind–Body Problem, in S. Stich and T. Warfield (eds) *The Blackwell Guide to the Philosophy of Mind*, Malden, MA.: Blackwell.

Maher, B. (1974) Delusional thinking and perceptual disorder, *Journal of Individual Psychology*, 30: 98–113.

——(1988) Anomalous experience and delusional thinking, in T. F. Oltmanns and B. Maher (eds) *Delusional Beliefs*, Chichester: John Wiley and Sons.

——(1999) Anomalous experience in everyday life: its significance for psychopathology, *The Monist*, 82: 547–70.

Maibom, H. L. (2008) The mad, the bad, and the psychopath, *Neuroethics*, 1: 167–84.

Malenka, R. C. (2004) The addicted brain, *Scientific American*, 290: 78–85.

Margolis, E. and Laurence, S. (2003) Concepts, in S. Stich and T. Warfield (eds) *The Blackwell Guide to Philosophy of Mind*, Malden, MA: Blackwell.

Marks, I. and Nesse, R. (1994) Fear and fitness: an evolutionary analysis of anxiety disorders, *Ethology and Sociobiology*, 15: 247–61.

Maslow, A. H. (1950) Self-actualizing people: a study of psychological health, *Personality Symposium*, 1: 11–34.

Matthews, E. (2007) Suspicions of schizophrenia, in M. Chung, K. Fulford and G. Graham (eds) *Reconceiving Schizophrenia*, Oxford: Oxford University Press.

Maudsley, H. (1867) *The Physiology and Pathology of Mind*, London: Macmillan.

May, R. (2004) Making sense of psychotic experience and working towards recovery, in J. Gleeson and P. McGorry (eds) *Interventions in Early Psychosis: A Treatment Handbook*, Chichester, UK: Wiley.

McCauley, R. N. (1996). Explanatory pluralism and the co-evolution of theories in science in R. N. McCauley (ed.) *The Churchlands and Their Critics*, Oxford: Blackwell.

McGinn, C. (1999) *The Mysterious Flame: Conscious Minds in a Material World*. New York: Basic Books.

McKay, A., McKenna, P., and Laws, K. (1996) Severe schizophrenia: what is it like?, in P. Halligan and J. Marshall (eds) *Method in Madness: Case Studies in Cognitive Neuropsychiatry*, East Sussex, UK: Psychology Press.

McKay, R. T. and Dennett, D. C. (2009) The evolution of misbelief, *Behavioral and Brain Sciences*, 32: 493–510.

Mellor, C. S. (1970) First rank symptoms of schizophrenia, *British Journal of Psychiatry*, 117: 15–23.

Metzinger, T. (2003). *Being No One: The Self-Model Theory of Subjectivity*, Cambridge, MA: MIT Press.

Mill, J. S. (1969). *Autobiography*, J. Stillinger (ed.), Boston: Houghton Mifflin.

Moore, M. S. (1980) Legal conceptions of mental illness, in B. Brody and T. Englehardt (eds) *Mental Illness: Law and Public Policy*, Dordrecht: Reidel.

Morrison, A. P. (1998) Cognitive behavior therapy for psychotic symptoms of schizophrenia, in N. Tarrier, A. Wells and G. Haddock (eds) *Cognitive Therapy for Psychosis: A Formulation-Based Approach*, London: Brunner-Routledge.

Morse, S. J. (2011) Addiction and criminal responsibility in J. Poland and G. Graham (eds) *Addiction and Responsibility*, Cambridge, MA: MIT Press.

Muneoka, K., Han, M., and Gardiner, D. (2008). Regrowing human limbs, *Scientific American*, 298: 56–63.

Munro, A. (2006) *Delusional Disorder: Paranoia and Related Illnesses*, Cambridge: Cambridge University Press.

Murphy, D. (2006) *Psychiatry in the Scientific Image*, Cambridge, MA: MIT Press.

Nesse, R. M. (1990) Evolutionary explanations of emotions, *Human Nature*, 1: 261–89.

——(2001) Motivation and melancholy: a Darwinian perspective, in J. French, A. Kamil and D. Leger (eds) *Evolutionary Psychology and Motivation*, vol. 47 Nebraska Symposium on Motivation, Lincoln: University of Nebraska Press.

Nesse, R. M. and Jackson, E.D. (2011) Evolutionary foundations for psychiatric diagnoses: making DSM-V valid, in P. Adriaens and A. DeBlock (eds) *Maladapting Minds*, New York: Oxford University Press.

Nesse, R. M. and Williams, G. (1996) *Why We Get Sick: The New Science of Darwinian Medicine*, New York: Times Books.

Nozick, R. (1974) *Anarchy, State, and Utopia*, New York: Basic Books.

Nussbaum, M. (2006) *Frontiers of Justice: Disability, Nationality, Species Membership*, Cambridge, MA: Harvard University Press.

Odean, T. (1998) Volume, volatility, price, and profit: When all traders are above average, *Journal of Finance*, 53: 1887–1934.

Olson, E. (1997) *The Human Animal: Personal Identity without Psychology*, New York: Oxford University Press.

——(2007a) There is no problem of the self, in B. Gertler and L. Shapiro (eds) *Arguing about the Mind*, Oxford: Routledge.

——(2007b) *What Are We?: A Study in Personal Ontology*, Oxford, Oxford University Press.

Ostwald, P. (1987) *Schumann: The Inner Voices of a Musical Genius*, Boston: Northeastern University Press.

Panksepp, J. (2009) A non-reductive physicalist account of affective consciousness, in S. Wood, N. Allen and C. Panelis (eds) *The Neuropsychology of Mental Illness*, Cambridge: Cambridge University Press.

Perry, J. (1979) The problem of the essential indexical, *Nous*, 13: 3–21.

Pickard, H. (2009) Mental illness is indeed a myth, in M. Broome and L. Bortolotti (eds) *Psychiatry as Cognitive Neuroscience: Philosophical Perspectives*, Oxford, Oxford University Press.

——(2011) Responsibility without blame: empathy and the effective treatment of personality disorder, *Philosophy, Psychiatry, and Psychology*, 18: 209–23.

Pinker, S. (1997) *How the Mind Works*, New York: Norton.

Place, U. T. (1999) Ryles behaviorism, in W. O'Donohue and R. Kitchener (eds) *Handbook of Behaviorism*, San Diego: Academic Press.

Poland, J. (2001) Review of DSM-IV Sourcebook, vol. 1. On-line at *Metapsychology*. http://mentalhelp.net/books.php?type=de&id=557.

——(2007) How to move beyond the concept of schizophrenia, in M. Cheung, K. Fulford and G. Graham (eds) *Reconceiving Schizophrenia*, Oxford: Oxford University Press.

——(2013) Deeply rooted sources of error and bias in psychiatric classification, in J. Sullivan and H. Kincaid (eds) *Psychiatric Classification and Natural Kinds*, Cambridge, MA: MIT Press.

Poland, J., Von Eckardt, B. and Spaulding, W. (1994), Problems with the DSM approach to classifying psychopathology, in G. Graham and G. L. Stephens (eds) *Philosophical Psychopathology*, Cambridge, MA: MIT Press.

Powell, G. (2000) Cognitive assessment, in M. Gelder, J.J. Lopez-Ibor and M. Andreasen (eds) *New Oxford Textbook of Psychiatry*, vol. 1, Oxford: Oxford University Press.

Price, C. (2010) The rationality of grief, *Inquiry*, 53: 20–40.

Proust, J. (2006) Agency in schizophrenia from a control theory viewpoint, in N. Sebanz and W. Prinz (eds) *Disorders of Volition*, Cambridge, MA.: MIT Press.

Putnam, F. W. (1989) *Diagnosis and Treatment of Multiple Personality Disorder*, New York: Guilford Press.

Quine, W. V. (1969) Speaking of objects, in W. V. Quine, *Ontological Relativity and Other Essays*, New York: Columbia University Press.

Radden, J. (2007) Defining persecutory paranoia, in M. Chung, K. Fulford and G. Graham (eds) *Reconceiving Schizophrenia*, Oxford: Oxford University Press.

——(2009) *Moody Minds Distempered: Essays on Melancholy and Depression*, Oxford: Oxford University Press.

Ramachandran, V. S. (2003) *Reith Lectures: The Emerging Mind*, lecture 5. BBC Radio 4, April 30, 2003. Available at the website of the BBC: www.bbc.co.uk/radio4/reith2003/lecture5/transcript/html.

Ratey, J. and Johnson, C. (1998) *Shadow Syndromes*, New York: Random House.

Rawls, J. (1971) *A Theory of Justice*, Cambridge, MA: Harvard University Press.

Reed, E. (1996) *Encountering the World: Toward an Ecological Psychology*, Oxford: Oxford University Press.

Reimer, M. (2011) A Davidsonian perspective on psychiatric delusions, *Philosophical Psychology*, 24: 659–77.

Rescher, N. (1987) *Ethical Idealism: An Inquiry into the Nature and Function of Ideals*, Berkeley: University of California Press.

Reznek, L. (1987) *The Nature of Disease*, London: Routledge & Kegan Paul.

Richardson, R. (2007). The adaptive programme of evolutionary psychology, in P. Thagard (ed.) *Philosophy of Psychology and Cognitive Science*, Handbook of the Philosophy of Science: General Series, Amsterdam: Elsevier.

Robinson, T. (2004) Addicted rats, *Science*, 305: 951–53.

Robinson, T., and Berridge, K. (2003) Addiction, *Annual Review of Psychology*, 54: 25–53.

Rogers, M. (1999) Apraxia, in J. Beaumont, P. Kenealy and M. Rogers (eds) *The Blackwell Dictionary of Neuropsychology*, Malden, MA: Blackwell Publishers.

Rosch, E. (1978) Family resemblances: studies in the internal structure of categories, in R. Rosch and B. Lloyd (eds) *Cognition and Categorization*, Hillsdale, NJ: Lawrence Erlbaum Associates.

Ross, D., Sharp, C., Vuchinich, R., and Spurrett, D. (2008) *Midbrain Mutiny: The Picoeconomics and Neuroeconomics of Disordered Gambling*, Cambridge, MA.: MIT Press.

Russell, B. (1989/1917) A free man's worship, in T. Penelhum (ed.) *Faith*, New York: Macmillan.

Sadler, J. (2004a) A Madness for the Philosophy of Psychiatry, *Philosophy, Psychiatry, and Psychology*, 4, 357–59

——. (2004b) Diagnosis/Antidiagnosis, in J. Radden (ed.) *The Philosophy of Psychiatry: A Companion*, Oxford: Oxford University Press.

Samuels, R. (2009) Delusions as a natural kind, in M. Broome and L. Bortolotti (eds) *Psychiatry as Cognitive Neuroscience: Philosophical Perspectives*, Oxford: Oxford University Press.

Sass, L. (1992) *Madness and Modernism: Insanity in the Light of Modern Art, Literature, and Thought*, Cambridge, MA.: Harvard University Press.

——(1999) Schizophrenia, self-consciousness and the modern mind, in S. Gallagher and J. Shear (eds) *Models of the Self*, Thoverton, UK: Imprint Academic.

Sass, L. and Parnas, J. (2007) Explaining schizophrenia: the relevance of phenomenology, in M. Chung, K. Fulford and G. Graham (eds) *Reconceiving Schizophrenia*, Oxford: Oxford University Press.

Satel, S. (2008) Science and sorrow: a review of A. Horwitz and J. Wakefield "Loss of Sadness", *New Republic*, February 27: 37–43.

Schaff, P. (1918) *The Person of Christ*, New York: American Tract Society.

Schoeman, F. (1994) Alcohol addiction and responsibility attributions, in G. Graham and G. L. Stephens (eds) *Philosophical Psychopathology*, Cambridge, MA: MIT Press.

Schopenhauer, A. (1841/1965) *On the Basis of Morality*, trans. E. Payne, Indianapolis: Bobbs-Merrill.

Schweitzer, A. (1948/1913) *The Psychiatric Study of Jesus*, trans. C. Joy, Boston: Beacon Press.

Searle, J. (1983) *Intentionality*, Cambridge: Cambridge University Press.

——(2001) *Rationality in Action*, Cambridge, MA.: MIT Press.

——(2007) *Freedom and Neurobiology: Reflections on Free Will, Language, and Political Power*, New York: Columbia University Press.

Sellars, W. (1997) *Empiricism and the Philosophy of Mind*, Cambridge, MA: MIT Press.

Silverman, H. (1995) Review of Kluft and Fine, *Clinical Perspective on MPD*, *Contemporary Psychology*, 40: 589.

Simonton, D. K. (1994) *Greatness: Who Makes History and Why*, New York: Guilford.

Slavney, P. and McHugh, P. (1987) *Psychiatric Polarities: Methodology and Practice*, Baltimore: Johns Hopkins University Press.

Soble, A. (2004). Desire: paraphilia and distress in DSM-IV, in J. Radden (ed.) *The Philosophy of Psychiatry: A Companion*, New York: Oxford University Press.

Spanos, N. (1996) *Multiple Identities and False Memories: A Sociocognitive Perspective*, Washington, DC: American Psychological Association.

Stephens, G. L. and Graham, G. (2000) *When Self-Consciousness Breaks: Alien Voices and Inserted Thoughts*, Cambridge, MA: MIT Press.

——(2004) Reconceiving delusion, *International Review of Psychiatry*, 16: 236–41.

——(2007) The delusional stance, in M. Chung, K. Fulford and G. Graham (eds) *Reconceiving Schizophrenia*, Oxford, Oxford University Press.

——(2009a) Mental illness and the consciousness thesis, in S. Wood, N. Allen and C. Pantelis (eds) *The Neuropsychology of Mental Illness*, Cambridge, Cambridge University Press.

——(2009b) An addictive lesson: a case study in psychiatry as cognitive neuroscience, in M. Broome and L. Bortolotti (eds) *Psychiatry as Cognitive Neuroscience*, Oxford, Oxford University Press.

Stich, S. (1983) *From Folk Psychology to Cognitive Science*, Cambridge, MA: MIT Press.

Stone, T. and Young, A. W. (1997) Delusions and brain injury: the philosophy and psychology of belief, *Mind and Language*, 12: 327–64.

Strawson, G. (1997) The self, *Journal of Consciousness Studies*, 4: 405–28.

Strawson, P. F. (1962) Freedom and resentment, *Proceedings of the British Academy*, 48: 1–25.

——(1966) *The Bounds of Sense: An Essay on Kant's Critique of Pure Reason*, London: Methuen.

Styron, W. (1990) *Darkness Visible: A Memoir of Madness*, New York: Vintage Books.

Swoyer, C. (2008). Abstract entities, in T. Sider, J. Hawthorne and D. Zimmerman (eds) *Contemporary Debates in Metaphysics*, Malden, MA: Blackwell.

Szasz, T. (1960) The myth of mental illness, *American Psychologist*, 15: 113–18.

——(1972) Bad habits are not diseases, *The Lancet*, 128: 83–84.

——(1974) *The Myth of Mental Illness*, New York: Harper and Row.

——(1982) The psychiatric will: a new mechanism for protecting persons against "psychosis" and "psychiatry", *American Psychologist*, 37: 762–70.

——(2001) Mental illness: psychiatry's phlogiston, *The Journal of Medical Ethics*, 27: 297–301.

Taylor, C. (1976) Responsibility for Self, in A. Rorty (ed.) *The Identities of Persons*, Berkeley: University of California Press.

Taylor, M. A. (1999) *The Fundamentals of Clinical Neurology*, New York: Oxford University Press.

Taylor, S. E. (1989) *Positive Illusions: Creative Self-Deception and the Healthy Mind*, New York: Basic Books.

Taylor, S. E. and Brown, J. (1988) Illusion and well-being: a social psychological perspective on mental health, *Psychological Bulletin*, 103: 193–210.

Torrey, E. Fuller (1995) *Surviving Schizophrenia: A Manual for Families, Consumers, and Providers*, 3rd edn, New York: HarperCollins Publishers (2001, 4th edn).

Vaillant, G. (1977) *Adaptation to Life*, New York, Little Brown.

Van Inwagen, P. (2009) *Metaphysics*, 3rd edn, Boulder, CO: Westview Press.

Velleman, D. (1991) Well-being and time, *Pacific Philosophical Quarterly*, 72: 48–77.

Von Wright, G. E. (1963) *Varieties of Goodness*, London: Routledge.

Wakefield, J. C. (1997) Diagnosing DSM-IV – part I: DSM-IV and the concept of disorder, *Behavioral Research in Therapy*, 35: 633–49.

——(1999) The measurement of mental disorder, in A. V. Horwitz and T. L. Scheid (eds) *A Handbook for the Study of Mental Health: Social Contexts, Theories, and Systems*, New York: Cambridge University Press.

Watson, P. and Andrews, P. (2002) Toward a revised evolutionary adaptationist analysis of depression: the social navigation hypothesis, *Journal of Affective Disorders*, 72: 1–14.

Weiskrantz, L. (1986) *Blindsight: A Case Study and Implications*, Oxford: Clarendon.

——(1991) Introduction: dissociated issues in A. D. Milner and M. D. Rug (eds) *The Neuropsychology of Consciousness*, London: Academic Press.

West, R. (2006) *Theory of Addiction*, Oxford: Blackwell.

Whittle, S., Yucel, M., and Allen, N. B. (2009) The neurobiology of the emotion response: perception, experience, and regulation in S. Wood, N. B. Allen and C. Pentelis (eds) *The Neuropsychology of Mental Illness*, Cambridge, Cambridge University Press.

Wilkes, K. (1988) *Real People: Personal Identity without Thought Experiments*, Oxford: Oxford University Press.

——(1991) How many selves make me?, in D. Cockburn (ed.) *Human Beings*, Cambridge: Cambridge University Press.

Wilkinson, S. (2000) Is "normal grief" a mental disorder?, *The Philosophical Quarterly*, 50: 289–304.

Wittgenstein, L. (1958) *Philosophical Investigations*, Oxford: Blackwell.

Wolterstorff, N. (1988) Suffering love, in T. Morris (ed.) *Philosophy and the Christian Faith*. Notre Dame, Indiana: University of Notre Dame Press,

Woodward, J. (2003) *Making Things Happen: A Theory of Causal Explanation*, New York: Oxford University Press.

World Health Organization (1992) *ICD-10: International Statistical Classification of Diseases and Related Health Problems*, 10th revd edn, Geneva: World Health Organization.

——(2002) *Mental Health Global Plan: Close the Gap, Dare to Care*, Geneva: World Health Organization.

World Mental Health Survey Consortium (2004) Prevalence, severity, and unmet need for treatment of mental disorders in the World Health Organization World Mental Health Surveys, *Journal of the American Mental Health Association*, 291: 2581–90.

Young, A. W. (2000) Wondrous strange: the neuropsychology of abnormal beliefs, in M. Davies and M. Coltheart (eds) *Pathologies of Belief*, Oxford: Blackwell.

Young, A. W. and Leafhead, K. (1996) Betwixt life and death: case studies in the Cotard delusion, in P. Halligan and J. Marshall (eds) *Method in Madness: Case Studies in Cognitive Neuropsychiatry*, East Sussex, UK: Psychology Press.

Zimmerman, D. (2003). Material People, in M. Loux and D. Zimmerman (eds) *The Oxford Handbook of Metaphysics*, Oxford: Oxford University Press.

Index